Financing Higher Education Worldwide

Financing Higher Education Worldwide

Who Pays? Who Should Pay?

D. Bruce Johnstone
and
Pamela N. Marcucci

The Johns Hopkins University Press
Baltimore

© 2010 The Johns Hopkins University Press
All rights reserved. Published 2010
Printed in the United States of America on acid-free paper
9 8 7 6 5 4 3 2 1

The Johns Hopkins University Press
2715 North Charles Street
Baltimore, Maryland 21218-4363
www.press.jhu.edu

Library of Congress Cataloging-in-Publication Data

Johnstone, D. Bruce (Donald Bruce), 1941–
    Financing higher education worldwide : who pays? who
should pay? / D. Bruce Johnstone and Pamela N. Marcucci.
        p. cm.
    Includes bibliographical references and index.
    ISBN-13: 978-0-8018-9457-2 (hardcover : alk. paper)
    ISBN-10: 0-8018-9457-3 (hardcover : alk. paper)
    ISBN-13: 978-0-8018-9458-9 (pbk. : alk. paper)
    ISBN-10: 0-8018-9458-1 (pbk. : alk. paper)
    1. Education, Higher—Finance.   2. Education, Higher—
Costs.   3. Education, Higher—Economic aspects.
4. Universities and colleges—Finance.   5. College costs.
6. Higher education and state.   7. Government aid to
education.   I. Marcucci, Pamela Nichols.   II. Title.
    LB2341.98.J64   2010
    378.3′8—dc22   2009026925

A catalog record for this book is available from the British
Library.

*Special discounts are available for bulk purchases of this book. For
more information, please contact Special Sales at 410-516-6936 or
specialsales@press.jhu.edu.*

The Johns Hopkins University Press uses environmentally
friendly book materials, including recycled text paper that is
composed of at least 30 percent post-consumer waste, whenever
possible. All of our book papers are acid-free, and our jackets
and covers are printed on paper with recycled content.

Contents

Preface

This book has had a very long gestation. The beginning goes back to the early 1970s, when Bruce Johnstone took a project specialist assignment at the Ford Foundation, which had just committed to a serious study of what was then known as the *Yale Plan for Tuition Postponement*: the first experiment with income contingent student lending. In this to-be-totally-self-financed plan (although Yale University had sought capitalization from the Ford Foundation), the repayment obligation was not expressed as a fixed schedule of repayments set to amortize each borrower's indebtedness at a certain rate of interest over a certain time period. Rather, it was to be defined as an obligation to repay a certain percent of earnings over an unspecified time period until the combined indebtedness of the cohort of fellow borrowers who had begun repaying at the same time had repaid their combined debt at a certain rate of interest (in the case of the Yale Plan, this was a rate set to fully amortize the cost of capital without further subsidization).

The principal advantage of such a plan is that no borrower incurs an unmanageable debt. This plan has, with significant variations, been adopted in a minor way in the United States and in a major way in such countries as

Australia, Chile, New Zealand, South Africa, Thailand, and the constituent countries of the United Kingdom. In the Yale Plan, which was to be self-financing, the shortfalls from low-earning borrowers—who, by the time that the cohort had repaid the combined debt in full, would have repaid less than the break-even rate for the cohort as a whole—were compensated for by the high-earning borrowers who would have repaid an effective interest premium.

In the various international, government-sponsored, income continent loan schemes established since that early, short-lived private experiment, the shortfalls from the low-earning borrowers are made up by taxpayers, with most borrowers simply repaying their loans at the contractual rate of interest (which is most commonly the government's borrowing rate). Low earners in these recent plans simply repay the maximum percent of earnings until some maximum repayment period has passed, at which time they are forgiven from any remaining debt. These borrowers are, in effect, receiving an eventual governmental subsidy on the basis of *their own* low lifetime earnings, as opposed to the prevailing scheme of most means-tested financial assistance programs, which is to subsidize a student on the basis of their *parents'* low earnings at the time the student is studying.

This was Johnstone's first experience with the fascinating combination of higher educational finance, student financial assistance, state and federal governmental policies toward the financing of both institutions and students, and the politics and ideologies of higher educational finance. These elements blend such compelling (but not necessarily compatible) goals as institutional financial viability, the efficient use of public resources, an appropriate balance between public and private higher educational sectors, the elusive goal of more equitable access to higher education by socioeconomic class, and the frequently counterintuitive consequences of governmental subsidies in pursuit of these multiple aims.

In the early 1980s, Johnstone integrated the presidency of the State University of New York College at Buffalo with a continuation of the research begun a decade or so earlier on student financial assistance policies at the University of Pennsylvania. During a sabbatical from the presidency of Buffalo State College in 1985, he decided to apply an international perspective to a theme he had developed in an article written for the College Board. Out of that work came the book *Sharing the Costs of Higher Education: Student Financial Assistance in the United Kingdom, the Federal Republic of Germany, France, Sweden, and the United States* (Johnstone 1986), which, as recounted by Maureen Woodhall (2007), is generally credited with popularizing the term *cost-sharing*. Cost-sharing refers both to the fact that higher educational costs are borne by governments, parents, students, and philanthropists, as well as to the political struggles among these alternative bearers of costs and, in many countries, to the apparent drift of this burden toward greater shares borne by students and their families.

Johnstone left Buffalo State College in 1988 to serve a term as chancellor of the State University of New York system, during which time he continued to write on higher educational finance, governance, and policy in both US and international perspectives. In 1994, he left the chancellorship and joined the Higher and Comparative Education doctoral programs at the University at Buffalo. With this opportunity to engage in full-time research and teaching unencumbered with administrative responsibilities, and with the advantage of international graduate students and generous support from the Ford Foundation, in January of 2000 he established the International Comparative Higher Education Finance and Accessibility (ICHEFA) Project, with the aim of compiling a body of theoretical, descriptive, and empirical works on the growing phenomenon of cost-sharing, its implications for higher educational participation and for the financial health of universities and other institutions of higher education, and for the policy tools of tuition fees, grants, and student loan schemes.

Pamela Marcucci entered the story as the project manager planning and directing the project's first international conference in Dar es Salaam, Tanzania. Marcucci had just returned to Buffalo from a position in Rome, where she had managed conferences in Africa, building on her graduate studies in international relations. Marcucci and a team of international graduate students established the ICHEFA Project's Web site and compiled a rich annotated bibliography of works on student finance, tuition policies, student loans schemes, and similar topics. The successful 2002 conference in Tanzania was followed by others on international higher educational finance and cost-sharing in Prague in 2003, Moscow in 2004, and Wuhan in 2005. By 2008, as the Ford Foundation support was drawing to a close, the ICHEFA Project had produced a substantial literature collection in international comparative higher educational finance and cost-sharing, most of it published in journals and books; compiled (and kept up to date) some 50 country descriptions of higher education systems and the costs borne by parents, students, and taxpayers; and provided a scholarly home not only to Johnstone's doctoral and master's students engaging in research on higher educational finance and accessibility, but also to doctoral students and established scholars from other US and international universities.

The ICHEFA Project took a special interest in East Africa. Beginning in the early 2000s, this region had begun testing the *dual track tuition fee* concept, which retained free or very low tuition fees for increasingly limited numbers of the most able entering students, but then took in substantial numbers of additional fee-paying students. Thus—as in most of the previously Communist countries of the former Soviet Union and Eastern and Central Europe—the governments were able to preserve a legal (and politically important) semblance (or pretense) of free tuition while providing desperately needed revenues to the universities. Conferences were held in Nairobi in 2006 and 2007 on the access and equity implications of this concept, followed by a workshop on student loans in the winter of 2008 that included student loan teams from the East African countries of Burundi, Ethiopia, Kenya, Rwanda, Tanzania, and Uganda.

Under Marcucci and a team of international students and scholars, the project collected data from students in Egypt, Ethiopia, Kenya, and Morocco, testing hypotheses on student behavior and attitudes toward various means of financing their higher educational expenses. Johnstone and Marcucci, under contract from the World Bank and again assisted by international graduate students, developed technical papers for Morocco (in 2006) and Romania (in 2008) on ways to enhance revenue from cost-sharing and student loans while preserving accessibility and enhancing capacity and educational quality. In these ways, plus in scores of conference presentations and individual lectures, the authors of this volume have sought to advance the theoretical underpinnings of higher educational finance and cost-sharing, as well as the policy implications for countries through out the world. This book is the fruit of such labors.

REFERENCES

Johnstone, D. Bruce. 1986. *Sharing the Costs of Higher Education: Student Financial Assistance in the United Kingdom, the Federal Republic of Germany, France, Sweden, and the United States*. New York: College Entrance Examination Board.
Woodhall, Maureen. 2007. *Funding Higher Education: The Contribution of Economic Thinking to Debate and Policy Development*. Washington, DC: World Bank.

Financing Higher Education Worldwide

Introduction

This is a book about the financing of higher education from an international comparative perspective. In particular, it is about a form of higher educational finance that has come to be popularly labeled *cost-sharing*. Cost-sharing has less to do with institutional financing and budgeting, or with financial management, or with governmental policies and formulas for allocating tax revenues to institutions of higher education—although all of these perspectives are important background themes and will be dealt with later—and more with the costs of higher education that are borne by parents and/or students. The book considers the impact of this cost-sharing on institutional finance, capacity, and quality as well as its effect on access to higher education and the social equitability of that access.

The costs of instruction that are borne by students and/or parents in the form of tuition fees may be more properly termed *prices* (or *net prices*, after grants, scholarships, and institutional discounts have been factored in) and are generally considerably less than the true, full *costs of instruction*. Some of these instructional costs (or much, or nearly all of them, depending on the institution and the country) may be borne by governments or, especially in the United

States, by endowment revenue or current philanthropic donations. Similarly, the cost of student living, or *maintenance*, that is reflected in the concept of cost-sharing may not be a true cost of higher education, as most of such costs, or expenses, must be borne anyway. But to the students and parents having to meet the costs of food and lodging during university attendance, such expenses are virtually indistinguishable from the costs (or prices) associated with tuition and other fees.

Many of the theoretical concepts and much of the descriptive literature on cost-sharing has been developed by the International Comparative Higher Education Finance and Accessibility (ICHEFA) Project at the Center for Comparative and Global Studies of Education at the State University of New York at Buffalo.[1] This project has been directed by Bruce Johnstone and managed by Pamela Marcucci. By means of papers and monographs (both published and unpublished), country descriptions, international conferences, visiting scholars, and doctoral students (including a dozen Ph.D. dissertations), from 1999 through 2009 the ICHEFA Project complied a substantial volume of theoretical and descriptive works—as well as empirical studies on the setting of governmental cost-sharing policies, their rationales, the political and ideological contestation of these policies, and worldwide trends in cost-sharing.

The term *cost-sharing*, as it has been developed in large part through these ICHEFA works (Johnstone 1986, 2004, 2006; Marcucci and Johnstone 2007), refers to a shift of at least some of the higher educational cost burden from governments, or taxpayers, to parents and students. Cost-sharing is thus both a statement of fact—that is, that the costs of higher education are shared among governments (or taxpayers), parents, students, and philanthropists— and also a reference to a policy shift of some of these costs from a predominant (sometimes a virtually exclusive) reliance on governments and taxpayers to being increasingly shared by parents and/or students in addition to taxpayers.

Cost-sharing is mostly associated with tuition fees and *user charges*, the latter fees often applying to what was formerly, in many countries, governmentally or institutionally provided food and lodging (in American parlance, *room and board*). However, a policy shift in the direction of greater cost-sharing can also take the form of encouraging (and sometimes even partially subsidizing) a largely tuition-fee-dependent private sector. It can also take the forms of reducing grants or other subsidies, or simply freezing them (especially in inflationary economies), or of raising the effective interest rates on student loans.

The Spread of Cost-Sharing

Cost-sharing thus appears in many different forms. But in whatever form or forms, cost-sharing—meaning a shift toward greater shares borne by parents and/or students—is generally increasing throughout the world in the early years of the twenty-first century (Johnstone and Marcucci 2007).

The United States: In the United States, the underlying instructional costs of higher education—generally higher than in most other nations to begin with—have been rising even faster in the share borne by parents and students (in the form of tuition fees) as compared to the share borne by governments, or taxpayers, as the latter share in most states has been steadily diminishing. In 2008–9, public sector tuitions and mandatory fees in the United States for in-state students varied widely by state and type of institution (i.e., low at community colleges and considerably higher at flagship research universities), but they ranged from a low of less than $2,000 at some community colleges, to an average of more than $5,700 at public master's degree colleges, to an average of almost $7,500 at doctoral campuses (some at more than $10,000); for out-of-state students, public-sector tuitions and fees averaged almost $17,500. There has been an even greater disparity in private-sector tuitions and fees, from as little as $12,000 or even less for nonselective, low-cost colleges, to a 2008–9 average of just over $25,000, to tuition fees as high as $30,000 and more at elite, selective, private colleges and universities (College Board 2008a). The actual expenses, of course, particularly to students from middle- and low-income families, are generally a great deal lower because of the various forms of financial assistance, including grants, fee discounts, and loans. However, in light of the worldwide trend toward a continuing shift in expenses away from governments, or taxpayers, and onto parents and students, the more significant and politically controversial aspect of cost-sharing in the United States has been in the sharp yearly escalation in these public sector tuition fees, revealing not simply the very high (by world standards) share of total costs borne by parents and/or students at any recent point in time, but also, and more significantly, a very pronounced year-by-year shift of these costs to ever-greater shares borne by tuition fees and thus by parents and/or students.

In spite of these high and rapidly increasing costs, however, both public and private US higher education feature extensive programs of financial assistance that, in 2007–8, totaled an estimated $143 billion, including grants from all sources (almost $29 billion in governmental grants, another $29 billion in college and university grants and discounts, and another $10.5 billion in private and employer-provided grants), governmentally sponsored loans (more than $65.5 billion), and an estimated $7 billion in education tax credits (College Board 2008b). The extent of financial assistance in the United States is such that all students (at least all who are of traditional college-going age and who are willing to assume some debt and some part-time employment) can afford at least a public college or university, even with no financial support from their parents. And the most academically able students, regardless of the incomes of their families, will frequently be offered sufficient financial assistance to attend even the most expensive private institution (albeit generally with both loans and some part-time employment).

The United Kingdom: In 1997, the United Kingdom became the first European country to impose more than a nominal tuition fee. Shortly afterwards, the constituent countries of the United Kingdom began to separate in their higher educational policies. First in Scotland in 2001, then in England in 2006 followed by Wales in 2007, what came to be referred to as an *up-front* tuition fee—that is, a tuition fee that was paid prior to enrollment, and mainly by parents—was changed to a *deferred* tuition fee, or *loan*, which was paid mainly by students on the basis of their later incomes, or earnings, at a rate of interest equal to the then-prevailing rate of inflation, or what has come to be called a *zero real* interest rate. At the same time, what used to be the most generous means-tested cost-of-living grants in the world were shifted in the 1990s to another form of loan.

Australia: Australia in 1989 inaugurated the Higher Education Contribution Scheme (HECS), described as a fair and equitable way of ensuring that students contribute to the cost of their higher education. The tuition fee can be deferred (i.e., borrowed) and repaid as an income contingent loan at a rate of interest that mirrors the prevailing Australian rate of inflation (as in the United Kingdom, at a zero real interest rate, or repaying in real terms what was borrowed). Although Australia does not use the terms "tuition fees" or "loans" per se, and although some parents pay up front at a discount, HECS clearly shifted a significant portion of the higher educational cost burden from the government, or the Australian taxpayer, mainly onto students. Significantly, revenue to the Australian universities increased substantially; that is, the new tuition fees supplemented, rather than substituted for, governmental revenue, with no evident loss of enrollments or accessibility.

Japan: Japan, like Korea and the Philippines, relies on a large, tuition-fee-dependent private sector to absorb much of the substantial demand for higher education. Tuition fees at its national universities have also been rising; in addition, Japan has been turning to a corporatization of its public universities to force greater reliance on nongovernmental revenue. Japan also features several governmentally sponsored student loan programs, but it relies mainly on an unusually high parental willingness to contribute to the costs of higher education, both public and private.

Russia: Similar to many formerly Communist countries, including most of the now-independent countries of the former Soviet Union as well as the transitional countries of Eastern and Central Europe, Russia, by its constitution, requires all education to be without cost to the student or family. At the same time, the very great need for additional revenue has given rise to the strategy of limiting this privilege of free (or very low) tuition fees to those student who score the highest on an admissions examination. The cutoff score is established not by any meaningful level of requisite proficiency—and ignoring, for purposes of this illustration, the fallibility of any such high-stakes examination, not to mention the significant potential for socioeconomic bias as well as outright corruption—but simply to let in just the number of students the government has enough revenue to support. Other applicants can then be admitted, but only for a tuition fee. In addition, the once-generous provision of free or very low-cost food and lodging has been shifted to a combination of user fees and maintenance grants that, in turn, have been frozen or reduced. The combination of the inauguration of a *dual track* tuition fee system plus the reduction or freezing of maintenance grants has resulted in a very significant shift of higher educational costs at the national level from governments, or taxpayers, onto parents and students (all the while allowing the government to continue professing allegiance to free higher education for all *regular* students).

China: China, like Russia and most other post-Communist countries first employed a dual track tuition fee policy. However, in 1997 China declared tuition fees to be fair and ideologically appropriate according to official Chinese Communist Party ideology (as revised) and began charging tuition fees—as well as fees for food and lodging—to nearly all students. Since then, the Chinese higher educational system, fueled by a combination of public revenues and tuition fees, as well as by a deep cultural reverence for education and a pervasive social climate of growth and change, has become the largest in the world, topping 20 million students, and it has a growing student loan system.

Continental Europe: Still a bastion of very low tuition fees (sometimes even no tuition fees, as in the Nordic countries), Continental Europe has been edging in the direction of greater cost-sharing for most of the first decade of the twenty-first century. The Netherlands in 2008 charged a more-than-nominal tuition fee of €1519 [US$1,688].[2] And as of 2008, in an even greater great political shift, many of the German Länder began charging tuition fees between €500 and just under €1000 [US$561–$1,124]. At least 18 European countries were charging at least some tuition fees by 2008, many of which are nominal and all of which are low in comparison to US public universities, but the shift is both politically and financially significant.

Latin America and East Asia: Similar to Japan, cost-sharing and revenue diversification in much of both Latin America and East Asia more frequently have taken the form of increasing reliance on a tuition-fee-dependent private higher educational sector (with the public universities continuing to feature very low fees). Much as in Russia and the other dual track tuition fee countries, this system of an inexpensive but limited and generally elite public sector and a less-selective but expensive private sector leads to the seeming anomaly of students from upper- and upper-middle-income families—frequently benefiting from vastly superior (and often private) secondary education and thus able to pass the rigorous public university entrance examinations—attending high-quality and highly subsidized public universities, while students from middle- and lower-middle-income and rural families are either excluded altogether or are forced to pay for tuition-fee-dependent, and frequently inferior, higher education. This questionable equity continues to put pressure on these countries' governments to enlarge the capacity of their public universities, perhaps by increasing public revenue through cost-sharing, while at the same time attempting to maintain or even heighten equitable participation in this expanding public sector in spite of the higher costs to parents and students.

These are but a few examples of the emergence of policies during the last years of the twentieth and early years of the twenty-first centuries that have shifted some of the very high and rapidly rising costs of higher education from taxpayers to parents and/or students. We will present summaries of cost-sharing according to categories of economic development (that is, highly industrialized, transitional, middle income, and low income) in chapter 9 and provide more detailed country summaries in the appendix. For now, we wish simply to make the point that governments throughout the world are embracing—however reluctantly, tentatively, and frequently with euphemisms and political spin—some version of cost-sharing in the form or forms of tuition fees, user fees, the reduction of maintenance grants, and official encouragement of tuition-dependent private higher education.

Cost-Sharing and the Furtherance of Participation and Accessibility

Tuition fees and other forms of cost-sharing are only a part of the story of the growing worldwide shift of higher educational costs from governments to families. Virtually all governments, in spite of a greater need to supplement limited public revenue with private revenue to keep up with the surging costs of higher education, also remain committed to equitable access to the benefits of higher education. At the very least, equitable access means providing some measure of higher educational accessibility to the bright and ambitious who are also poor—or from ethnic or linguistic-minority groups or other marginalized sectors of the population—and who are likely to be excluded from higher education absent some policies to assure them otherwise. Thus, alongside the worldwide trend in the direction of greater cost-sharing—that is to say, increasing the financial burdens borne by parents or students or both—governments and institutions of higher education throughout the world are planning and implementing policies and instruments to assure higher educational accessibility by compensating for these additional costs that low-income parents cannot afford.

The two most prevalent measures of compensating for rising costs that cannot be covered by parents or extended families are grants (sometimes called *stipends*, or *bursaries*) and loans (sometimes euphemistically called *deferred fees*). In later chapters we will examine the considerable complication arising from the fact that most student loans also contain a component of grants—in the form of the present discounted value of repayment subsidies. For the purpose of this introduction, it will suffice to point out that loans are technically complex, costly even in the best cases, and financially disastrous in the (not infrequent) worst cases. Student loans are also frequently politically contested, either because they are perceived to be too costly or a financial failure from the standpoint of the government, or—in sharp contrast—because they are viewed by students and the political Left both as a repudiation of their entitlement to free higher education and as a part of a cost-sharing plot to reduce government expenditures on higher education and shift these costs to students.

The first complexity, in connection with grants, stipends, and other direct or indirect subsidies (including most student loan schemes) is the need to have an instrument for *means-testing*, that is, targeting these grants and other subsidies so that scarce public revenues—this scarcity, after all, is the reason for pursuing cost-sharing policies in the first place—are used on students for whom such subsidies will make a difference, whether in initial matriculation, in persistence and completion, or in the decision to go on to more advanced levels of higher education. However, means-testing, which to an American is a relatively simple matter of filling out a form drawing on information already compiled and entered onto a federal 1040 form for the annual payment of income taxes, is for much of the rest of the world a matter of both great complexity and significant resistance, as well as a process that lends itself to considerable manipulation and dissembling.

The second critical instrument in reconciling the competing needs of revenue supplementation with the goal of increasing participation and more equitable access is a means to defer the student's share (if there is to be any) of the costs until after his or her graduation and entry into the adult workplace, presumably when that person would be earning a higher salary. In short, cost-sharing, if it is to include students, requires a program of student loans. However, for student loans to successfully shift a portion of costs to students, these loans must be properly designed to recover all or most of the costs of capital plus all or most of the costs of collection—that is, designed at an appropriate and minimally subsidized rate of interest—and they must also be cost-effectively recovered, or collected. But politics frequently intrudes into the design of student loan schemes, resulting in excessive interest subsidization, so that the loans, even if collected, cannot recover more than a fraction of the initial cost of the capital. Furthermore, students are inherently high-risk borrowers, generally with no credit histories, little or no collateral, and at an exceptionally mobile and frequently unstable phase of their lives. For all of these reasons, student loans, which are indispensable in any policy of shifting higher educational costs to students, are financially complex and technically difficult; they will occupy the attention of chapters 6 and 7.

At a more inclusive and politically sophisticated level, of course, truly equitable access to higher education also requires compensatory policies and instruments to overcome the effects of economic and social deprivation—for example, poor schools, rural isolation, the absence of educated family or peers, linguistic marginalization, and the like—occurring far prior to a decision to attend college. Policies and instruments might include investing in better schools, communicating the advantages and possibilities of tertiary education to students while they are in secondary school, creating appropriate short-cycle programs with transfer opportunities, expanding higher educational capacity, and creating sensitive and politically robust policies of affirmative action, or compensatory preferences—all in addition to financial assistance policies. As this book is concerned broadly with cost-sharing, however, we limit our treatment of accessibility mainly to added revenue from cost-sharing and its potential to contribute to expanded capacity as well as to greater financial assistance, both of which are indispensable, albeit insufficient in and of themselves, to assure full accessibility and equity in higher education.

NOTES

1. As of 2009, the International Comparative Higher Education Finance and Accessibility Project Web site was at www.gse.buffalo.edu/org/IntHigherEdFinance/.

2. Throughout the book, conversions to the US dollar will use the global purchasing power parity estimates that were produced within the context of the World Bank's 2005 International Comparison Program (ICP). Purchasing power parity (PPP) estimates are used rather than exchange rates because, unlike exchange rates, PPP estimates not only convert prices to a common currency, but they also equalize the purchasing power of the different currencies and eliminate distortions due to currency speculation, short-term capital movements, and government interventions (OECD Statistics Directorate 2008; World Bank 2008). They are, therefore, more appropriate for comparison purposes.

REFERENCES

College Board. 2008a. *Trends in College Pricing*. Washington, DC: College Board.
———. 2008b. *Trends in Student Aid 2008*. New York: College Board.
Johnstone, D. Bruce. 1986. *Sharing the Costs of Higher Education: Student Financial Assistance in the United Kingdom, the Federal Republic of Germany, France, Sweden, and the United States*. New York: College Entrance Examination Board.
———. 2004. The Economics and Politics of Cost-Sharing in Higher Education: Comparative Perspectives. *Economics of Education Review* 20 (4):403–410.
———. 2006. *Financing Higher Education: Cost-Sharing in International Perspective*. Boston: Boston College Center for International Higher Education and Sense Publishers.

Johnstone, D. Bruce, and Pamela N. Marcucci. 2007. *Worldwide Trends in Higher Education Finance: Cost-Sharing, Student Loans, and the Support of Academic Research.* Commissioned Paper Series. Paris: UNESCO Forum on Higher Education, Research, and Knowledge.

Marcucci, Pamela, and D. Bruce Johnstone. 2007. Tuition Fee Policies in a Comparative Perspective: Theoretical and Political Rationales. *Journal of Higher Education Policy and Management* 29 (1):25–40.

OECD Statistics Directorate. 2009. Purchasing Power Parities. www.oecd.org/std/ppp/.

World Bank. 2005. *ICP Methodologies Handbook.* http://web.worldbank.org/.

CHAPTER ONE

Diverging Trajectories of Higher Education's Costs and Public Revenues Worldwide

Higher education in the twenty-first century has become increasingly important,[1] not only to individuals—bringing enriched lives, enhanced status, and greater earning power—but also to society at large, fostering economic prosperity generally, as well as the advancement of democracy and social justice. This expanding importance is reflected in a rising demand for higher education, as well as heightened expectations on the part of students (and potential students), parents, citizens generally, and taxpayers. Significantly, the increasing demand for higher education in many countries may actually exceed the growth of employment opportunities requiring this level of education. But the demand is fueled not simply by a (possibly misplaced) certainty of greater productivity and higher earnings, but by the near certainty of greater social status, increased odds of attaining a well-paying position, and the attraction of a pleasant lifestyle with new freedom and the company of similarly inclined youth.

Higher Education's Rising Demand

In the United States, where public colleges and universities have been of high quality, commodious, and substantially subsidized (more so in the past, but still to the extent of covering 60 to 75 percent of the costs of undergraduate instruction), the continued strength of a considerably more expensive private sector is testament not only to the strong demand for higher education but to the belief in its high private returns. Such a substantial demand for private higher education is mirrored in other countries, such as Japan, Korea, the Philippines, and much of Latin America. In countries where the supply of free or very low tuition fee slots in public universities is greatly constrained—generally by insufficient public resources—and where a private higher educational sector is allowed to operate, an escalated demand for higher education can be signaled by the sudden and unprecedented emergence of new, private, fee-dependent institutions of higher education. This has occurred in most of the formerly Communist, or *transitional*, countries, as well as in many of the very low-income countries of sub-Saharan Africa and Asia.

A similar example is the emergence—also in the post-Communist world as well as in East Africa—of separate, privately supported, tuition-fee-paying tracks within the otherwise public universities, available to those students not eligible for one of the highly subsidized but limited regular places. In both the new private institutions as well as the new privately supported tracks within public institutions, the programs tend to be low cost to the university (such as law, social science, or humanities) or in high demand (such as business, computer science, or the study of English); without the traditional academic trappings of campuses, student activities, research, or faculty governance; and sometimes of questionable quality. These two recent developments are further vivid demonstrations of the very high private demand for higher education, as well as its presumed private worth revealed by the market (which, after all, is the paramount signal of worth in a market economy).

At the same time, the great public value of higher education is also signaled by the creation and continued funding of public universities and other state-supported nonuniversity institutions of higher education. Universities supported by the state have been heavily subsidized because of this high perceived public value, in spite of the very great (and continuously increasing) cost to the taxpayer and despite the willingness of parents and/or students to pay a tuition fee if necessary. Some of this public value has been the obvious need for trained professionals and civil servants, but much of it stems from the conviction that a highly educated citizenry, whether elite or popular, is necessary to sustain a liberal democratic society. Part of the public value of higher education reflects a perceived need for research to support the economy, the military, and, at least in more affluent countries, the advancement of knowledge for its own sake. And some of the public worth attributed to higher education, especially to a developing or newly independent country, reflects the important symbolic value of a national university that can preserve (or, in some cases, purposefully change) a country's national heritage and accommodate its precious educated elite. In recognition of all of these public values, virtually all countries have provided students with public, low-tuition-fee institutions of higher education. (And in the former days of the Soviet Union, Eastern and Central Europe, and Old China, as well as in much of sub-Saharan Africa under the ideology of African socialism, the most academically able students were favored with free tuition, free food, free lodging, and pocket money.)

The demand for higher education is thus both public and private, and little good comes from attempts to argue the case for it being just one or the other. Clearly, some forms of higher education are more public than private: for example, training professionals for certain kinds of public service (teachers or social workers) or to serve in socially important but less-remunerative venues (such as physicians serving in remote areas), or advanced training for basic research. Yet all of these occupations (and there are many other examples) are characterized by insufficient or uncertain private returns and thus would almost certainly not be able to generate the needed numbers and quality of graduates and practitioners without substantial public subsidies, mainly in the forms of low tuition fees, financial assistance, and the continued support of academic and research employment.

Additionally, a case can be made for social justice and the public benefits of a society that is not only well educated, but in which access to this education, even at the highest levels, is available on the basis of interest and academic ability rather than family wealth, ethnicity, or social connections. Again, these public benefits require either subsidized tuition fees, or financial assistance, or some combination thereof, to be made available at public expense.

On the other hand, there is no point in arguing that there are not very great private benefits to higher education as well—for which both parents and the students themselves are manifestly willing and able to pay (albeit in some cases only with the assistance of publicly sponsored loans). Certainly, if one were to ask students or their parents if they wish to pay for something that the public (i.e., the taxpayer) seems, or in the past has seemed, willing to pay for instead, the response is likely to be in the negative. But the clear evidence of substantial private returns to higher education, amply buttressed by the obvious willingness of most parents (at least those who are financially able) and most students (at least those with access to part-time employment and/or student loans) to pay at least something for higher education, should set aside any argument that all benefits are properly public or that the case for cost-sharing is made only by arch-conservatives or so-called neoliberals.[2]

Whatever the mix of forces, the demand for higher education is growing at an accelerating pace worldwide, fueled by both rising public and private demands. The UNESCO Institute for Statistics (2006) reports some 132 million students worldwide in tertiary education in 2004—up from 91 million since 1991, for a 45 percent increase in just 13 years! This is the underlying reality behind the search for additional revenues in support of higher education. And the still miniscule participation rates in much of the low-income world means that such rates of increase are likely to continue.

Increasing Costs Per Student

A fundamental fact of higher education everywhere, and one underlying the theme of this book, is the very high (and, even more so, the continuously increasing) costs of instruction. These expenses are significant and constantly increasing, even in the absence of the rising demand and increasing enrollments described above.

Costs of instruction are those expenses reflected in college and university budgets that support the institution's instructional mission. They are mainly the costs of faculty and staff compensation, but they also include the direct costs of student services as well as the indirect costs of libraries, administration, and the operation and maintenance of the physical plant that are appropriately allocated to instruction (as opposed to, say, research or public service). Instructional costs also contain some indirect but very real costs that in some countries (as well as in some US states) may not commonly be included in public institutional budgets at all, such as expenditures for separately budgeted health insurance or public contributions to pensions, as well as the costs of that portion of capital depreciation that could be (but rarely is) budgeted at all, much less allocated to instruction. Aside from these real but frequently hidden expenses, the costs of instruction will generally exclude the costs of both externally sponsored and separately funded research, as well as the costs of public services, hospitals, revenue-producing clinics, and auxiliary enterprises such as university dormitories and restaurants.[3]

These *unit*, or per-student, costs of instruction (i.e., before taking into account the additional costs of expanding enrollments) follow a trajectory of annual cost pressures, where the natural and quite appropriate rate of increase is the rate by which faculty and staff wages and salaries go up, which in turn tends to track the rate of increase of wages and salaries in the general economy —or, if there is any real growth in the economy, at a rate described as *inflation plus*. This is sometimes called the *cost disease*, or the phenomenon of rising relative unit costs in the labor-intensive, productivity-immune (or at least productivity-resistant), sectors of the economy—which include symphony orchestras, schools, and universities. This phenomenon was first articulated by Baumol and Bowen (1966) and then applied specifically to higher education by, among others, W. Bowen (1968), H. Bowen (1980), and Johnstone (1999, 2001).

Accelerating this natural rate of increase in unit (or per-student) instructional costs are other factors peculiar to colleges and universities that further heighten annual costs in varying degrees in different countries, depending mainly on available revenues. These additional cost drivers include:

- *Technology*: In higher education, technology tends not to be a productivity enhancer and cost reducer—that is, substituting capital for labor and driving down unit costs, as it does in the private, for-profit, goods-producing sectors—but an add-on to higher education's unit costs, altering the very nature (and supposedly improving the value) of the product, but still requiring more, not less, revenue.

- *Competition and ambition*: These naturally and rapidly rising costs are accelerated by faculty and administrative ambitions—ones often supported by politicians and business and civic leaders—to be content not simply with a constant share of prestige or of the enrollment market, but (at least for the elite institutions) to seek greater scholarly recognition, better and more academically qualified students, and higher rankings on such international-league tables as the Times Higher Education Supplement's *World University Rankings* or Shanghai Jiao Tong University's *Academic Ranking of World Universities*.

- *Consumer demand*: Particularly in the United States, where competition is so keen, and where parents are prepared to spend significant amounts on their children's higher education, students and parents alike demand attractive accommodations and grounds, an up-to-date gymnasium and student center, and a totally wired campus.

- *Change*: The natural inflation-plus rate of increases in unit costs is even further accelerated as new programs are added faster than old programs or former faculty can be shed or retrained (quite contrary to a popular and political misconception of higher education as being resistant to change), also clearly adding to continuing cost increases.

Higher educational finance, then, is burdened with a natural unit cost trajectory that in normal years will exceed the average rate of increase of consumer prices generally: that is, it will naturally exceed the rate of inflation, year-in and year-out. Not, as some politicians, journalists, and other critics would have it, at a rate that "just can't continue to rise like this," but at a rate of increase that very well can, and probably will, continue to rise at such levels as long as either taxpayers or parents or students—or all of them together—are willing to pay.[4] The natural unit cost increase of inflation plus is not a mark of managerial ineptitude or of faculty inefficiency. It is, rather, the entirely natural consequence of the nature of the production function of higher education— along with the fact that in any set of measures that are to be averaged, approximately one-half of them will be above, and about one-half below, this average. And since an official rate of inflation is nothing more (or less) than an average of many price increases, it should be no surprise that the rising costs of about one-half of the goods and/or services produced in any economy will be in this "greater than" half—or that higher education, with its limited capacity for replacing faculty with technology, will generally experience cost increases exceeding the prevailing rate of inflation.[5]

Rising Enrollments and the Acceleration of Cost Increases

To this natural trajectory of continuously rising unit, or per-student, costs must be added the cost-accelerating effect of increasing enrollments, which are a function of three forces that vary greatly among countries. The first of these is demographics: specifically, the change (generally the growth) over time in the number of youths within the conventional college- or university-age cohort (ages 18 through about 24). Some countries—such as Germany, Italy and other countries in southern Europe, Japan, and Russia—are experiencing demographic declines. Most countries, however, are encountering an expansion of the traditional university-age cohort.

The second force affecting enrollments is the growing participation rate of this (generally increasing) university-age cohort. Increasing participation rates, in turn, are a function of three factors: (1) an increasing proportion of youth completing their secondary education; (2) changing employment opportunities and a perception of greater competition for fewer *good* jobs, the attainment of which is likely to be enhanced by higher education; and (3) an increasing regard for social and economic mobility and justice, leading to policies designed to boost higher educational participation—particularly among those who are traditionally underrepresented, primarily on account of poverty, but increasingly as well on account of other reasons for historically low participation rates, including gender, ethnic and linguistic-minority status, poor secondary schools, or any of a number of conditions associated with marginalized populations.

As academic potential is generally thought to be distributed fairly evenly throughout a population, the lower the participation rate is at any given point in time, the more that young people with potential are being deprived of a chance to participate in higher education. This participation rate can rise more steeply once secondary enrollments begin to rise, higher educational capacity starts to expand, and financial assistance begins to be made available to redress the purely financial barriers to higher educational participation. Similarly, although it is unlikely that any country has had their traditional university-age participation rates reach literal saturation, it is likely that these rates will rise much more slowly as participation moves above, say, 50 or 60 percent of the appropriate age cohort, as it has in most highly industrialized countries. The point of this observation is to call attention especially to those countries— predominately low-income ones—experiencing both of these enrollment accelerators, that is, steeply increasing participation rates coupled with sharply rising numbers of university-age youth. The result is extreme enrollment pressures upon what is most likely to be a highly constrained university capacity.

A final factor enlarging enrollments, particularly in the more economically advanced countries (which may be experiencing much less of the aforementioned demographic and participation-rate phenomena), is the greater amount of higher education per entering student. This, too, is an accelerating factor, as graduates with their first degree perceive a need for even higher levels of education to be competitive (e.g., the growth of MBAs and other professional master's degrees), and as professions (especially licensed occupations such as teachers and the non-MD health professions) endeavor to raise their stature and limit the numbers allowed to practice by raising the academic standards required for practice and licensure.

The impact of these growing enrollments, driven by any or all of these factors, on the financing of higher education is to accelerate the natural rate of increase of higher education's per-student costs and thus to escalate—steeply and continuously—the public resources required to maintain the quality of the higher educational product.[6] And should these increasing public resources not be forthcoming—which we will argue is the case in almost every country, including the most industrialized and affluent but especially comprising most of the low-income, or developing, world—the inevitable result is greater higher educational austerity, bringing with it both decreased quality and diminished equity.

Faltering Governmental Revenues

The final step in outlining diverging cost and revenue trajectories in a worldwide context, a topic which will be expanded upon in the rest of our book, is to account for the (almost) universal phenomenon of faltering governmental (tax) revenues available to meet these rapidly growing higher educational costs. Again, there are several reasons, differing considerably by country, for the inability of governmental revenues to keep up with the steeply rising trajectory of higher educational costs and revenue needs. For example, governments everywhere struggle more and more under escalating burdens of seemingly nondiscretionary increases in public spending obligations: pensions, the rising costs of elementary and secondary education, health care, public infrastructure, national security, and interest on national debts. Electorates in many highly industrialized countries have been getting more conservative, particularly in their distaste for continually rising taxes and what some perceive to be wasteful government spending. Many European countries, with their high social-welfare costs—typically spending from one-third to more than one-half of their national gross domestic products (GDPs) in the public sector—are trying to shift productive resources to the private sector and reduce public deficits to comply with the requirements of the European Community and the Euro Zone. Russia, the rest of the countries that have emerged from the former

Soviet Union, and the formerly Communist countries of Central and Eastern Europe all labor under the enormous costs of building an internationally competitive, productive infrastructure and weaning a labor force away from its deeply rooted dependence on state enterprises and governmental employment. The United States struggles with an overconsuming, under-saving population that is unwilling to tax itself for the public benefits it demands.

Taxation in developing countries, where production and incomes (and thus theoretically taxable wealth) tend to be low anyway, and where the most steeply rising enrollment pressures are felt, is also technically difficult. The financial challenge to such governments is how to get a share of purchasing power when relatively little wealth comes from large, stable enterprises that can be taxed and that can also be counted upon to withhold taxes from their employees. For example, in an analysis of taxation, tax capacity, and needed tax reforms in sub-Saharan Africa, researchers from Norway's Michelson Institute found the tax-to-GDP ratio to be around 21 percent in sub-Saharan Africa (as low as 10% in Tanzania and Uganda) compared with an Organisation for Economic Co-operation and Development (OECD) average of some 32 percent, suggesting what might simply be an inadequate tax effort. However, while the Norwegian researchers found considerable room for improvements in fiscal management in the public sectors and cited many examples of ineffective, costly, and coercive tax-collection efforts, especially at the local levels, they warned that "attempts to squeeze additional revenues from poorly designed taxes may exacerbate the negative effects of the tax system on the economy and the society in general." Additionally, they concluded that "it is unlikely that a substantial widening of the tax base can be achieved without increasing the tax burden of the poorer segments of the society" (Fjelstad and Rakner 2003).

Former Communist countries, once dependent on easy and extensive turnover taxes on state-owned enterprises, now need to tax personal or corporate incomes, retail or commercial transactions, and property. All such assessments are difficult to calculate, expensive to collect, and relatively easy to evade. Businesses and individuals in many countries seem increasingly able to hide or shield incomes and the value of their taxable assets. And even in affluent, highly industrialized countries with efficient tax systems, the expanding globalization of the world economy encourages productive enterprises and wealthy individuals to flee to countries with lower taxes.

Finally, governments everywhere are contending with competing new needs for increasingly scarce public dollars—needs that may be more politically and socially compelling than a voracious public higher educational sector (especially one that most citizens' children in low-income countries will probably not see and that most citizens in affluent countries may believe to be too costly to begin with). In much of the developing world and in many transitional countries, for example, the competitors for meager public revenues include the replacement of decrepit public infrastructure, unfunded pension obligations, the need for a workable social safety net, and the cost of reversing generations of environmental degradation. In sub-Saharan Africa, competition for the extremely scarce public dollar is truly formidable, comprising, in addition to the needs listed above, public health (including the old scourge of malaria and the new pandemic of HIV-AIDS), elementary and secondary education, and assistance to generally faltering economies. As a result, although the government (or the taxpayer) will continue to be the principal revenue source for public higher education throughout the world, most or even all of whatever limited additional revenue can be squeezed out of public treasuries will be absorbed by the need to accommodate at least some of the inevitably expanding higher educational enrollments, leaving little (or nothing, or worse) to maintain faculty and staff salaries, improve faculty-student ratios, and meet the needs of deteriorating physical plants.

Higher Educational Austerity

Most of the world, from highly industrialized to low-income countries, and including countries embracing market capitalism, socialism, or combinations thereof, is experiencing a divergence between the trajectories of steeply rising higher educational costs and the flat or even declining trajectories of available public revenues. As we have seen, these diverging trajectories are a function of three principal forces: (1) rapidly increasing unit, or per-student, costs; (2) escalating higher educational enrollments, in turn caused by a combination of population growth and the mounting higher educational participation rates of this expanding population; and (3) a dependence on what in most countries is increasingly inadequate governmental revenue. These forces vary by country, but the result in most countries—and especially in low- and middle-income countries—has been far greater austerity in both universities and other institutions of higher education, as well as in national systems of higher education. This nearly universal—and growing—higher educational austerity in turn has affected

- *universities and other institutions of higher education*—manifested by, among others, overcrowding in lecture theaters, restive and over-worked faculty, insufficient library holdings, outdated computing and telecommunications devices, deteriorating physical plants, less time and support for faculty research, and a widely assumed loss in the quality of both teaching and learning, as well as of scholarship;
- *national systems of higher education*—manifested by capacity constraints, the inability to accommodate all graduates of academic secondary levels who are capable and desirous of further study, a loss of the most talented faculty to countries with fewer financial troubles, and an increasing inability to compete in the global knowledge economy; and
- *students*—who are facing tuition fees where there used to be none, or very rapidly rising fees in places where they already existed, in addition to the rising costs of student living; all of which contribute to a requirement to work and earn while studying or a need to go into debt, or both, for those fortunate enough to find a place at all (with many having left the system long before completing secondary school, never experiencing even the possibility of tertiary education).

This austerity has been most crippling in sub-Saharan Africa (Task Force on Higher Education and Society 2002; Ng'ethe et al. 2003; Sawyerr 2004), but it is also serious throughout developing countries and in many transitional countries, especially those emerging from the former Soviet Union. But the kind of austerity exhibited by severe overcrowding can been seen as well in much of Europe and Latin America, with students unable to find seats in lecture theaters, and with instruction reduced to didactics and only rarely open to discussion or the opportunity to ask questions. And the kinds of austerity evident in the loss of secure faculty positions and faculty morale, or in deteriorating physical plants, or in students leaving higher education with burdensome levels of debt, can be seen in countries as affluent as Canada, Sweden, the United Kingdom, and the United States.[7]

In addition to this sheer austerity, and especially noticeable in countries that have moved toward the political Right, there is a diminution of trust in government and in the public sector generally, including (at times, it would seem, *especially*) in public universities. This mood both reflects and accounts for the loss of some of the esteem in which public universities were once held. It has led to calls for additional and frequently burdensome forms of accountability and other governmental intrusion into the management of universities (sometimes contradicting the more general trend away from overregulation and toward greater university autonomy). And it has contributed to the growing underfunding both of universities and of student financial assistance.

The link between this mood—what might described as a curious mixture of fiscal conservatism and populist antielitism—and the burgeoning underfunding of higher educational budgets is the sense among some (generally, but not always, politically conservative) political, business, and civic leaders that public colleges and universities are both wasteful and insufficiently responsive, either to their clients (students and parents), to businesses and other enterprises that employ their graduates, or to the taxpayers who pay so much of their costs. Worse, university leaders and faculty are perceived, especially by politicians and much of the press, as being out of touch with realities, aloof, and sometimes arrogant. To some degree, particularly in the United States and a number of other highly industrialized countries, a measure of the austerity in public higher education can be ascribed not simply to a scarcity of public revenues or to other public priorities, and certainly not to an underappreciation of the importance of higher education, but rather to a political perception of much-needed fiscal discipline: the kind of tough love that a parent might impose on a wasteful child by cutting his or her allowance.

Similarly, cuts in student financial assistance budgets (or, just as likely, a failure to increase financial assistance budgets enough to accommodate growing numbers of eligible students as well as the escalating expenses of college attendance) are rationalized in part by the belief that too many of the students on the margin of these expanding enrollments—that is, those who are now endeavoring to enter postsecondary education who would not have completed an academic high school with such aspirations a decade or two or three ago—are not academically worthy enough. And politicians, especially on the political Right, might point to declining performances on entrance and exit examinations or to the greater numbers of drop-outs (or *wastage*) to buttress their view that participation rates in higher education have increased not only beyond the needs of the economy, but also beyond the abilities or true academic interests of marginal entering students.

The Political and Ideological Context of Austerity and Its Policy Solutions

The political responses to the increasing condition of higher educational austerity that so affect the financial fortunes of colleges and universities, as well as the accessibility of higher educational opportunities, occur within political and ideological contexts that are both country-specific and global. At the risk of oversimplification, views and proposed solutions at the extreme political and ideological Left tend to be those accepting the appropriateness of governmental ownership of virtually all institutionalized means of production (including universities and colleges), in addition to governmental allocation of resources, the establishment of prices, and the remuneration of workers. However, as the one-time *command economies* (e.g., the former Soviet Union, the Communist block of Eastern and Central European countries, as well as China and other Asian countries exhibiting similar political and economic systems) have given way to *transitional economies*, which accept a large role for private enterprise and the useful place of markets in the allocation of resources and rewards, one way the political Left has become characterized is less by its adherence to an old Soviet system of production, distribution, and reward and more by its continuing advocacy of high levels of taxation, governmental regulation, and public employment, plus its criticism of the income disparities, economic instability, savage competition, and commercialism associated with markets and capitalism. This *critical Left* is preoccupied with what it sees as the pervasive and continuing role of socioeconomic class—along with race, ethnicity, and gender—in the distribution of power, status, and wealth in those countries that embrace markets and private enterprise. It also tends to view poor countries (similar to the way it views poor people) as victims—of the World Bank and other agencies of international finance, and of the investment and trade policies of the advanced industrialized nations (especially of the United States).

At the other extreme are the views associated with the Far Right that would diminish public employment and the size of the public sector generally, including publicly owned and financed higher education. The political Right tends to view government, including both politicians and civil servants, as less productive and more self-serving, preoccupied with maintaining the salaries and other emoluments that go with governmental employment, and generally oblivious to the view that governmental employees must live off the goods and services created mainly in the private sector (the claims on which have come into the possession of state employees through direct and indirect taxes or by inflationary deficit financing). In keeping with this mistrust of governmental institutions (including public universities) and governmental employees (including faculty and staff of these public universities), those on the Right tend to be more critical of what they perceive to be governmental waste and more insistent on greater measures of accountability. At the same time, the political Right is more accepting of the economic instabilities and disparities in income and wealth that follow capitalism, holding such conditions to be the necessary price for the dynamism and high productivity of private enterprise. In America, members of the right wing generally prefer private higher education—although most will accept some governmental cash transfers to *their* private institutions in order to level the playing field and provide constructive examples (mainly of efficiency) to the public universities. The political Right also tends to view merit and ambition as the appropriate criteria for selection to the most prestigious institutions of higher education—with no exceptions (or preferences, or affirmative action) to compensate for the possible influence of social class or other attributes, such as race or gender, on academic merit or ambition as conventionally measured. (Correspondingly, the Right tends to downplay the role[s] of race, class, and gender in the determination of who comes into power, privilege, and remuneration.)[8]

As in any portrayal of a range, most countries and governments and polities are somewhere near the center, generally vacillating between a Center Right and a Center Left, but always feeling pressures from the extremes. Universities—especially public ones, but private universities as well—always operate in a country-specific political and economic context, although they also follow their own historical context and exist in an increasingly globalized international context. Institutional financial problems, as well as possible solutions and the likelihood of their adoption all occur within these larger contexts. At the same time, unlike many scholars of comparative higher education (most of whom are not economists and are mainly to our political Left), we believe that the factors most directly affecting the financing of higher education and described in the preceding chapter—namely, the inexorably rising per-student costs, the growing rates of participation and consequently expanding enrollments, the limits on governmental taxing capabilities in most countries, and the lengthy queue of socially and politically compelling yet competing public needs—are beyond politics and ideologies.

Politics and ideology, however, are not immaterial. The aggressively capitalistic United Kingdom and United States, for example, have usually had different priorities and put forth different solutions to the problems of austerity in higher education than did the former Soviet Union under its Marxist-Leninist command economy, and they will probably continue to differ from the new transitional countries, with their socialist market systems, or from the social welfare democracies of Scandinavia. However, the expanding reach of tuition fees and other forms of revenue diversification, as well as the increasing pressures for accountability or for more institutional autonomy, owe far more to a virtually universal underlying higher educational production function, to the escalating demand for higher education, and to demographics than to political abstractions like globalization or capitalism (academic or otherwise) or to any prescriptions of the World Bank, multinational corporations, or a hegemonic Anglo-America.

Solutions to Growing Higher Educational Austerity

In response to these financial pressures and increasing demands for accountability, universities and national systems have sought solutions. Some of the *cost-side* solutions—for example, enlarging class sizes and teaching loads, deferring maintenance, substituting lower-cost part-time faculty for higher-cost full-time faculty, dropping low-priority programs, and cutting or freezing financial assistance—are both difficult, academically problematic, and heavily contested, especially by the faculty and their political allies. Both groups frequently reject outright the claims of insufficient public revenues and, even if they accept the basic economic principle of scarcity, may have very different notions of proper academic priorities from either their governments or their university leaders.

Solutions on the *revenue side*—instituting tuition fees (or rapidly raising them), encouraging faculty and institutional entrepreneurship, promoting philanthropy, and allowing or encouraging a demand-absorbing private sector— tend to be favored more by faculty and staff, but such responses are also difficult, politically contested (especially cost-sharing, or the shift of costs to students and/or parents), and not always as successful as hoped for or planned. And increased cost-sharing—which moves expenses from either taxpayers or parents to students, in the form of greater indebtedness—may be causing new and unintended burdens upon heavily indebted graduates, in forms such as a loss of credit, disincentives to marriage, reluctance to take low-paying public service employment, or the erosion of responsible borrowing behavior.

Two Worldwide Issues

What emerges from this worldwide confluence of surging demand for, and rapidly rising costs of, higher education, coupled with increasingly limited public revenues and the political and ideological context in which governmental policy is made, are two large, complex, and interrelated issues. First, *How can this escalating demand for greater (but still high-quality) higher educational capacity be financed?* Policy responses to this dilemma include those that attempt to maximize higher educational productivity—for example, merging institutions for economies of scale, enlarging student-faculty ratios, freezing (or simply not paying) staff salaries, or substituting very low-paid, part-time faculty for better-paid, full-time faculty—and those that attempt to supplement limited public revenue with private revenue, such as tuition fees, philanthropic donations, and institutional and faculty entrepreneurship. The higher educational reform agendas of most countries contain elements of both of these broad strategies.

The second overarching issue is, *How can higher education resist (and possibly reverse) its natural inclination to reproduce and even to exacerbate existing social disparities and inequalities, whether by parents' social class, ethnicity or kinship affiliation, region, language, or religion?* Access to higher education everywhere is limited by the level and quality of secondary education, including whatever a combination of parental assistance and private tutors can do to further enhance the academic preparedness of an aspiring student. (This is especially true where capacity is limited and entrance to the best universities is extremely competitive, as in Brazil, China, or India.) Where there are tuitions and fees to be borne in addition to living costs and the opportunity costs of lost earnings, parental income is an even greater predictor of higher educational participation, especially where means-tested financial assistance and generally available student loans are limited. Thus, substantial parental income, a white-collar or professional occupation, membership in a dominant ethnic and linguistic group, access to the best secondary schools, and residence in a metropolitan area are each likely to enhance the probability of higher educational participation and completion. And because these attributes are so strongly correlated in most countries, higher education often seems to reinforce and even accentuate existing social stratifications, even while a few of the very brightest and luckiest of the poor or the rural or linguistic or ethnic minorities are able to use higher education to escape from their social and economic marginalization.

This, then, is our book's worldwide context, which tells of a mounting shift in the higher educational cost burden from governments and taxpayers to parents and students, and of the policies that countries have designed to maintain (and perhaps even to enhance) higher educational participation rates in spite of this shift. It is a story that combines economic and financial realities with the realities of politics and competing ideologies. But it is the story of a common struggle: to accommodate the rising demand, both public and private, for a very expensive—and increasingly so—product, the costs of which are everywhere shared among the government (or taxpayers), parents, students, and philanthropists.

NOTES

1. The term *higher education*, as used in this introduction and throughout this book, refers more generally to the larger universe of postsecondary or tertiary or even post-compulsory education. By the International Standard Classification of Education (ISCED), we are referring to levels 5 A&B.

2. The term *neoliberal* has been co-opted, largely by noneconomists on the political Left who are generally against private ownership of the means of production, markets, competition, and individualism. They use the term neoliberal to designate a disdain for those individuals or policies that either advance market economics or the privatization (or partial privatization) of what formerly may have been entirely public or tax-supported.

3. The research expenditures that are normally excluded from calculations of instructional costs are (a) expenditures on grants, contracts, and other forms of externally funded activities, and (b) the expenditures of ongoing, publicly funded, public service and research activities, such as the University of California's Lawrence Livermore Laboratories or the John Hopkins University's Applied Physics Laboratory (for which instruction is a minor part of the mission, and even then it is limited to advanced training). However, in the better-funded public research universities throughout the world, much of the support for research, especially outside of sciences and engineering, is paid for by the provision of faculty time away from teaching (by way of light teaching loads), plus the libraries, computers, and other overhead expenses that cannot easily be disaggregated from the cost of instruction and therefore drive up the per-student costs, particularly of undergraduate education.

4. This does not mean that spending will increase. Indeed, it usually does not—and this is the widespread condition of austerity that we are trying to explain. In short, this

natural per-student expenditure is what it would take to truly keep up and not be plagued by the aforementioned manifestations of austerity.

5. This explanation for the escalating costs of higher education does not take into consideration the possibility that the price of the higher educational product may be increasing because the quality of the product is improving. Or that the cost of the product (say, public higher education) may actually be decreasing—either as labor costs are cut through wage and salary freezes and the substitution of cheap part-time labor for fully qualified (but expensive) full-time labor, or as productivity is forced to expand simply by "speeding up the line" through larger class sizes or increased teaching loads (see Johnstone 1999, 2001).

6. At the same time, increasing enrollments also make it at least theoretically more possible to take the kinds of management actions—for example, raising student-faculty ratios, or implementing new and more cost-effective pedagogies—that are otherwise extremely difficult in a mode of stable or declining enrollments, where such measures inevitably mean terminating jobs and encountering the extraordinary levels of resistance and demoralization that attend any downsizing of an institution.

7. This chapter was begun in 2008, just before the global financial meltdown so evident as we went to press in 2009. The current recession, then, is greatly exacerbating the financial austerity described in this chapter.

8. Curiously, considerable academic concern with the inequities stemming from intergenerationally (and thus unequally) transmitted social and cultural capital is especially evident in aggressively capitalistic and individualistic America and Britain—perhaps because of a general recognition of both widespread inequalities and deeply ingrained racism in their societies—while inhabitants of former Communist countries (even those who would think of themselves as politically Left) seem, at least to the authors, to be far less concerned about the effects of class or ethnicity on success or less inclined toward compensatory practices to reduce the disparities of access and success that are statistically evident in their own countries.

REFERENCES

Baumol, William J., and William G. Bowen. 1966. *Performing Arts: The Economic Dilemma.* New York: Twentieth Century Fund.
Bowen, Howard R. 1980. *The Costs of Higher Education.* San Francisco: Jossey Bass.
Bowen, William G. 1968. *The Economics of Major Private Universities.* New York: Carnegie Commission on Higher Education.
Fjelstad, Odd-Helge, and Lise Rakner. 2003. *Taxation and Tax Reforms in Developing Countries: Illustrations from Sub-Saharan Africa.* Bergen, Norway: Michelsen Institute.
Johnstone, D. Bruce. 1999. Financing Higher Education: Who Should Pay? In *American Higher Education in the Twenty-First Century: Social, Political, and Economic Challenges,* ed. Philip G. Altbach, Robert O. Berdahl, and Patricia J. Gumport. Baltimore: Johns Hopkins University Press.
———. 2001. Higher Education and Those "Out-of-Control" Costs. In *In Defense of American Higher Education,* ed. Philip G. Altbach, Patricia J. Gumport, and D. Bruce Johnstone. Baltimore: Johns Hopkins University Press.

Ng'ethe, Njuguna, N'Dri Assié-Lumumba, George Subotzky, and Addy Essi-Sutherland. 2003. *Higher Education Innovations in Sub-Saharan Africa: With Specific Reference to Universities.* Paris: Association for the Development of Education in Africa.

Sawyerr, Akilagpa. 2004. *Challenges Facing African Universities: Selected Issues.* Accra, Ghana: Association of African Universities.

Task Force on Higher Education and Society. 2002. *Higher Education in Developing Countries: Peril and Promise.* Washington, DC: World Bank and UNESCO.

UNESCO Institute for Statistics. 2006. Global Education Digest 2006. Montreal: UNESCO Institute for Statistics.

CHAPTER TWO

Financial Austerity and Solutions on the Cost Side

We have outlined the worldwide diverging trajectories of higher educational costs and available public revenues and the consequent condition of rising higher educational austerity throughout much of the world. We now turn to one set of solutions to this austerity, which we call *solutions on the cost side*.

Financial Austerity

The diverging trajectories of costs and available revenues were described in chapter 1 as a function of three principal forces: (1) rapidly increasing unit, or per-student, costs; (2) escalating tertiary-level enrollments, greatly exacerbated in many countries by the combined forces of university-age population growth and the rising higher educational participation rates of these expanding cohorts (what the Europeans have termed *massification*); and (3) a financial dependence on what in most countries has become increasingly inadequate governmental revenue. These forces vary by country, but the result in most countries—and especially low- and middle-income countries—has been growing austerity in both universities and other institutions of higher education, as well as in national systems of higher education. The consequences of this austerity (again, varying considerably by country) have included

- increasing student-faculty ratios, which generally mean larger classes, overcrowded lecture theaters, and less use of faculty-intensive pedagogies such as small seminars, classroom discussion, written assignments, and essay-type examinations;
- increasing employment of part-time and other nonregular faculty, and in some countries and some universities, using regular faculty for teaching overloads;
- reducing expenditures on almost everything other than faculty and staff compensation, such as on library acquisitions, laboratory equipment, and technology;
- deferring costly maintenance on the physical plant (a practice that is akin to borrowing, as the deferred maintenance usually costs more when expenditures are ultimately made); and
- in many countries, providing insufficient public university capacity— with the consequent need to raise admission standards—simply to deny entry to many otherwise-qualified students or to allow parallel, tuition-fee-supported tracks in the public universities.

The reminder of this chapter will explore the solutions advanced, and in some cases implemented, to solve this gap on the cost side—that is, by slowing the cost trajectory and imposing cost-cutting and other efficiency measures on universities and other institutions of higher education.

Although this is a book devoted mainly to cost-sharing, which by definition is the supplementation of increasingly inadequate governmental revenues with funds from parents and students—or *revenue-side solutions*—we begin our account of cost-sharing with this examination of solutions on the cost side for two reasons. In the first place, policies turning to such politically unpopular fiscal enhancements as tuition fees and other charges upon students and parents are strengthened by already having vigorously pursued alternative cost-side solutions to the aforementioned diverging trajectories of university costs and revenues. In the second place, responding to the political and other downsides of cost-sharing, it is important for both political and more substantive reasons to continue pressing for cost-side solutions even as (or especially when) cost-sharing solutions are being sought that will shift the financial burdens more and more onto parents and students.

Traditional Cost-Side Solutions

Cost-side strategies deal with the diverging trajectories of expenses and revenues by lowering instructional costs (or at least flattening or lessening their otherwise anticipated increases). At the most drastic, simplistic, and least strategic level, governments may cut university costs by seriously delaying or not paying the salaries of faculty and staff who are remunerated directly by the central government (as happened to university personnel, and all other civil servants, in Russia in the early days after the collapse of the Soviet Union). Or the universities themselves may not pay salaries or other obligations when they become due. This can occur in cases where governmental appropriations simply do not materialize as anticipated, either from a deliberate overestimation of tax revenue at the time the budget was made (in order to protect the government from having to make politically unpopular cuts), or from declining tax collections due to a genuinely unexpected downturn in the hoped-for tax base—for example, when individual and corporate tax bases disappear by those concerned going bankrupt or out of business, or fleeing the tax jurisdiction. And only slightly less simplistic, but still potentially damaging and decidedly nonstrategic, are such relatively easy expense-cutting actions as freezing salaries or student bursaries (especially when increases are expected and counted upon, as in a highly inflationary economy); terminating part-time or less-senior staff, regardless of their contributions to the mission of the university; eliminating expenditures on books, equipment, and other current nonsalary expenses; or reducing all maintenance and repair work.

All of these cost-cutting measures have been documented in universities and national systems of higher education in the poorest of developing nations (Ziderman and Albrecht 1995; Task Force on Higher Education and Society 2002). Providing a more contemporary example, a 2008 World Bank staff report on tertiary education in Madagascar provides a glimpse into the effects of these extreme cost-cutting measures and the consequent higher educational privation in one of the poorest countries in the world. On the cost side, the government of Madagascar has enforced a strict hiring freeze for more than ten years, driving up student-faculty ratios and greatly increasing the teaching loads of the remaining faculty, who were willing to add on many complementary teaching hours to compensate for their extremely low salaries. With no new faculty having been hired, the average age of the remaining faculty has risen alarmingly, with 81 percent aged 50 or above and 22 percent older than 60 in 2008. Very little has been spent on anything other than personnel, including on maintenance, and the infrastructure has deteriorated badly. Some of the regional universities were reported to have had no phones and no electricity for many hours daily for want of paying the bills. Supplies were not available, and the library was reported to have not purchased a single textbook in years. Anomalously, these cuts coexist alongside what still seems to be substantial higher educational waste and mismanagement after all of the easy cuts had long since been made. The main university, with only 500 full-time faculty, carries a nonteaching/administrative staff of nearly 2,200, and the World Bank report describes many of the university management practices as "weak and incomplete" (World Bank 2008).

Cost-side solutions have also been employed—albeit for shorter periods of time and with fewer deleterious effects—by governments in affluent countries during times of fiscal stress. For example, at the state level in the United States, this generally occurs in an economic downturn, when retail sales, property values, and other sources of state and local taxes decline precipitously, as in the 2008–9 recession. At such a time, public higher education can sometimes be made to absorb what appears (at least to the administration, faculty, and students of public colleges and universities) to be a disproportionate share of the necessary state budget reductions. Part of the problem in the United States during economic downturns is that public higher education is the responsibility of the states, and most state constitutions mandate balanced budgets (that is, they forbid the deficit financing of state operations). At the same time, even though state tax revenues may be declining, most US states have what are virtually mandatory expenditures, such as interest on debts, aid to local schools, and federally mandated health and welfare expenditures, which then force the necessary cuts into the supposedly discretionary parts of the state budget, such as public higher education. Since public higher education—however important it may be to local elected officials—is such a large part of the operating budget of any state, a substantial cut in this budget can go far toward solving the state's immediate financial crisis. Last, but not least, public higher education is eminently fiscally vulnerable in a time of public retrenchment, especially in the United States. Public higher education always seems as though it can survive just one more necessary cut—particularly as public colleges and universities, unlike local school districts, can always turn to the revenue side, such as tuition fees and philanthropy!

Other, more strategic types of expenditure reductions at the institutional level—whether to meet an aggregate budget reduction or to free up revenue for reallocation and investment—attempt to reduce the largest university expense, which is invariably salaries and benefits (constituting total compensation), thoughtfully and over a longer period of time, doing so in ways that maintain high-priority programs and eliminate faculty and staff who are the least productive or least central to the core mission(s) of the university. Of course, the least productive or least central faculty may well be some of the most senior and politically powerful members, whose scholarly productivity or teaching effectiveness may have seriously declined. Or they may be administrative staff whose days may be spent in hard work, but in work that no longer adds commensurate value to the mission of the institution. Eliminating faculty and staff positions may be both politically and legally difficult, and at times impossible. Strategic cost-cutting cannot ignore contractual obligations or be oblivious to sensitivity and decency when it comes to the excruciatingly difficult task of terminating faculty and staff. At the same time, if the future needs of the university and the quality of the instructional programs are to take precedence, universities must be allowed to make such difficult decisions. In short, they must be able to maintain mission and quality, even, if necessary, at the cost of losing lower-priority programs (as well as losing popularity, political support, and smooth labor relations).

The management of governmental agencies and the norms of civil-service employment—both of which prize continuity of employment above all else—are generally incompatible with strategic cost-side solutions to financial problems. Typical problems with government agencies are laws, contracts, and political considerations that forbid terminating staff for any but the most egregious causes, hiring part-time or temporary staff in place of full-time workers, contracting out services, carrying unspent funds forward from one fiscal year to the next, or shifting available funds from one budget category to another (Johnstone 1999–2000).

Yet there has been a clear shift in such management-constraining laws and regulations in the last decade or two—especially in Europe (e.g., the Netherlands and the United Kingdom, and extending to France and Germany in 2008–9), many Canadian provinces and American states, and, beginning in 2004, in Japan—all in the direction of giving greater managerial autonomy and flexibility to public universities. Frequently, this entails transforming universities from governmental agencies to public corporations possessing the attendant authority to own and dispose of property, execute contracts, issue debt, and sue and be sued. These new trends in the direction of greater managerial autonomy and flexibility—essentially moving toward managerial models associated with private enterprise—are collectively referred to as *New Public Management* (NPM) and are designed to maximize the university's outputs of teaching and research for the public, or taxpayer, dollar, as well as to provide incentives for maximizing other-than-governmental revenue (Almaral, Meek, and Larson 2003; Herbst 2006).

In NPM, the university, rather than the ministry or the state budget office, may be given the authority, for example, to

- establish wage and salary policies (formerly reserved to the ministry or parliament and to the government's financial, personnel, and civil-service bureaucracies);
- reallocate expenditures from one category to another in response to institutionally determined priorities (formerly disallowed in many countries);
- carry forward unspent funds from one fiscal period to the next, thus encouraging savings and institutional investment and discouraging spending for no reason other than the avoidance of loss or the appearance of an excessive budget (formerly disallowed in many countries);
- enter into contracts with outside agencies and businesses expeditiously and competitively (formerly too frequently politicized and prolonged); and
- receive and own assets and sometimes even borrow and incur debt (not allowed in ordinary government agencies).[1]

With such authority increasingly being strengthened and vested in a president or chief executive officer selected by a governing board, rather than the faculty-elected rector model still prevailing on the European continent, cost-side solutions to financial shortfalls may seek to lower the average per-student costs of instruction in any of the following ways:

1. *Substituting lower-cost junior or part-time faculty for higher-cost senior faculty.* This allows more instructional faculty for the available instructional budget. The advantage to this strategy is that faculty-student ratios need not be

compromised by the budget reductions. In turn, this assures the maintenance of prevailing instructional workloads and an allocation of time between teaching and research, at least for the regular faculty, as well as a mix of class sizes and instructional modalities (e.g., between seminars and large lectures). The disadvantage of this strategy, at least with regard to using part-time faculty, is that it reduces the size of the regular, full-time, scholarly oriented faculty, which presumably diminishes the scholarly output of the university as well as the academic mentoring of students, especially at advanced levels that require the time, institutional commitment, and expertise of full-time, regular faculty. In addition, smaller numbers of regular faculty decrease the contributions to institutional and departmental governance that can only be done by regular faculty.

2. *Lowering the faculty-student ratio by increasing average class size.* The advantage of such a strategy is that it may seem possible, at least on paper, to reduce per-student costs with minimal alterations in the nature of, or the fundamental scholarly expectations upon, the faculty, as well as in the time and attention they are expected to devote to research. The disadvantage of a strategy of higher student-faculty ratios and larger average class sizes is that it diminishes the time a professor can spend with individual students and limits possible instructional modalities—favoring large lectures (perhaps enhanced by instructional technologies), fewer examinations, and fewer or shorter written assignments over small classes, discussion-centered pedagogies, and more written exams and assignments. The most practical disadvantage, however, is that this strategy has already been used (some would say used up) throughout much of the higher educational world, which is now experiencing greatly overcrowded classes and diminishing interest in the academic profession. There are arguably few further productivity, or cost-side, gains to be made in most institutions in most countries (even if the detrimental impact on instructional quality is to be ignored).

3. *Increasing teaching loads.* A third way to lower average per-student costs is to change the currently prevailing mix of instructional and research expectations upon all faculty and to place a greater premium on instruction. Such a change would require altering the most basic reward structure of the university: not just those rewards under the control of an institution, such as salaries and the requirements for gaining tenure and promotion, but also, or even more importantly, the kinds of rewards that are bestowed by the community of scholars outside the institution, which are mainly prestige and reputation.

(In partial support of such cost-side strategies in some institutions in some countries is the view that many institutions that are called—or prefer to call themselves—*universities*, particularly regional institutions in low-income countries, may lack a critical mass of genuinely research-trained faculty or the equipment, supplies, library resources, advanced students, or even time for faculty to do genuine scholarly research after teaching the overloads that are sometimes necessary to earn a living.)

4. *Differentiating faculty workloads.* A strategy of differential workloads would expect more teaching (and less research) only from some faculty—presumably those deemed less productive in their scholarship. This strategy could, in theory, lower average instructional costs and still preserve the fundamental scholarly orientations of universities and, at least for most faculty, maintain the prevailing teaching loads and instructional paradigms. It would require more instruction only from those faculty who have, for whatever reason, become unwilling or unable to contribute to the dominant research orientation of a classical research university. Those faculty from whom more instruction would be expected would include those who would simply prefer to teach more and be expected to produce less genuine research, as well as (and more controversially) those whose scholarly productivity was judged by university leaders or their peers to be insufficient to justify a workload and a salary that presuppose a continuous level of high-quality research.

Whether such cost-side solutions are right may be less important than whether they are even possible, or whether they may have already run their course. In most countries—with the exception of a handful of well-endowed private research universities in the United Kingdom and the United States, a few particularly well-funded European universities, and a few universities selected for major upgrading in China, Japan, and elsewhere—expansions of average class sizes and teaching loads have already taken place.[2] Further across-the-board increases in teaching loads (sufficient to lower the average per-student cost of instruction) may be possible, although, in most universities in the world, almost certainly with a concomitant greater deterioration in the quality of teaching and learning. But a more important limitation on such cost-side strategies is that they would also clearly change the nature of the institutions. The result would not necessarily be more productive institutions than it would simply be very different institutions—and, inevitably, far less scholarly and less attractive ones to future scholars.

Solutions to higher education's financial austerity that rely only on expenditure reductions, or cost-side savings, continue to appeal to politicians—mainly (but not exclusively) those on the political and economic Right who are more likely to believe that public universities are wasteful if for no other reason than that they are public, and who will therefore resist claims from faculty and from most on the political Left that the problem can be solved with more public revenues. And there may be (or, more likely, may once have been) elements of truth to many of the portrayals of waste, bad management, and unproductive faculty—at least in some universities in some countries, and however much exaggerated. At the same time, in most nations several decades of budget cuts and of absorbing more students and instituting new academic programs with little or no additional public funding has arguably taken most (if not all) of the low-hanging fruit of obvious reductions in waste and budgets.[3] It is always possible to make higher education cheaper by forcing faculty to teach more and/or larger classes, substituting part-time inexpensive faculty for more expensive full-time faculty, and letting the plant, equipment, and library holdings run down. However, cheaper is not the same as more efficient or more productive, and it is at least an arguable proposition that most of the easy expenditure reductions have been already forced upon most universities in most countries.

For example, the major limitation of the cost-side strategies of increasing teaching loads mentioned above is that, aside from some of the top research universities of the world (mainly in the United States), faculty workloads have already been substantially expanded and/or effectively differentiated. Student-faculty ratios—and especially the ratio of students to regular, full-time faculty—have been enlarged at universities throughout the world. In the United States and other countries where undergraduate degrees are awarded according to accumulations of course credits, and therefore where small classes are considered especially costly, a great many low-enrollment classes have already been cancelled and students have been driven to take larger and presumably more cost-effective classes. More and more teaching at research universities throughout the world is being conducted by adjunct, part-time, or other nonregular (or nontenured or non-tenure-track) faculty. Finally, the very low faculty salaries attributable to higher educational austerity in low-income and many transitional countries are leading more and more faculty, and especially those without special grants or other sources of income, to take on teaching overloads, which effectively both increase and differentiate their teaching loads.

New Cost-Side Solutions

There remains, however, a view in many countries that much more fundamental changes must still be made—if not necessarily to all institutions, then
at least to some institutions or to some sectors of some postsecondary educational systems—to lower per-student costs and provide some cost-side solutions
to the otherwise steeply rising trajectory of higher educational expenditures.
Some of the more fundamental, radical, and systemic changes might include
the following:

1. *More radical sector diversification.* Sector diversification—or a shift from a
preponderance of higher educational institutions being (or at least aspiring
to be) research universities toward a cadre of short-cycle, less-expensive, less-
selective, more vocationally oriented, and more hierarchically managed institutions, whose faculty are oriented to teaching rather than to research—is
commonly viewed as at least a partial answer to higher education's increasing
austerity. The presumably lower per-student costs of these *nonuniversity* alternatives to the classical research university lie in their higher teaching loads,
which in turn are a consequence of reduced expectations for research, a less-
extensive involvement in university governance, and the presumption of a
lower reliance on expensive equipment, laboratories, libraries, and technology, as well as a shorter duration of study for their students.[4] The form and
extent of these alternatives to a classical university vary throughout the world.
Among the best known are the German technical universities, or Fachhochschulen (FHs); Dutch higher technical schools (HBOs); French Instituts Universitaires de Technologie (IUTs); Japanese public and private junior colleges, and American community colleges. Some would also add the American
master's-level, *comprehensive* colleges and universities, most of which attempt
to provide tertiary-level education that is shorter in duration, more practical,
less academically rigorous, and less costly.

Some countries, such as Italy and Spain, have resisted the nonuniversity
movement altogether. Britain actually erased what was once a clear binary line
dividing the classical research universities, both old and new, from the nonuniversity polytechnics. It now exhibits the *research drift* so prevalent in the
United States, where colleges and universities that once featured bachelor's
and master's degrees and a teaching emphasis now frequently strive toward
more research and the addition of advanced-degree programs. Sector diversification will continue to meet resistance from university students and faculty,

who frequently see alternatives to the classical university as lower in status and designed mainly to track less-well-prepared students—who are more likely to be from poor or otherwise marginalized families—into forms of tertiary education that will limit their opportunities. Nevertheless, sector diversification will likely remain prominent on the agenda of international higher educational reform both for its supposed greater relevance and usefulness to many students (and employers), as well as for its presumed greater cost-effectiveness.

2. *Mergers.* Mergers, at least in theory, can lower unit costs by increasing the scale of operations and achieving savings on such overhead expenditures as the physical plant, libraries, and administration. However, actual savings from mergers still require cutting faculty and staff, including top-level, highly paid administrators, as well as closing facilities, eliminating some academic programs, and giving up precious institutional identity—measures that are often bitterly resisted, both institutionally and politically. If the merger is only nominal—that is, retaining most facilities, programs, and faculty, and merely eliminating a president or rector and a few other top-level administrators—the result may simply be more complicated and less-effective management, a demoralized faculty (for both institutions), and a failure to realize the potentially significant savings of either a genuine merger or the outright closure of one of the supposedly merged institutions. At the same time, institutional mergers may be both necessary and possible. They already have occurred in countries where many universities and colleges developed on very small and frequently narrow scales for historical reasons that are no longer relevant or that have been discredited—for example, South Africa's apartheid division of higher educational institutions by race, or the old Soviet Communist model of small and academically narrow universities owned by and oriented to the research and employment needs of a single industrial sector or production ministry.

3. *Technologically assisted instruction, distance learning, and virtual universities.* In most countries, there has been an explosion of interest in both technologically assisted and distance learning, although the most successful applications have been principally at the margins, or peripheries, of higher education rather than radical transformations of existing universities. New virtual universities sometimes arise with great fanfare and then subside, as most students of traditional university age seem to continue to want a fuller university experience (and some speculate that many enrollments in distance learning programs or virtual universities may consist more of initial matriculates than those who will persist and complete a course of study or a degree). However, there will

undoubtedly continue to be great interest on the part of existing universities in instructional technologies of all sorts—largely to supplement traditional modes of instruction, but also to deliver true distance learning to older or returning students as well as to midcareer professionals needing efficient refresher learning (perhaps to maintain licensure, as might one day be required of physicians, teachers, and lawyers). In developing and low-income countries, the potential of technologically mediated distance learning may lie more in serving traditional-age students in remote locations, where the principal costs of higher education are their living expenses away from home (although a lack of personal computers and good Internet connectivity will continue to be major barriers).

Whether new developments in instructional technology can ease the financial austerity of institutions is unclear, although experiences from more affluent, industrialized countries suggest that instructional technologies may enrich teaching and learning, but they rarely lower—and more frequently substantially increase, at least in the short run—the per-student costs of instruction. In theory, of course, one professor, with considerable technological investment and extensive staff support, can offer instruction to many locations, and possibly to far more students, than he or she could teach "face-to-face" at a single site. And if the goal is to reach out to otherwise place-bound students, unable to travel to a common site for any number of reasons but able to get to remote sites to receive a transmission, distance learning can extend access at a considerable savings over the alternative of placing faculty and a full-scale facility at each remote site. In countries with surging enrollments, financially unable to build and staff more institutions, virtual universities or distance-learning programs may be a key to relieving some of their enrollment pressures, especially in areas remote from metropolitan centers. China, India, Indonesia, Turkey, and sub-Saharan Africa (the African Virtual University) all claim large enrollments in distance learning and in virtual universities (World Bank 2002; Herbst 2006). However, for a single institution, or even a national system, seeking to cope with diverging trajectories of costs and revenues, most applications of distance learning can enrich learning but may actually cost more rather than less.

In the end, while cutting instructional expenses needs to be part of the answer to higher education's underlying financial dilemma, cost-side solutions alone will be insufficient for both substantive and political reasons. Most are too divisive and too easily politicized from both sides (i.e., from those on the outside who believe that there are far more cuts yet to be made, as well as those on the inside who believe that the cuts that have already been made were unnecessary and have virtually destroyed their universities). But more importantly, the gap from the diverging trajectories of higher educational costs and available revenues is simply too wide to be closed by further cuts in expenditures, even with some of the more radical cost-side solutions. In short—and as a segue to the next section—higher education in almost all countries must turn to nongovernmental revenues to supplement the increasingly insufficient funds available from governments.

NOTES

1. The experience of the State University of New York (SUNY), of which Johnstone was chancellor from 1988 to 2004 and president of its largest college from 1979 to 1988, is a vivid demonstration of the adoption of the principles of NPM in an American public university system. From the late 1980s through the mid-1990s, New York abandoned its formerly rigid control over lines (or authorizations to hire), job titles, interfund transfers, and the confiscation of unspent funds at the end of a fiscal year. Notably, however, SUNY still lacks the ability to set tuition fees (and retain the revenue), own and dispose of real property, issue debt, employ faculty and staff, or negotiate labor contracts.

2. For example, Herbst (2006, pp. 34–35) cites increases in student-faculty ratios in German universities from 47:1 to 55:1 between 1960 and 2000 (as compared to the ratios in US universities of between 10 and 25 students to 1 faculty member).

3. Johnstone, with the experience of nine years as president of the largest comprehensive college of the State University of New York system and another six years as chancellor of that system, wrote: "In almost every one of those fifteen years, from 1979 to 1994 (and frequently more than once in a single fiscal year), I and my administrative team had to cut faculty, staff, and operating expenses (on more than one occasion extending to the removal of tenured faculty), totaling approximately 20 percent of the full-time faculty and staff of the state-operated system" (2001, p. 174). And this was the state of New York, in the most affluent country in the world!

4. Some of these commonly assumed efficiencies may not apply to many of what much of the world refers to as institutes or technical universities. Many of these short-cycle, vocationally oriented institutions feature small and very specialized classes and call for less reading and writing and more practical instruction, which may actually be more costly than some university instruction and more like university-level science, with it costly inputs of equipment and technology.

REFERENCES

Almaral, Alberto, V. Lynn Meek, and Ingvild M. Larson, eds. 2003. *The Higher Education Managerial Revolution?* Dordrecht, The Netherlands: Kluwer Academic Publishers.

Herbst, Marcel. 2006. *Financing Public Universities: The Case of Performance Funding*. Dordrecht, The Netherlands: Kluwer Academic Publishers.

Johnstone, D. Bruce. 1999–2000. The Challenge of Planning in Public. *Planning for Higher Education* 28 (Winter):57–64.

———. 2001. Higher Education and Those "Out-of-Control" Costs. In *In Defense of American Higher Education*, ed. Philip G. Altbach, Patricia J. Gumport, and D. Bruce Johnstone. Baltimore: Johns Hopkins University Press.

Task Force on Higher Education and Society. 2002. *Higher Education in Developing Countries: Peril and Promise*. Washington, DC: World Bank and UNESCO.

World Bank. 2002. *Constructing Knowledge Societies: New Challenges for Tertiary Education*. Washington, DC: World Bank.

———. 2008. *Madagascar: Financing and Governance of Tertiary Education*. Washington, DC: World Bank.

Ziderman, Adrian, and Douglas Albrecht. 1995. *Financing Universities in Developing Countries*. Washington, DC: Falmer Press.

CHAPTER THREE

The Perspective and Policy of Cost-Sharing

Thus far we have attempted to establish four key points:

1. The growing importance of, and demand for, higher education throughout the world
2. The rapidly and continuously escalating costs of higher education, propelled by the combination of rising per-student costs and expanding enrollments
3. A trajectory of cost increases in most countries—especially in developing or low-income countries—that greatly exceeds the trajectory of conceivable boosts in tax revenues, therefore leading to a serious and worsening higher educational austerity, with consequences for the financial viability of institutions and a perpetuation of inequalities in access
4. The inability of cost-side solutions alone to solve the problem of these diverging trajectories of costs and available public revenues

These lead to a fifth point: the imperative of developing a robust stream of nongovernmental revenues for higher education. The most efficient and robust revenue stream—that is potentially sizeable, continuous, and least likely to divert the faculty from their mission of instruction—comes from a parent and/ or student, via tuition and other fees. In fact, tuition fees, along with the financially self-sufficient provision of food and lodging and the rise of tuition-fee-dependent private institutions, are growing phenomena in most countries of the world. This chapter goes more deeply into the concept of, as well as the parties to, cost-sharing; resistance to policies of cost-sharing; and forms of and rationales for such policies, especially the implementation of tuition fees. We will leave more detailed discussions of financial assistance to chapter 4, and of tuition fees to chapter 5.

Cost-Sharing as Perspective and Policy

Cost-sharing is first of all a perspective: that the costs of higher education can usefully be viewed as being shared by a limited number of parties, or bearers, in a kind of zero-sum game in which a reduction of the burden on one party must either result in its shift to one or more other parties or to a loss in revenue, either to institutions or to the higher educational system as a whole. This perspective was first articulated and extended internationally by Johnstone (1986) in his study of tuition fees and student finance in the United Kingdom, Germany, France, Sweden, and the United States, and it has been developed and documented further by the Johnstone and Marcucci through the International Comparative Higher Education Finance and Accessibility Project at the University at Buffalo.[1] As the term *cost-sharing* has entered into common parlance in the discourse of higher educational policy, it has also come to refer to a policy shift of the higher educational cost burden—including both the institutional costs of instruction and the costs of student maintenance—from governments, or taxpayers, to a relatively greater financial reliance upon parents and/or students. In her summary for the World Bank, subtitled *Contributions of Economic Thinking to Debate and Policy Development,* Woodhall (2007) observed: "Within a few years, Johnstone's [1986] study had a significant impact on policy decisions in three of the five countries [i.e., the United Kingdom, Germany, and Sweden]."

As set forth in our introduction, cost-sharing (as policy) is associated primarily with tuition fees, although it applies as well to the imposition of user charges for what may formerly have been governmentally or institutionally provided food and lodging. A policy shift in the direction of greater cost-sharing can also take the forms of encouraging a larger, fee-dependent private sector; reducing or simply freezing (especially in inflationary economies) grants or other subsidies; or increasing the effective interest rates on student loans. We turn next to the distinction between, and some implications of, these policy shifts, especially between sharing the costs of instruction and sharing the costs of student maintenance.

Sharing the Costs of Instruction

This policy shift commonly comes about with the introduction of tuition fees (where higher education had formerly been free), or a very sharp rise in tuition fees (where they have long been accepted, either as appropriate or inevitable), or the encouragement of a larger, fee-dependent private sector. Thus the costs referred to in cost-sharing are most often the costs of instruction—which, as developed in chapter 1, tend to rise over time at rates that are considerably in excess of the rates of growth of available public revenues. These instructional, or *institutional*, costs, particularly as reflected in the budgets of public institutions of higher education, are the costs that most often drive policy concerns. They are the costs that tend to rise at rates considerably above the prevailing rates of inflation—a rate of increase that too many politicians, not recognizing that the rate of inflation is merely an average, above which, by definition, about one-half of all price increases must fall, become convinced is *ipso facto* excessive. These are the costs that, particularly in the absence of any sharing of this burden by parents and/or students, fall entirely on governments, which are generally under political pressure from taxpayers to reduce taxes, just as they are always under pressure from competing interests to have these same scarce tax dollars be used elsewhere. And these are also the costs—at least in public institutions of higher education—that politicians are frequently convinced are wasteful, thus leading them (or providing a convenient excuse for them) to resist both the additional tax dollars that are called for by the growing per-student costs and the inauguration of, or an increase in, politically unpopular tuition fees, which would ease some of the cost-revenue squeeze on public institutions of higher education.

Sharing the Costs of Student Living, or Maintenance

In addition to these ever-expanding instructional costs, covered in the public sector mainly by governmental revenues, there are two other costs, more frequently falling directly on students and their families, that are related to instructional costs but generally do not flow through governmental or institutional budgets. These are the educationally related expenses of books, supplies (today including laptop computers), and travel or the expenses of commuting, which are generally borne by students and/or their parents, but which are as much a part of the necessary expenses of higher education as tuition fees. Even more significant are the expenses of student living, or maintenance, including food, lodging, and other necessary expenses of student life. In one's late teens and early twenties, the latter might include a mobile telephone, an automobile (and auto insurance), health insurance, entertainment, clothing, and the like, expenses that would also appropriately be borne by students and/or parents. In fact, the costs of student living, at least if these are incurred outside of a parent's home, are likely to be much higher—and far more of a potential barrier to higher educational accessibility—than are any public tuition fees.

Most of these student living expenses are not, strictly speaking, part of the costs of higher education per se, as they would be incurred anyway if a high school graduate was to have gone directly into the adult workforce. At the same time—and particularly as we are interested in the total expense that must be met in some way by a parent, student, or taxpayer if the student is to spend most of his or her time for a number of years in study and therefore out of the full-time adult workforce—it may be quite immaterial to the student and parent whether it is a tuition fee, or the necessary costs of books and other educationally related expenses, or the costs of food and lodging, that the family can or cannot afford. Similarly, it is (or ought to be) immaterial whether the government (that is, the taxpayer) is subsidizing the costs of food and lodging, or subsidizing the costs of instruction, or covering either the costs of grants or much of the cost of a student loan scheme. While these different expenditures may make the same net contribution to the total higher educational expenses facing the family, and while they may incur the same opportunity costs to the public budget, they may nonetheless have quite different political, as well as cash flow, implications for governments.

The cost (or expense) of student maintenance is also an important but complex and even controversial cost, especially in the degree to which it may (or may not) constitute a financial barrier to attendance. The complexity lies in the seeming subjectivity, or flexibility, of maintenance costs. On the high side, the costs of student living, or maintenance, may be viewed as the same as the living expenses of any young person of college age who is living independently of his or her parents and who is out in the workplace. In the 1970s and 1980s, politically active students in affluent northern Europe, frequently a year or two older than their American counterparts and accustomed to the greater levels of transfer payments and generally flatter income distributions of the European welfare state, proclaimed what they believed to be the justice of the *study wage*: the idea being that they (the students) were doing society a service by attending a university and that society (i.e., the government) therefore owed them a wage similar to the wages being earned by their non-student-age peers.

The concept of the study wage never caught on. However, the growing affluence of high-income countries (i.e., OECD countries and most of the petroleum-exporting countries), plus the concentration of upper-middle- and upper-class students in traditional universities, has allowed many students to enjoy a relatively high standard of living: not from the generosity of their governments, but from a combination of affluent parents (other than in the Nordic countries, where parents are not officially expected to contribute to any of their children's higher educational expenses), increasing possibilities of part-time employment, and—in countries like Canada, Scandinavia, the United Kingdom, and the United States—the widespread availability of student loans.

The other extreme is the traditional, if dated, notion of a student working his or her way through college, supported by low wages and possibly a modest scholarship, and living in genteel student penury in a cheap flat shared by two or three other students, all of them getting by on public transportation. This portrayal of the bright and earnest but impecunious student has a long tradition: a student's willingness to sacrifice, whether for an intense love of learning or for the more modern notion of higher education bringing substantial monetary and nonmonetary returns. In many developing countries—where cost-sharing and market economies have replaced the former tenets of socialism and the financially unsustainable policies of free higher education and greatly subsidized food and lodging—many students are indeed living in poverty, and even sacrificing health and jeopardizing their parent's assets in coping with the rising costs of food and lodging and, frequently, the addition of new tuition fees, with generally insufficient student assistance or student loans.

What emerges from the above sketches is a very great—and probably an increasing—range, or spread, of seemingly appropriate student living conditions and commensurate expenses and an increasing difficulty (or perhaps a growing irrelevance) in stipulating with any precision a reasonable minimum level of income required to maintain a student. In a sense, then, the appropriate student maintenance budget depends very much on what is available, which is not a particularly satisfying basis for establishing a student grant or subsidy policy. The other implication, particularly for the United States—which is characterized by a wide range of public and private tuition fees, living arrangements (i.e., living at home, or in a university dormitory, or in high- or low-cost private housing), and borrowing possibilities—is that the costs of student living can be said to be highly elastic: that is, capable of being much higher or much lower, depending on the revenue from parents, the student's inclination toward (and possibilities of) term-time employment, and the student's tolerance for debt.

This variability in living expenses, in turn, makes it much more difficult to calculate empirically a meaningful *elasticity of tuition prices*: that is, the percent change in enrollment (or in gross tuition revenue) in response to a change in tuition prices (or a change in tuition prices *net* of changes in financial assistance). The standard application of price elasticity is the change in demand, or total revenue, from a change in price—such as the changing quantity of bananas demanded as a result of a change in their price in the marketplace. Research on tuition price elasticity (as well as on behavior in general) that is associated with changes in the costs of higher education to students and their families is discussed in chapter 8. What is relevant here is the overall conclusion: tuition fees are relatively price inelastic, although low-income students and students for whom the decision to matriculate may have been made with some ambivalence are assumed to be considerably more sensitive to increases either in tuition fees or other expenses associated with higher educational attendance (Heller 1997; Vossensteyn 2005; Vossensteyn and de Jong 2006). However, at least in the United States, the more common response either to an increase in tuition fees or to a rise in the cost of rent, food, or gasoline is not a decline in enrollment, especially among those already enrolled, but rather an absorption of the impact of the price increase by various means: obtaining additional revenue from parents, additional borrowing or employment, or spending less on the costs of student living—for example, moving back home for a semester or two, moving out of a high-cost university dormitory to a low-rent student apartment with four or five roommates, or simply spending less on gasoline or entertainment or Starbucks coffee in order to absorb the higher expense of higher education (Simpson 2005). In short, the variability, or flexibility, of student living costs serves to cushion the impact of rising higher educational expenses, whether in tuition fees or in the costs of student living, and to help preserve the overall price inelasticity of higher education.

The Parties to Cost-Sharing

Cost-sharing begins with the assertion that the costs of higher education in all countries and in all situations can be viewed as being borne by four principal parties: the government (or taxpayers), parents (or spouses or extended families), students, and individual or institutional donors. We will examine each party in turn.

Government

Economists in market-oriented economies prefer to view the source of most public revenue not as government, but as people who pay taxes. The exception is countries that have large stocks of revenue-producing resources owned by the state—oil being the best example, although publicly owned land can yield many resources, as it did for at least the first century of the United States, where the sale and lease of federally owned land provided the bulk of the federal government's budget. But most governmental revenue in most countries comes from taxation (or from borrowing or printing money—both of which, as will be discussed below, having essentially the same impact, or *incidence*, as taxation).

Taxes can be paid by most citizens directly and visibly, as in taxes upon earnings, property, retail sales, general consumption, or special goods such as gasoline, cigarettes, alcoholic beverages, airline travel, or imported goods. Or taxes can be paid indirectly and largely invisibly (at least to the average citizen), originating with taxes on businesses or enterprises, which then pass them on to consumers in the form of higher prices on the products they buy. In this way, the tax incidence, or ultimate burden, is not unlike the incidence of direct taxes on retail sales generally. If both prices and wages are governmentally controlled, as was the case in the former Soviet Union and in most of the other command economies of China, the other Communist countries of Asia, and Central and Eastern Europe, and if the enterprises are therefore unable to pass along their very high value-added, or *turnover*, taxes in the form of higher prices, then these enterprise taxes must instead be borne by employees in the form of lower wages and salaries—with the tax incidence, again, being not unlike that of a flat income tax or a general sales tax.[2]

Governments can also obtain purchasing power by borrowing, whereby the purchasing power flows from individual and institutional savers (this is increasingly the case in China and other countries with high savings rates) to the borrowing government, which must then repay its debt from taxes levied upon its future citizens. Finally, a government may take purchasing power from both its current and future citizens not by taxation at all, but by merely printing money, thus shifting purchasing power to the government via deficit-driven inflation and the resulting erosion of the actual value of wages and assets of an average citizen. The average citizen whose wages have been effectively confiscated by inflation, of course, is very much like the average citizen whose wages are effectively confiscated by the higher prices paid to cover taxes on the businesses or enterprises whose products or services he or she buys— or like the average citizen whose wages are directly taxed by income or sales taxes.

Governments may attempt to tax only the rich, or only large multinational corporations, or only their export-earning extractive industries. But such highly progressive income taxation is very difficult and becoming even more so. Not only can income be effectively hidden or shifted (and, generally, the higher the income, the greater the opportunities for shifting or hiding it), but increasing economic globalization allows high-income individuals and profitable enterprises to simply move to jurisdictions with lower taxes if they perceive their tax burdens to be too high. In the end, then, and in most countries, governmental revenue comes largely from the ordinary citizen, whom we are calling the *taxpayer.*

Parents

The second party to the cost-sharing paradigm is the parent (or the spouse or members of the extended family) who may pay some of the costs of higher education by providing funds for tuition fees or cover some or all of the costs of student living, either through paying the expenses of room and board or bearing the more indirect expense of keeping the student at home. Parents can cover these extra costs from their current income, in part from savings (or past income), or even in part through borrowing (that is, drawing on future income). Grandparents or other members of an extended family, or even members of a village or a church, can also be considered parents when it comes to supporting a student.

A successful *expected parental contribution*—that is, when most parents do indeed cover at least part of the higher educational expenses of their children, to the extent of their financial ability, and normally through the first degree or until some equivalent age—is a function of both history and culture. In Canada, China, Japan, and the United States, for example, this expectation extends to a portion of the cost of instruction (i.e., tuition fees in both public and private universities) as well as to the costs of student living, or maintenance. In addition, in both Japan and the United States, parents are used to the very high tuition fees of the private sector and consider themselves financially fortunate if all they face as parents are the not-insignificant tuition fees of the public sector (as opposed to their friends and neighbors who may be facing the much more expensive tuition fees of the private sector). In most of continental Europe, the expectation of a parental contribution extends only to the expenses of student maintenance, as most countries (through 2008) mainly had only nominal tuition fees. This officially expected, means-tested contribution to students' living expenses may even, as in Germany, be legally enforceable.[3]

A parental contribution may also be explicitly denied, both culturally and legally, as it is in the Nordic countries of Denmark, Finland, Iceland, Norway, and Sweden. The absence of an officially expected parental contribution in the Nordic countries leaves only students as an alternative to taxpayers in supporting of the costs of higher education, and then only for the costs of student living, or maintenance, as there are still no tuition fees. In short, the burden borne by parents in the Nordic countries is, at least officially, only through parents also being taxpayers—which, in light of the high and relatively equal participation rates, extensive and generally available student loans, and relatively flat income distributions, seems to be a stable and economically justifiable policy.

The constituent national entities of the United Kingdom represent a sociopolitical culture that struggled with the concept of an officially expected parental contribution in the early 2000s, pulled between the Nordic tradition of no such expected contribution, the intense dislike of tuition fees on the part of the Labour government's political left wing, the economic realities that seemed to need the revenue from tuition fees, and the socioeconomic realities of higher educational participation that was still substantially correlated with socioeconomic class. Before its national devolution, the United Kingdom had been the first European country to embrace more than a nominal tuition fee (in 1997, with a tuition fee of £1500 [US$2,310]). However, in 1998 in Scotland, in 2006 in England, and in 2007 in Wales, voters abandoned the up-front tuition fee that is generally paid by parents and shifted this part of the cost burden (£3000 [US$4,615] in England and Wales) to the student via a deferred tuition fee to be repaid as a student loan (with Scotland having abandoned tuition fees altogether in 2008).[4] In such cases—that is, in countries and cultures that have rejected an officially expected parental contribution—the defining cultural construct is not parental irresponsibility or unconcern for their children's higher educational future or a lack of paternal generosity, but rather the notion of a university-age son or daughter being more properly viewed as an independent adult rather than as a financially dependent child. (This notion is also culturally appealing to most students, even though it generally means more student debt.)

Students

The third party to share the burden of higher educational costs is the student, who can bear some of these costs through earnings (generally part-time during the term or during summer vacation) or through loans. The loans, in turn, can be paid back when the student has graduated and is employed, in monthly installments similar to an auto loan, or, in some loan schemes, they can be repaid through deductions that the employer removes from the graduate's pay and forwards to the lender, similar to income-tax withholding or contributions to an insurance or pension fund. Depending on the loan scheme, the repayment obligation can be *fixed*, as in a conventional loan, with a contractually stipulated interest rate and repayment period, or it can be *income contingent*, with the repayment obligation set at a certain percentage of (generally monthly) earnings. In an income contingent repayment obligation, which will be discussed more fully in chapter 6, the majority of students will still repay the loan at the contractually stipulated rate of interest, but the repayment period becomes a variable, with high-earning borrowers repaying in shorter periods of time than low-earning borrowers. In this form of loan, the required monthly payment is usually (but not always) deducted from the borrower's wages by the employer in the same way that the employer deducts a certain amount or a certain percentage for income taxes, social security or pension contributions, and perhaps for health insurance or other pretax deductions.

Similarly, the borrower can repay the loan after leaving a university and entering the workforce (assuming the loan was borrowed from, and therefore owed to, the government) through an additional tax on earnings until the loan has been repaid, also at a contractually stipulated rate of interest.[5] In all loan schemes—conventional fixed-schedule paid in equal installments, conventional but with installments graduated over time, or income contingent— what is most critical to the student (or at least what ought to be in an informed and rational world) is not the form of the repayment obligation, but, first, the discounted present value of the total anticipated payments, and, second, the number of years required to repay the loan (which, coupled with the interest rate, defines the monthly repayment burden). These and other forms of student loan schemes will be discussed more fully in chapter 6.

Individual or Institutional Donors, or Philanthropists

The fourth party to cost-sharing is the donor. Donations, or philanthropic contributions, are a significant and widespread bearer of instructional costs (that is, beyond government, parents, and students) only in the United States, where these brought some $29.75 billion in new money into the coffers of its public and private colleges and universities in 2007, including $6.6 billion from alumni (Council for Aid to Education 2008).[6] The 2007 survey of US public and private colleges and university endowments conducted by the National Association of College and University Business Officers (2008) revealed 76 institutions with endowments of more than $1 billion (including 25 public universities, public university systems, and public university foundations) and 373 institutions and foundations with endowments of more than $100 million. In 2004–5 (the most recent comprehensive statistics), US private colleges and universities spent more than $30.4 billion and public colleges and universities more than $7 billion from their investments, mainly earned from endowments representing past donations (National Center for Education Statistics 2008).

America's success in capturing huge sums both from returns on endowments and from new philanthropic gifts are the envy of the highly industrialized nations, and most OECD countries have the beginnings of higher educational philanthropy on their agenda of university financial reforms. However, successful higher educational philanthropy on a scale anywhere near that of the United States requires not only a substantial concentration of wealth and favorable tax treatment for philanthropic gifts, but a tradition of giving to colleges and universities—a tradition that is not encouraged by cultures (such as those of continental Europe) that have historically viewed higher education as the financial responsibility solely of the government (Johnstone 2005b).

To the degree to which donations, or philanthropic contributions, have any significance in the financing of higher education, such contributions may go to the institution to supplement other sources of revenue and improve the quality of the university—and thus the educational experiences of all. Or contributions may be applied toward the institutional budget to reduce the amount that must be covered by parents and students through tuition fees, but not necessarily to add to the net institutional revenue. Finally, philanthropic contributions may assist students in the form of grants or scholarships, generally based on a combination of financial need (established by family income and assets), academic merit, and other attributes that the receiving student is thought to be able to bring to the institution. The donors may long since be deceased, with their past gifts to the university preserved as endowments (as is common in the United States)—where only the income is spent for scholarships or other institutional needs and the principal, or corpus, is preserved. Such donations, in effect, go on in perpetuity. Or donors may be individuals, corporations, or foundations giving to support current institutional operations.

The university itself may seem to be a donor through institutionally awarded scholarships, stipends, and discounts. But such institutional scholarships, or grants, are of three quite different forms, not all of them constituting institutional donations as such. The first is a scholarship or grant from a *designated* (or *restricted*) *gift*, either in the form of an endowment or a current gift. By law, donor designations must be followed, so there is therefore no true *opportunity cost*—in the form of foregone expenditures (other than the foregoing of an alternative recipient)—attached to such a scholarship. The original donor remains clearly the donor, even though he or she may have left the actual awarding of the scholarship or grant up to the institution.

On the other hand, a grant or scholarship taken from otherwise unrestricted institutional funds, while looking much like and possibly having the same effect as a designated, or restricted, grant or scholarship, is more appropriately viewed as a *spending decision* by the institution—not unlike a decision to fund an additional faculty position or purchase new laboratory equipment. Such spending choices carry opportunity costs in the form of the foregone next-best alternative expenditure or expenditures. These grants, or discounts, are, in effect, strategic expenditures designed to induce certain students to matriculate in order to strengthen the institution's student profile in a way that will enhance the appearance and reality of its quality. Such high-value students may be high-achieving secondary school graduates, to boost the institution's academic profile. They may be minority students, to achieve greater racial or ethnic diversity. Or the value they bring may be their athletic prowess, musical talent, leadership skills, or any other attribute that strengthens the college or university's reputation and market position. The cost of such scholarships, at least in the American example of private elite colleges or universities, is best viewed as being borne either by the institution's general endowment or by the parents of wealthier students—who may be paying more than would otherwise be required simply to meet the institution's average instructional costs, but who also perceive the college's or university's ability to give such discretionary scholarships as essential to maintaining or enhancing the quality and prestige of the institution and thus the value of its degrees.

A third kind of institutional scholarship, first articulated by Bowen and Breneman (1993) and prevalent in less-well-endowed, tuition-fee-dependent institutions without strong applicant pools, is the *price discount*, which is strategically designed not to attract a particular kind of student but simply (or at least mainly) to maximize net tuition fee revenues. Such pricing is not unlike the sale prices advertised in any retail outlet, reflecting nothing more eleemosynary than a motive to augment revenue or market share (or to fill what would otherwise be unfilled student places). Such scholarships, or tuition fee discounts, have little or no real opportunity costs in the form of foregone alternative institutional expenditures. But they do lower the net revenue impact of tuition increases by the amounts of additional financial assistance, or discounts, needed to preserve enrollments. In the United States, with a great many minimally endowed and minimally selective private colleges, a high level of institutional aid—in the form of discounts that are given simply to maintain enrollments—is considered to be a measure of financial fragility.

Resistance to Cost-Sharing

In spite of the significant expansion of cost-sharing throughout the world in the last decade of the twentieth and first decade of the twenty-first centuries, the rationales for cost-sharing and the forms it is taking are still contested ground, technically and strategically as well as politically and ideologically. Very simply, not all policymakers, observers, or stakeholders share the notion that increased cost-sharing—that is, a further shift of the cost burden to the student and family—is correct or necessary or even expedient. Opposition to cost-sharing, and especially to cost-sharing in the form of tuition fees, can stem from three quite different sources, with variations on each as well as combinations of them.

Ideological Opposition

A shift in the higher educational cost burden from governments and taxpayers to students and families may not be easily accepted, especially in countries or within parties holding sociopolitical ideologies that believe higher education to be another social entitlement that ought to be free—that is, taxpayer supported—at least for those fortunate enough to make it through a rigorous academic secondary system. This ideology, in turn, can stem from a view that society is the major beneficiary of higher education, which therefore ought to override the demonstrably high private benefits received by graduates and their families.

The economic assertion that society is the sole or even the primary beneficiary of higher education would not be accepted by most economists (Bowen 1977; Woodhall 2007), but it provides good theoretical cover for student, parent, and faculty self-interest in the preservation of low or no tuition (although the rational for faculty opposing all cost-sharing is probably less out of self-interest and more out of political ideology).[7] Understandably enough, students, regardless of ideology, tend to resist the imposition of, or an increase in, tuition fees. And students can be a formidable political force, especially in Africa, Europe, Latin America, and some countries in Asia, where they are frequently allied to, and financially supported by, various (mainly leftist) opposition parties and can be counted upon to disrupt the university and embarrass a government that proposes tuition fees or other vestiges of cost-sharing. At the same time, parents of students and would-be students, especially in low-income countries, may be politically powerful elites who may not truly require, but who may benefit most from, free higher education, especially when the supply is greatly constrained (as in most of Africa) and partaken of predominantly by middle- and upper-middle-class families like themselves. This may explain why many students and their families, from affluent to low income and from Left to Right in their political inclinations, tend to oppose tuition fees, even as most economists and policy analysts, including those on both the political Left and Right, tend to approve of at least some degree of cost-sharing and do so in substantial measure on the grounds of its allegedly greater social equity.

In opposition to assertions of greater efficiency and market responsiveness as rationales for increased cost-sharing, many academic leaders assert that a proper higher education is supposed to be removed, or at least substantially insulated, from commercialization and market forces. According to many academic traditionalists, following what paths students believe they themselves want, or what politicians or businesses think they want students to take, is the road to academic mediocrity—even when such opposition tends to buttress the domination of the classical university model over shorter-cycle, and arguably more economically and vocationally appropriate, forms of higher or postsecondary education. The World Bank and the other regional development banks, as well as country-specific and international development agencies, have long had sector diversification on their reform agendas, pointing to a frequently outmoded curricula, even in the most academic subjects at universities; the high dropout, or wastage, rates in spite of the seemingly rigorous selection criteria for university admittance; and the high unemployment rates of university graduates throughout much of the developing world (World Bank 1994, 2002; Task Force on Higher Education and Society 2002).

The two agendas of sector diversification and cost-sharing are related in their stance that too much of what passes for university education in much of the developing world is both cost-ineffective and insufficiently relevant to the needs of struggling economies and students alike. While the arguments for sector and revenue diversification are similarly situated in economic theories of markets, tradeoffs, and the high opportunity costs of governmental expenditures—especially in the developing world, with its long queue of public needs—these agendas are also quite distinct. However, both agendas tend to be rejected by the academic and the political Left, which look upon markets with suspicion, especially when promoted by international entities they believe to be associated with capitalism, globalization, and the Western legacy of colonial exploitation.

Technical and Pragmatic Opposition

The view that higher education ought to be free, or at least very highly subsidized, may also be a predominantly *technical* or *pragmatic* (i.e., regardless of, or independent from, any ideological or political opposition) position. Technical opposition to, or the argument against, cost-sharing is not that it should not work, but that it most often does not and probably cannot work—at least not in much of the developing world (Colclough and Manor 1991). For cost-sharing to succeed as its proponents argue it can and should—that is, supplementing governmental revenue but not diminishing, and quite likely enhancing, equitable access to higher education—requires both need-based (or *means-tested*) grants in order to make up for the presumably missing parental funds from those parents too poor to contribute, and loans where students can borrow against their future (presumably greater) earnings. Highly industrialized countries have the technical means to accomplish these two policy instruments, including the following:

- extensive and generally workable income-tax systems with high degrees of voluntary compliance that capture most sources of taxable income and allow a reasonably reliable calculation and monitoring of family means, or financial need;
- ways to keep track of people's movements, including wide-ranging postal and telephone systems with skip-tracing capabilities, as well as official and enforceable requirements for employee identification;
- systems for income tax, pension, and insurance withholding at the point of wage and salary payment that can also facilitate student loan repayments (especially of the income contingent varieties); and
- effective systems of student loan guarantees as well as primary and secondary private-capital markets that, together, are able to allow private savings to supplement public revenue (thus providing a real alternative to dependence on tax revenue).

Opponents of cost-sharing (Colclough and Manor 1991; Buchert and King 1995) maintain that an absence of such advanced systems makes need-based grants and widely available student loans either unworkable or too costly. Proponents of cost-sharing and student loans even in very low-income countries claim that systems to estimate family means, or need, can still be worked out—at least with some degree of rough justice, even in the absence of reliable measures of incomes and assets, with the onus of demonstrating financial need placed upon the family that is claiming it and with clear penalties for misrepresentation (Tekleselassie and Johnstone 2004; Johnstone 2006a). Also, proponents of student loans in developing countries (Woodhall 1989; Ziderman and Albrecht 1995; Johnstone 2004b, 2006a, 2006b; Johnstone and Teferra 2004) claim that the minimization of interest subsidies and vigorous collection efforts, as discussed further in chapter 6, can greatly improve student loan recovery rates. Improved recovery rates, in turn, increase the real discounted present value of the loan notes: even if these notes are only obligations to repay a percentage of future earnings, or an *income surtax*, and even if these income contingent obligations must remain on the government's books with no private buyers. At the same time—and in at least partial support of the claim that cost-sharing is far more technically complex and difficult to implement in most low-income countries than is sometimes alleged—it is true that a demonstration of means, or need, is both difficult and unreliable in most developing countries. Furthermore, as we shall see in chapter 6, the absence of a private-capital market for student loan notes in all but a handful of countries (principally the United States) does restrict the volume of new student lending mainly to the volume of current repayments plus whatever the government can provide out of current taxation or deficit financing, thus limiting the ability of student loan schemes to supplement scarce current public revenues in any substantial way.

Like the technical opposition described above, another essentially pragmatic form of opposition to the efficacy of cost-sharing (as it was presented at the beginning of this chapter) might begin with an acceptance of the notion that means-tested financial assistance and loans could, at least in theory, preserve accessibility to the socioeconomic mainstream even in the face of rising tuition fees and diminishing taxpayer subsidies. However, this strain of opposition claims that children of the very poor, or from ethnic or linguistic minorities, or marginalized in whatever other way—potential students whose parents may have had very little education and who probably have few college- or university-educated role models—may not understand that a high tuition can be offset with financial assistance. Hence such children might not aspire to a university education during their middle- and secondary-school years, when the absence of such an aspiration may effectively limit their secondary-school performance and choice—and thus constrain or even preclude any options for postsecondary education.

Similarly, some opponents of cost-sharing assert that children of working-class or peasant or certain religious backgrounds may resist the borrowing that some tuition fee policies and other forms of cost-sharing generally require; such children may do so less from personal economic calculations than from a cultural aversion to debt (Callendar 2003).[8] This opposition, at least to forms of cost-sharing that require borrowing, does not deny the theoretical arguments in favor of tuition fees but maintains that families who are culturally debt-averse must be accommodated. We will consider the claims of debt aversion more fully in chapter 8, when we consider the broader issue of behavioral responses to tuition fees, financial assistance, and debt. At this point, we will only observe that aversion to debt is not the same as a refusal to borrow if borrowing, or deferring payments, is the accepted means of accessing higher educational opportunities. Furthermore, even if, in isolated cases, a deeply seated cultural aversion to any form of debt were to preclude some higher educational opportunities, this cultural exception to what is now a feature of modernity (not unlike higher education itself) should not obviate all forms of cost-sharing that call for some contribution from the student in the form of debt or of deferred tuition fees.

Political and Strategic Opposition

Resistance to a shift of higher educational costs from governments and tax-payers to students and parents may also be based on political strategy. Such opposition to cost-sharing may recognize that political authorities do not nec-essarily allocate scarce taxpayer dollars on a rational assessment of the costs and social benefits of all competing claims, but rather on the basis of which claims can muster the greatest political pressure. Given this realpolitik, even those who accept the rationales for cost-sharing in theory may worry that higher tuition fees may lead neither to more resources for the university, nor to additional need-based aid and greater participation among the hitherto bypassed, nor even to a reallocation of public resources to other socially worth-while programs, but simply to a shift in taxpayer resources from higher educa-tion to some other claims that may be more politically forceful, including tax cuts for the wealthy. Thus, it may be neither inconsistent nor irresponsible for higher education's stakeholders, even if they accept the theoretical justifica-tions for cost-sharing, to advocate for higher subsidies and for low or no tu-ition fees—even to the exclusion of other public purposes that are assumed to have their own fierce advocates—hoping at the end of the political day at least to have minimized budget cuts and tuition fee increases and maximized the offsetting effect of additional financial assistance.[9]

Another example of what might be termed a political and strategic rather than a strictly ideological opposition to cost-sharing is an objection to tuition fees and other vestiges of cost-sharing based not on a belief that all resources belong to the state and that the state should therefore fund all of higher edu-cation, but on a simpler and less ideological view that fees, if enacted, would simply find their way into the pockets of corrupt politicians, or even corrupt university leaders, rather than actually expanding either higher educational capacity or quality. Such an opposition is particularly salient in light of the widespread perception of corruption in many low-income countries. Some's study (2006) of student leaders in Burkina Faso, for example, found that many of them were more inclined to accept the theoretical justifications for tuition fees when the perception of corruption was mitigated and their politicians would accept some sacrifice and transparency.

Finally, in a combination of ideological and strategic opposition to cost-sharing—a major plank in the Far Left, or *critical*, opposition to higher educa-tional cost-sharing—is the assertion, contrary to the view presented in chapter 2, that taxes *can* always be raised, both substantially and progressively, if there is but the political will and the leadership to do so. Such a position would further argue that higher education should be near the head of the queue for these additional tax revenues—which would pay for the costs of additional capacity and whatever financial assistance is necessary to remove all barriers to higher educational aspiration, matriculation, and completion, regardless of competing public needs. Moreover, proponents of this view would aver that doing so would obviate the need for tuition and other forms of cost-sharing; it would also avoid the danger of losing enrollments (particularly among the poor) and risking failure in possibly ineffective and expensive financial aid and loan schemes (Colclough and Manor 1991; Buchert and King 1995).

In the end, opposition to cost-sharing and to the imposition of at least some tuition fees rests mainly on these three assertions:

1. Government can cost-effectively and progressively raise additional taxes (or greatly reallocate taxes away from some current, allegedly wasteful expenditures, such as corruption or military adventures).
2. Higher education stands sufficiently high on the queue of claims to this additional public expenditure that these extra (or reallocated) public revenues will be able to fund the inevitably and perpetually rising trajectory of revenue needs without recourse to cost-sharing.
3. Financial assistance will be insufficient to maintain and enhance access and equity, less because of flaws in liberal economic theory, but because of formidable cultural and technical obstacles—in particular to fair and cost-effective means-testing and to workable, generally available, and affordable student loans that provide genuine cost recovery.

And liberal advocates of cost-sharing would have arguments to counter these assertions:

1. The annually increasing revenue needs of higher education—especially in the developing world, where such needs are propelled by a combination of swiftly expanding numbers of secondary school finishers and rapidly rising proportions of these students seeking tertiary education—will continue to outrun the already scarce available public revenues. This inability to tax sufficiently and progressively, and without unintended damage to the underlying economies, has nothing to do with the World Bank, the International Monetary

Fund, structural adjustment, globalization, capitalism, or a simple right-wing opposition to taxation.

2. Even if additional revenues should materialize in the developing world, and even granting a compelling need to direct further resources to higher education, other, even higher-priority needs would claim most or all of the additional public revenues.

3. Many parents will pay for the higher education of their children, as proven by the rising numbers doing so in the emerging private sectors, as well as in the fee-paying tracks of public universities in those countries with dual track systems.

4. The technical problems of means-testing and workable student loan schemes are indeed formidable, but they can be resolved—as will be demonstrated throughout the remainder of this book.

At the same time, in spite of what has been reported as a worldwide trend toward greater cost-sharing, and despite our belief that this trend is mainly both inevitable and desirable, cost-sharing does not diminish the powerful case for a substantial—and, in most countries, an increasing—share of public revenue for higher education, whether publicly or privately "owned." Some amount and form of higher education is still fundamental to individual opportunities and for the personal fulfillment of most persons, regardless of the private returns captured in greater earnings. Publicly funded higher education is still essential to most forms of basic research, to the preservation and transmission of culture, and to the strengthening of civic society. Cost-sharing cannot achieve these things.

The politics of cost-sharing, then, like the politics of almost everything else, is a veritable stew of differing priorities and ideologies, self-interest, trust in government (or the absence thereof), and a belief in the capacity of government to implement policy with integrity and cost-effectiveness (or a skepticism over its ability to do so). In the end, cost-sharing may be better viewed as a concept and a general policy direction than as a specific policy prescription or agenda. There have been many false starts and even failures, particularly in the realms of tuition policies and student loan programs. But the extraordinary need for and general popularity of higher education, plus the apparent limitation of public revenues and the ever-more-fierce competition for these scarce revenues, means that the goal of cost-sharing will continue to intrigue politicians and policy analysts, even in the face of inevitable political opposition.

Forms of Cost-Sharing

Having developed a rudimentary theory of cost-sharing and discussed its political and ideological ramifications, it is time to provide more specifics about the form or forms that cost-sharing can take. Cost-sharing, as set forth at the beginning of this chapter, is primarily associated with tuition fees and other fees, or user charges, mainly on governmentally or institutionally provided room and board. However, a policy shift in the direction of greater cost-sharing —that is, a shift from governments, or taxpayers, to parents and/or students— can take one or more of seven main forms.

1. *The beginning of tuition fees (where higher education was formerly free)*. This would be the case in Britain in 1997, for example, or China in 1997, or Austria in 2001.

2. *The addition of a special tuition-paying track while maintaining free or very low-cost higher education for an increasingly limited number of regularly admitted, state-supported students.* Such a dual track tuition fee preserves the political appearance of free higher education, which is particularly important (and frequently enshrined in a constitution or a framework law) in formerly Communist countries such as Russia, most of Eastern and Central Europe, other countries that were once part of the former Soviet Union, and in most of countries of eastern Africa.[10]

3. *A very sharp rise in tuition fees (where public-sector tuition fees already exist).* A shift in the direction of greater cost-sharing requires that the rise in tuition fees be greater than the rise in institutional costs generally in order for the government's, or taxpayer's, share to be lessened and the parents' or family's and the student's shares to rise commensurately. This has been the case recently in the United States, where many state governments have failed to maintain their former share of public university expenses and where public university tuition fees have been increased very rapidly to fill in the gaps left by the withdrawal of state government funding.

4. *The imposition of user charges, or fees, to recover the expenses of institutionally provided and formerly free or greatly subsidized residence and dining halls.* Similar to the establishment of a dual track tuition fee in most of the former Communist or Socialist countries since the early 1990s, the concurrent establishment of fees for institutionally provided food and lodging reflected both a newfound appreciation of the significance of the market as well as a great need to supplement the collapsing tax revenues in transitional countries in the early

post-Communist period. Thus, food and lodging fees began rising precipitously in the 1990s in Russia, most of Eastern and Central Europe, other countries that were once part of the former Soviet Union, and many post-Socialist countries in Africa and Asia.

5. *A diminution of the value of student grants or other stipends.* This is sometimes accomplished simply by freezing grant or loan levels, or holding them constant in the face of general inflation, which then erodes their real value. This happened to the once very generous grants in Britain in the 1990s (which were later abandoned altogether); it has happened as well to the value of maintenance grants in Russia and most of the rest of the former Soviet republics, as well as in the countries of Eastern and Central Europe. A recent study by Ait Si Mhamed (2006), confirmed by a report to the World Bank (Johnstone, Ait Si Mhamed, and Marcucci 2006), illustrates the effect of such a freeze, shifting student maintenance expenses from the Moroccan government to parents and students in that country.

6. *An increase in the effective cost recovery on student loans.* This means of shifting taxpayer-borne costs to the student could be accomplished through a reduction of subsidies on student loans (similar to a reduction in the amount spent by the government on nonrepayable grants), which might be achieved either by a rise in interest rates or by a decrease in the length of time that interest is not charged, or through a reduction in the numbers of loans for which repayments, for any number of reasons, are forgiven. This effective cost recovery might also be accomplished by tightening collections, or reducing the instances of default, with no change in the effective rates of interest for those who were already repaying their loans.

7. *A limitation on capacity in the low-tuition or tuition-free public sector, together with official encouragement (and frequently a public subsidization) of a tuition-dependent, private higher educational sector.* A number of countries—notably Brazil, Indonesia, Japan, Korea, the Philippines, and other countries in Latin America and East Asia—have avoided much of what would otherwise have had to have been governmental expenditures on higher education by keeping a limited (and usually elite and selective) public sector and transferring much of the cost of expanded participation to parents and students through the encouragement of private (sometimes profitmaking) institutions of higher education.[11] This realignment in higher educational costs from the government to parents and students, then, comes from the increasing proportion of students being shifted from public to private higher education, supported largely by tuition fees.

The Rationales for Cost-Sharing

There are three principal rationales behind this worldwide shift from a dominant and at times near-exclusive reliance on governments and taxpayers to a sharing of costs with parents and students, and they differ considerably in their underlying economic, political, and ideological assumptions.

The Need for Revenue

The first, and least ideologically contested, rationale is the sheer need for other-than-governmental revenue. Following the diverging cost-revenue trajectories model developed in chapter 1, this need begins with the ascending trajectory of underlying per-student instructional costs, accelerated in most countries by the sharply rising public and private demand for higher education, which is increasingly recognized as a primary engine of national economic growth and individual opportunity and prosperity. These realizations lead to escalating secondary-school completion rates, which in turn increase the numbers of those wanting to go on to higher education, compounded by an growing number of adults who were formerly bypassed because of their lack of sufficient secondary-school preparation or higher educational capacity or financial wherewithal, or who had some higher education but now need retraining as the underlying economies and job opportunities have dramatically changed. Finally, these expanding participation rates are further accelerated in many countries, and in virtually all of the developing countries, by the sheer demographic explosion in the traditional college-age cohort. But an increasing demand for higher education will still be found even in affluent, highly industrialized countries—some of which are experiencing either flat or declining population growth, and most of which are already at mass or near-universal participation rates—as a result of immigration from low-income countries and because the average student is consuming ever-larger amounts of higher (or at least postsecondary) education over his or her lifetime.

The imperative for other-than-governmental revenue to meet this rapidly rising trajectory of higher educational revenue needs, then, emerges from the limited ability of governments to raise taxes at these same rates, reinforced by the simultaneously expanding competition from other public needs such as health, infrastructure, elementary and secondary education, and other politically and socially compelling needs. Thus, as established in chapter 1, the main driver behind the worldwide movement in the direction of tuition fees and other manifestations of cost-sharing—however reluctantly and tentatively and with such political battles—is the sheer need for revenue. It is in light of these forces and the consequent financial struggles that national systems of higher education and institutions nearly everywhere in the world are supplementing their limited governmental revenues not only with forms of cost-sharing, as noted above, but with entrepreneurial activities such as the sale of faculty services, the sale or lease of university facilities, a vigorous pursuit of grants and contracts, and fundraising from potential donors. However, tuition fees have an advantage over other forms of revenue supplementation because of increasing examples of success, as well as being able to substantially augment scarce public revenues without simultaneously adding new costs or diverting faculty from their core teaching responsibilities, which is generally not the case with supplementing revenues via grants and contracts or other forms of faculty entrepreneurship (Johnstone 2002).

The objection that imposing tuition or raising it at a rapid rate might exclude potential students from poor or rural or otherwise disadvantaged families can be met, it is argued, by a promise of generally available loans (a topic to which we return in chapter 6) or by means-tested student grants that can be paid for, at least in part, by the augmented revenue from tuition fees. In fact, the proponents of cost-sharing are likely to argue that the alternative to some form of substantial public revenue supplementation is continued or worsening austerity in the public higher educational system, the likely result of which would be limitations on enrollment or increasingly shabby and underfunded universities. And because the sons and daughters of the wealthy will always have alternatives (in the private sector or through higher education abroad), the students, or potential students, who will be hurt most are the very disadvantaged students that a resistance to tuition fees is supposed to protect.

The Allegedly Greater Equity of Cost-Sharing

The second rationale for tuition and other forms of cost-sharing, based less on need or expediency than on principle (however ideologically contested), is the notion of equity: the view that those who benefit should at least share in the costs.[12] Four observations make this principle more vivid and compelling. The first is that "free" higher education is actually paid for by all citizens, whether or not they know that they have been taxed (or have had their purchasing power effectively confiscated by inflation brought on by the printing of money, as explained in chapter 1). Second, most taxes—notwithstanding public policy declarations to the contrary—are collected through levies that are at best proportional and frequently regressive (such as taxes on sales, production, or individual incomes that cannot be otherwise hidden), or through even-more-regressive governmentally induced inflation. Third, a very disproportionate number of the beneficiaries of higher education are from middle-, upper-middle-, and upper-income families who could and would pay at least a portion of the costs of instruction if they had to, thus demonstrating the value to them of the higher educational opportunity and signaling the benefits that are thought to be private as opposed to public. Such students and families would probably prefer that much or all of this particular personal benefit be paid for by the general taxpayer. But whether higher education is subsidized or not—that is, whether tuition is zero, moderate, or high—should make little or no difference in the enrollment behavior of students from more affluent families. In this instance, the higher public subsidy required by low or no tuition can be said (at least by the proponents of cost-sharing) to resemble a transfer payment from the average taxpayer to middle- and upper-middle-class families. Fourth, to the extent that there are potential students who would be excluded from higher education by the presence of tuition, a portion of the collected tuition fees can easily (at least in theory) fund the means-tested grants and loan subsidies that can (again, at least in theory) maintain and even enhance accessibility.

One example out of very many that could be cited is the 1988 report of the Wran Committee in Australia, as it made a case for cost-sharing in the form of restoring some kind of tuition fees.

> Higher education in Australia provides its users with an opportunity to improve their economic and social circumstances. Graduates can expect higher lifetime incomes, on average, than the rest of the population . . . but since the abolition of fees in 1974, students have not contributed directly to the costs of their tuition. . . . The fundamental inequity in our present system of financing higher education is that the small and privileged section of the community who benefit directly make no contribution to their tuition [instructional] costs. (quoted in Woodhall 2007)

The Allegedly Greater Efficiency of Cost-Sharing

A third rationale for cost-sharing in higher education is the economic notion that a tuition fee—a price, as it were, on a valuable and highly demanded commodity—brings to higher education some of the virtues of the market.

The first such virtue is the presumption of generally greater efficiency: the payment of some tuition will make students and families more discerning consumers, and universities more cost-conscious providers, of this expensive product, or service. The second virtue attributed to the market is producer responsiveness: the assumption that the need to supplement public revenue with tuition, gifts, and grants will make universities more responsive to individual and societal needs. A variation on this theme is directed at the alleged problem of academic malingering—that is, students supposedly taking more years or more courses (or both) than are necessary or even useful merely or largely because the courses and sometimes even the living expenses are paid for and because the alternative may be the considerably riskier and less-pleasant task of making one's way out in the real world. Germany, the Netherlands, and the United States have responded in part by eliminating or reducing student aid after insufficient progress is made toward the degree, and some US states have begun charging the higher, out-of-state tuition fee after an in-state student accumulates so many excess credits.

The Worldwide Spread of Cost-Sharing

From country to country, the rationales for cost-sharing are mixed. Further, they are made unclear by the complex and contested ideologies that frequently—especially on the part of political actors—obscure the motives for shifting costs that were formerly governmental to parents and/or students. But the spread of cost-sharing is unmistakable and seemingly inexorable. Clearly, the combination of rising higher educational cost pressures; ascendant liberal, or market-oriented, ideologies; and the success of cost-sharing policies in expanding higher educational revenues with little or no loss in accessibility have combined to advance the worldwide shift of higher educational costs from being mainly or even exclusively the responsibility of governments (taxpayers) to being shared as well with parents and students.

In short, cost-sharing is a global trend. And it brings with it the need to coordinate policies regarding tuition and other fees that are needed to augment scarce governmental revenues with the politically sensitive and technically difficult policies of targeting grants and loans in order to preserve (and desirably increase) equity and accessibility. We turn in the next chapter to a discussion of this delicate combination of tuition fee, grant, and loan policies, before turning in later chapters to the topics of tuition fees and student loans themselves.

NOTES

1. Maureen Woodhall of the United Kingdom, whose 1968 work is credited with being the first international study of student loan schemes, noted that although the word cost-sharing had been used previously, "the term was much more widely used after the publication of Johnstone's study in 1986" (Woodhall 2007, pp. 24–25). The International Comparative Higher Education Finance and Accessibility Project Web site is at www.gse.buffalo.edu/org/IntHigherEdFinance/. For key theoretical papers, see especially Johnstone 2003, 2004a, and Marcucci and Johnstone 2007; for a book of published papers, see Johnstone 2006a.

2. The Soviet worker, for example, might not have felt himself or herself literally taxed, as did the American worker after paying property, sales, and income taxes. But the Soviet worker (or workers in any economy in which virtually all production occurred in state-owned enterprises and in which wages and prices were closely controlled by the state) might have wondered why there was so little left in the form of wages for the workers after these enterprises taxes were paid.

3. As of 2009, six of the German states, or Länder, have adopted tuition fee policies.

4. For more on the UK experience, see Richards 2002; Woodhall 2002; Johnstone 2005a; Rees 2005; and Woodhall and Richards 2006.

5. An income contingent loan repayment that is withheld by the employer and sent to the government-as-lender through what is effectively a *withholding surtax*, is sometimes mistakenly called a graduate tax. However, the *graduate tax*, properly named, is a simple surtax on university graduates (as well as sometimes on those who attended and left prior to graduation), but without regard to amounts borrowed or declining balances. Through 2008, there has never been an actual trial of a graduate tax, although the term has sometimes been applied to an income contingent loan scheme—as in the graduate tax adopted in 2006 by Ethiopia. See Woodhall 1989; Glennerster 2005.

6. Some oil-rich countries might claim that their states' contributions to higher education constitute a form of philanthropy, although the distinction between governmental and philanthropic revenue may be somewhat gray where the country's treasury has been effectively expropriated by an extended ruling family, blurring the distinction between governmental and philanthropic spending.

7. In fact, Woodhall (2007), in her recapitulation of the debates of the 1970s when returns to higher education were first being seriously studied, cites the frustration (and even cynicism) of economists with the seeming lack of good evidence on any of these alleged social benefits.

8. Evidence on debt aversion is mixed. Students from low-income or rural or ethnic minority families in many countries and cultures do appear to be more generally negative and anxious about debt. However, as most of the research is on students who are borrowing, it is less clear that this dislike of, or aversion to, debt is having a real impact on enrollment behavior—at least of the individuals under study.

9. Johnstone (1993) wrote in opposition to the high tuition–high aid policy that was favored by many higher education economists and leaders in private higher education, as well as by many conservative politicians, who tended to favor the private to the public sector. He acknowledged that a policy of high tuition, combined with generous means-tested aid, might be more efficient in theory, allowing the available public subsidies to be more effectively targeted. However, he was concerned that high tuition can be imposed

for short-term political expediency, while high aid requires a longer-term ideological commitment—and the result can easily be a de facto policy, not of high tuition–high aid but rather a policy of high tuition–low aid or high tuition–high loans only.

10. Interestingly, China, which began with a dual track tuition fee, changed to a universal tuition fee in 1997.

11. The distinction between nonprofit and for-profit institutions of higher education, while quite precise in advanced industrialized countries with well-developed tax laws, accountancy, and systems of institutional accreditation, is much less clear in many transitional and developing countries, where ownership, governance, and management are intertwined and profits can be hidden in salaries and bonuses rather than in dividends.

12. Some classic expositions of this equity argument include Hansen and Weisbrod 1969; Carnegie Commission on Higher Education 1973; Jallade 1978; Psacharopoulos and Woodhall 1985; and Hearn, Griswold, and Marine 1996.

REFERENCES

Ait Si Mhamed, Ali. 2006. Cost-Sharing in Moroccan Higher Education: Perceptions and Attitudes of Students and Parents. Ph.D. diss., Department of Educational Leadership and Policy, State University of New York at Buffalo.

Bowen, Howard R. 1977. *Investment in Learning*. San Francisco: Jossey Bass.

Bowen, William G., and David W. Breneman. 1993. Student Aid: Price Discount or Educational Investment? *College Board Review* (167):2–6.

Buchert, Lene, and Kenneth King, eds. 1995. *Learning from Experience: Policy and Practice in Aid to Higher Education*. The Hague: CESO/NORRAG.

Callendar, Claire. 2003. *Attitudes to Debt: School Leavers and Further Education Students' Attitudes to Debt and Their Impact on Participation in Higher Education*. London: Universities UK and Higher Education Funding Council for England.

Carnegie Commission on Higher Education. 1973. *Higher Education: Who Pays? Who Benefits? Who Should Pay?* New York: McGraw-Hill.

Colclough, Christopher, and James Manor. 1991. *States or Markets? An Assessment of Neo-Liberal Approaches to Education Policy*. Oxford: Clarendon Press.

Council for Aid to Education. 2008. Contributions to Colleges and Universities Up by 6.3 Percent to $29.75 billion. www.cae.org/content/pdf/VSE 2007 Survey Press Release .pdf.

Glennerster, Howard. 2005. A Graduate Tax Revisited. *Higher Education Review* 35 (2): 25–40.

Hansen, W. Lee, and Burton A. Weisbrod. 1969. *Benefits, Costs, and Finance of Higher Education*. Chicago: Markham.

Hearn, James C., Carolyn P. Griswold, and Ginger M. Marine. 1996. Region, Resources and Reason: A Contextual Analysis of State Tuition and State Aid Policies. *Research in Higher Education* 37 (3):241–278.

Heller, Donald E. 1997. Student Price Response in Higher Education: An Update to Leslie and Brinkman. *Journal of Higher Education in Africa* 38 (6):624–659.

Jallade, Jean-Pierre. 1978. Financing Higher Education: The Equity Aspects. *Comparative Education Review* (June):209–325.

Johnstone, D. Bruce. 1986. *Sharing the Costs of Higher Education: Student Financial Assistance in the United Kingdom, the Federal Republic of Germany, France, Sweden, and the United States.* New York: College Entrance Examination Board.

———. 1993. The High Tuition–High Aid Model of Public Higher Education Finance: The Case Against. Office of the SUNY Chancellor [for the National Association of System Heads]. www.gse.buffalo.edu/FAS/Johnston/HIGHAID.htm.

———. 2002. Challenges of Financial Austerity: Imperatives and Limitations of Revenue Diversification in Higher Education. Special international issue of *Welsh Journal of Education* 11 (1):18–36.

———. 2003. Cost-Sharing in Higher Education: Tuition, Financial Assistance, and Accessibility. *Czech Sociological Review* 39 (3):351–374.

———. 2004a. The Applicability of Income Contingent Loans in Developing and Transitional Countries. *Journal of Educational Planning and Administration* [New Delhi, India] 18 (2):159–174.

———. 2004b. The Economics and Politics of Cost-Sharing in Higher Education: Comparative Perspectives. *Economics of Education Review* 20 (4):403–410.

———. 2005a. Fear and Loathing of Tuition Fees: An American Perspective on Higher Education Finance in the UK. *Perspectives* 9 (1):12–16.

———. 205b. A Political Culture of Giving and the Philanthropic Support of Public Higher Education in International Perspective. *International Journal of Educational Advancement* 5 (3):256–264.

———. 2006a. *Financing Higher Education: Cost-Sharing in International Perspective.* Boston: Boston College Center for International Higher Education and Sense Publishers.

———. 2006b. Higher Educational Accessibility and Financial Viability: The Role of Student Loans. In *Higher Education in the World 2006: The Financing of Universities,* ed. J. Tres and F. López-Segrera. Barcelona: Palgrave Macmillan.

Johnstone, D. Bruce, Ali Ait Si Mhamed, and Pamela Marcucci. 2006. *Reforming the Moroccan University Student Financial Aid System: A Technical Report to the World Bank.* Washington, DC: World Bank.

Johnstone, D. Bruce, and Damtew Teferra, eds. 2004. Cost-Sharing and Other Forms of Revenue Supplementation in African Higher Education. Special issue of *Journal of Higher Education in Africa* 2 (2).

Marcucci, Pamela, and D. Bruce Johnstone. 2007. Tuition Fee Policies in a Comparative Perspective: Theoretical and Political Rationales. *Journal of Higher Education Policy and Management* 29 (1):25–40.

National Association of College and University Business Officers. 2008. *2007 NACUBO Endowment Study.* Washington, DC: NACUBO.

National Center for Education Statistics. 2008. Revenues of Public Degree-Granting Institutions, Table 338, and Revenues of Private Not-for-Profit Degree-Granting Institutions, Table 342. Washington, DC: National Center for Education Statistics. http://nces.ed.gov/programs/digest/d07/tables/dt07_338.asp and http://nces.ed.gov/programs/digest/d07/tables/dt07_342.asp.

Psacharopoulos, George, and Maureen Woodhall. 1985. *Education for Development.* Oxford: Oxford University Press for the World Bank.

Rees, Teresa. 2005. *Fair and Flexible Funding: A Welsh Model to Promote Quality and Access in Higher Education; Final Report of an Independent Study into the Devolution of the Stu-*

dent Support System and Tuition Fee Regime in Wales (The Rees Review). Cardiff: Department for Education and Training, Welsh Assembly Government.

Richards, Ken. 2002. Reforming Higher Education Student Finance in the UK: The Impact of Recent Changes and Proposals for the Future. Special international issue of *Welsh Journal of Education* 11 (1):48–63.

Simpson, Bobby Jo. 2005. The Effects of the Increase in SUNY Undergraduate Tuition in the 2003–2004 Academic Year on Undergraduates at the University at Buffalo. Ph.D. diss., Department of Educational Leadership, State University of New York at Buffalo.

Some, Touorouzou. 2006. Cost-Sharing in Francophone West Africa: Student Resistance and Institutional Stability at the University of Ouagadougou, Burkina Faso. Ph.D. diss., Department of Educational Leadership and Policy, State University of New York at Buffalo.

Task Force on Higher Education and Society. 2002. *Higher Education in Developing Countries: Peril and Promise.* Washington, DC: World Bank and UNESCO.

Tekleselassie, Abebayehu, and D. Bruce Johnstone. 2004. Means-Testing: The Dilemma of Targeting Subsidies in African Higher Education. *Journal of Higher Education in Africa* 2 (2):135–158.

Vossensteyn, Hans. 2005. Perceptions of Student Price-Responsiveness. University of Twente, Enschede, The Netherlands. http://www.utwente.nl/cheps/publications/.

Vossensteyn, Hans, and Uulkje de Jong. 2006. Student Financing in the Netherlands: A Behavioural Economic Perspective. In *Cost-Sharing and Accessibility in Higher Education: A Fairer Deal?* ed. Pedro N. Teixeira, D. Bruce Johnstone, Maria J. Rosa, and Hans Vossensteyn. Douro Series, Higher Education Dynamics, vol. 14. Dordrecht, The Netherlands: Springer.

Woodhall, Maureen. 1989. *Financial Support for Students: Grants, Loans, or Graduate Tax?* London: Kogan Page.

———, ed. 2002. Paying for Learning: The Debate on Student Fees, Grants and Loans in International Perspective [editorial]. Special international issue of *Welsh Journal of Education* 11 (1):1–9.

———. 2007. *Funding Higher Education: The Contribution of Economic Thinking to Debate and Policy Development.* Washington, DC: World Bank.

Woodhall, Maureen, and Ken Richards. 2006. Student and University Funding in Devolved Governments in the United Kingdom. In *Cost-Sharing and Accessibility in Western Higher Education: A Fairer Deal?* ed. Pedro N. Teixeira, D. Bruce Johnstone, Maria J. Rosa, and Hans Vossensteyn. Douro Series, Higher Education Dynamics, vol. 14. Dordrecht, The Netherlands: Springer.

World Bank. 1994. *Higher Education: Lessons of Experience.* Washington, DC: World Bank.

———. 2002. *Constructing Knowledge Societies: New Challenges for Tertiary Education.* Washington, DC: World Bank.

Ziderman, Adrian, and Douglas Albrecht. 1995. *Financing Universities in Developing Countries.* Washington, DC: Falmer Press.

CHAPTER FOUR

Parental Contributions, Means-Testing, and Financial Assistance

Cost-sharing, as presented in the previous chapter, is both a statement of fact—that is, that the costs of higher education are shared among governments (or taxpayers), parents, students, and philanthropists—and a reference to the policy shift of some of these costs from a predominant (sometimes a virtually exclusive) reliance on governments and taxpayers to being shared among parents and students in addition to taxpayers. Cost-sharing in this latter policy sense can be seen throughout the world in the introduction of tuition fees where they did not previously exist; a sharp increase in tuition fees in places where they have long been accepted; a rise in other fees to recover what may previously have been governmentally subsidized food, lodging, and other services, such as public transportation; a reduction in or at least a freezing of what may once have been generous student maintenance grants; more effective cost recovery on student loans; and a policy shift of some of the demand for higher education to tuition-dependent private institutions.[1]

The purpose of this chapter is to explore the introduction of parental contributions, means-testing, and financial assistance into the cost-sharing paradigm. This requires an examination of the linkages between parental contributions, financial assistance, and various forms of governmental subsidization, as well as into the possible beneficiaries and the intended and unintended consequences of cost-sharing. First, however, we must explore the differences between a shift of higher educational costs to parents as opposed to a cost shift to students—a difference that we have heretofore obscured by a reference to parents *and/or* students when, in fact, there are important political and cultural differences in the appropriateness of expecting parents as well as students to contribute either to the costs of instruction (i.e., to tuition fees) or to the expenses of student living, or to both.

Parents or Students?

The first question that policymakers must face when contemplating a shift of some of the costs of higher education from governments and taxpayers to parents and students is, Which party? Parents or students or both? The economic rationale behind the case for students bearing a portion of the costs of their higher education is that there are substantial private benefits, both monetary and nonmonetary, that accrue to the student from higher levels of education, and that these benefits therefore justify a tuition fee—especially one that can be deferred and repaid through a loan or through some form of surtax upon future earnings. This premise is generally accepted, at least in theory, by most analysts and even most politicians (other than those convinced that higher education can continue forever as an entitlement, provided free of all charges).

The case for parents bearing a share of the costs of their children's higher education (entailing financial responsibility for up-front tuition fees or the costs of student maintenance or both), however, is based on quite different rationales. The first is that parents, too, benefit from this phase of their children's education—as demonstrated by the fact that so many parents throughout the world take great pride and pleasure in the higher education of their children and willingly buy them the best they can afford, as well as by the fact that older adults in many (especially lower-income) countries may sense that they will someday become financially dependent on their (adult) children. The second is the cultural notion that parents (at least those who are financially able) have a financial obligation to pay something toward the higher education of those students who can plausibly be thought of as *financially dependent children*—at least to some age (say, age 22 or 23) or through some level of postsecondary education (say, through a bachelor's degree). Thus, an officially expected parental contribution for both the costs of instruction (that is, for tuition fees) and the costs of student living is the veritable bedrock of cost-sharing in Canada, China, Japan, the United States, and growing numbers of other countries. And except for the Nordic countries, most of continental Europe (which continues to feature nominal or no tuition fees) still considers student maintenance a parental responsibility; in Germany it is even a legally enforceable obligation.

The monies derived from Americans and others who share the cultural notion of the appropriateness of an expected parental contribution, especially for tuition fees, are substantial, and to lose or forego this revenue would cause significant changes. Either governmental revenue to public colleges and universities would need to be greatly augmented—with all of the tax burden and opportunity-cost issues arising from annual increases to an enterprise that is already taking large portions of available public revenues—or the financial burdens on their children—who, in many countries, are already assuming the brunt of their living costs though part-time employment or loans or both—would be compounded. This expected parental contribution, then, is almost easy money, although it still allows governmental revenue to be tapped for a major portion of the per-student costs of instruction (public-sector tuition fees, even in the high-tuition-fee United States, tend to be no more than 25%–40% of underlying costs, relying on the government for the rest) and for the costs of access (i.e., targeted, or means-tested, governmental grants and subsidized loans taking the place of parental contributions for those unable to pay).

Lastly, many affluent families in the United States spend considerable sums —upwards of $120,000 and more per child for four years of private higher education and $60,000 or more for a selective public alternative—with no expectation of grants or subsidized loans. Thus the mix of costly tuition fees (for both public and private institutions) plus substantial amounts of grant aid and governmentally subsidized loans for the needy and the middle class, combined with a very high level of income inequality but a ready acceptance of these high prices on the part of the upper-middle and upper classes in order to access selective private colleges and universities, serves—quite informally but usefully— an *income redistribution function*.[2]

However, a parental contribution is not at all the expectation in the Nordic countries, where there are no public-sector tuition fees (and no private college or university sector to speak of) and where parents are not even officially expected to contribute to their children's student living expenses. Cost-sharing (at least as official policy) in the Nordic countries, then, means that students pay all or most of the costs of student living, or maintenance, mainly through student loans; the costs of instruction are considered to be the financial responsibility not of parents but of taxpayers. A parental contribution in the form of up-front tuition fees is also strictly voluntary in Australia and New Zealand, where the sizeable de facto tuition fee in these countries is deferred, to be paid by the student via a loan (unless the parents choose to pay up front). In Britain, it was opposition less to the principle of a tuition fee and more to the expectation that such fees should be paid up front by parents that lead to the virtual abandonment of up-front, parentally borne tuition fees and their replacement by deferred, student-borne fees in the constituent countries of the United Kingdom, which for a short while (from 1997 until Scottish devolution in 1999) had been the only European country with a more-than-nominal tuition fee. It is true that much of the opposition to tuition fees in the United Kingdom was from the Labour Party's left wing, which had simply never accepted the end of free higher education. But equally or more damaging to Britain's short-lived, up-front tuition fee—even though it was means-tested and not imposed on the poor—was this cultural opposition to thinking of university students as dependent children (Johnstone 2005, 2006).

Means-Testing

To pursue cost-sharing in countries where some parental financial responsibility for the higher education of their children is assumed (and this is most countries, whether for the costs of tuition fees, if any, or for some or all of the costs of student maintenance), and where there is also a commitment to financial assistance for those for whom these expenses would constitute a financial barrier to their children's higher educational opportunities, there needs to be some fair and cost-effective system for targeting this assistance: that is, for assessing a family's ability to pay for higher education and providing governmental assistance to fill in for the expected contribution from those families whose incomes are insufficient to pay it themselves. This is the concept of *means-testing*, which is familiar to families in the United States and in virtually all other countries in which parents are expected to contribute, according to their respective financial means, to the expenses of their children's higher education. In fact, the combination of an expected parental contribution and means-tested financial assistance to preserve higher educational accessibility in cases of low income or other extraordinary expenses (such as other dependent children in school, or unusual medical expenses) is the essence of the two main rationales for cost-sharing, which are

- *efficiency*—in that the combination of tuition fees plus means-tested financial assistance targets more of the taxpayers' assistance where it makes a difference (that is, targeting by financial means reduces some of the subsidization to families whose children will attend a college or university anyway); and
- *equity*—in that parents are expected to pay what they can, but higher educational accessibility is not jeopardized because means-tested financial assistance helps make up for a lack of funds.

Means-testing, however, is complex, difficult, and costly. Two particular complexities are (1) the treatment of assets and (2) the stipulation of the parental or family unit that is deemed to have financial responsibility.

The Treatment of Assets

The first complication in any means-testing scheme is the treatment of assets: that is, anything over and above a consideration of current income (Tekleselassie and Johnstone 2004; Johnstone 2006a). Assets—whether in the form of savings and investments or ownership of a home, business, or farm—add to the financial strength of the family and to its presumed ability to contribute toward the costs of higher education, and thus are frequently part of a means test for targeting subsidies. The consideration of assets in determining an expected parental (or family) contribution, while almost always controversial, is used in at least two quite different ways.

First, in so far as assets in most cases correlate reasonably well with current income, some appraisal of assets can serve to corroborate other measures of income and thus signal any suspected underreporting of income. This is particularly useful in countries in which much of one's current income goes unreported—which probably includes most countries outside of the highly industrialized countries in the Organisation for Economic Co-operation and Development (and may include a few within the OECD club). In this respect, the use of assets is similar to other *categorical indicators*—such as occupation or neighborhood or type of secondary school—that may be only approximations of true financial means but are also difficult to disguise and relatively easy and inexpensive to monitor. Thus, mere possession of a home or, in some low-income countries, a car or a telephone landline or even indoor plumbing, may be sufficient to indicate enough probable financial means to contribute something to a child's higher education. The use of assets (especially real property, which has the advantage of being more difficult to hide than liquid assets, which can be held in an unreported account in another country)—at least as a corroboration of current income and overall means to pay—may be especially useful in developing countries, where measures of current income are so notoriously unreliable. It is also true that asset measurements may be unreliable, especially in nations where there has not been a free market in operation with a sufficient number of transactions to establish the proper valuation of assets, and where assets can be hidden from authorities. However, a combination of several unreliable measures may still be better than depending on only a single unreliable measure of current earnings.

Second, sufficient assets, especially investments and other liquid forms of savings, may serve not only as a corroboration of reported current income or earnings, but may in fact be assumed to be a part of the actual parental contribution. In this case, a means test converts a portion of these assets (with various exclusions and exceptions) toward a kind of *current income equivalence*, implicitly assuming that asset-rich families can either contribute some of their current income toward the costs of their children's higher education or, as a choice, liquidate or borrow upon a portion of their assets and apply this toward their parental contribution. This is a source of considerable controversy, especially when the assets that are thus effectively taxed for the expected parental contribution are not in the form of savings or other liquid investments, but rather are in the form of a home, family farm, or family-owned small business. These latter assets are not easily converted into the cash that would be needed for an actual parental contribution toward the costs of college or university (at least, not without selling the asset and severely diminishing the home ownership or means of livelihood).

Means-testing in the United States either excludes such assets altogether or counts their values only after allowing a considerable exemption. For example, the official governmental means test known as the *Federal Methodology* ignores all assets for families with incomes under $50,000 and excludes home equity from consideration altogether (US Department of Education 2008a, 2008b).

In contrast, the *Independent Methodology*—which is used by many of the very expensive private colleges and universities for their own grants and price discounts and is operated by the independent, nongovernmental College Board —considers all liquid and nonliquid assets, including home assets, for all applicants for financial assistance (College Board 2008a, 2008b). The Federal Methodology relies on the principle that homes and family farms are nonliquid assets, the consideration (or *effective taxation*) of which might require families to liquidate these assets and disrupt their lives in unacceptable ways in order to finance their expected share of their children's higher educational costs. In contrast, the Independent Methodology of the College Board assumes that both assets and income contribute independently to the financial strength of the parents or families and that a family that has chosen to hold its assets in the forms of home ownership ought not to be treated more favorably (i.e., assigned a lower expected parental contribution) than a family that has chosen to rent its home and to hold most of its assets in the form of savings or investments that are easier to liquidate.

Most US families have access to high-quality and relatively affordable public colleges and universities, and the ease of obtaining a home equity loan in the United States means that a family owning its home virtually never has to sell the home to meet an expected parental contribution for public (or even most private) tuition fees. Therefore, in a 1992 amendment to the Higher Education Act, Congress stipulated that home equity be excluded from consideration in the official calculation of family means. (Middle-class parents seemed, at least then, to have more political clout in Congress than their student children.) This served to shift what was formerly a greater parental share of the expected family contribution either to the college or university (in the form of additional institutional aid) or toward the student (in the forms of additional debt burdens or more part-time employment).

Another example of assets that might be excluded from the means test is savings that have been made over the years explicitly for the college expenses of children (or grandchildren). The rationale for such an exclusion, at least in the United States, is that the costs of a college or university education in both the public and private sectors are so great that the officially expected parental contribution is already beyond the amounts that can reasonably be expected to come from most families' *current* income (and even beyond the amounts that can be expected from current plus *future* incomes, or from parental borrowing). Moreover, this discrepancy will become even greater as time goes on.

Therefore all but the very wealthiest of parents who are aspiring to send their children to expensive public or private colleges and universities—especially if they wish to shield their children from very large amounts of student debt— will have to begin saving for these future college costs far in advance of the actual event (that is, contribute from past income as well as from current and future incomes).[3] According to proponents of college savings programs, one way to encourage such savings is to shield them from being considered as part of the family means that are effectively taxed to arrive at the officially ex- pected parental contribution.

Of course, any such exclusion raises issues of *horizontal* and *vertical equity*: that is, the need to treat families in similar financial circumstances alike and to treat families in disparate financial circumstances differently. Using assets to calculate family financial means leads to the effective taxation of those means in the officially expected parental contribution. So, quite apart from the use of financial assistance for aims that have nothing to do with financial or social equity—merit scholarships, for example, or grants to athletes or children of alumni—the differential treatment of assets in means-testing suggests a depar- ture from equity that is likely to be controversial. In the United States, for ex- ample, not only are most *529 Plans* (including both college savings plans and prepaid tuition plans) shielded from inclusion in those assets that go into the determination of family means, but in most cases they also carry state and/or federal tax advantages over other forms of savings or investments.[4] Obviously, wealthy families are better able to set savings aside in federal and state tax- advantaged college savings plans. But all families who do so become eligible for lower taxes, even if they simply move savings from a non-tax-advantaged savings vehicle to a tax-advantaged one, a strategy that has no impact what- soever on their total net savings or on the college plans of their children. The extraordinary popularity of these savings plans in the United States from the mid-1990s through the time of this writing (2009) is almost certainly a func- tion of the combination of rising middle- and upper-middle-class tuition anxi- ety, coupled with a peculiarly American middle- and upper-middle-class tax aversion (Griswold and Marine 1996). At the same time, the net effect of these plans—that is, the likely absence of any significant impact on college or uni- versity enrollment behavior, but an almost certain increase in the intergenera- tional transmission of inequality through the medium of higher educational enrollment decisions—is much like the expansion of *merit* (i.e., non-income- dependent) financial aid in the United States, and similar to the practice of *enrollment management,* where financial aid decisions at private colleges are made to maximize the matriculation of high-achieving students rather than to bolster the socioeconomic diversity of the class.

The Stipulation of the Parental or Family Unit

The means-testing, or targeting, of financial assistance in advanced industrialized countries where parental contributions are expected is based on the means (however defined and however measured) of the immediate, or nuclear, family. Assuming that a student is appropriately considered a financially dependent child for the purpose of an expected parental contribution (i.e., that the student has not been living independently or is not over a certain age limit, such as 24 years old), the means test for that family effectively considers the current incomes, and sometimes the assets, of the parents and generally also of the student him- or herself. One complication, which arises in the event of divorce or legal separation, is fixing the financial responsibility of the noncustodial parent. In most cases this will have been established in the legal agreements or court orders stipulating the financial responsibility associated with child support. Accordingly, it is important that the courts be prepared to take legal action against a noncustodial parent who has sufficient means but who refuses to acknowledge a legally established financial responsibility for the higher educational expenses of children from earlier relationships.

In very low-income countries or in very low-income (generally rural or remote) regions of middle-income countries, stipulating the appropriate unit for calculating an expected family contribution to higher educational expenses may be even more complex. Financial responsibilities may be shared within extended family units that may include not only several generations, but also the combined families of siblings. The principal breadwinner may be employed outside of the country, making substantial remittances to the family, but also making verification of that income difficult. Older siblings may also be sending money home, which in some low- and middle-income countries may represent a substantial portion of the assets of many families, and these too may need to be taken into consideration in determining family means.

Means-testing in low-income countries can entail further complications. For example, the tradition of polygamy in many, albeit scattered, parts of the developing world creates difficulties in defining the financially responsible family unit. Not only do polygamous fathers have many children, but many of these progeny are of the same or very close ages, potentially raising the aggregate financial burden at the time of the children's possible college or university participation. At the same time, anecdotal reports suggest an association between the practice of polygamy and family wealth (especially in land and cattle), making the practice of polygamy a signal of current income and likely other assets that would be sufficient to contribute to the costs of the children's higher education.[5] Finally, it has been reported that in very low-income countries, at least early in the period of expanding higher educational participation, there may be only one young person from a small village fortunate enough to be given the chance to go to a university—which may or may not entail tuition fees, but which almost always involves living expenses. In such cases, it may be the village that assumes financial responsibility, further complicating— albeit enriching—the determination of need and the awarding of aid.

Expected Parental Contributions, Means-Testing, and Effective Taxation

Means-tested financial assistance provides a benefit in the form or forms of a grant, a tuition fee discount, access to subsidized food or lodging, or access to a subsidized loan, all of which are targeted either to families or directly to students with minimal financial means in order to fill in for what would be a parental contribution from families with more substantial means. The system may simply provide a benefit the student/family unit either is entitled to or is not. Or the system may call for financial benefits that rise with diminishing family means (or, from the opposite perspective but with the same consequence, financial benefits that diminish with increasing incomes or measured means).

A system in which the student either is or is not entitled to the full benefit, based on some estimate of family means, has the advantage of being simple to calculate, easy to dispense, and relatively inexpensive to monitor. At the same time, such a system is usually inefficient, because it probably oversupports those who are just barley eligible, at least relative to those who are needier, and probably undersupports those in greatest need. Furthermore, it places great financial stakes on whether one is entitled to the benefit or is not, especially for families whose calculated means are close to the tipping point. Thus there is a substantial incentive for and payoff to shifting family incomes or earnings out of the period on which the entitlement is to be based, or suppressing or simply not reporting income altogether. Such an all-or-nothing system, while benefiting from the simplicity of rough justice, compromises the policy goal of vertical equity, with families of quite different means being entitled (or not) to the same benefit.

A more ideal and equitable system of means-testing provides a more continuous relationship between the officially calculated financial means of the parental or family unit and the value of the means-tested financial benefit (or, conversely, the size of the expected family financial contribution). Such a targeting system, then, resembles an income tax in which, at least between some maximum grant (or minimum family contribution) and a phasing out of the grant altogether (at the point of maximum family contribution), there is a defined relationship between increases or decreases in calculated means and increases or decreases in the grant or the expected parental contribution.[6] Such a system has an advantage over the all-or-nothing system by reducing the incentives to alter the tipping point for the family's calculated means and providing what is probably a more equitable system of targeting. At the same time, such a system is both complex and difficult and expensive to police, and it still—as in any system of income taxes—rewards tactics such as income-shifting or underreporting for all of the family units who are eligible for some financial assistance, rather than only those near the tipping point.

In the end, developing countries that are just at the point of beginning to employ cost-sharing and targeted subsidies, and that are most often without an efficient and ubiquitous system of income reporting, may have to implement a simpler system under which the student/family unit is either entitled to the subsidy or is not, perhaps on the basis of a categorical indicator that is simple to discern—such as full-time employment, or home ownership, or even place of residence. Tekleselassie and Johnstone (2004) and Johnstone (2006) reported on means-testing systems in sub-Saharan Africa from the late 1990s that relied on categorical indicators of high income in excluding families from financial assistance, such as

- professional or high-ranking civil service occupations;
- most occupations requiring a higher education;
- ownership of an automobile or an executive, managerial, or professional position with a car and driver; or
- children in private, fee-paying secondary schools.

These authors also examined categorical indicators of low-income families qualifying for financial assistance, such as

- farming as their principal occupation, with limited acreage under cultivation or a limited number of livestock;
- housing without electricity or running water or a landline telephone; or
- a father with only a primary education or less.

Moreover, declarations of current income and other data (such as number of dependents) should be added to information on categorical indicators, all of which may be combined to lead to eligibility or ineligibility for financial assistance, and any system of means-testing must be enforced with spot checks and penalties for violations. Therefore, along with improvements in the calculation and verification of family financial means, the installation of a more sophisticated system of income taxation, a system of audits and spot-checks, and fair and consistent penalties for violations, developing countries might work toward a means-testing system with a more continuous relationship between calculated means and targeted financial assistance.

Means-Testing and Cost-Sharing

In short, cost-sharing that depends on parental contributions requires means-testing of the parents' income or assets to preserve accessibility to higher education for the children of the poor. However, means-testing is not only technically difficult, sometimes imperfect, and expensive to monitor, but it also demands an official reporting of earnings and assets that some individuals and some cultures consider intrusive and unwarranted. Officially expected contributions also require rules to determine how long, or to what age of the dependent student, the expectation for contributions are to continue: that is, through the first degree, or to a certain age, or via some other decision rule? Divorce, separation, and arrangements for custody and child support create further complications. None of these requirements and complications is insurmountable, of course, but they add to the administrative burdens and expenses of means-testing and also inject an element that is prone to error, manipulation, and possible unfairness that may require constant adjudication.

At the same time, most parents in the United States, as well as in most countries (outside of the Nordic countries and elsewhere in northern Europe), willingly contribute either to tuition fees or to the costs of student living. The absence of such funds from these parents would necessarily add significantly to the monies required of either students (i.e., their children), or taxpayers, or both. Thus, although higher education in Scandinavia is without tuition fees, students bear a very considerable debt burden though their cost-of-living loans. And the shift from an up-front tuition fee paid mainly by parents to a deferred tuition fee paid mainly by students—as occurred in Scotland in 2001 and in England and Wales in 2006—amounts to a transfer of costs from parents to students, not, as might have originally been intended (at least by the students and some of the political Left) to the government. As complex and sometimes unreliable as expected parental contributions and means-testing are, the net contributions from parents in the United States and other countries that rely heavily on tuition fees and parental contributions to the costs of student living are enormous and almost certainly irreplaceable.

Financial Contributions of Government

Whether a portion of the total costs of higher education (i.e., the costs of instruction, including tuition fees, if any, plus the costs of student maintenance) are to be borne by parents or students or both, as well as by the government, these total costs, regardless of the quality of the instruction or the kind of living arrangements, are sufficiently high in any country to require the financial participation of government if higher education is to be accessible to any but the very wealthy. Governmental contributions to the costs of instruction plus the expenses of student maintenance may take many forms, but for publicly owned and largely publicly financed colleges and universities, they consist principally of the following:

1. Direct contributions to the underlying costs of instruction (both operating and capital expenses), generally ranging from a high of bearing the entire set of costs—that is, requiring no or negligible tuition fees—to a low of providing only 60 or 70 percent of the costs of undergraduate instruction, requiring tuition fees for most of the remaining costs (which can range from $5,000 to $10,000 and even more in countries with high public tuition fees, such as the United States)

2. Direct contributions to subsidized (that is, low-fee) food and lodging

3. Governmentally financed financial assistance in the forms of grants and student loan subsidies

In addition, governmental contributions may take less direct forms, including, for example:

1. The extension of child allowances to families whose older children are full-time students (significant in Europe)
2. The tax deductibility of gifts, which an institution can then either apply to capital or operating expenses to lower the total costs of instruction that must be covered by parents, students, or direct governmental support, or designate such gifts as part of the funds used for institutionally awarded financial assistance (significant in the United States)
3. The tax deductibility of tuition fees (controversial and unusual, as such support flows predominantly to higher-income families who can afford substantial tuition fees, particularly in the private sector)
4. The tax deductibility of interest on student loans (may become significant as aggregate debt rises)
5. Tax-advantaged parental savings plans (increasingly popular—and controversial—in the United States)

The focus of this section is the place of financial assistance in the cost-sharing paradigm. Governmentally awarded financial assistance is principally in the form of grants or stipends (which are nonrepayable) and loans (which, as will be discussed in greater detail in chapter 6, are composed of a true loan plus an effective grant in the form of a stream of interest subsidies). In most countries this aid is allocated mainly, although not exclusively, on the basis of financial need—primarily according to the financial means of the parents—in order to increase accessibility, although governmental financial assistance can also be awarded for other public policy aims, such as targeting certain kinds of students (ethnic or linguistic minorities, for example, or females or older students), rewarding military service, rewarding academic achievement, or providing monetary incentives for students to enroll in certain institutions or academic programs.

Institutionally awarded financial assistance, on the other hand, which in high-tuition-fee colleges and universities, both public and private, may take the form of targeted discounts, mainly serves the purpose of achieving institutional rather than social or political goals. These institutional goals may be to attract particular students whose matriculation would be of high value to the institution: the very academically able, for example, or an applicant with special talent, or the child of a politically powerful governmental official or a potential donor, or (especially in the United States) a promising athlete. As discussed in chapter 3, this kind of expenditure has an opportunity cost to the institution: not unlike that for a star professor or some new equipment, it is in essence an institutional decision to spend money for a particular purpose. On the other hand, as Bowen and Breneman (1993) pointed out in their classic paper, institutional financial assistance may be nothing more than the discount necessary to fill the space in the class, with no true opportunity cost to the institution.

Table 4.1 shows the basic allocation of the total costs of higher education, including both the costs of instruction and the costs of maintenance plus other family-borne educational expenses (e.g., books and supplies), among the parties to cost-sharing, and it illustrates the role of financial assistance. Such a table necessarily simplifies the great variations both between and within countries by kind of institution (e.g., university or college) or federal division (e.g., between central governments and states or provinces). But this simplified model also illustrates the basic point of the cost-sharing perspective: a given level of governmental, or taxpayer, contribution (assuming a given level of total instructional costs to be covered) can, at least in theory, be shifted among two extremes, either (a) low or no tuition fees, which then requires substantial direct governmental contributions to the public institutions and leaves little or nothing for targeted assistance to the financially needy for the high costs of student maintenance, or (b) some tuition fees, which then requires means-tested financial assistance in the form of grants or loans, but which can also generate additional revenue, part of which can fund the targeted assistance to low-income students to help with meeting the costs of tuition fees and student living.

Direct Assistance to Institutions or Indirect Assistance to Students?

A perennial public policy issue is whether a given amount of governmental, or tax-originated, assistance to the cost of instruction in public colleges and universities is better spent through direct institutional subsidies or (at least partially) indirectly via financial assistance to students, who can then better afford tuition fees. Public colleges and universities that are permitted to charge tuition fees and that have strong applicant pools on the strength of established institutional reputations might prefer some of their governmental assistance to be via portable student assistance, which ensures them of both the tuition-

Table 4.1 Total costs of public higher education borne by government/taxpayers, parents, and students, illustrating governmentally borne financial aid through grants and loan subsidies

	Costs of instruction	Costs of maintenance and family-borne costs of education (e.g., books and supplies)
Costs directly borne by government and taxpayers	Direct support of costs of instruction (operating and capital expenses)	Government-subsidized food/lodging
Costs *faced* by parents and students	Tuition fees (up-front and deferred)	Student living costs, books, supplies, etc.
Financial aid via government grants and loan subsidies	Grants and loan subsidies	Grants and loan subsidies
Costs *borne* by parents	Up-front fees net of financial aid	Maintenance and other family-borne costs paid by parents
Costs *borne* by students	Deferred fees/loans net of subsidies	Maintenance and other costs paid by student's earnings and loans net of subsidies
Total costs borne by government/taxpayers	Direct support of instructional costs; Financial assistance	Subsidies for food/lodging; Financial assistance

fee-paying students from middle- and upper-middle-class families and, through governmental financial assistance, some tuition fees and the presence of high-value students from low-income families. Private colleges and universities might lean toward direct governmental subsidies, but few countries provide this for private institutions, so these entities almost universally prefer governmental assistance through student aid over governmental assistance only to public institutions, as this gives them a chance to compete for students who would otherwise be unable to afford their higher tuition fees. Finally—and most significant politically—those fiscally conservative politicians and political influentials who favor lower taxes, more reliance on markets, and the privatization of public institutions generally also favor the efficiency and competition that comes with what is frequently described as the *high tuition–high aid* model of public college and university finance.

On the other hand, public colleges and universities that do not enjoy deep applicant pools and the advantages of selectivity generally prefer the lowest possible tuition fees and direct governmental subsidization, which frees them from financial reliance on tuition fees and the need to compete for students against more selective colleges and universities, public or private. In addition, those on the political Left, including very many academics and most students, who favor a more extensive public sector generally and who perceive many academic downsides to aggressive academic capitalism (Slaughter and Leslie 1997), as well as those who fear the transmutation of high tuition–high aid to high tuition–low aid, or high tuition–loans only (Johnstone 1993), may also resist a policy of cost-sharing that is represented by tuition fees, parental contributions, and means-tested financial assistance.

Governmentally awarded financial assistance comes in three main forms: (1) *grants*, awarded on some combination of financial need and other criteria; (2) the *grant component*, or the subsidized portion, *of student loans*; and (3) *student loan repayment forgiveness*, based either on low lifetime earnings or on the borrower's willingness to practice a certain profession (e.g., teaching or the practice of medicine), oftentimes in a particularly high-need venue (e.g., a remote village or an urban slum).

Complementing governmentally awarded financial assistance in its various forms are other indirect forms of governmental contributions to the costs of higher education, such as the extension of child allowances to certain families, or the tax deductibility of gifts or tuition fees, or tax-advantaged parental savings plans.

These forms of direct and indirect financial assistance are shown in table 4.2, along with their targets, public or institutional purpose, and policy implications.

Consequences and Beneficiaries of Cost-Sharing and Financial Assistance

The consequences and beneficiaries of the additional revenue from parents or students or both, as modified by financial assistance, are complex and, as with so many instruments of public policy, are subject to unintended consequences. For example, advocates of high tuition–high aid policies in the public higher educational sectors of the United States purport to be in favor of increasing net tuition revenue without sacrificing accessibility for students from low-income families. But who actually benefits? If the higher aid for the low-income students merely compensates for their now even higher tuition fees, the low-income students and their families can be said to have been held financially unharmed, but they are still no better off, while the high-income families will be paying more.

If, however, some of the additional revenue also goes toward qualitative improvements, then the low-income students clearly benefit; the high-income students may also benefit, providing the added quality (including the greater diversification and overall quality of their classmates) is worth the extra price. If the state is in a period of fiscal retrenchment, then the additional revenue may add little or nothing, but it may save the public colleges and universities from what would otherwise have been a budget cut.

Alternatively, the additional net revenue from new tuition fees may go into greater public-sector capacity. In the kinds of supply-constrained public systems typical of countries in which the free or very low-tuition openings are limited and academically selective, and in which students unable to earn a place are forced either into a more costly, less selective, demand-absorbing private sector (e.g., Argentina, Brazil, Japan, Korea) or into the fee-paying tracks of the public sector (e.g., Russia or the dual track tuition fee countries of East Africa), the principal beneficiaries of an enlarged capacity made possible by increased tuition fee revenue may be middle-class parents, whose children can now move from the private sector or the fee-paying tracks of the public universities into the expanded free or low-fee track, saving them the higher tuition fees that may have been a great financial sacrifice. (The additional

Table 4.2   Forms of governmental financial assistance

Form of governmental financial assistance	Target
1. Direct grants or discounts based on low income or assets of family (means-tested on parents' income and/or assets)	Financially dependent children of low-income parents
2. Direct grants or discounts based on student's own low income and/or assets	Adult or independent students with low income or assets
3. Direct grants based on attributes (other than parents' income) associated with underrepresentation (such as ethnicity, gender, or regional location)	Underrepresented ethnic minorities (in some countries, females)
4. Direct grants based on academic promise or prior high school achievement (merit)	High-achieving secondary school students
5. Direct grants based on academic achievement while in college or university (merit)	Students who achieve academically while in college/university
6. Grants to parents in the form of extended child allowances	Parents of full-time students
7. Subsidized food and/or lodging based on low income or assets of family (means-tested)	Financially dependent children of low-income parents; requires institution to be in the food and lodging business
8. Direct grants for living costs based on low income or assets of family (means-tested)	Financially dependent children of low-income parents; operates through private-sector food and lodging
9. Deferred tuition fees but up-front subsidy (effective grant) to all borrowers because of low interest rates	All students (other than those whose parents choose to pay up front)
10. Up-front subsidy (effective grant) to borrowers in the form of low interest rates based on low income of family	Targeted students who nonetheless must borrow for some or all of the private costs

Public or institutional purpose to be served	Policy implications
Reduce financial barriers, enhance student participation, and preserve accessibility	Necessary if parents are officially expected to contribute to tuition fees; requires cost-effective and verifiable means-testing
Reduce financial barriers and enhance student participation; also enhance student's independence	Conceptually complex as all independent students have need and the case for grants as opposed to loans is not clear
Reduce financial barriers and enhance targeted student participation	Likely to be effective in combination with low parental income, but increasingly politically controversial
Enhance academic effort of many secondary school students (public); enhance institutional prestige	Grants have a minimal effect on student enrollment behavior and do little or nothing for the policy goal of accessibility
Enhance academic effort in post-secondary institutions (public); may enhance timely progress to degree	Similar to #3; unclear how much influence such rewards have on grades
Encourage parents to support child in college financially and in other ways	Child allowances may have a minimal effect on student enrollment behavior or access
Reduce financial barriers, enhance student participation, and preserve accessibility	
Reduce financial barriers, enhance student participation, and preserve accessibility	
Politically popular and may minimize debts in high-borrowing countries, but may have a minimal effect on access	
May reduce debt aversion and awkwardness of defaults; may increase willingness to borrow	Expensive and trades off with direct grants; not clear that interest rates factor into any debt aversion or willingness to borrow

continued

Table 4.2   Continued

Form of governmental financial assistance	Target
11. Forgiveness of remaining debt (effective grants) based on borrower's own low lifetime income (income contingent)	Students whose low lifetime income makes it impossible to repay the entire debt—and who are eventually released from further repayments
12. Debt reduction (effective grants) based on academic performance while in college (merit)	Good academic performance while in college
13. Debt reduction (effective grants) based on borrower's postgraduation choice of professional practice or venue (e.g., a teacher practicing in a remote school)	Students who practice targeted professions (e.g., nursing) or in targeted venues (e.g., inner city or rural venues)

capacity, of course, does nothing for students already enrolled and therefore not eligible for additional financial assistance; they or their families will have to pay more because of the higher fees.)

Similarly, the introduction of tuition fees when there formerly were none (as in China or the United Kingdom) or the addition of fee-paying tracks in dual track tuition fee systems (as in most of the former Communist states as well as the East African countries) can also add significant revenue, whether to the operating budgets of the universities or simply to the treasuries of the states. Again, who benefits? In low-income and transitional countries, the beneficiaries of these additional revenues may be the faculty, whose low salaries and very high teaching loads may have been bearing the brunt of the fiscal austerity that this new form of cost-sharing may alleviate somewhat. Students may also share in the benefits of extra revenue from the implementation of newly created tuition fees: with better faculty, or less faculty turnover, or faculty less distracted by the need to teach double loads or moonlight on other, outside jobs simply to earn a decent living.

In all of these examples, however, critics and skeptics of tuition fees may claim that the very possibility of the implementation of, or a substantial rise in, tuition fees may also have had a hand in the very low level of (or even a

Public or institutional purpose to be served	Policy implications
Reduce risk of unmanageable debt and possible debt aversion; may increase willingness to borrow	Basing subsidies on a student's own low lifetime income may be preferable to basing subsidies on the parents' low income at the time of initial borrowing
May enhance academic effort in post-secondary institution (public); may enhance timely progress to degree	Unclear whether academic performance responds to the prize of debt reduction; rewards those who least need rewarding
Enhance number of targeted professionals and/or those who will serve in less-desirable venues	Unclear as yet how cost effective this is (compared to direct bonuses or direct income supplements)

decrease in) governmental support that preceded the advent of new or augmented fees. This has surely been the case in the clear diminution of state governmental support for public colleges and universities in the United States and the constituent countries of the United Kingdom. In such instances—where an increase in tuition fees is matched or preceded by a decrease in governmental tax support—one can argue that the additional revenue from parents and/or students goes not to faculty or elsewhere in the universities, or even to students, but rather to other, higher-priority public expenditures (or at least to alternative public expenditures with greater political salience), or even into the hands of taxpayers or businesses through the tax cuts or the avoidance of the tax increases that may have been made possible by the increased cost-sharing.

Even more cynical critics may claim that the beneficiaries of cost-sharing are not the faculty or the students or even other worthy public expenditures, but rather the university administrators—or worse, the politicians whose wastefulness and corruption may have occasioned a turn toward cost-sharing in the first place. This was the finding of Touorouzou Some (2006) in his study of the attitude of university student leaders in Burkina Faso toward the imposition of tuition fees. The resistance of student leaders was hardly surprising in that impoverished Francophone country where there had never been tuition fees. However, the basis of this resistance was much more strongly rooted in the perception that the beneficiaries would be university leaders or corrupt politicians than it was grounded in any kind of Marxist ideology or belief in the imperative of higher education as a permanent, publicly funded entitlement.

A final beneficiary of higher tuition fees in the public sector—in addition to public institutions or systems, public-sector faculty, taxpayers, or other public priorities—may be private institutions of higher education (or, in the case of proprietary schools, their owners), which might, with higher tuition fees than their public competitors, find themselves at a lessened market disadvantage relative to a time when public institutions charged low or no tuition fees. For example, the United States has a very large and high-priced private sector that, even with its far larger tuition fees, still competes favorably with its public rivals. The elite private colleges and universities do so with a combination of current gifts and endowment returns to support institutionally funded financial aid, governmental assistance through subsidized grants and loans to students, tax advantages to their donors, and indirect-cost recovery on their governmental research grants. Expensive private colleges and universities in the United States also benefit from an extensive upper- and upper-middle-class population, much of which (rightly or wrongly) equates *private* and *high-priced* with higher educational quality—and can afford to pay the price. At the same time, the US private sector is far larger than its handful of elite private colleges and universities; most private institutions are minimally selective and do indeed compete with similarly selective (or nonselective) public institutions that are far lower in price. These mainstream private colleges and universities (numbering well over 1,500) almost certainly harbor some delight in the loss of public support that has been forcing considerable increases in tuition fees at public colleges and universities and narrowing, even if only slightly, the tuition fee gap that such private institutions perceive as so threatening to their competitive position.

In short, while the preceding chapter made a strong case for at least some cost-sharing—whether based on a presumption of the greater efficiency of markets and prices; or on the greater equity of having students and their parents, who are better off financially than the average taxpayer, assuming at least a portion of the high and rising cost of higher education; or on the sheer need for additional revenue—the beneficiaries of cost-sharing may be unclear and depend on other policies and assumptions. However, those who advocate cost-sharing in any form do so under two presuppositions. The first is that a shift of some of the costs of higher education from a predominant reliance on governments, or taxpayers, to parents and/or students will complement—not substitute for—governmental assistance. The second is that cost-sharing will be accompanied by financial assistance in the forms of grants and loans so as to preserve accessibility in the face of these higher costs to either the parents or the students or both. Under these assumptions, greater revenues from cost-sharing can serve such widely supported public policy aims as

- the increased quality of institutions, whether through more faculty (permitting smaller classes), improved faculty salaries (permitting fewer overloads and other distractions as well as less turnover), more equipment and technology, or better and expanded facilities;
- an enlarged public-sector, higher educational capacity—that is, lecture theaters, faculty, and dormitory rooms—permitting expanded enrollments (which tends to favor those heretofore excluded, whether by costs or by the severity of the entrance examinations, and therefore to improve access and equity);
- more means-tested, or targeted, grants to expand access to children from low-income or rural families or others marginalized by, for example, ethnic or linguistic-minority status;
- a greater volume of lending, or lower interest rates on existing student loans;
- repayment relief for those unable to repay their loans because of unemployment, low-paying jobs, or other legitimate reasons, or to give incentives to graduates with student loan debts who agree to practice certain professions in certain venues (e.g., teaching in remote areas or in challenging schools); or
- subsidies to the private sector, arguably (although controversially) providing more higher education for the governmental dollar than the much more costly and less philanthropically supported public colleges and universities.

The Total Package of Policies

The lesson of this chapter is that public policy in support of the financial aspects of higher education cannot responsibly look only at tuition fees or only at student loan schemes, but must consider the entire package:

1. Tuition fees—with all of their variations, which is the topic of the next chapter—or the absence of (or only nominal) tuition fees, which imposes all or nearly all of the costs of instruction on the government, or taxpayers, as opposed to sharing those costs with parents and/or students

2. Grants or discounts (both means-tested as well as those based on other criteria)

3. Student loans (or any other kind of deferred obligation), which will be considered more fully in chapter 6

4. The effective-grant component of student loans (or the stream of subsidies contained within the terms of the student loans)

5. Public subsidies toward the costs of food and lodging

6. Public subsidies to private colleges and universities

If we now assume that the total annual volume of public, or governmental (or tax generated) revenue is limited and inadequate to meet all of higher education's needs, then the policy question is: How should this revenue best be spent to achieve the aims of public spending on higher education? In other words: How should scarce revenues be allocated among the various possibilities?

1. Low or no tuition fees in public colleges and universities limit both the quality and the capacity of the public sector and reduce participation and access in most countries (and in virtually all of the middle- and low-income countries).

2. Higher up-front tuition fees can be paid mainly by parents and coupled with a limited number of means-tested grants or discounts to enhance access.

3. Higher up-front tuition fees can be paid mainly by parents and coupled with minimally subsidized loans to both parents and students, most of which should be recoverable. This makes it possible for the same sum of public dollars to provide a greater volume of lending than do means-tested grants—and allows considerably more participation and accessibility than low tuition fees for all.

4. Higher, but deferred, tuition fees can be paid mainly by students after they complete their education and are out into the adult job market, presumably earning a premium because of the higher

education that they partially financed (on top of whatever portion of the costs of their student maintenance they may also have covered with loans). Such an arrangement foregoes most of what might have been borne by parents, but it still provides more revenue—at least in the form of the present discounted value of reasonably anticipated repayments—than full governmental (taxpayer) financing for the costs of instruction.

In theory, then, a principal question for a policy analyst—desirably sharpened, if not fully answered, by an exposition such as this chapter—is the amount of accessibility that can be obtained by additional dollars spent, for example, on lowering tuition fees for all as opposed to the same resources expended on targeted grants for the poor, or disbursed to cover repayment risk and tap the private capital market in providing loans to many students. Yet accessibility, however important, is not the only legitimate policy aim for the public dollars spent; the analyst, and ultimately the final decision-makers, must also weigh increments in additional accessibility (however measured) against other public policy aims that might have been procured with the same resources: increased capacity, or investments in altogether new sectors (such as more short-cycle higher education), or additional investments in a few flagship universities to better compete on the international level.

Clearly, the metrics of more accessibility, greater capacity, improved instructional quality, or additional scholarly prestige are exceedingly difficult to stipulate and even more difficult to compare. Some will maintain that additional accessibility cannot be measured, much less compared with enhanced quality or augmented prestige. But comparisons must be made, and, in the end, decisions must be arrived at that unavoidably reflect the harsh reality of tradeoffs. Such decisions must, of course, also take into account history and culture. In the process, the social and political costs of gaining the resources to invest in one sector or one institution or one program, as laudable as such an investment may be, at the expense of losing part or all of another institution or program need to be weighed—and compromises and politics are legitimate complications in a democracy. But the task of the analyst, like the task of the scholar and the task to which this book is endeavoring to contribute, is to clarify

- the underlying costs involved in higher education and its various policy aims;

- the tradeoffs and opportunity costs of the options in front of the decision-makers; and
- the consequences of the choices that must be made.

In the next chapter we turn to the topic of tuition fees as the paramount, although not the sole, example of cost-sharing, that is, the shift of a portion of higher education's cost burden to parents and/or students.

NOTES

1. This book is more about the privatization of public higher education than the emergence of distinct private sectors of higher education. However, cost-sharing as a policy shift necessarily encompasses both. The emergence of private sectors in higher education is a long-established tradition in Latin America and parts of East and South Asia, but it is a relatively recent phenomenon in the formerly Communist, or transitional, countries and in Africa. A public policy to shift enrollment towards a more tuition-dependent private sector begins with allowing such sectors: via accreditation and degree authorization; sometimes by direct governmental subsidies; but more frequently by indirect governmental subsidies, such as portable financial assistance (including loans) for private-sector students, access to subsidized capital (e.g., a tax exemption on the interest from construction bonds), and income-tax-deductible donations.

2. Barr (2005) claims that a high tuition–high aid system (such as in the United States) is an inefficient way both to redistribute income and to subsidize students: that is, based on their parents' low incomes at the time they were in college or university, rather than on their own low incomes over their working lifetimes (via the income contingent debt obligations held by most students).

3. Assets also make borrowing possible—that is, paying from future income—without having to liquidate assets through collateralizing parental loans. This is especially critical in the United States and a few other advanced industrialized countries (such as Canada, Japan, or the United Kingdom), where officially expected parental contributions can be high and where borrowing is relatively simple and inexpensive as long as there is good collateral, such as home equity or similar assets.

4. A *529 Plan* (authorized by Section 529 of the US Internal Revenue Code) is a tax-advantaged college savings plan (including prepaid tuition plans sponsored by private colleges or universities) designed to encourage saving for future college costs. By 2007, all fifty states and the District of Columbia, and a number of private colleges and universities, were sponsoring at least one type of 529 plan (US Securities and Exchange Commission 2007).

5. This from some Francophone African graduate students referenced in Tekleselassie and Johnstone 2004 and Johnstone 2006, pp. 175–200.

6. For examples of the relationship between family means and the expected parental contribution, see US Department of Education 2008a, 2008b.

REFERENCES

Barr, Nicholas. 2005. Financing Higher Education. *Finance and Development* 42 (2). www .imf.org/external/pubs/ft/fandd/2005/06/index.htm.

Bowen, William G., and David W. Breneman. 1993. Student Aid: Price Discount or Educational Investment? *College Board Review* (167):2–6.

College Board. 2008a. *Trends in College Pricing.* Washington, DC: College Board.

———. 2008b. *Trends in Student Aid 2008.* New York: College Board.

Griswold, Carolyn P., and Ginger M. Marine. 1996. Political Influences on State Higher-Tuition, Higher-Aid, and the Real World. *Review of Higher Education* 19 (4):361–389.

Johnstone, D. Bruce. 1993. The High Tuition–High Aid Model of Public Higher Education Finance: The Case Against. Office of the SUNY Chancellor [for the National Association of System Heads]. www.gse.buffalo.edu/FAS/Johnston/HIGHAID.htm.

———. 2005. Fear and Loathing of Tuition Fees: An American Perspective on Higher Education Finance in the UK. *Perspectives* 9 (1):12–16.

———. 2006. *Financing Higher Education: Cost-Sharing in International Perspective.* Boston: Boston College Center for International Higher Education and Sense Publishers.

Slaughter, Sheila, and Larry Leslie. 1997. *Academic Capitalism: Politics, Policies, and the Entrepreneurial University.* Baltimore: Johns Hopkins University Press.

Some, Touorouzou. 2006. Cost-Sharing in Francophone West Africa: Student Resistance and Institutional Stability at the University of Ouagadougou, Burkina Faso. Ph.D. diss., Department of Educational Leadership and Policy, State University of New York at Buffalo.

Tekleselassie, Abebayehu, and D. Bruce Johnstone. 2004. Means-Testing: The Dilemma of Targeting Subsidies in African Higher Education. *Journal of Higher Education in Africa* 2 (2):135–158.

US Department of Education. 2008a. Free Application for Federal Student Aid (FAFSA) Web site. www.fafsa.ed.gov.

———. 2008b. *Managing the Price of College: A Handbook for Students and Families.* National Institute on Postsecondary Education. www.ed.gov/pubs/collegecosts/cover.html.

US Securities and Exchange Commission. 2007. An Introduction to 529 Plans. www.sec .gov/investor/pubs/intro529.htm.

CHAPTER FIVE

The Spread of Tuition Fees

In the worldwide shift toward some form or forms of cost-sharing, either the inauguration of tuition fees where they did not previously exist (whether for some or for all students) or the sharp increase of tuition fees in countries where they had become accepted, has become the principal form of supplementing governmental revenue and also the political and ideological flashpoint for debates over the need for, and the propriety of, cost-sharing in all of its forms. This chapter examines this greater reliance on tuition fees, the variations in this form of cost-sharing, and the fundamental questions that must be addressed when considering a policy of tuition fees.

Definitions: Tuitions, Fees, and Tuition Fees

To define our terms, in the United States, the word "tuition" refers to a fee for instruction. In the United Kingdom and most of the rest of the world, however, the word tuition means "instruction," so a fee for instruction is therefore called a tuition fee. As much of the readership of this book is likely to be from outside the United States, we will employ the British term tuition fee, even though it may sound slightly redundant to the American ear.

We will reserve the term tuition fee to designate a fee paid to cover part of the cost of instruction, as discussed in chapter 1. The distinction between a tuition fee and other kinds of fees is imprecise; in fact, the use of the term "fee" is sometimes deliberately intended to hide what could just as well be termed a tuition fee (or, in the United States, simply called tuition) because of either legal obstacles or political opposition to the very concept of a tuition fee. However, a *tuition fee* properly refers to a mandatory charge levied upon all students (paid by themselves or their families) covering some portion of the general underlying costs of instruction (Marcucci and Johnstone 2007). *Fees*, on the other hand, can consist of several types of charges. Fees generally refer to charges levied to recover all or most of the expenses associated with particular institutionally provided goods or services that are frequently (although not always) partaken of by some (but not all) students and that might, in other circumstances, be privately provided. Such fees, for example, might cover some or all of the costs of food and lodging, or of health and transportation services, or of some special expenses associated with instruction, such as consumable supplies in an art class or transportation associated with a special internship experience. There are other charges—such as application fees, examination fees, and Internet or athletic fees—that are considered fees (to be differentiated in the United States from tuition costs), despite the fact that they are levied on all students. Such fees, because they are presumably based on the actual expense of the particular institutionally provided good or service, may be supported in whole or in part from that fee revenue. Finally, a third set of charges, generally also referred to as fees, are those that are levied on all students and that are associated with noninstructional programs or services that the students themselves have a major hand in allocating among competing programs and services (usually through an elected student government).

Tuition Fee Policies

Should There Be a Tuition Fee?

The first question in considering the adoption of a tuition fee policy, of course, is whether there ought to be any tuition fees at all (or any more-than-nominal fees) for all or most students in public colleges and universities. This question goes to the fundamental political and ideological acceptability of tuition fees—as altered and sometimes distorted by the harsh economic realities of higher educational finance. As we have seen in preceding chapters, the answer has been yes (in some cases reluctantly and with considerable obfuscation) in most of the highly industrialized world outside of continental Europe: such as Australia, Canada, Japan, New Zealand, and the United States, along with England, Wales, and Northern Ireland of the constituent countries of the United Kingdom. Much of Asia accepts tuition fees, particularly (in addition to Japan) in Korea and the Philippines—both of which (not coincidentally, along with Japan) have extensive private higher educational sectors; this makes at least some portion of their respective populations quite accustomed to the notion of a tuition fee. In India, the state universities charge substantial tuition fees. Tuition fees, albeit only of a dual track nature (a distinction that will be discussed at greater length below), have been accepted in Russia and the other countries emerging from the former Soviet Union, as well as in the former Communist countries of Central and Eastern Europe. Tuition fees have also been accepted in the formerly Communist (now more Socialist market) economies of China, Vietnam, and Mongolia (the latter having, as a percentage of its per-capita income, probably the highest tuition fees of any country in the world). Until the turn of the last century, on the other hand, Western Europe was the last major bastion of free or very nearly free higher education. Yet by 2009 (although positions change rapidly), nearly all of Europe, with the exception of the Nordic countries and Switzerland, now has tuition fees (most of them still nominal by American standards), or dual track tuition fees, or other-than-tuition fees that are actually tuition fees in all but name.

Two Forms of Tuition Fees

The second question relates to the form of tuition fees: whether the tuition fee, if there is to be one, is to be charged *up front*—payable at the time of matriculation and thus most frequently paid for by the parents (insofar as they are financially able)—or is to be a tuition fee that is *deferred*—as a loan generally repaid by students after graduation and entry into the adult workforce. Unfortunately, and the source of much policy confusion, this question is quite distinct from the ancillary issue (dealt with at length in the next chapter) of what is to be the form of the *repayment obligation*: that is, whether the deferred obligation, or loan, is to be repaid on a predetermined fixed schedule or on a schedule that is based on the graduate's later earnings or income.

The distinction between an up-front and a deferred tuition fee is not un-important and has, in fact, become the topic of much policy debate in a number of countries. But the essential difference, as we saw in chapter 4, is that an up-front tuition fee is based on the premise of an officially expected parental contribution and the assumption that they are able to provide it. The (under-graduate) student is thus considered financially dependent on his or her parents (or sometimes on the extended family) with respect to a tuition fee obligation. A deferred fee, on the other hand, is based on the premise that a student is a financially independent adult, responsible for his or her expenses, including the share of instructional costs that is represented by a tuition fee. There are clearly financial implications to the designation of tuition fees as either properly up front or deferred. But the designation is largely cultural. The Australians and the British are generally comfortable with deferred tuition fees and with the notion of most undergraduate students being financially independent young adults (which, of course, implies higher average debt loads). The Americans, Canadians, Chinese, Japanese, and most other countries having tuition fees, on the other hand, seem more comfortable with up-front fees and with the underlying expectation of a parental or family contribution. Interestingly, the Australians cover both bases and feature their well-known deferred-payment Higher Education Contribution Scheme, but they make it attractive for families to pay these tuition fees up front by offering a 20 percent discount for an up-front payment. England, on the other hand, with a similar deferred tuition fee, makes no such provision.

After the deeply contested implementation of tuition fees in the United Kingdom in 1997, political resistance converged around an opposition less to the principle of cost-sharing than against the concept of a tuition fee at the point of entry. Much of the British animus toward a tuition fee, then, was that it was to be paid up front by parents. This was apparently offensive to some British students, who preferred to be viewed (like their Nordic counterparts) as financially independent (even if impecunious) young adults rather than as financially dependent children. Also, others claimed (albeit with mainly anecdotal evidence) that some parents were refusing to contribute even the means-tested expected parental contribution—allegedly, for example, for university-age daughters in certain immigrant cultures. Consequently, Scotland in 2001, followed by England and Wales in 2006 and 2007, replaced up-front tuition fees with deferred tuition fees (which Scotland then abandoned altogether in 2008). But for our analysis of tuition fees, the distinction between up-front or deferred is not that one is a tuition fee and the other is something fundamentally different, or that one represents cost-sharing and the other does not, but rather simply who—either the parent or the student—most generally pays (Johnstone 2004).

Unitary or Dual Track Tuition Fees?

For those tuition fees that are to be paid up front, another distinction is whether all students in similar programs at the same or similar institutions pay essentially the same fee, or whether there are two tracks of students with respect to tuition fees: one track charged no or very nominal tuition fees and the other track charged a substantial tuition fee for pursuit of the same degree program at the same institution. In Russia and the other countries of the former Soviet Union, the post-Communist countries of Central and Eastern Europe, and some of the countries in East Africa, free higher education is guaranteed by their constitutions or framework laws, or is otherwise so deeply ingrained in their political culture that tuition fees charged to all students would be politically impossible. However, as tuition fee revenue is crucial to the financial viability of their universities, Russian universities, along with most universities in formerly Communist Eastern and Central Europe as well as other countries emerging from the former Soviet Union, have adopted a *dual track*, or parallel, tuition fee policy. This policy essentially limits admission to the free (or very low tuition fee) openings to only the number of students that the state can afford to support, while allowing a second track of matriculates, generally scoring below an admissions examination cutoff score, admission if they pay a tuition fee (and sometimes a very high one). By 2006 or so, more than one-half of all Russian university operating revenue was said to come from tuition fees—even as the Russian Constitution continued to guarantee free higher education (conveniently interpreted to mean only for all regular-track students). In Romania, about one-half of the higher educational students in 2008 were eligible for free, state-supported places, while the other half were required to pay tuition fees averaging 1,760 Ron per year [US$1,239].

A dual track tuition fee policy also exists in most of East Africa. It was first implemented with striking fiscal success by Uganda's Makerere University in 1992, followed by the University of Nairobi in 1998, and then by most of the universities in the region (Court 1999; Kiamba 2003; Ssebuwufu 2003).

The public university system in Australia also has a form of dual track tuition fee policy, although this fact is generally eclipsed by worldwide fascination with the country's *Higher Education Contribution Scheme* (HECS). Under Australia's Commonwealth Grant Scheme, each of the 37 public universities enters into an annual funding agreement with the government that sets out the number of places being funded and the discipline mix. Students who are eligible for Commonwealth-funded openings can defer payment and take out loans via the Higher Education Contribution Scheme, or they or their parents can pay up front and receive a 20 percent discount. However, since 1989 universities may also offer fee-paying places to Australian undergraduates who are not within the pool of Commonwealth-funded students, as long as these institutions have met their enrollment targets for Commonwealth students and limit the number of up-front, fee-paying students to no more than 35 percent of the total number of places available within the university. The fee-paying students pay tuition fees that are more than twice those paid (or deferred) by the Commonwealth-funded students. In 2006, there were 13,757 Australian undergraduates in full-fee-paying slots (Department of Education 2008). A similar, but slightly different dual track tuition policy is used in a number of countries, whereby some high-demand programs are offered at a costly tuition fee while regular courses remain free (or nearly so). In Egypt, for example, programs taught in French and English are more than ten times as expensive as the same programs offered in Arabic. In the Czech Republic, tuition fees are charged for courses taught in English but none at all for regular university courses.

The four columns shown in table 5.1 summarize the variations in the forms of tuition fee policies thus far portrayed, which are

- up-front tuition fees
- deferred tuition fees
- no (or only very nominal) tuition fees
- dual track tuition fees

Within the framework shown in table 5.1, many countries continue to struggle with the fundamental questions of whether to have a tuition fee at all (or more than a nominal one) and, if so, how to reconcile the need for a stable policy that produces a predictable (and preferably an increasing) stream of revenue with what is oftentimes a continuing popular and political resistance to tuition fees. Sometimes political winds affect disparate sectors or various regions of the same country differently. In Nigeria, for example, in May 2002 the government announced that the 24 federal universities were forbidden to charge tuition fees, although universities established by the Nigerian state

Table 5.1 Forms of public tuition fee policies

Up-front tuition fees	Deferred tuition fees	No or only nominal tuition fees	Dual track tuition fees
Austria	Australia	Argentina	Iceland	Angola	Lithuania
Belgium	England	Benin	Ireland[5]	Australia	Madagascar
Botswana	Ethiopia	Bolivia	Lebanon	Bulgaria	Malawi
Bulgaria	Lesotho	Brazil	Mali	Cambodia	Mauritius
Burkina Faso	Namibia	Burundi	Malta	Czech Rep.	Poland
Canada	New Zealand	Cameroon	Mauritania	Egypt	Romania
Chile	Rwanda	Cape Verde	Mexico	Estonia	Russia
China	Swaziland	CAR	Morocco	Ethiopia	Rwanda
Colombia	Tanzania	Chad	Niger	Ghana	Senegal
Costa Rica	Wales	Congo-Brazza.	Nigeria (F)[6]	Hungary	Tanzania
Côte d'Ivoire		Congo-Dem.	Norway	Jordan	Uganda
Ecuador		Cuba	Paraguay	Kazakhstan	Zambia
Gambia		Cyprus	Peru	Kenya	Zimbabwe
Germany[1]		Denmark	Saudi Arabia	Latvia	
Hong Kong		Eritrea	Scotland[7]		
India		Finland	Slovakia		
Indonesia		France[3]	Slovenia		
Italy		Gabon	Sudan		
Japan		Germany[4]	Sweden		
Jordan		Ghana	Syria		
Kenya		Greece	Togo		
Korea		Guatemala	Tunisia		
Liberia		Guinea	UAE		
Lichtenstein		Honduras	Uruguay		
Luxembourg					
Malaysia					
Mongolia					
Mozambique					
Netherlands					
Nigeria (S)[2]					
Philippines					
Portugal					
Serbia					
Sierra Leone					
Singapore					
South Africa					
Spain					
Switzerland					
Taiwan					
Turkey					
United States					
Vietnam					

1. Seven Länder now have tuition fees in their universities.
2. State universities in Nigeria.
3. As of 2009, French universities have no tuition fees as such (as the 1958 Constitution requires), but they charge registration fees of €230 per year [US$251] to cover certain administrative and health costs.
4. Nine Länder have retained free tuition.
5. While Ireland's universities do not charge tuition fees, they do charge a yearly student service fee of €750 [US$735].
6. Federal universities in Nigeria.
7. Scotland changed from up-front to deferred tuition fees in 1999 but abandoned them in 2008 for new entering students.

governments were allowed to continue doing so. Similarly, in Mexico many of the public state universities charge a modest tuition fee, but the attempt to introduce even a nominal tuition fee in Mexico's flagship National Autonomous University (UNAM) resulted in violent demonstrations that closed the university for a year and ended up with the government backing down and restoring the previous tuition fee that amounted to pennies per year (Preston 1999).

In Europe (i.e., the 27 European Union countries in 2009 plus Norway and Switzerland), some 17 countries now have some form of tuition fee, but only Austria, Belgium, Italy, the Netherlands, Portugal, and some of the Länder (states) in Germany have what Americans would consider more-than-nominal tuition fees (CESifo Group 2007). The advancement toward cost-sharing in Europe has been tentative and contested. Ireland, for example, abolished its tuition fees in 1997 but established what were simply called fees (some €825 [US$809] in 2007), which were clearly tuition fees under a different name. By 2008, outright tuition fees were back on the policy table in Ireland (albeit very contested), reportedly to address the major university deficits brought on by a 32 percent decline in state tax revenue from 1995 to 2005, with insufficient income in the form of the fees alone to close the gap between available governmental revenue and the increasing revenue needs of the universities (Flynn 2008).

Until 2005, the federal higher educational framework law (Hochschulrahmengesetz) in Germany imposed restrictions on an individual Länder's authority to charge tuition fees, and the former Social Democratic government banned all tuition fees throughout the country for the first university degree. At the same time, certain exceptions were made, and several states (Baden-Württemberg, Bavaria, Berlin, Brandenburg, Lower Saxony, and Saxony) implemented the special forms of fees that were allowed, such as tuition fees for students who exceeded the normal duration of a certain program plus four semesters and tuition fees for students enrolled in a second degree. However, in January 2005, after several years of political debate, Germany's Supreme Court overturned the ban in a case brought by six Länder and ruled that individual Länder could introduce tuition fees. As of 2008, seven of the German Länder have established tuition fees of up to €1,000 [US$1,124] in their universities (an amount that Americans might still consider nominal, but that in Germany is a major—albeit painful and still contested—step in the direction of cost-sharing).[1]

In Africa, the acceptance of tuition fees is mixed, with tuition fees fully (if controversially) accepted in South Africa, the dual track concept accepted in East Africa, and most of West and Central Africa together with North Africa and the Middle East (with the exception of Israel) still politically unable to accept anything other than very nominal tuition fees at best. Latin America also displays a great ambivalence about tuition fees. Most countries there continue to maintain public sectors that are largely free or charge only nominal tuition fees and are thus limited in capacity (and therefore academically selective and arguably elitist) alongside a large number of private colleges and universities, a few of which are selective and of high quality, and many of which are of marginal quality and essentially demand absorbing.

This ambivalence is reflected, for example, in Colombia, which has all of the attributes of a country that is poised to implement a program of cost-sharing, including

- a rapidly increasing population of youth completing high school and seeking some form of higher or postsecondary education;
- aspirations to compete (in terms of public university quality) with the leading public universities in Argentina, Brazil, Chile, and Mexico;
- substantial revenue needs in the public universities that are unlikely to be met with additional public revenue;
- a well-established student loan system (ICETEX);
- a well-established and sophisticated system of general means-testing, whereby additional grants or loans could be effectively targeted to make a maximum difference in student enrollment behavior;
- a well-established, tuition-dependent private sector; and
- a government (in 2009) that is politically receptive to markets and to liberal economic reforms.

In spite of this apparent readiness, Colombia (as of 2009) does not yet seem politically able to pursue additional higher educational revenue supplementation via tuition fees, using grants and loans to maintain accessibility.

Setting the Tuition Fee

Once the fundamental issue of whether to have a tuition fee at all has been decided in the affirmative, as well as the form it should take—that is, up-front, deferred, or dual track—the next obvious question is the proper amount of the fee. This, however, cannot be answered independently of a cluster of other policies and contextual circumstances:

1. The cultural and historical acceptability of public-sector fees generally
2. The existence of other kinds of nondiscretionary, supposedly non-tuition fees in addition to what is acknowledged to be the official tuition fee
3. The underlying per-student costs of instruction that are taken as a basis for the tuition fee
4. The mix of private as opposed to public benefits perceived to be attached to the institution or academic program (which is almost the same as identifying the market value attached to an institution or program)
5. The prevailing costs of student living (net of institutional or governmental subsidies for food, lodging, and other expenses)
6. The amount and coverage of student financial assistance

Let us consider each factor in our search for the proper tuition fee and then examine related issues: how this tuition fee (or fees) can or should vary, how it can be increased over time, and by what authority or combination of authorities a tuition fee is first established and then enlarged.

The cultural and historical acceptability of tuition fees, as well as the general principle of fees for any publicly provided service, is partly a function of history, as many countries had fee-supported universities long before there was any thought of higher education as an appropriately public enterprise. It also depends on currently prevailing political ideology—that is, one supporting high taxes, large government, and extensive entitlements as opposed to lower taxes, smaller government, and fewer entitlements. Thus some of the more aggressively market-oriented countries that take the appropriateness of public-sector tuition fees for granted (e.g., Canada, England, and the United States) will probably also feature higher tuition fees (i.e., based on a percentage of underlying instructional costs), whereas those countries that are more social welfare-oriented and in which acceptance of the very idea of a tuition fee continues to be widely contested (e.g., France, Germany, and Ireland) may begin with a very nominal tuition fee, merely to establish the principle.

Secondly, the appropriate amount of a tuition fee will also be affected by the presence of other kinds of nondiscretionary fees in addition to what is acknowledged to be the official tuition fee. These other-than-tuition fees may be one-time fees (such as for application or registration), or they may be semester or annual fees (such as for student programs, athletics and recreation, or Internet connectivity). Ireland, for example, got rid of tuition fees—to considerable political fanfare—but then established registration and other fees (allegedly not tuition fees) that were as high as some of the emerging tuition fees in Europe. Japanese universities at one time charged very expensive, one-time application fees (as much as the acknowledged tuition fees in many countries), and these fees were over and above their own already high tuition fees. Similarly, for many years the state of California was notorious for maintaining very low tuition fees only because of its very high other-than-tuition fees.

As a final example, and close to our institutional home, most of the colleges and universities within State University of New York system charge high auxiliary fees (e.g., the State University of New York at Buffalo's annual fee of $1,950 in 2008–9 in addition to the official, legislatively established tuition fee of $4,660) because the politics of New York State, like the politics of most states and most countries, tend to get paralyzed and totally irrational over the topic of tuition fees, so the easier alternative (from the standpoint of the system or the 29 senior colleges and universities within the system) is to garner supplementary revenue through the convenient euphemism of "fees," over which the individual campus administrations and the system trustees have full authority. In short, although the difference between a tuition fee and most other fees is genuine—even if imprecise and easily blurred—setting a tuition fee may depend in part on how much the university or the system has already closed the cost–revenue gap with other, less politically volatile fees.

In most countries, a third factor in determining the proper amount for a tuition fee is the per-student cost of instruction at the particular higher educational institution, system, or program in question. Instructional costs vary substantially across countries or systems, individual institutions, and academic programs. Thus if the establishment of a tuition fee is justified by the principle of sharing these underlying costs, it stands to reason that the proper amount of the tuition fee or fees should bear a close relationship to the calculated per-student costs of instruction. Following this reasoning, tuition fees—at least for undergraduate, or bachelor's degree, students[2]—should be higher in colleges and universities—and, possibly, in any given institution's academic programs—with high instructional costs. An additional argument for establishing a tuition fee in relation to some percentage of the underlying per-student costs of instruction is that the rationale for establishing the tuition fee in the first place also provides the reason for subsequent enlargements in the tuition fee, as the components of these underlying costs—principally faculty and staff salaries, but also the costs of technology, utilities, books, and journals—inevitably rise over time, calling for comparable periodic increases in tuition fees merely to preserve a constant share.

One problem with this construction, however, is that a calculation of per-[undergraduate]-student costs of instruction, particularly at research universities, depends on some partly arbitrary assumptions and accounting conventions: for example, how indirect costs, or institution-wide expenditures, are apportioned among bachelor's degree as opposed to graduate instruction; or how pension costs, or the costs of health insurance, or the costs of capital are allocated to undergraduate instruction, especially when most of the faculty (at least at a true research university) believe their principal missions to be scholarship and teaching future scholars at advanced levels. In addition, per-student costs vary considerably among the different degree programs in accordance with prevailing faculty-student ratios, equipment needs, and other program-specific costs—for example, among programs in science, history, or undergraduate teacher education. Particularly when the establishment of, or an increase in, a tuition fee in most countries continues to be so contested, these complications, although resolvable, can cause considerable delay and prolong the necessary decisions. This is by no means a sufficient cause for rejecting tuition fees; it only shows that the quest for an incontestably correct tuition fee is probably impossible.

A fourth factor used in the search for the proper, or correct, amount for a tuition fee is the perceived mix of private and public benefits attached to particular institutions and academic programs. Regardless of the underlying instructional cost differences, it is commonly thought to be appropriate (or perhaps merely more expedient, or more feasible) to recover a higher percentage of these instructional costs from those programs and degrees believed to bring the greatest private return to the student in the form or forms of future earnings, prestige, job security, or anything else valued in a profession or vocation. Thus, in the world of private higher education, as well as in public higher educational institutions where tuition fees are permitted, tuition fees for medical and other advanced health professional programs are generally expensive, reflecting not only the greater instructional costs of this education but also the high market value of the degree, which in turn is associated with the substantial income and elevated prestige of these professions. Similarly, since most of the former Communist, centrally planned economies have accepted market forces for setting prices in accord with supply and demand, the demand for higher education in such academic programs as economics, management, law, computer and information science, and the English language has risen greatly— and so, too, have tuition fees in most of these programs when fees are permitted to vary.

We should note a complication in the search for the proper tuition fee that is caused by the occasional disconnect between two factors: (a) instructional costs, and (b) the perceived mix of public and private benefits. For example, it is conventionally thought that classic research universities are more costly per student than shorter-cycle, more vocationally oriented, less research-intensive institutions, so that a similar percentage of costs to be charged to students and their parents would require a higher tuition fee in a research university, reinforced by the common presumption of greater prestige and market value attached to a university degree. However, although the presumption of higher unit costs in research universities may be true for laboratory sciences and engineering, particularly at advanced levels, it is probably not true for the undergraduate programs in many of the social sciences or the humanities and may not be true in some of the advanced professional programs (like law or business) that tend to feature higher tuition fees but can also be rather inexpensively delivered. In fact, while certain laboratory science and engineering programs are both high cost and bring greater-than-average prestige—which might suggest elevated tuition fees—they are not, in general, associated with substantial market demand or particularly high incomes, which might suggest a larger public benefit component and therefore a lower tuition fee. In countries that are legally able to differentiate undergraduate tuition fees by academic program and commonly do so, markets seems to trump instructional costs; hence tuition fees are generally more expensive in very high-demand programs, regardless of the underlying instructional costs.[3]

A fifth factor that might influence what is thought to be the proper amount of tuition fees in public undergraduate education involves the costs associated with student maintenance, especially the expenses of food and lodging. These are mainly a function of the degree to which it is possible to live at home— which, in turn, is a matter of the proximity of the college or university to the home, the availability of inexpensive transportation, and, to some degree, especially in wealthier countries, the cultural acceptability or nonacceptability of living with one's parents well into one's 20s. State policies in the United States generally aim at putting at least a public community college within commuting range of most families (which generally assumes automobile ownership). This is clearly not feasible in many parts of rural America, or the more remote regions of many countries, where traditional college-going must assume living in a university residence or with relatives or independently. But even where living with parents is possible, general cultural acceptability may vary among countries, with such an arrangement allegedly being more countenanced, for example, in France than in England or Germany.

If a student cannot live at home, the cost of student living is most affected by the degree to which residence halls and/or canteens are publicly subsidized or otherwise made accessible at minimal cost. This creates a possible clash between two forms of cost-sharing: (1) charging a tuition fee to cover some of the costs of instruction and shifting a part of these costs from governments or taxpayers to parents or students, and (2) charging more nearly break-even fees for governmentally or institutionally provided residence halls or canteens. Both forms of cost-sharing have the fiscal purpose of shifting costs from governments to families. As discussed in chapter 3, for what can be a comparable fiscal impact, higher fees to lessen the public costs of subsidized food and lodging tend to elicit less political resistance than the establishment of, or an increase in, tuition fees. Thus the existence of many indirect forms of student subsidies, such as subsidized food, lodging, and public transportation, might be thought of as associated with setting higher tuition fees, in a kind of fiscal compensation; whereas the absence of indirect forms of student subsidies might, in similar fashion, be thought of as associated with lower tuition fees and a more direct subsidy of the costs of instruction.

An examination of countries with higher and low tuition fees, and direct and indirect subsidies, however, does not bear out this relationship. Some countries with high indirect forms of subsidy, like Germany (Schwarzenberger 2008), still contest the very principle of tuition fees, while some countries with low indirect subsidies, such as the United States, feature very high public tuition fees. Expressed another way, prevailing political ideology appears to be a stronger factor in influencing what is assumed to be a proper amount of tuition fee than a mix of *direct subsidies* (i.e., subsidies to the universities, presumably affecting the need for supplemental tuition fees) and *indirect subsidies* (i.e., subsidies for food and lodging, reflecting more of a general welfare-state ideology than an analytical decision about where to place public subsidies).

A final factor in establishing what is thought to be a proper, or correct, tuition fee is the amount and targeting of financial assistance, as discussed in chapter 4. Clearly, the more extensive, effectively targeted, and generous the financial assistance, the less traction it gives to the expected political resistance to tuition fees on the grounds that such fees may exclude the sons and daughters of the poor. Countries with extensive financial assistance (including both grants and loans), the policies and personnel to deliver that assistance, plus the appropriate instruments for cost-effective targeting, or means-testing, are better able to establish and protect substantial public-sector tuition fees.

In the end, the proper amount for a tuition fee is best established as some percentage of underlying instructional costs, with due regard to all of the above-mentioned factors. To make a significant contribution to revenue supplementation—that is, to be an instrument of cost-sharing—policies establishing tuition fees in public higher education generally aim for tuition fees (before financial assistance) in the neighborhood of one-fifth to one-third of the instructional costs.[4]

Tuition fees for public higher education in the United States range widely between states, of course, but also by region, with such fees generally greater in the Northeast and less so in the South and West. They also vary by degree level and selectivity, with tuition fees high for selective research universities and low for open-admission community colleges. Public colleges and universities in the United States are able to charge relatively expensive tuition fees because of

- a long history of extensive, mainly private, fee-supported colleges and universities;
- a prevailing political-economic acceptance of markets and market-determined prices and of the ideological appropriateness of tuition fees—even in the public sector; and
- a well-established and abundantly funded array of grants and loans, as well as means-testing instruments to target these financial assistance resources effectively.

Variations in Tuition Fees

Tuition fees vary among countries according to the above factors. But tuition fees also vary within each country, as we saw in the dual track tuition fee institutions and sectors. Thus a tuition fee policy is not just about a single tuition fee, but generally about many fees, which will vary not just among individual institutions, for example, but also by

- the cost of the program, following per-student cost differences (e.g., among engineering, the social sciences, biology, and law);
- the faculty (e.g., among faculties or schools of arts and letters, education, law, and medicine);
- the level of the degree (e.g., among bachelor's degrees, master's degrees, and doctorates);
- the sector (e.g., among junior or community colleges, comprehensive colleges, and research universities);
- the market demand for the degree, as mentioned above, with expected variations (e.g., among management, medicine, law, and social work); and
- the academic ability of the entering student (e.g., among the two tracks of students in the dual track tuition fee institutions or systems).

Table 5.2 presents some examples of differing tuition fees in selected countries.

In a number of countries (Australia, for example, and Hungary for fee-paying students), tuition fees are set according to the course of study, while in others (Austria, Luxembourg, the Netherlands, and Portugal), university tuition fees are uniform throughout the country. Tuition fees at the undergraduate level are also generally uniform throughout an institution in the United States, where entering students frequently do not know and do not need to declare their program (or major, or concentration) at the start of their studies; they may not even take courses in their intended program for the first year or two. This delay is due to the peculiarly American undergraduate requirement that many courses during the first two years be taken outside of the student's major program: for example, in general education or a foreign language; or in elective courses that undergraduates in the United States are encouraged to take; or in courses to bring their basic skills in writing or mathematics up to college standards. These requirements make it difficult to charge

Table 5.2   Tuition fees for public sector institutions in various countries, for first degree, in recent academic year

Country	Public institution fees			Special fee-paying track
	Low	Medium	High	
Australia (2008)	$3,665	$5,223	$6,114	$6,530
Austria (2007)	$856	$856	$856	NA
Brazil (2006)	0	0	0	NA
Canada (2007–8)	$3,867	$6,231	$8,519	NA
Chile (2003–4)	$5,094	$6,293	$8,331	NA
China (2007)	$1,749	—	$2,940	NA
England (2008–9)	$4,838[1]	$4,838	$4,838	NA
Ethiopia (2006–7)	$386	—	$888	NA
Hong Kong (2002–3)	$7,402	$7,402	$7,402	NA
Hungary (2006–7)	0	0	0	$1,427–$6,370
India (2008)	$16[2]	$204[3]	$613[4]	NA
Japan (2005)	$4,200	$4,200	$4,654	NA
Korea (2004–5)	—	$3,883[5]	—	NA
Luxembourg (2009–10)	$217	$217	$217	NA
Mongolia (2002–3)	$719	—	$1,078	NA
Netherlands (2006)	$1,687	$1,687	$1,687	Set by institutions
Portugal (2004–5)	$913	$1,047	$1,062	$3,849
Romania (2005–6)	0	0	0	$1,240
Russia (2001–2)	0	0	0	$1,530–$3,768
Singapore (2008–9)	$5,888	$5,888	$6,055	$23,546
South Africa (2005)	$1,730	$2,266	$4,960	NA
United States (2004–5)	$4,350	$9,000	$12,400	NA
Vietnam (2008–9)	$380[6]	$380	$380	$1,060[7]
Wales (2008–9)	$4,838	$4,838	$4,838[8]	NA

Note: National currencies converted to US dollars by the World Bank's 2005 International Comparison Program purchasing power parity estimates.

1. Maximum level allowed by the government. Most universities in England charge this level of tuition fee.

2. Central university.

3. University or government college.

4. State university.

5. Annual average tuition fee.

6. Maximum allowed.

7. There appears to be a disconnect between the Ministry of Education and Training in Vietnam, which allows universities to collect higher fees for high-quality training courses, and the state financial inspection agencies, which claim that this practice is not supported in legal regulations. http://english.vietnamnet.vn/ [accessed 14 October 2008].

8. All Welsh students are entitled to a fee grant of up to £1,890 to be paid directly to the institution.

varying tuition fees for different programs when so many students have not yet declared—or will change—their undergraduate program, or when students in different programs are sitting side by side in the same general education classes. In addition, there is a reluctance to charge higher tuition fees for the more costly programs in engineering and science, because of what is believed to be too few Americans (and especially too few women) taking such programs already. At the postbachelor's level, however, especially in advanced professional programs such as law or business administration, there are no such inhibitions, and very great demand, combined with the high starting salaries (making students' debts easier to pay off), frequently leads to considerably higher tuition fees.

At the same time, it is common for different sectors in the same public system—for example, research universities versus comprehensive colleges—to charge different (in this example, more expensive) tuition fees, both because of the presumably greater underlying costs of a research university as well as for what is generally (but not always) a greater market demand for a university over a comprehensive college. This is the case in Mexico, Vietnam, and most public higher educational systems in the United States.[5]

In Canada and the United States, tuition fees are lower for students who come from the state or province where the higher educational institution is located. A New York State resident undergraduate, for example, paid $2,175 per semester in 2008, while an out-of-state student had to pay $5,305 per semester. In Canada, the tuition fees for students from another province can be twice as much as the fees paid by students from the province in which the university is located.

Universities in a number of countries (the Czech Republic, Denmark, Greece, Ireland, Luxemburg, Malta, Scotland, and Spain; and for state-sponsored students in Estonia, Hungary, and Latvia) have no tuition fees for a first degree, but they charge for a second or higher degree and/or charge tuition fees to students who take longer than some standard time stipulated by law to finish their initial degree. In the Czech Republic, for example, the fee for a second degree in 2006 was approximately CZK 2,890 [US$200] per year, and the cost of needing an additional six months to finish a first degree was CZK 4,340 [US$300].

In some European countries—Denmark and Finland (beginning in 2009 with master's programs), Sweden (beginning in 2010), plus Cyprus, Ireland, Malta, and Slovakia—university tuition fees are not charged for their own nationals but apply for international students from non-European Union countries. In other countries—Australia, Austria, Canada, England, Singapore, and the United States, among others—international students (again, in the case of the EU, excluding those students who are from EU or European Economic Area countries) pay substantially higher tuition fees than do the citizens of that country: twice as much in Austria and more than eight times greater in England (European Commission 2007; OECD 2007). Tuition fee policies toward nonnationals are even more complicated in Scotland, where Scottish students pay no tuition fees (deferred or otherwise), as the deferred graduate endowment contribution was abolished in 2008, but students from other UK constituent countries and from the EU pay £1,700 [US$2,615] per year and international students from outside the EU pay considerably more.

Increases in Tuition Fees Over Time

Once a tuition fee has been established in some form and in some amount (or amounts), with a policy created for that tuition fee to vary (or not), it becomes essential to initiate a policy whereby the fee can be increased over time. Chapter 1 posited that the underlying per-student costs of instruction rise at a rate roughly equal to the rate of increase in faculty and staff compensation (including the rate of increase in benefits costs), or generally at a rate in excess of inflation. Therefore, unless the purchasing power of a tuition fee is to decrease over time and the share of costs borne by the parent and/or the student is to be commensurately eroded, tuition fees must increase over time. Those governments, governing boards, or institutions responsible for changing (i.e., raising) the tuition fee over time need a policy, or a principle, for such increases that balances the institutions' need for their revenues to expand more or less in accord with their rising costs against their need to maintain student accessibility and hold down cost increases that are not absolutely necessary. Elected officials can be expected to resist being constrained by mere principles on matters as costly and as politically volatile as proposals to raise tuition fees in public colleges and universities. However, absent at least some guiding principles for associating tuition fees with escalating instructional costs, the entire debate over the need for, or the ideological appropriateness of, tuition fees will come back onto the policy table. Thus some set of principles is strategically useful and, if built into law, can allow tuition fees to grow at an appropriate rate without having to replay the entire tuition fee debate.

From the standpoint of institutional financial viability, tuition fees should be allowed to increase over time in general accord with the rising per-student costs of instruction. Such a policy would maintain tuition fees at a constant share of the underlying costs of instruction, and, assuming that government also increased its share of instructional costs, the college or university would be insulated from the erosion of budgetary purchasing power by escalating wages and salaries and other expenses over which it may have little control. A number of US public college and university governing boards have established policies that are nonbinding, but that ask parents and students to anticipate tuition fee hikes pegged to the rising costs or revenue needs of the institution (and that indirectly ask governors and legislators to allow such increases).

On the other hand, since the normal rise in per-student instructional costs, as emphasized in chapter 1, is in excess of the prevailing rate of inflation and also in excess of likely increases in wages or salaries for many families, such a policy essentially guarantees that college expenses for a number of them will continue to rise at rates exceeding both the cost of living and the rate of increase of their own wages and salaries. Furthermore, such a policy seems, to many politicians, to purport to hold public colleges and universities harmless from the financial ups and downs that public sectors are expected to go through, and to accept as a given that colleges and universities are unable to expand their productivity or to insist on similar increased efficiencies from their faculty and staff. Thus, other guiding principles for tuition fee increases have been proposed, such as raising them only at (rather than above) the prevailing rate of inflation or at the rate of increase in the state's operating budget. In the end, what is important is that, first, politicians recognize the underlying pressures from expanding costs and are made aware of the revenue needs of their public colleges and universities, and that, second, some guiding principle is at least politically acknowledged, even if the exigencies of politics, taxes, and competing needs will ultimately determine the budgetary outcome.

The Locus of Authority to Set (and to Increase) Tuition Fees

The authority to set and to raise tuition fee levels is vested in different entities in different countries: in some nations it rests in the central government (e.g., Austria and Hong Kong); in others, in the state or provincial government (e.g., Canada, India, Spain, and the United States); and in still others, in the institutions themselves (Chile, Indonesia, South Africa, South Korea, Switzerland, and Taiwan). In the United States, tuition levels for public colleges and universities are set at the state level, but the authority or authorities responsible for establishing tuition fees differ from state to state and may include governors, legislatures, state higher education coordinating councils, system-wide governing boards, individual institutions, or combinations thereof. With so many entities involved in what is generally so politicized a process, it is often difficult to establish exactly who set (or who blocked) any particular tuition fee or tuition fee increase.

For example, in New York State (to take a very personal but illustrative example), only the State University of New York (SUNY) system trustees (the governing board) have the authority to set tuition fees for any of the 29 state-operated colleges and universities in the system. However, the state legislature, disliking tuition fees and mistrusting the governing board, placed a provision in New York State's higher educational framework law stating that the trustees cannot establish any tuition fee until the SUNY system's budget for the year in question has been passed by the legislature and signed by the governor. Thus, if the trustees establish a tuition fee that is insufficient to generate the revenue required for SUNY's state-approved budget—which the legislature has clearly passed with a specific tuition fee in mind, although this is nowhere stipulated—the State Division of the Budget will be forced to demand that the university system make budget cuts to bring its authorized spending in line with the new lower revenue estimate: in effect, to unilaterally cut the SUNY budget (and quite appropriately to blame the trustees and the system chancellor for what the politicians will portray as an unnecessary cut). If, on the other hand, the trustee-established tuition fee is greater than the tuition fee contemplated by the governor and the legislature in the construction of the SUNY budget, then (a) the university system will have more revenue than it will be allowed to spend and will be forced to return it at the end of the fiscal year; (b) the next year's budget will almost assuredly start out with less tax funding; and (c) the governor and the legislature are likely to be very angry at the SUNY trustees and chancellor.

In several countries (e.g., Australia and England), the government sets the *maximum* tuition fee that may be charged, under which the universities are free to determine their fee amounts. In Japan, a major reform in 2004 authorized the national universities to set their own tuition fees. However, these universities may not exceed 110 percent of the standard fee established by the

Ministry of Education and the Ministry of Finance. Local authorities, none-theless, continue to determine the tuition fee levels at Japan's local public institutions.

In a number of countries, the authority to set tuition fee levels is split be-tween the central and state governments or between the state and the institu-tions. In the Netherlands, for example, the government establishes tuition fees for those students eligible for student support, while the institutions them-selves set tuition fees for the students who are not eligible (Jongbloed 2005). In Germany, after the Supreme Court ruling reaffirming the right of the Länder to establish tuition fees, the North Rhine–Westphalia Länder passed such a law, allowing their universities to determine tuition fees, but setting a maxi-mum fee and restrictions on how the tuition fee revenue can be used. In 2007, the University of Cologne, Germany's second largest, established a new tuition fee of €500 per semester [US$560]. However, even though no one doubted the serious and prolonged underfunding of this university, its great need for ad-ditional faculty, or the benefits that tuition fee revenue could bring, the North Rhine–Westphalia law permitting it to charge a tuition fee restricted the use of the revenue to teaching only—which the Ministry in 2008 interpreted as disal-lowing the use of that revenue to hire any professor who would be expected to perform any research (or be given any time away from a teaching overload to do so). For a prestigious German university, such a restriction is tantamount to denying the mission of the university and virtually precluding the hiring of a professor whose role would be acceptable to the rest of the faculty (Wilhelm 2008).

Tuition Fees: A Summary

Although the many variations and dynamic histories of tuition fees worldwide make summary generalizations a bit risky, we can discern a number of trends and rules of thumb about tuition fees from the vantage point of 2008–9.

1. Along with other forms of cost-sharing, tuition fees—meaning fees to cover a portion of the underlying costs of higher education—are being intro-duced (or are being increased, sometimes at rates in excess of increases in these costs) in most countries, covering most or all students, in most or all public institutions of higher education.

2. Tuition fees are almost everywhere contested. The opposition to tuition fees is especially bitter in Europe, which has had a long tradition of no such

fees but where relatively modest tuition fees are clearly encroaching in the first decade of the twenty-first century. The transitional countries emerging from the former Soviet Union and their Eastern and Central European counterparts still strongly oppose tuition fees—a legacy of the state-controlled economies that once guaranteed free higher education (along with free food and lodging, health care, and jobs), but now find that difficulties in taxation and mounting competition from other public needs are forcing cost-sharing everywhere, including tuition for students not passing entrance exams with a high enough score. Opposition is also strong (and sometimes violent) in most African countries, which share European colonial legacies (with their traditional opposition to tuition fees) and the legacy of African socialism, which at one time had assumed state control and financial responsibility for education and other services, but was unable to tax sufficiently to support them. Finally, most Latin American countries strongly oppose tuition fees; here, socialist and populist legacies combine with private nonprofit, proprietary, and church-supported universities to preserve limited, generally free, but elitist public systems.

3. Although opponents of tuition fees frequently decry what they portray as a neoliberal ideology that rejects the notion of public or social benefits to higher education, tuition fees even in the United States and other countries that follow the Anglo-American financing model are generally between 15 and 35 percent—and only rarely more than 40 percent—of full instructional costs, reinforcing widespread acceptance among politicians and economists alike of the concepts that there are substantial public benefits to higher education as well as an obligation to continue public support.

4. Tuition fees are only one—and oftentimes the smallest—of the costs confronting students and parents, who also face the generally far higher expenses of food, lodging, and other costs of student living, as well as traditionally privately borne educational expenses (such as computers, books, and Internet access) that sometimes give rise to a host of other fees that are difficult to distinguish from tuition fees. However, the fact that tuition fees are politically determined and are symbolic of a larger political and ideological contest between state ownership, state control, and heavy taxation on the one hand, and privatization and markets on the other, combined with the fact that in many countries the university is the intellectual center of much of the political opposition and leftist ideology in these nations, have made tuition fees a political flash point in this larger political/ideological arena.

5. Although the equity argument for some cost-sharing—and thus for some tuition fees to be borne by some or most students and/or parents (less any targeted financial assistance)—is set forth by most economists and policy analysts, a more powerful case for tuition fees is the less ideologically and politically contestable combination of several factors: (a) the very high costs of instruction; further propelled in most countries by (b) the even more rapidly rising cost pressures of expanding higher educational demand; both of which are confronted by (c) the severe limitation of available public revenues, especially in most low-income countries, together with (d) the increasingly socially and politically compelling case made by other competing public needs (again, especially in most low-income countries).

6. The combination of the continuing strong opposition to tuition fees expressed in #2 above, alongside the strong case for tuition fees as suggested by #5, has lead to a variety of euphemisms and obfuscations, such as (a) a reluctance to use the term "tuition fees" and to use instead simply "fees," which seems to invoke less political resistance; (b) a shift in the burden of tuition fees from parents to students and a softening of their impact by deferring the fees as loans—and possibly a further softening (or obfuscation) of the nature of these loans by calling them "income contingent obligations" or "graduate taxes"; (c) the retention of very low or no tuition fees for regular students, while rationing these places to certain students only—generally the most academically well prepared—and charging high tuition fees to students who do not attain this standard.

7. To the degree to which tuition fees for public institutions are charged up front and are therefore expected to be paid primarily by parents (at least for traditionally aged first degree students), a policy of up-front tuition fees requires a system of means-testing and financial assistance, as discussed in chapter 4.

8. To the degree to which tuition fees for public institutions are deferred and are therefore expected to be paid by students, these deferred tuition fees need a system of available loans (whether income contingent or fixed schedule) if cost-sharing is any part of the rationale for tuition fees in the first place.

9. Political resistance to tuition fees will be less in countries where means-tested financial assistance in the form of grants and/or loans can assure higher educational opportunities for students with low-income parents. The following chapter will discuss the various types of loan schemes that countries have

either put in place or are contemplating in order to mitigate the impact of cost-sharing on higher educational enrollments, to increase enrollments, and/or to improve access to higher education for certain populations.

10. Political resistance to tuition fees in public institutions of higher education is generally less for nonuniversity vocational, graduate-level, or advanced professional education, or for programs that are subject to enrollment limitations (*numerus clauses*), than it is for general first degree university studies. Political resistance may also be somewhat less in countries like Japan or the United States, which have substantial and popular private higher education.

We conclude this chapter as we began it. Tuition fees are increasingly important in most countries as the trajectory of revenue needs continues to outpace the trajectory of likely available public revenues. At the same time, tuition fees are but one of the forms of cost-sharing; they are also, in most countries and for most students, far from the most costly element in the total packages of expenses to be met by students, perhaps with the help of parents and extended families, and perhaps also with the help of financial assistance. One of these forms of financial assistance is the student loan scheme, to which we turn in the next chapter.

NOTES

1. An article by Wilhelm (2008) about the beginning of tuition fees (€500 per semester [US$560]) at the University of Cologne, Germany's second largest, illustrates the political pain evidently felt in the acceptance of tuition fees in Germany, even though no one doubts the serious and prolonged underfunding of German universities or the benefits that tuition fee revenue could bring.

2. Advanced professional programs, which in the United States include law and graduate business programs, are exceptions: their costs often can be quite low, while the market demand and tuition fees are generally very high. Advanced Ph.D. programs, on the other hand, tend to be very costly, yet most Ph.D. students in most of the advanced industrialized countries are employed in teaching or research assistant capacities by the university in which they are enrolled, making tuition fees less fiscally relevant to either the student or the institution.

3. Tuition fee differentiation at the undergraduate level is not a common practice in US college and universities, due in large part to the mostly common curricula for most bachelor's degree students during at least their first two years of study. With business majors and social work majors sitting side by side in many of their classes, differential tuition fees based on the market demand for academic majors is generally considered unworkable.

4. The Carnegie Commission on Higher Education (1973) found that historically, tuition fees in the United States have averaged approximately 25 percent of per-student

instructional costs. The Commission proposed a policy of slowly increasing tuition fees as a proportion of costs, rising from its 1973 level of 24 percent to a recommended steady-state level of one-third of costs. While the Commission's recommendation never became policy as such, tuition fees in the United States did indeed rise as a proportion of total revenue throughout the latter decades of the twentieth century, and some state tuition policies began to link tuition fees to a designated fraction of underlying costs (Johnstone 1992). Interestingly, China has also set maximum tuition fee levels at a proportion of instructional costs, officially aiming at 25 percent, although here tuition fees are applied mainly to undergraduate instruction.

5. Most public systems in the United States feature higher tuition fees in their research universities than in their comprehensive (nondoctoral) colleges and universities. The State University of New York system, however, is forbidden by state law from charging different tuition fees in different institutions for the same programs, thus requiring the same tuition fee for, say, an undergraduate economics major in one of the colleges and a similar major in one of the research universities. This frustrates the leaders of the research universities, who believe that their programs are more costly as well as of higher quality, both of which could justify considerably higher tuition fees. The leaders of the colleges, on the other hand, argue (1) that the underlying per-student grants from the state to the colleges and universities already greatly favor the research universities, compensating for whatever higher costs may be associated with their instructional programs; (2) that the undergraduate instruction in the research universities is not necessarily of any better quality; and (3) that some of the press from university leaders and faculty pertaining to higher undergraduate tuition fees is no more than a marketing device in the hopes that the public might associate a higher tuition fee with better quality. As of 2009, there is no resolution to this issue.

REFERENCES

Carnegie Commission on Higher Education. 1973. *Higher Education: Who Pays? Who Benefits? Who Should Pay?* New York: McGraw-Hill.
CESifo Group. 2007. Tuition Fees in Europe 2007/2008. *CESifo DICE Report [Database for Institutional Comparisons in Europe]* 4/2007. www.cesifo-group.de/portal/page/portal/ifoHome/b-publ/b2journal.
Court, David. 1999. *Financing Higher Education in Africa: Makerere; The Quiet Revolution.* Washington, DC: World Bank.
Department of Education. 2008. *Higher Education Report 2006.* Canberra: Australian Department of Education, Employment and Workplace Relations.
European Commission. 2007. *Key Data on Higher Education in Europe.* Luxembourg: Office for Official Publications of the European Communities.
Flynn, Sean. 2008. Fees Re-Introduction "Not Part of Green Party Policy." *Irish Times,* 11 August. www.irishtimes.com/newspaper/breaking/2008/0811/breaking18.html.
Johnstone, D. Bruce. 1992. Tuition Fees. In *The Encyclopedia of Higher Education,* ed. Burton R. Clark and Guy R. Neave. London: Pergamon Press.
———. 2004. Cost-Sharing and Equity in Higher Education: Implications of Income Contingent Loans. In *Markets in Higher Education,* ed. Pedro Teixeira, Ben Jongbloed,

David Dill, and Alberto Amaral. Dordrecht, The Netherlands: Kluwer Academic Publishers.

Jongbloed, Ben. 2005. Higher Education Funding in the Netherlands: Recent Developments. *IAU Horizons, World Higher Education News* 11 (1):9.

Kiamba, Crispus. 2003. The Experience of Privately Sponsored Studentship and Other Income Generating Activities at the University of Nairobi. In *Improving Tertiary Education in Sub-Saharan Africa: Things that Work; Report of a Regional Training Conference Held in Accra, Ghana,* ed. Burton Bollag. Washington, DC: World Bank.

Marcucci, Pamela, and D. Bruce Johnstone. 2007. Tuition Fee Policies in a Comparative Perspective: Theoretical and Political Rationales. *Journal of Higher Education Policy and Management* 29 (1):25–40.

OECD. 2007. *Education at a Glance.* Paris: Organisation for Economic Co-operation and Development.

Preston, Julia. 1999. University Officials Yield to Student Strike in Mexico. *New York Times,* June 8, A12.

Schwarzenberger, Astrid, ed. 2008. *Public/Private Funding of Higher Education: A Social Balance.* Hanover: Higher Education Information Systems (HIS).

Ssebuwufu, John P. M. 2003. University Financing and Management Reforms: The Experience of Makerere University. In *Financing of Higher Education in Eastern and Southern Africa: Diversifying Revenue and Expanding Accessibility,* ed. Burton L. M. Mwamila, Issa Omari, and Eva Mbuya. Dar es Salaam: University of Dar es Salaam.

Wilhelm, Ian. 2008. German Universities Cope with a Novelty—Tuition. *Chronicle of Higher Education,* April 4, A27.

CHAPTER SIX

Student Loan Schemes in Purpose, Form, and Consequence

Students, in addition to taxpayers and alongside their parents, can also shoulder a portion of the costs of higher education, including a portion of the costs of instruction and other educationally related expenditures as well as some or all of the cost of student living. Students can assume these expenses in two main ways: by working and earning the necessary funds, either during term time or vacations, or by borrowing. This chapter is about borrowing—or, from the vantage point of governmental policy, about the establishment of student loan schemes either (or both) to further a shift of higher educational costs to students or to maintain accessibility in the face of higher educational expenses borne, for whatever reason, by the student and his or her family.

Variations in Student Loan Schemes

Student loan schemes vary enormously. They can differ in purpose: borrowing to cover the student borrower's share of tuition fees, or borrowing to cover all or some of the cost of student living, or borrowing for both reasons. Similarly, student loan schemes can vary in ultimate benefit or impact. A loan scheme can benefit some students by providing opportunities for a higher education that were not heretofore possible, or by allowing students who would have been attending anyway the option to devote less time to outside employment or to improve their standard of student living, or perhaps to become financially independent from their parents. The extra revenue made possible by the additional fees that in turn were made possible by the student loan scheme might, on the other hand, primarily benefit the university and the faculty via higher wages or lighter loads or more opportunities for research. The additional revenue might allow for expanded system capacity, the benefits of which would accrue to aid the marginal students who were formerly excluded by capacity constraints. Student loans can also benefit mainly the government, such as when new revenue from the tuition fees that are covered by new loans allow the government to decrease its share of current operating funds, or when the repayment stream is never capitalized at all but simply becomes a future additional revenue stream for the government, like any other future stream of taxation. Finally, financial benefits from student loans can accrue to the parent, for instance when an up-front fee paid mainly by parents is shifted to a deferred fee (i.e., a loan) paid mainly by the student (as in the example of England and Wales discussed in the previous chapter).

Student loan schemes also vary in the nature of the lender, including borrowing from a bank, from the government, from a public student loan agency, or from a university (which presumably would immediately sell the note to a bank or student loan agency). Schemes also differ in the act of borrowing, depending on whether the student borrower literally receives a loan in cash and then pays college or university tuition fees or the expenses of lodging or food, or whether the borrower is merely incurring a repayment obligation simply by virtue of college or university attendance, with the deferred tuition fee, or loan, never passing through his or her hands but still obligating that student to a stream of future payments.

One last significant variation in student loan schemes may be in the relationship between borrowing as a principal form of the student bearing a portion of the costs of higher education and the extent to which parents are also expected to contribute either to the costs of instruction or the expenses of student maintenance, as discussed in chapters 4 and 5. The arguments for the student bearing a portion of the costs of higher education are somewhat different from the reasons for the parents to contribute, as discussed in chapter 4. In either case—a parental or a student contribution—the rationales are also different when applied to the costs of instruction (i.e., the expenses incurred by universities and other institutions of higher education) as opposed to the costs of maintenance, or student living (primarily food and lodging, but extending as well to all other expenditures, including clothing, entertainment, transportation, and all else that is thought to constitute at least a minimum standard of living for a young full-time student). Furthermore, as discussed throughout the preceding chapters, countries and cultures differ in their beliefs and policies regarding the appropriateness of parents and/or students—as opposed to governments or taxpayers—bearing a portion of either of these sets of costs.

These patterns of higher educational costs being shared by parents and/or students and the consequent need for the student's share to be deferred, or borrowed, are portrayed in table 6.1. The question that was developed in the preceding chapters on cost-sharing and tuition fees is fundamental to these differing patterns: specifically, if there are to be more than the most nominal of tuition fees, are such fees to be paid up front and mainly by parents (at least to the degree to which the family is financially able), as in Canada, China, Japan, or the United States, or are these tuition fees to be deferred and paid mainly by students (i.e., treated as a loan), as in Australia, New Zealand, England, Scotland (from 1999 though 2008), Wales, Ethiopia, South Africa, and Tanzania?

In those countries featuring an officially expected parental contribution to up-front tuition fees, the rationale for such fees, as discussed in chapter 5, begins with the generally accepted proposition that higher education offers very substantial returns to the student—both monetary, in the form of higher lifetime earnings, as well as nonmonetary, through enhanced status and richer life choices—such that parents will naturally want to maximize the chances for their children to obtain these considerable benefits. Additionally, the parents themselves are also presumed to benefit from the higher education of their children, both through their children's higher status that then rubs off on themselves, and from the enhanced security of having children who are more likely to be affluent and therefore to be in a better position to care for them financially, if need be, in their old age.

Students of traditional university age in the United States and other countries that feature an up-front expected parental contribution to the costs of instruction are thus assumed (at least for the purpose of sharing the costs of higher education) to be financially dependent children—either through the uninterrupted completion of an undergraduate degree, or until some age

Table 6.1 Differing patterns of student borrowing for and parental sharing of higher educational costs

| | Costs of instruction | | Costs of student living |
	Up-front tuition fees	Deferred tuition fees	No tuition fees	
Student	May borrow if financially independent or to supplement parental contribution	Deferred obligation (loan), the value of which is discounted by the present value of repayments	No obligation	May borrow if financially independent or to supplement parental contribution
Parent	Main contributor where tuition fees are up front	No official expectation, but may pay up front in lieu of student debt	No obligation	May pay all or part, either via an allowance or directly to the institution—or by assuming the expenses of a student living at home
Government (taxpayer)	May supplement parent if need is demonstrated	May supplement student via subsidized interest rates	Government (taxpayer) must assume full costs	May subsidize food and/or lodging, or subsidize interest rates on loans

generally corresponding to the age at which that first degree should have been completed, or until the occurrence of some traditionally adult event such as marriage or military service that signals the departure of the child from the home of the parents. However, even in countries that emphasize an officially expected parental contribution to the costs of instruction through an up-front tuition fee, there will still be a need for student contributions—and thus for student loans—in cases where the parent is financially unable or unwilling to contribute, or where the student has attained an age of independence or otherwise so desires financial independence from parents that he or she has demonstrably left the family (e.g., is no longer counted as a dependant by the parents for tax purposes) before entering into a college or university and thus needs a way to assume (but probably to defer and thus have to borrow) his or her share of whatever costs of instruction are passed on as tuition fees. And in US private higher education, where tuition fees plus the expenses of student living can be in the range of $30,000 to $50,000 a year, even most families able to afford these prices will require the student to bear a considerable portion of these costs over and above the parents' contributions—and thus will require student loans.

Also, in the case of Canada, the United States, and other countries where there are sharper divisions (and likely to be actual breaks) between undergraduate and graduate or advanced professional levels of education—for example, between the bachelor's degree and entry into law or medical school, or returning for a master's degree in education or business administration—tuition fees at these advanced levels tend to fall more on the student regardless of the official expectation of parental contributions at the undergraduate level. At graduate or advanced levels, parents contribute more infrequently and usually unofficially, depending both on their affluence and their willingness and financial ability to cushion their adult children from too much debt. In such cases, generally available student loan schemes—preferably unsubsidized or minimally subsidized and without regard to the income of the parents—are imperative if adult students, now financially independent from their parents, are to have access to advanced professional and graduate levels of higher education.

In countries like Australia, New Zealand, England, Wales, and Scotland (in the latter case only from 1999 though 2008), where traditional-age students themselves, rather than their parents, are expected to pay tuition fees in the public institutions of higher education (albeit in most instances with these fees deferred, or in the form of loans), the rationale is that students are major beneficiaries of what in all cases are costly programs of higher education. Students receive these benefits throughout their lifetimes in a variety of ways, including higher earnings, more career options, greater prestige, and the not inconsiderable consumption benefits that are part of the collegiate experience. Thus it is thought to be fair that students bear some of the costs of this expensive higher education—but only after completion of their studies when, at least in part because of this higher education, they are assumed to be employed at better jobs and at higher salaries. In such countries, then, most students will finish their studies having borrowed at least some amount of money, with the aggregate level or burden depending on the amount of tuition fees that were deferred, the number of years the student made use of such deferred obligations, and the rate of interest charged on the accumulated debt. This, however, considers only the indebtedness incurred through deferred tuition fees, which will be over and above whatever indebtedness a student may have accumulated during the years of study to pay his or her share of lodging, food, and all of the other maintenance expenses.

As in the case of higher educational systems in countries like Canada, China, Japan, and the United States that feature up-front tuition fees paid mainly by parents (or governments on behalf of parents who are financially unable to contribute), toward which many students must also contribute and thus need the ability to borrow, countries such as Australia, New Zealand, and the constituent countries of the United Kingdom that feature deferred tuition fees paid by students also allow parents to contribute, either by paying up front (in spite of not being officially expected to do so) or by helping out on repayments after the student has completed his or her education and may need assistance managing a debt burden. Thus, as shown in table 6.1, countries or systems in which tuition fees are part of the financing of public higher education generally place some of the instructional cost burden on both parents and students. The relative shares of this burden are determined partly by an official stipulation whereby the tuition fee is required either up front and mainly from parents or deferred and mainly from students, but the actual division of expenses is determined by the families, through a kind of negotiation in which both parents and students share in bearing the portion of the costs of instruction that is not covered by the government, or taxpayer.

Students—as well as parents and governments—also contribute to the cost of student living, or maintenance, as shown in table 6.1. They cover their share of these expenses, like their share of tuition fees, through term-time or vacation earnings, or loans, or both. Student loans to cover maintenance costs are likely to pass directly through the students' hands and thus be perceived more clearly as loans. This may be unlike their obligations to repay deferred tuition fees, which probably will not have passed through their hands and thus may be viewed more like a future tax or pension obligation in countries like Australia or the United Kingdom. This perception is reinforced by a requirement that employers deduct the repayment obligations from wages and salaries, similar to income-tax withholding or employee contributions to insurance or pensions (hence the common but incorrect appellation of *graduate tax* to refer to a repayment obligation that is treated like an income surtax upon college and university graduates).

In countries where political and ideological opposition to cost-sharing is strong yet where cost-sharing measures, including student contributions, are deemed essential to supplement otherwise insufficient tax revenues, governments may disguise a tuition fee by referring to it only by a euphemism, such as *deferred obligation*—which neither parents or students supposedly need worry about at the time of attendance. Governments may also minimize the consequent repayment obligation by making the monthly salary deduction equal to only a certain percentage of earnings, as though this income contingent, or income related, obligation was fundamentally different from a loan. In fact, an income contingent obligation is just like a conventional loan for most student borrowers, since they will repay it at the same level of interest—and therefore repay the same discounted present value of payments—as if the repayment obligation was on a fixed schedule of payments. This distinction between conventional fixed-schedule and income contingent loans will be discussed later in this chapter. For now, the point of table 6.1 is that there are a variety of student loan forms, including

- borrowing from a bank, a public student loan agency, or from a university (which presumably would immediately sell the note to a bank or student loan agency);
- borrowing to cover the student borrower's share of tuition fees, or borrowing to cover all or some of the costs of student living, or borrowing for both purposes;
- the student borrower receiving a loan and then paying college or university tuition fees, or the student borrower incurring a repayment

obligation simply by virtue of college or university attendance, with the deferred tuition fee, or loan, never passing through his or her hands; and

- having the deferred obligation, or loan, benefit the institution like any tuition fee paid with a bank loan (that is, the government, which would be the lender in the case of a deferred tuition fee, sending the deferred amount to the college or university as new revenue), or having the deferred obligation contribute little or nothing in the form of new revenue to the college or university, but instead merely become another future tax stream for the government.

Our use of the term *student loan*, then, covers all of these instances—in other words, all cases in which the student incurs an obligation for some of the costs of instruction or some of the expenses of student living or both, whether or not such sums actually pass through his or her hands; and in which the obligation is deferred to the future, when the student is in the adult workforce, presumably able to repay and presumably earning more than he or she would have in the absence of a higher education that has been procured, in part, through the loan.

The Need for Student Loans

The perspective, and the policy, of cost-sharing lead to the need for a governmentally sponsored student loan scheme. Borrowing, at least in theory, can provide a substantial amount of money in support of higher education, essentially adding a "third leg" to cost-sharing that supplements revenue from parents and taxpayers. Thus a functioning student loan program can provide revenue to higher education that, in its absence, would presumably not be there at all. Assuming (or to the degree that) borrowing does indeed *supplement* rather than *supplant* higher educational revenue from taxpayers and parents, the additional revenue from borrowing can make possible: (a) enhanced institutional quality, (b) additional capacity and thus greater participation and accessibility, (c) more higher educational choices for students, and/or (d) a better style of student living. Expressed another way, if additional revenue from governments or taxpayers is unlikely—either because a government is at its effective tax capacity or because other public needs would take precedence even if taxes could be raised—and if parental contributions are also at their likely maximums, then the other major possible source of additional revenue for the general operation of a university or for the costs of student living would seem to be the deferred, or borrowed, contributions of the students themselves.

From the perspective of the student, the ability to borrow toward at least some of the costs of his or her higher education gives young persons a chance to invest in their own futures. While many or most students might prefer all of the money to come either from parents or (preferably) from taxpayers, in light of the demonstrable private benefits from higher education that accrue to the student—including both monetary (i.e., higher future earnings) and nonmonetary ones (e.g., elevated status, access to generally more interesting and pleasant jobs, and greater choices for occupations, mates, and places to live)—such an investment is perfectly reasonable. In fact, given the limits on both parental and governmental contributions as well as on part-time employment possibilities, for some students borrowing will mean the difference between having and not having access to higher education.

Borrowing is particularly necessary in the absence of (or to supplement insufficient) parental contributions. This lack may be the obvious consequence of low family income, or of the parents' disinclination to provide further financial support, or of the student's disinclination to be financially dependent on his or her parents; and all of these reasons are more compelling the older the student or the more advanced the degree. Or the absence of any officially expected parental contribution may, as in the Nordic countries, be the prevailing sociopolitical norm: where the high taxes that support a university education without the supplementation of tuition fees are assumed to be the parental contribution, but where the costs of student living must be born by the students themselves through borrowing. In the case of a dual tuition country such as Russia, borrowing also allows (or in theory ought to allow) students to attend a university or other higher educational institution when they are capable of the academic work but did not pass the entrance examination with a high enough score to earn tuition-free admission—and whose parents cannot afford the tuition fee.

In other cases, borrowing is not so much the difference between participating or not participating in higher education, but rather the provision of additional choices for the student, such as living independently instead of living at home and commuting, or attending an expensive private college or university instead of a less-expensive public institution, or accepting more debt but working fewer hours or not at all, or living at a somewhat higher standard than what is often thought of as the appropriate lifestyle of student poverty. In these examples, borrowing (and saving and lending) are economic expressions of time preferences for money. The saver is one who has more claims on goods and services than he or she needs at a given moment and who, as (or through) a lender, is willing to rent these claims for a fee that we call interest. The borrower, in turn, is one who has a present need for claims (i.e., money) that he or she does not yet have, but who is reasonably certain to have these claims in the future and thus is willing to return these claims with interest (i.e., a payment for the use of this borrowed money). In this way, the ability to borrow makes possible the choice of a higher standard of living for students who are confident of their eventual higher incomes and who thus would apply higher subjective discount rates to their future repayment obligations.

Purposes of Student Lending

Student loan schemes can have a number of different purposes. However, some of these purposes may be less than fully compatible or even contradictory, such as, for example, the aim of simply putting money into the hands of students—which is always a politically popular goal to profess, especially if the loans can be portrayed as much less costly to the government's budget than outright grants or stipends (which may or may not in fact be the case)—as opposed to the less politically popular goal of increasing revenue to higher education by moving some expenses to students rather than to governments or even to parents. The last-mentioned aim may in fact be what a higher educational system needs most, particularly if, as in most countries, the revenue requirements of higher education (including both the costs of instruction, the costs of additional capacity, and the costs of student maintenance) are rising rapidly and annually at rates considerably in excess of the likely rates of expansion in the government's higher educational budget.

Student loan schemes in any country thus include several principal purposes.

1. *To put money in the hands of financially needy students in a way that expands participation.* Such a purpose requires a student loan scheme that is both means-tested (or need-based) and generally available. In other words, loans would be made available to all or most students who have a remaining financial need after considering all other sources of revenue, including officially expected contributions from parents (and, in some countries, extended families). In this way, the loans would not be available simply to provide a higher student living

standard or to allow students to become financially independent of parents who would otherwise be providing at least some financial assistance. Such a loan scheme, however, requires a functioning system of means-testing, the difficulties of which were discussed in chapter 4. Also, as the loan recipients in some countries would be mainly from low-income and frequently rural families who may not have been exposed to a modern credit culture and who may be unwilling or unable to even co-sign a loan, the scheme should anticipate a relatively high rate of default.

2. *To put money in the hands of all students.* Student loan schemes that are generally available to all students without regard to the incomes of their parents can serve not only to make higher educational participation possible, but also to further students' financial independence from their parents. This is essentially the system in Australia and in the constituent countries of the United Kingdom, where generally available deferred contributions (i.e., loans to cover tuition fees) are available to all. In the United Kingdom, partially means-tested cost-of-living loans, in addition to means-tested grants, are also generally available to cover maintenance expenses. In the Nordic countries, where the government assumes the costs of instruction (i.e., no tuition fees) but where the parents are not officially expected to contribute to living expenses, student loans are made available to virtually all students, without regard to the means of their parents, to cover the costs of maintenance, which are thus borne principally by students (with some assistance from governmental subsidization of the loans and, presumably, with some voluntary assistance from at least some parents). In the United States, subsidized student loans are made available to students with financial need (i.e., means-tested), but all students have access to governmentally sponsored student loans, with those from families not deemed to be in financial need required to take unsubsidized loans.

Student loans that are made available for the primary purpose of simply putting money in the hands of all students necessarily feature large amounts of lending. Lending, even to students, does not necessarily entail a significant cost to taxpayers. Loans themselves are assets. The government's cost in sponsoring student loan schemes comes through interest subsidies (including in-school, grace period, and repayment period subsidies) and defaults. As we shall discuss more fully later in this chapter, these costs can be reduced, although probably not entirely eliminated, through minimizing interest subsidies, using aggressive and cost-effective collection practices, and sharing the financial burden of defaults by means of cosignatory requirements. Most student loan schemes throughout the world do not fare well by these measures and thus remain costly—in some cases approaching the cost of direct, nonrepayable grants (Shen and Ziderman 2007).

The nearly $60 billion worth of governmentally sponsored student loans made generally available (i.e., without regard to the creditworthiness of the borrower) to student borrowers in the United States in 2006–7 represent a relatively cost-effective form of financial assistance, because of

- relatively minimal interest subsidization even on the subsidized loans;
- virtually no interest subsidization on the unsubsidized loans;
- cost-effective systems of means-testing and loan origination; and
- a relatively low incidence of defaults (especially considering the substantial amount of student borrowing by academically at-risk students in short-cycle and proprietary schools, which experience considerably higher default rates, and the absence of parental co-signatories and risk rating).

The governmentally borne costs of student lending in the United States could, in theory, be reduced even further by eliminating or reducing the in-school and grace period interest subsidies (i.e., making the terms of the current subsidized loans more like the terms for unsubsidized loans); and requiring cosignatories so as to further reduce the government's exposure to defaults. However, insofar as governmentally sponsored student loan schemes in the United States help preserve officially expected parental contributions, and in so doing help preserve the relatively high tuition fees in all of America's public colleges and universities, student loans play an important role in the furtherance of cost-sharing. In this way, the accessibility of governmentally sponsored student loans for most students in the United States is not only financially affordable, but probably cost-effective—at least compared to countries that lack an acceptance of public-sector tuition fees, parental contributions, a minimal subsidization of loans, and cost-effective student loan collections. However, in middle- and low-income countries—which are usually burdened with socially and politically competing needs for scarce public revenues, in addition to high rates of default and oftentimes the politically imposed, excessive subsidization of student loans—the opportunity costs of loans for all students is almost certainly too great.

3. *To implement a degree of cost-sharing by shifting some of the costs of instruction and/or student maintenance from either the government or the family to the student.*

Clearly, the nearly $60 billion worth of governmentally sponsored student loans in the United States in 2006–7 allowed a far greater flow of total revenue to higher education than would have been conceivable with only governmental and parental contributions. These student-borne contributions permitted a larger total number of students, more equitable participation in higher education, and a greater number of enrollments in the more costly private sector; they also almost certainly allowed a higher overall standard of student living or more independence from students' families.

The advent of student-loan-supported deferred tuition in Australia, for example, expanded both capacity and participation. And the similar concept of a deferred tuition fee/student loan in the constituent countries of the United Kingdom, which also provide partially means-tested cost-of-living loans, has similarly expanded both capacity and participation, even though some of the additional burden on students has probably decreased the contributions of some parents and also diminished the burden borne by the British taxpayer.

In theory, a student loan scheme can also allow an increase in food and lodging fees. This could lower governmental subsidization of student maintenance and shift these savings to other higher educational needs, such as expanded financial assistance, enlarged capacity, or heightened quality, but still maintain accessibility by allowing students, if need be, to borrow the funds to cover the raised fees. Similarly, a student loan scheme could permit a hike in some or all of the tuition fees paid in the fee-paying tracks found in the dual tuition countries of the former Soviet Union, Eastern and Central Europe, and East Africa—again, by allowing the funds for such increases to be borrowed, thus maintaining accessibility. Also, universities in countries where tuition fees are most resisted might find that fees could be charged for at least some of the most selective, high-cost, and highly remunerative advanced graduate programs, such as medicine or graduate management training—again maintaining accessibility through student loans while requiring students to contribute more to the programs with such manifestly high private returns.

A student loan scheme that is linked to revenue supplementation as well as to accessibility requires loan recovery to be maximized; in other words, the two principal sources of losses—interest subsidies and defaults—must be kept to a minimum. The enhanced revenue made possible by cost-sharing, in turn, may be used to expand capacity, enhance quality, provide more targeted (i.e., means-tested) financial assistance, substitute for tax-based governmental revenues, or any or all of the foregoing.[1]

4. *To influence institutional or program selection.* Eligibility for student loans can be made contingent upon the recipient selecting certain institutions (e.g., rural, or newer, or nonuniversity institutions) or particular high-need programs (e.g., teacher education, nursing, or engineering). Thus, just as loans can be rationed, or targeted, by financial need or by ethnic or linguistic-minority status or by region or rural schools in order to expand certain kinds of participation (as set forth in purpose #1), loans can also be rationed, or targeted, to achieve other public purposes—such as manpower needs (e.g., for teachers or nurses) or regional planning needs (e.g., to induce students to select colleges or universities in remote territories)—or to provide special assistance to certain higher educational sectors (e.g., private or nonuniversity institutions). Unlike targeting low-income or rural youth in order to improve their accessibility to any college or university, as discussed above, targeting loans to certain institutions or academic programs is meant to make these institutions or programs relatively more attractive than those that are not so targeted. Thus the aim is not simply to remove a barrier or to make attendance possible, but to steer a student—probably already destined for higher education of some kind—toward a particular program, institution, or sector (e.g., two-year colleges instead of universities). And such steering by student loan eligibility, therefore, is likely to be effective when loans for the targeted programs or institutions are substantially more subsidized, or simply more available, than loans for the nontargeted programs or institutions.

5. *To encourage academic progress and/or success by forgiving portions of the principal based on the number of years of academic success.* This aim is less a loan scheme, or even a system of rewards that relies on a loan scheme, than it is a simple monetary reward wrapped in the form of repayment forgiveness. Such a program is expensive and depends on the assumption that desirable academic behaviors—for example, achieving high grades or, less ambitiously, simply finishing on time—respond cost-effectively to the prospect of a future reward in the form of repayment forgiveness (as opposed to other methods of eliciting the desired behavior). Such a provision could be thought to be cost-*in*effective if—as is usually the case—many or even most of the student borrowers who are academically able to avail themselves of this reward would finish their academic program with distinction anyway, with or without any loan forgiveness. In fact, as the most academically able and academically responsible students are likely to be disproportionately from the middle- or upper-middle classes and thus have been taught such behavior in their homes,

the effect is very similar to a system of merit awards or to merit selection in a supply-constrained system: likely to reward those who do not need the reward financially and who do not need the reward to behave in the desired manner. At the same time, after the end of apartheid, South Africa found that the completion rates of black and colored students, who were the overwhelming participants in the National Student Financial Aid loan scheme, were so low that a substantial subsidy in the form of debt reduction was thought to be a cost-effective measure for improving completion rates (Jackson 2002).

6. *To influence a postgraduation practice or venue.* Finally, a student loan can be given with the aim of influencing a student's choice as a graduate to practice a certain profession or to practice in a particular target venue: the practice of medicine or nursing, for example, or teaching in a rural district. This can be accomplished by granting or even requiring most students in the appropriate academic programs (e.g., medicine or nursing or elementary education) to complete their education with a relatively high level of indebtedness, portions of which can then be forgiven for each of several years of practice in the target venue. Sometimes called *workforce contingent student loans* in the United States, the practice dates back to the early days of the National Direct (then National Defense) Student Loan program in the late 1950s and 1960s where the government forgave 20 percent of the outstanding principal for each year of full-time teaching. The program was tightened in the 1980s and 1990s to provide forgiveness only for teaching in certain urban schools with high levels of attrition and violence, and then extended to other health professions practicing in high-need venues (Kirshstein et al. 2004).

As in the schemes of repayment forgiveness to elicit desired academic behavior described above, workforce contingent student loans assume that professionals will be motivated to do what they would not be likely to do otherwise (i.e., teach or practice medicine in a remote village for a small salary) because of the prospect of debt forgiveness. Furthermore, the public policy assumption is that student-debt forgiveness is more cost-effective (or more politically feasible) than alternatives such as higher salaries, first-year bonuses, subsidized housing and transportation, and other incentives that might target public resources to achieving the same end. However, the idea of coupling substantial tuition fees with student loans and some kind of workforce contingent repayment forgiveness is especially compelling in low-income countries, where, for example, an expensive higher education in medicine or dentistry, or even in nursing or teaching, may have been entirely covered by the average taxpayer but where the recipients are likely to practice only in major cities—or, most unfortunately and even more inequitably, to emigrate to Europe or North America, with these nations benefiting from the advanced professional education paid for by the taxpayers of a low-income country. In such cases, the imposition of a high tuition fee that would be forgiven simply by such students remaining in the country for a period of years, and perhaps spending a couple of years in a rural village, would serve the health needs of the country and provide a much more equitable means of financing their advanced professional education.

The Need for Government Participation

The simple case for student borrowing as a personal investment that will pay off in higher incomes, greater status, and more life choices does not, in itself, make the case for governmental participation in this lending. That is, if student loans were no more than the bringing together of student borrowers, who wish to invest in their higher education, and lenders, who have the savings to lend, or *rent*, for the price of interest, it is not immediately clear why governmental participation (beyond the normal regulations and consumer protections applied by governments to borrowing and lending generally) should be needed. Particularly in a market economy, banks and other private financial institutions lend (on behalf of savers) for the purposes of business expansion, working capital, or the purchase of homes or automobiles. They cover the costs of money, administration, and all other expenses, as well as allowances for defaults, with the *interest rate spread*, or the difference between the interest paid to savers and the interest charged to borrowers.

In fact, there are many examples in many countries of strictly private—that is, neither governmentally subsidized nor guaranteed—loans to students. Private lending in the United States, for example, rose very sharply in the 2000s to a high of $17.892 billion in 2006–7 (almost 24 percent of all US student lending). In part this was a reflection of the general credit boom (some would say recklessness) in the United States prior to the 2008 economic downturn, but it was also in response to the continuing rapid increase in public and private tuition fees and stagnant loan limits on lower-interest, governmentally sponsored loans (Loonin 2008). However, private loans in normal times and in most countries will generally be limited to students in elite colleges or universities or in advanced professional programs such as medicine or law, where the likelihood of high future earnings and the imperative of building a good credit reputation lower the risk of default, in combination with the desirability of attracting such students as future bank customers. Private loans thus allow credit to be extended to such students at favorable terms without governmental subsidization or guarantees.

However, *generally available* lending to students—that is, lending to all or most students without tests or conditions of creditworthiness and without requirements for creditworthy cosignatories or other collateral—is another matter altogether. In the absence of creditworthy cosignatories or other guarantors, the risk of default on student loans is considerable—probably high enough to force the student's interest rate to entirely unacceptable levels without governmental intervention, either in the form of a governmental guarantee or an interest rate supplement to the lender (both of which, of course, imply costs to the government). What makes the risk of default especially great in lending to students is the absence of collateral that can be recovered in the event of nonpayment. Unlike a business loan in which machinery or inventory can be repossessed in the event of default, the only collateral stemming from an investment in higher education is in the form of knowledge and learned behaviors that cannot be repossessed in order to recover a defaulted loan. Further increasing the likelihood of default, and raising the costs of collection even in the absence of default, the typical student borrower usually cannot begin repayment until the end of his or her studies and the beginning of gainful employment. This leaves a long period of time between the origination of the loan and the beginning of repayment—long enough for the borrower to have forgotten the debt or to have moved residence three or four times and possibly to another country, leaving little trace of his or her whereabouts (along with little recollection of the promise to repay).

Such a risk, then, from generally available student lending calls either for a governmental guarantee or for a substantial up-front payment to the lender (or a discount on the purchase of student loan obligations), thus enabling a student loan program to tap the private capital markets of banks, pension funds, and other major sources of savings. Or, the inherent risk of student lending calls for the government itself to be the lender, effectively originating new student lending (net of any repayments from former lending) either from current tax revenue, like any other governmental expenditure, or from revenue borrowed from national or international capital markets and added to all other governmental borrowing, to be repaid from future tax revenues.

Of course there are limits on the borrowing capacity of any government, especially a government whose ability to tax or to maintain the value of its currency may be suspect in the views of domestic and international capital markets—as in most developing and some transitional countries. But these very limitations may apply as well to the worth of a governmental guarantee: a government that might not be able to repay its debts to domestic bondholders or international lenders may be as unlikely to be able to cover the defaulted debts it has guaranteed. In such cases (again, applying mainly to developing as well as to some transitional countries with limited taxing capabilities), the need to cover the risks of generally available student lending can at least be lessened through a judicious use of cosignatory requirements, with the government as a primary guarantor only for families with insufficient collateral, and only as a secondary guarantor for families who are able to co-sign the loan, thus limiting, if only slightly, the government's risk exposure. However, in the end, generally available student loans are inherently risky, and governments will always be required to at least share in the risk of a student loan program that is widely available to all or most students in need.

At the same time, the need for government to bear a substantial portion of risk does not in itself also mean the need for government to heavily subsidize the loans—or to collect the repayments, or even to originate the loans. If a government decides to subsidize student borrowing—for example, by covering the interest payments during the in-school years and perhaps for a period of time afterwards while the student (hopefully having graduated) is seeking employment, or by charging an interest rate that is less than the cost of money to the government for the entire life of the loan—it is making an effective policy decision that the cost of the subsidies, which can be very considerable, is worth the expense in terms of the greater or more equitable higher educational participation that such borrowing can generate. It must be kept in mind, however, that a high level of subsidization for student borrowing—which is already costly to service and which carries the additional burden of absorbing some level of default in the best of circumstances—can be extremely expensive. In fact, Ziderman and Albrecht (1995) and Shen and Ziderman (2007) describe scenarios in which a combination of numerous defaults, high levels of subsidy, and significant expenses in servicing and collecting yields student loan programs that bring an effective negative return: in other words, governments would have saved money by giving the money out in nonrepayable grants in the first place.

Thus in the provision of generally available student loan schemes, the need for government—or for that matter, the need for any of the possible agents in such student lending—is best seen in an alignment between these possible agents and the necessary functions of student lending. The agents include (a) governments and ministries, (b) public agencies, (c) banks and other sources of private capital, (d) universities and other institutions of higher education, (e) cosignatories, and (f) collection and servicing agents. The functions of (governmentally sponsored) student lending include: (a) setting the terms, (b) originating the loans, (c) bearing the risk of default, (d) subsidizing, if loans are to be subsidized, (e) providing the capital, and (f) servicing the loans and collecting the repayments.

These agents and functions are shown in table 6.2. As can be seen, the functions that absolutely require government participation are the setting of terms, the absorption of all or the greater part of the risk, and the provision of subsidies (if any). Governments can also originate the loans (by receiving promises of repayment for deferred tuition fees) and provide the capital—but they do not have to. In the case of developing countries, where credit is limited, having governments or public agencies originate the loans and provide the capital (i.e., be the lender) directly impacts the government's operating budget and thus has opportunity costs not unlike those for any other governmental expenditure. However, with the government covering the risk, which it must do (or at least share in) anyway, banks or any other holder of savings can originate loans and provide capital.

Loans can also be originated by the colleges and universities themselves, as in the US direct loan program, provided that most of the risk is absorbed by the government (thus enabling the loans to tap private capital markets) and provided that any subsidies are also supplied by the government. Similarly, governments or banks (or even universities) can collect the loans—but again, they do not have to, as this is a function that can be assumed by private debt collectors or by any agency with the experience and the necessary computing and skip-tracing capabilities.

In short, and particularly important in the case of developing countries contemplating new student loan schemes, governments must set forth the rules of the game (e.g., eligibility, rates, terms, and maximum amounts to be borrowed), must pay for any subsidization, and must at least share substantially in guaranteeing the loans (or covering defaults). Only banks and other agencies of the larger capital market, however, are appropriate in the long run

Table 6.2 Agents and functions of governmentally sponsored, generally available student lending

Functions of student lending	Agents of student lending					
	Governments and ministries	Public agencies	Banks and other sources of capital	Universities and colleges	Parents or other cosignatories	Collection and servicing agents
Setting terms, such as eligibility, rates, and repayment periods	Must set terms of loans					
Originating loans	Can originate, but not ideal for the purpose	Can originate if the agencies can tap private capital sources	Can originate if the risk is borne by other agents	Can originate and bear some (but not all) default risk		
Bearing the risk of default	Must bear the risk via a guarantee or up-front payment		Will bear the risk only for creditworthy borrowers	Can bear some risk for creditworthy borrowers	Can bear some or all risk if creditworthy	
Subsidizing loans	Only significant source (if any) of subsidy					
Providing capital	From public budget or public borrowing	Can be a conduit for capital via securitization	Purchase loans or securitize agency paper			
Servicing and collecting	Can service, but generally inefficient efficient	Can service if sufficiently inefficient	Can service inefficient	Can service, but generally		Can service

for the provision of capital. Either public agencies or the colleges and universities themselves can originate the loans (and then sell the notes to the providers of capital). Finally, any entity with collecting experience can service the loans, generally under contract to the holders of the obligations themselves. But it is often advisable for governments not to attempt to do all of the origination, provision of capital, or servicing of the loans.

Forms of Student Loans

Student loans may take one of two basic forms, with many variations of each and with hybrids of the two also possible.[2] Although the most important feature of student loan schemes is the degree of cost recovery, the form of the loan—especially whether the repayment obligation is fixed or is based on the borrower's income—has come to dominate the political discourse about student loan schemes.

The Fixed-Schedule, or Conventional Mortgage-Type, Loan

A *fixed-schedule*, or conventional mortgage-type, loan obligation carries all of the following:

- A rate of interest, expressed as an annual percentage of the amount borrowed
- A repayment period, or the amount of time the borrower has to repay, or amortize, the loan
- Repayment terms, such as whether the payments are to be in equal monthly installments, or in installments that begin small and increase over time, or in some other arrangement that yields a stream of payments sufficient to amortize the loan at the contractual rate of interest

The rate of interest may be fixed or variable (e.g., linked to the government's borrowing rate or to the prime commercial rate); and, after any subsidies (usually from the government), must cover the cost of money plus the cost of servicing and collecting and, sometimes, an amount to cover the costs of defaults (portions of which may also be covered by subsidies or through cosignatories). Sometimes, there will be an up-front fee attached to the loan (for example, borrowing and paying interest on $1,000 but receiving only $850), which is actually a hidden boost in the rate of interest.

The Income Contingent Loan

A second common form of student loan is the *income contingent* (or income related, or contingent repayment) loan.[3] This type of loan carries the following contractual repayment obligations:

- A percentage of earnings or income must be paid generally until the loan is fully repaid at the contractual rate of interest. This percent-of-income may be set as a flat rate on all income or earnings; or may be progressive (i.e., higher percentages at higher levels of income); or may achieve a measure of progressivity by applying a flat rate only to income over some threshold level—such as a minimum wage or, even more progressively, the median income for beginning college or university graduates. (The third option, then, would normally require a higher percent-of-income after this threshold level in order to return a sufficient amount to amortize the debts.)
- A contractual rate of interest is assigned, which, as in a fixed-schedule obligation and after any subsidies (usually from the government), must cover the cost of money plus the costs of servicing and collecting and, sometimes, the costs of defaults (which may also be covered by subsidies or through cosignatories).
- A maximum number of repayment years is stipulated, after which the low earner is to be released from any further obligation, regardless of the amount or the effective rate of interest (or discounted present value) that has been repaid.
- A limit is set for the high earner, which is generally when the borrower has repaid his or her debt at the contractual rate of interest. A *mutualized income contingent loan plan*, in which the shortfalls from low earners must be recovered from the interest premiums paid by high earners, will require high earners to continue paying even after their original obligation has been met. To date there has been only one such operational plan, the Yale Plan for Tuition Postponement (in the early 1970s), but this plan still had a maximum aggregate repayment for the very high earner beyond which no further payments were to be required.[4]

In a fixed-schedule (or conventional) loan, the repayments, the interest rate, and the repayment period are all fixed in the repayment obligation, or loan note. What varies—mainly according to the income of the borrower, including periods of low or no income, as in unemployment—is the burden of the payments. In an income contingent loan, in contrast, the monthly or annual repayment burden is fixed (at least as far as the burden is considered to be a function of earnings). What varies in this type of contract—mainly as a function of changing levels of lifetime income, or earnings—are the repayment periods (for those who eventually repay their loans in full) and the ultimate cost of the loans (for some low-earning borrowers who ultimately are unable to fully repay their loans). The Australian, New Zealand, South African, English, Welsh, and (formerly) the Scottish student loan programs, as well as several new loan schemes in Africa (such as those in Ethiopia and Rwanda) and some schemes in other countries, all feature income contingent repayments. In addition, the United States has a minimally subsidized Income Contingent Repayment (ICR) option within its Direct Loan Program, and in mid-2009 it inaugurated an additional Income-Based Repayment (IBR) program specifically for borrowers having difficulties repaying their fixed-schedule loans, taking into account both their total incomes and their total indebtedness. The IBR is more of a hybrid program, as discussed below, in which payments based on incomes are to apply to borrowers whose combination of high debts and low levels of current income yield repayments that are limited to a maximum percentage of earnings.

As in conventional student loan programs, an income contingent loan program is likely to subsidize all of the borrowers to the extent that even those who repay "in full" will generally have repaid their loans at a somewhat subsidized rate—that is, at a rate that is generally set below the prevailing market rate of interest (or sometimes below the rate of interest charged to the best and most creditworthy borrowers or—lowest of all—to the government itself). For most income contingent borrowers, then, repaying their loans income contingently as opposed to conventionally merely affects the shape and length of each individual repayment period, rather than the ultimate amount (in present value) to be repaid. However, all income contingent loans have a provision for forgiving the remaining debts of some of the lowest-earning borrowers who reach some maximum repayment period or some maximum age with a debt still outstanding.

The present value of this low-lifetime-income subsidy for any particular lifetime earnings profile depends on the terms of the income contingent loan contract. For example, for any given set of assumed borrower lifetime earnings profiles, requiring a high percent-of-income for repayment, together with a long repayment period, will minimize the number and amounts of remaining debts to be forgiven and reduce the subsidy cost to be recovered (usually from the government). In contrast, a low percent-of-income plus a short maximum repayment period will (again, for any given set of assumed borrower lifetime earnings profiles) increase the number of borrowers who are likely to reach the end of their maximum repayment period with substantial debts to be forgiven—and, of course, add to the cost to the lender (presumably the government). The income contingent loan program in the United States, for example, features such high percent-of-income repayments and such a lengthy repayment period that only the very lowest lifetime earners are likely to be forgiven any debt; the merely moderately low earners will simply pay for a very long time (US General Accounting Office 2001).

In theory, the subsidy source might be the high earners who, in a mutualized plan, would finish their repayments having repaid at a premium rate of interest, thus effectively subsidizing their low-earning borrowing colleagues and providing the loan program with an average break-even interest rate over all of the loans. The principal flaw in this concept—perhaps explaining why, at least as of 2009, there are no such generally available mutualized plans in operation—is that students who reasonably anticipate high lifetime incomes will decline to participate, at least in any voluntary scheme, thus depriving the plan of most of its necessary source of subsidies to protect the low earners.

Therefore, in most cases the source of the subsidies that relieve the lifetime low earner from some of his or her debts in a generally available income contingent student loan scheme must be the government itself, which will ultimately forgive the remaining debts of these low earners in the same way that it might elect to make up the shortfalls from borrowers who simply default, or might provide other kinds of grants or subsidies to students on the basis of their low family incomes at the time they were in a university. Expressed another way, in such an income contingent loan program, the government is electing to subsidize ultimately those who turn out to have low lifetime earnings, just as it may, in a conventional need-based grant program, be electing to subsidize currently those whose parents had low incomes during the time the student was enrolled in a university. Those who advocate governmentally subsidized income contingent loans frequently claim that it makes greater sense to spend scarce tax dollars to subsidize those whose higher education, for whatever reason, has not paid off monetarily, than to provide a stream of repayment subsidies to individuals who had to borrow when they were students merely because their parents were poor—but who may later earn good incomes.

A variant on the income contingent loan is the *graduate tax*, whereby a student (sometimes only a graduated student), in return for governmental subsidization of higher education in the form of low or no tuition (and possibly of an additional student maintenance grant), becomes obligated to an *income surtax*, generally for the rest of his or her earning lifetime. A true graduate tax is just that: an income surtax on university graduates, without keeping individual borrower accounts or "balances owed" (Woodhall 1989). However, one purpose of a graduate tax, like any governmentally sponsored student loan plan, is to shift a portion of the costs of higher education from the government or taxpayers to students, albeit to be paid only after the student has finished (presumably graduated) and is earning an income (supposedly greater because of this higher educational experience). The financial success of the graduate tax would be measured by the discounted present value of this stream of future income surtax payments, just as the financial success of a governmentally sponsored, income contingent student loan program would be measured by the present discounted value of repayments that are based on a percentage of yearly income. Thus the mathematics and the practical effect on participating students of a graduate tax and an income contingent loan—assuming similar terms—are practically indistinguishable. Although Glennerster (2005) continues to be one of the few proponents of a graduate tax, a true graduate tax has never been implemented, due in part to the weakness of the correlation between lifetime earnings and the actual cost of the higher education received, as well as to the seeming impossibility of capitalizing or securitizing this form of obligation. (The Ethiopian graduate tax implemented in 2006, then, is not a true graduate tax at all, but merely another example of a deferred tuition fee that is to be collected via an income contingent repayment obligation.)

The Hybrid Fixed-Schedule–Income Contingent Loan

Lastly, a student loan program can combine features of conventional fixed-schedule and income contingent obligations in any number of what might be called *hybrid* fixed-schedule–income contingent loan plans, or what Usher (2005) calls *soft* income contingent loans. These would feature an underlying, or default, repayment obligation with a fixed schedule of payments that would be due, unless the monthly or annual repayments exceeded some maximum percentage of monthly or annual earnings—in which case the obligation would not exceed that maximum percentage. Amounts owed on the original fixed schedule of repayments would be deferred and become due only when the borrower's earnings or income rose and the repayment obligation could once again be made within the maximum percent-of-income limit. In such a scheme, most borrowers would simply repay according to the original fixed schedule (which might be graduated upwards over time to correspond better with anticipated earnings growth, but still on a fixed schedule of repayments). Some borrowers, particularly those experiencing a year or perhaps two or three of low income due to unemployment, would pay income contingently during these years but return to the fixed schedule of repayment obligations when they regained their employment and their earnings. These borrowers would have been granted the convenience of an automatic deferment of payments—similar to a refinancing—but not a subsidy, as such. However, a few borrowers who combined prolonged periods of unemployment or a low-paying job with high initial indebtedness might never get back on the fixed schedule. They would continue to repay their student loans on an income contingent basis, reaching the end of the original underlying repayment period with remaining indebtedness—which at some point would be forgiven, as though the entire student loan obligation had been income contingent from the beginning.

The advantage of such a hybrid version, as found in Canada and the Netherlands (Usher 2005a, 2005b) and recently initiated in the United States under the Income-Based Repayment option, is that most borrowers in most years would repay their loans on an administratively simpler fixed schedule, not requiring income verification, and the lender (presumably the government) could count on a flow of repayments (which could still be collected at the point of wage or salary payments by the employer if this is what government policy established). At the same time, borrowers would have the assurance that their repayments, by definition, would never become hopelessly burdensome and that they would be ultimately be forgiven some measure of their initial student indebtedness in the event that their higher education never paid off monetarily.

In the summer of 2009, the United States began a hybrid fixed-schedule–income contingent student loan plan under the Income-Based Repayment (IBR) option provided in the College Cost Reduction and Access Act of 2008. The

IBR option begins with a consolidation of all of a borrower's eligible, governmentally sponsored student loans and the assignment of an appropriate fixed repayment schedule (10 or more years, depending on consolidation and the size of the aggregate indebtedness). However, IBR limits loan repayments to 15 percent of the borrower's adjusted gross income in excess of 150 percent of the official poverty line (as adjusted annually and as applicable to the borrower's family size), thus moving borrowers with high debts and low incomes to an income contingent repayment schedule. If the borrower's income rises above the level that triggers the income contingent payments he or she returns to the original fixed repayment schedule. Any debts remaining after 25 years are forgiven. While the former Income Contingent Loan (ICL) option remains, the IBR provides a greater degree of protection for low earners. A separate but related provision adds a further workforce contingent element of subsidy by limiting the IBR payments to only 15 years before remaining debt forgiveness for borrowers working in a recognized public service capacity, such as public-interest law or many nonprofit organizations, goes into effect (Schrag 2008).[5]

The Role of Student Lending In Higher Educational Finance

In summary, student loans have the potential both to increase higher educational accessibility and to allow some portion of the costs of instruction or of the costs of living to be shifted to the student, to be repaid as he or she enters the workforce. In this way, student loans, at least in theory, can provide additional revenue to higher education for the purposes of enhancing capacity, quality, participation, or combinations thereof. Student loans can carry a portion of the costs of higher education when parents are financially unable to do so, or they can allow financial independence from parents (albeit at a cost). Thus student loans that make higher educational participation possible are properly viewed as personal investments that will usually pay off in some combination of higher lifetime earnings, greater personal status and respect, and a richer array of life options.

For countries contemplating a new or greatly expanded program of governmentally sponsored student lending, the possible beneficiaries of this new revenue from student loans—when appropriately discounted to a present value and adjusted for the not inconsiderable risk of default—will be some combination of

- the students themselves, to the degree to which the borrowed revenue allows a wider array of higher educational options, a lesser need for concurrent employment, a more satisfying standard of living, or earlier financial independence from parents;
- potential students, who previously would not have been able to access higher education for lack of either financial resources or institutional capacity, but who now can because of the additional revenue made possible by the student loan program;
- public colleges and universities or public higher educational systems that can benefit in any number of ways from the additional net revenue that a student loan scheme can at least make possible;
- private colleges and universities that can benefit from student loan schemes that allow their students to better afford their higher tuition fees (presuming private students are eligible to access the loans) and also benefit from potentially higher tuition fees in the public sector that can lessen the price disadvantage of their own tuition fees;
- parents, especially to the degree to which loans displace what might otherwise have had to have been parental contributions;
- governments, to the degree to which loans displace what might otherwise have been governmental contributions; and
- other public needs, to which governments might decide to shift the revenues freed up, as it were, by the additional revenue from the new student contributions.

To the degree to which a student loan scheme is the means by which the student assumes a share of the total higher educational cost burden, this share —and its beneficiaries, as outlined above—results partly from a kind of political negotiation between the government and families-as-voters. Within this family unit, then, the shares of family-borne expenses are allocated by a kind of negotiation between the share contributed by the parent or extended family (including the option of a parental assumption of some or all of the repayment obligation) and the share paid by the student. Finally, the portion of the student's share that is covered by loans (and thus by a mounting indebtedness) as opposed to summer and term-time employment, along with the degree to which the student accepts an old-fashioned life of student penury as opposed to a better but more costly lifestyle, is a personal financial decision that draws on aspirations, values, confidence, a tolerance for both debt and risk, and the ability to understand the meanings of financial obligations, compound interest, and the consequences of default.

Although student loans, when implemented for the first time, are frequently resisted by students, this resistance is mainly from those who do not accept the proposition that governmental revenues are limited (or that they at least have opportunity costs) and who therefore believe that they are entitled to free instruction, free food and lodging, and possibly even pocket money. Or, more strategically, a resistance to loans may be a part of a political game in which students may consider the presence of generally available loans to be a prelude to more tuition fees and less governmental support—and thus view the absence of a loan scheme as a possible defense against the imposition of additional cost-sharing.

Student loans, however, may also be resisted by more fiscally conservative politicians and legislators—especially by ministers of finance—who may view student loan schemes as too risky and too ultimately costly to the government. Some on the political Left, perceiving and fearing the shift of the cost burden to students, may also share in seeing student loan programs as costly and ineffective. And considering the array of failed student loan programs, especially in developing counties, they may understandably view student loans as offering all of the downsides of neoliberalism without even the additional revenue or presumed virtues of the market. Furthermore, some (especially in low- and middle-income countries where credit cultures are not strong) believe student loan schemes to be too frequently deceptive, in that politicians and governmental leaders may be led to believe that they have successfully passed costs on to students when they may not have—and students may be led to believe that their higher future earnings will enable them to repay their loans, when ignorance of personal finance, bad luck, and a sour labor market may instead result in them incurring unmanageable obligations.

Of course, adding to the higher educational revenue stream is not the only purpose of student loan schemes. Other aims, discussed at the start of this chapter, include: (a) putting money in the hands of needy students as a kind of transfer payment, only some of which may be returned; (b) allowing a higher standard of student living; (c) allowing financial and other forms of independence from parents; (d) supporting certain academic programs or certain institutions or sectors of higher education, including private and even proprietary, or profitmaking, institutions; and (e) influencing postgraduation behavior by the conversion of grants to loans, or visa versa, depending on whether the graduate with a potential repayment obligation pursues certain occupations or practices in certain venues.

In all of these purposes, however, there is a premium on the recovery of repayments. In other words, whether the aim is supplementing governmental and/or parental revenue with revenue from students, or any of the other legitimate aims of student loan schemes, the difference between a loan and a grant, and thus the virtual essence of a loan, is that the financial burden is on the borrower, and the success of the loan scheme—again, regardless of purpose—depends on repayment recovery, as measured by the discounted present value of the reasonably anticipated repayments. Thus student loans are an essential ingredient in any comprehensive policy of cost-sharing, but these loans must be repaid.

Successful loan recovery, in turn, depends on three elements:

1. *Design*, which is a function mainly of the interest rates and interest subsidies, which determine the discounted present value of the repayments, even in the total absence of defaults or excessive collection costs

2. *Execution*, or cost-effective collection, which is a challenge in any generally available student loan scheme

3. *Tapping the private capital market*, in the absence of which the loans must be made by governments and remain on the books of government, obviating the need for cost-sharing that almost certainly gave rise to the student loan scheme in the first place

It is to these elements of a successful student loan scheme, and to a number of current examples from various countries, that we turn in the next chapter.

NOTES

1. Ziderman (2002) differentiates the aim of revenue generation from the aim of university expansion, but otherwise he presents essentially the same portrayal of the policy aims of governmentally sponsored student loans.

2. This section draws on Johnstone 2006a, 2006b.

3. The literature on income contingent loans is extensive. See, for example, Johnstone 1972, 2004a, 2004b; Barr 2001; Palacios Lleras 2004; Usher 2005; and Chapman 2006a, 2006b.

4. The short-lived Yale Plan for Tuition Postponement is described in Johnstone 1972.

5. The US hybrid IBR student loan option was supported by the Rethinking Student Aid Study Group, a prominent coalition of economists and financial aid experts, in its 2008 report, *Fulfilling the Commitment: Recommendations for Reforming Federal Student Aid*. Addressing the huge and increasingly unwieldy set of financial aid programs in the United States, which included in 2007–8 nearly $29 billion worth of grants (mainly means-tested), nearly $67 billion in governmentally guaranteed loans (both subsidized and unsubsidized), plus federal tax credits worth more than $7 billion, the report recommended (among other proposals) (a) continuing fixed-schedule repayment obligations on federally sponsored student loans, with a default schedule that was graduated over time to approximate earnings growth, but with other repayment-schedule options available; (b) eliminating the current in-school interest subsidy on subsidized loans and shifting those dollars to help fund the more generous and more comprehensive Income Based Repayment (IRB) option; thereby (c) strengthening protection for low earners by limiting repayments to no more than 15 percent of one's annual income in excess of 1.5 times the official poverty level and by forgiving sums remaining after income based repayments have been properly made by low earners for 20 years (later changed to 25 years in the authorizing language).

REFERENCES

Barr, Nicholas. 2001. *The Welfare State as Piggy Bank: Information, Risk, Uncertainty, and the Role of the State*. Oxford: Oxford University Press.
Chapman, Bruce. 2006a. *Government Managing Risk: Income Contingent Loans for Social and Economic Progress*. London: Routledge.
——. 2006b. Income Related Student Loans: Concepts, International Reforms and Administrative Challenges. In *Cost-Sharing and Accessibility in Western Higher Education: A Fairer Deal?* ed. Pedro N. Teixeira, D. Bruce Johnstone, Maria J. Rosa, and Hans Vossensteyn. Douro Series, Higher Education Dynamics, vol. 14. Dordrecht, The Netherlands: Springer.
Glennerster, Howard. 2005. A Graduate Tax Revisited. *Higher Education Review* 35 (2): 25–40.
Jackson, Roy. 2002. The National Student Financial Aid Scheme of South Africa (NAFAS): How and Why It Works. Special international issue of *Welsh Journal of Education* 11 (1):82–94.
Johnstone, D. Bruce. 1972. *New Patterns for College Lending: Income Contingent Loans*. New York: Teachers College Press.
——. 2004a. The Applicability of Income Contingent Loans in Developing and Transitional Countries. *Journal of Educational Planning and Administration* [New Delhi, India] 18 (2):159–174.
——. 2004b. Cost-Sharing and Equity in Higher Education: Implications of Income Contingent Loans. In *Markets in Higher Education*, ed. Pedro Teixeira, Ben Jongbloed, David Dill, and Alberto Amaral. Dordrecht, The Netherlands: Kluwer Academic Publishers.

———. 2006a. *Financing Higher Education: Cost-Sharing in International Perspective*. Boston: Boston College Center for International Higher Education and Sense Publishers.

———. 2006b. Higher Educational Accessibility and Financial Viability: The Role of Student Loans. In *Higher Education in the World 2006: The Financing of Universities*, ed. J. Tres and F. López-Segrera. Barcelona: Palgrave Macmillan.

Kirshstein, Rita, Andrea Berger, Elana Benatar, and David Rhodes. 2004. *Workforce Contingent Financial Aid: How States Link Financial Aid to Employment*. Indianapolis: Lumina Foundation for Education.

Loonin, Deanne. 2008. *Paying the Price: The High Cost of Private Student Loans and the Dangers for Student Borrowers*. Boston: Student Loan Borrower Assistance Project, National Consumer Law Center.

Palacios Lleras, Miguel. 2004. *Investing in Human Capital: A Capital Markets Approach to Student Funding*. Cambridge: Cambridge University Press.

Rethinking Student Aid Study Group. 2008. *Fulfilling the Commitment: Recommendations for Reforming Federal Student Aid*. New York: College Entrance Examination Board.

Schrag, Philip G. 2008. Federal Student Loan Repayment Assistance for Public Interest Lawyers and Other Employees of Governments and Nonprofit Organizations. *Hofstra Law Review* 36 (27):27–63.

Shen, Hua, and Adrian Ziderman. 2007. *Student Loans Repayment and Recovery: International Comparisons*. Bonn: Institute for the Study of Labor.

US General Accounting Office. 2001. Details on Income Contingent Repayment in FDLP. Appendix IV in *Alternative Market Mechanisms for the Student Loan Programs*. Washington, DC: US General Accounting Office.

Usher, Alex. 2005a. *Much Ado About a Very Small Idea*. Toronto: Educational Policy Institute.

———. 2005b. *Understanding International Debt Management/Repayment Programs and Their Effect on the Repayment of Student Financial Assistance*. Toronto: Educational Policy Institute.

Woodhall, Maureen. 1989. *Financial Support for Students: Grants, Loans, or Graduate Tax?* London: Kogan Page.

Ziderman, Adrian. 2002. Alternative Objectives of National Student Loan Schemes. Special international issue of *Welsh Journal of Education* 11 (1):37–47.

Ziderman, Adrian, and Douglas Albrecht. 1995. *Financing Universities in Developing Countries*. Washington, DC: Falmer Press.

CHAPTER SEVEN

Student Loan Schemes in Practice

The preceding chapter dealt with the need for student loan schemes and their purposes, forms, and consequences (or beneficiaries). This chapter is about the actual construction of student loan programs, together with some examples of student loan schemes as they existed in 2008 in a number of countries.

Elements to Be Considered in Any Student Loan Program

Any of the forms of student loan programs described in chapter 6 need to answer the following eight questions, or design element—and the responses can then fully and unambiguously describe these programs.

1. *Purposes*: The first question in the actual implementation of a student loan scheme is to specify the purposes of the program (realistically and in priority order if there is more than one). The possible purposes (and there are various ways of enumerating aims) that were set forth and discussed in chapter 6 are: (a) to put money in the hands only of financially needy students for tuition fees, or the costs of student living, or both; (b) to put money into the

hands of all students (which is financially feasible only with unsubsidized interest rates or in countries without officially expected parental contributions, where the loans are actually the deferred tuition fees available to all eligible students); (c) to implement a degree of cost-sharing by shifting a portion of the costs (generally from government, or taxpayers) to the student; (d) to influence institutional or program selection through the criteria required for obtaining the loan; (e) to encourage academic progress and/or success by forgiving portions of the repayment (i.e., to provide effective grants) for such progress or success; and (f) to influence postgraduation behavior (e.g., the selection of a professional practice or a practice venue) by forgiving portions of the repayment for those making such selections.

2. *Eligibility*: Who is eligible to borrow? Are loans generally available to all students who want them? Or—as is common in developing countries where student loans as yet have little or no real asset value and thus little access to private capital—is the volume of new lending limited to the sum of current repayments plus new governmental appropriations, which is probably far below the need for new lending and which will thus require stringent rationing? Rationing, then, would have to limit either the number of new loans or the average amounts of the loans or both. If political pressure from students, parents, and opposition allies makes it difficult to limit the number of loans, which would then force the government to impose limits on individual loan amounts, is the government prepared to respond to what will inevitably be the inadequacy of these lower loan amounts?

If, instead, it is the number of loans that is to be rationed, might the loans be made available, for example, only to the very neediest students in the public sector? Or might loans be made available, like merit grants, only to the relatively more high-achieving students in the already substantially subsidized governmentally sponsored track? Finally, if the volume of new lending allows, might eligibility for governmentally sponsored student loans be one of the ways in which the government can support and indirectly subsidize a private higher educational sector? The crucial factor in any of these rationing schemes—and, of course, one directly related to the aforementioned question regarding the purposes of the loan scheme—is the relative importance of the criteria of *financial need* (usually determined according to the financial means of the parents) versus *academic merit* (which may refer either to academic promise or actual performance) or other criteria related to institutional or program selection.

3. *Source of capital*: There is no more elemental or critical question facing a student loan scheme than where the money is to come from. The capital for student loans may come from individual and institutional savers, made available to the student borrower via a bank or other form of credit institution. In a very similar fashion, the money can come from a governmental loan agency or even from a university, which then sells, or warehouses, the loans to a bank or other source of savings. Or the money to be lent may come from the government itself, in which case it may be obtained (a) from taxes, levied either directly upon the general citizenry or indirectly on business and passed on to the general citizenry through higher prices for their products or services; (b) from savers, via governmental debt; or (c) through the printing of money and the confiscation of purchasing power from the general citizenry because of the resulting inflation.

As the essence of lending and borrowing is a transaction between savers (the ultimate lenders) and investors (the borrowers), it is essential for the student loans themselves—that is, the individual repayment obligations, together with whatever provisions there may be for guarantees or cosignatories—to be treated as nearly as possible as assets. The value of these assets is the present discounted value of the reasonably anticipated payments (less defaults and other reasons for nonrepayment, such as mortality or permanent disability) and is set by the capital market. Student loans that have market or near-market rates of interest and that are guaranteed (or are otherwise deemed secure) can be sold or securitized, thus tapping private savings rather than governmental appropriations for the new lending.

4. *Origination and lender*: Who or what is to be the lender—that is, the entity from which the student actually receives the money and with which the student borrower (and any required cosignatories) make a legally enforceable contract? The originator may be a governmental ministry, a quasi-governmental public corporation, a private bank, or the higher educational institution itself. In some cases (e.g., in Germany or South Africa), the loan is that ultimately repayable part of a larger sum given to the student as study assistance—the other part being a grant, or bursary. For loans given to students at public institutions and which are limited to no more than the tuition due, no cash need actually change hands: the loan (e.g., in Australia) becomes whatever portion of the governmental allocation to the university that the student is to bear (i.e., the tuition); and which the student, with his or her parents, must choose

either to defer and repay as a loan, obligating the student, or to pay up front, in most cases obligating the parent.

5. *Ultimate risk*: Perhaps the most significant question in any lending transaction is, Who or what bears the ultimate risk? In other words, who or what loses in the event of default? With a private commercial loan, the risk is usually born by the lender, who (in addition to good lender practices) reduces this risk by requiring collateral, or assets that must be forfeited in the event of default, and who further covers what will still be some losses by an interest premium on riskier loans.

However, the default risk on most student loans that do not have governmental guarantees or cosignatories will be very high, due to the absence of collateral, frequent periods of unemployment, greater mobility, and lack of already established credit. For this reason, a truly market rate of interest on generally available student loans (that is, loans available to most or all students, rather than just to creditworthy, or low risk, individuals, such as medical or MBA students) would almost certainly have to carry a prohibitively high rate of interest. Therefore, most student loan programs pass most or all of the risk on to the government or to family cosignatories. This risk, and the resulting cost of student lending, may be largely hidden, such as when the government serves as the lender and simply fails to collect on many of its assets. Or the risk may be in the form of a guarantee to a private or quasi-private lender, who can collect from the government in the event of default, leaving the government with either the defaulted note and the task of finding, and trying to collect from, the defaulting borrower or the corollary simply absorbing the loss, as in any other governmental expenditure. Or the risk may be shared—either with parental or other cosignatories or with the higher educational institution itself, in addition to the state—in levels, or tranches, of guarantees. In any of these examples, controlling risk must be a central part of any student loan plan, whether the goal is to access private capital or simply to maintain credible governmental accounts.

6. *Loan amounts and limits*: How much can be borrowed? Part of the answer to this question depends on the amount of total available new loan capital, either from the private capital market or from the government-as-lender. In theory, and in perfectly functioning capital markets and proper governmental accounting, the cost to the government should be the same either way. That is, if the new lending is to come from the government or a public agency, the new cash outlay for a new lending year (that is, net of repayments received)

should, for proper accounting, be discounted by the present value of the reasonably anticipated future revenue stream from those outlays to provide an estimate of the government's real obligation in that lending year. If, on the other hand, the new lending is made available by banks, limited to the volume that the government can subsidize and guarantee, the real present value cost to the government is the discounted present value of the reasonably calculated streams of subsidies and defaults—which should (again, in theory and with proper asset accounting) be the same as in the preceding example. In either case, as discussed above under the section on eligibility, annual loan limits will be the starting point of a general plan to ration limited amounts of possible new lending.

In an ideal world, when available loan capital is adequate enough to significantly enhance accessibility (and not merely provide a better standard of student living or reduce the amount that might otherwise be contributed by parents), the maximum loan should be sufficient to cover at least the minimum expenses associated with university participation, less any reasonably expected means-tested contribution from parents and less any amount deemed appropriate (and possible) for the student to earn and save during academic terms or between academic years. At the same time, the resulting individual aggregate debt levels, along with the interest rates and repayment periods that together generate the monthly payments, must be in some kind of accord with the prevailing earnings of the graduates, so that repayment is possible without undue hardship (and thus a likely default).

7. *Amount and form of subsidization*: No element in the design of a viable student loan scheme is more important than the amount and form of governmental subsidization: that is, How much of the true cost of the loans is to be repaid by the borrower as opposed to the government or taxpayer? The costs of lending are (1) the cost of money to the lender, which will always be at some rate of interest in excess of the prevailing rate of inflation for there to be any real return to the saver or lender; (2) the cost of defaults or other sources of nonrepayment, such as death or disability; and (3) the costs of administration, or servicing and collecting the loans. The key issue in student lending is determining how much of this total cost is to be paid for by the student borrower through interest payments and how much by some source of subsidy, generally by the government (or taxpayer). As mentioned above under the treatment of risk, a generally available student loan program must cover much (if not all) of the costs of default through some combination of governmental

and cosignatory guarantees rather than through the interest charged to all of the borrowers, which would be prohibitively high. But the cost of money and the costs of administering student loans (which are, in comparison to most business or consumer lending, small and expensive to service and collect) must be recovered through a combination of interest charged to the student and possible additional subsidies from the government.

A few loan programs, such as the repayable portion of loans from the German Federal Education and Training Assistance Act, or BAföG,[1] charge no interest at all, which amounts to a very large governmental subsidy to all student borrowers. Others (e.g., in Ghana and Kenya) charge a flat rate of a few percentage points regardless of the interest rates prevailing in the market, which may still amount to a very large subsidy in an inflationary climate where the money that is eventually returned will have lost most of its value by virtue of inflation. Some student loan schemes—such as those in Australia, Sweden, and the United Kingdom—will occasionally be portrayed as not charging interest at all, but merely adjusting the amount owed upwards according to the prevailing rate of inflation so that the borrower repays in real terms only what he or she borrowed. This is still an interest rate, albeit what is frequently called a *zero real*, or inflation-adjusted, rate of interest, which, by definition is still moderately subsidized as money always has some real value, and true market interest rates will always be somewhat in excess of the prevailing rate of inflation. A still lesser degree of subsidization might be a rate of interest charged at the government's borrowing rate, which is generally the lowest nominally unsubsidized interest because of the large amounts involved (and thus lower cost per dollar borrowed) and the presumed security of government notes. Finally, an essentially unsubsidized student loan might be one that charged a rate of interest equivalent to the rate charged on consumer debt generally.

The inevitable political pressure for high subsidization (in addition to the recognition that greater rates of interest cause heavier debt loads and may thus contribute to higher default rates) will push for greater subsidization and lower student interest rates. On the other hand, high governmental subsidies impact governmental operating budgets and carry extensive opportunity costs: that is, forgone alternative governmental expenditures. Even restricting these foregone expenditures to those that might otherwise expand higher educational access and opportunity (i.e., excluding tax cuts or governmental expenditures on, for example, basic education, public health, or welfare), such forgone alternatives might include (a) more loans at lesser amounts of subsidy, (b) more grants, or (c) additional operating revenue to enlarge capacity and thus expand participation.[2]

In addition, high subsidies require rationing (as discussed above under eligibility), which needs to be mainly or entirely based on family financial need in order to prevent subsidized loans from simply displacing parental contributions and further subsidizing the upper-middle class. But rationing through forms of means-testing adds both administrative costs and opportunities for unfairness and corruption. A reasonable compromise is probably minimal subsidization: an interest rate high enough to assure some recovery, to discourage unnecessary borrowing, and to minimize the need for extensive family-income verification (which would probably be futile anyway in many countries), but still subsidized enough to be politically palatable and to control excessive student indebtedness.

Finally, a loan program must resolve how it will disburse its subsidies. For example, loan subsidies can be granted early in the borrowing process by subsidizing all interest during the in-school and grace periods. Or the loan subsidies can perhaps provide fewer front-end years of total interest forgiveness but allow a slightly more subsidized rate of interest during the actual years of repayment. Student loans can also provide both forms of subsidy, but for considerably more governmental expenditure. Income contingent loans can feature a substantial subsidy for all borrowers—as in the former Swedish and the current (as of 2008) UK plans, which feature a zero real rate of interest—or they can charge less-subsidized rates to the students who will repay but provide more substantial low-earnings protection (i.e., subsidies) to those who cannot, the latter by means of a smaller percent-of-income required for each individual payments and a shorter total repayment period, as discussed in the preceding chapter. None of these policy options is necessarily correct. But the differences are significant. And a student loan program cannot supply all forms of subsidization at generous levels and still be part of an overall policy of cost-sharing.

8. *The nature, shape, and duration of the repayment obligation*: Finally, some essentially technical questions must be resolved regarding the nature (or form), shape, and duration of the repayment obligation. A repayment period is defined precisely in a conventional fixed-schedule, or mortgage-type, loan; it is only implied in an income contingent loan—by the combination of percent-of-earnings required to be repaid, the average level of aggregate indebtedness, and the earnings profiles of the borrowers. With subsidized loans (as most

governmentally sponsored student loans are), the value of the subsidy to the borrower (and likewise, the cost to the government) increases as the repayment period expands, giving the government a reason to limit repayment periods. At the same time, the shorter the repayment period, all else being equal, the higher the individual payments and the more likely the payments are to be a burden to the borrower (and thus to be defaulted and result in an even greater cost to the government-as-guarantor). As in the resolution of the questions of the rate of interest to the student borrower and the degree of subsidization borne by the government, both discussed above, the resolution here is partly a compromise between several competing objectives—such as cost recovery, maximum participation, and accessibility—and the need to move toward some cost-sharing, even with more highly subsidized student lending.

Less politically charged and more technical matters having to do with the form of repayments must also be resolved. For example, conventional fixed-schedule loans generally feature equal, or level, installments. However, a fixed schedule of repayments can also be graduated upwards over time to correspond better with a borrower's likely increases in income or earnings: that is, made to approximate an income contingent repayment schedule. The terms of the loan must also stipulate whether the payments are to be paid directly to the lender by the borrower or whether they are to be (or can be at the discretion of the borrower or his or her employer) removed from the borrower's pay by the employer and paid directly to the government, similar to withholding for taxes or pension contributions.

An income contingent obligation must stipulate the percent-of-income that is required for repayment, as well as how "income" is to be defined—last year's actual or the current year's estimated income, or earnings only, or earnings plus taxable assets—and similar questions. Some income contingent obligations have an income threshold that must be exceeded before what is essentially a surtax takes effect, so that only income greater than this amount is subject to the repayment rate. Income contingent obligations must also stipulate how long this percent-of-income is to be paid: for example, until the loan is fully repaid at some rate of interest, or until the attainment of a certain age, or until some maximum number of years has passed since the beginning of repayments.

The point to be made is that these questions about the nature, shape, and the duration of repayment obligations are important and must be answered as a part of the design of any student loan scheme. At the same time, the elements of program purpose, risk, source of capital, and subsidization are the ones that contribute to the possible volume and sustainability of student lending and thus to the ability of the loan scheme to achieve a lasting level that makes any of its aims possible.

Implications of Student Loan Scheme Design

The above eight items to be considered are interrelated. For example, each of the elements in the design of a student loan scheme requires policy decisions that have implications to the overall costs of the program, which in turn have consequences for the volume of possible lending, the necessary (or possible) eligibility criteria, and the opening up of (or the need to forgo) other related choices, such as the level of tuition fees or the availability of nonrepayable grants. Table 7.1 illustrates some of these policy implications of the program design elements of alternative student loan schemes.

For example, a priority aim of expanding the participation of needy students requires a cost-effective system of means-testing, as discussed in chapter 4, as well as costly governmental guarantees. To many politicians as well as to some student-access analysts, a priority aim of accessibility requires substantial (and costly) nonrepayable grants or, if loans are necessary, substantial loan subsidies. Together, these requirements raise governmental costs and perforce limit the total volume of both the loans and the available grants. At the same time, it is not clear that student enrollment behavior is all that affected by interest rates, and whereas students will always prefer grants to loans and prefer low interest to high interest, it is less clear that governmental expenditure on highly subsidized interest rates is a cost-effective way of expanding access and participation. (The connection between tuition fees, financial assistance, and interest-rate subsidization and student-enrollment behavior is the subject of the following chapter.)

Cost-sharing, as a priority aim, requires minimal subsidization and effective cost recovery, which in turn may suggest parental cosignatories or *risk rating* (limiting eligibility to the lowest-risk borrowers), both of which run counter to the goal of expanding participation to low-income and other marginalized students. Influencing postgraduation behavior may require targeting postgraduate or advanced professional students, which does nothing to advance the policy goal of expanding undergraduate access but may be a cost-effective way of getting health professionals into remote regions.

Table 7.1   Implications of eight critical design elements

Element	Implications for program design
1. Aim(s) of student loan scheme	
• Expand participation of needy students	Means-testing necessary. Anticipate high defaults. Cost depends on eligibility and volume.
• Put money in the hands of all students	Requires large amounts of capital. Cost depends on limits, subsidization, and recovery.
• Cost-sharing: shift part of the costs to students	Requires low subsidization, high cost recovery, and tapping the private-capital market.
• Influence institutional or program selection	Questionable cost-effectiveness, unless coupled with program aim #6.
• Encourage academic success	Expensive, probably regressive, and questionably effective.
• Influence postgraduate practice or venue	Expensive, unless narrowly targeted to meet a significant shortage.
2. Eligibility	
• All higher educational students	Expensive, unless private capital is tapped. Some type of rationing is necessary.
• Only public-sector students	Expensive; cost-ineffective, especially with low or no tuition fees.
• Only needy students	More cost-effective; requires transparent and fair means-testing processes.
• Academically meritorious students	Cost-ineffective; probably regressive.
• Students studying in a particular field	Cost-effectiveness depends on whether the loans increase the number of graduates in that field.
3. Source(s) of capital	
• Governmental operating budget	Program breadth limited by current budget and competing needs for public finance.
• Governmental borrowing	Requires low interest and a long-term borrowing agreement.
• Private banking sector	Requires risk-sharing agreements with governments. Minimal subsidies.

• Capital markets via purchase of government loans	Depends on the market value of the loans as assets.
• Capital markets via purchase of bank agency loans	Depends on the market value of the loans as assets.
• Capital markets via purchase of loan agency bonds	Depends on the strength of the governmental guarantee backing the bonds.
• Capital markets via securitization of lending agency loan	Depends on the market value of the loans as assets and on the strength of the guarantee, if any.

4. Origination
• Lender

—Government agency	Effective if able to sell quickly to the capital market.
—Quasi-government agency	Effective if able to sell quickly to the capital market.
—Banks	Effective, though student loans are small and longer-term than banks prefer. Require guarantees.
—Higher educational institutions	Program breadth limited by institutional budget.

• Mode of disbursement

—To higher educational institutions	Must be made clear to student that he or she has taken a loan.
—To students	Students must be educated on the use of student loans.
—Tuition to institution and living expenses to student	

5. Ultimate bearer of default risk

• Lender	Unlikely beyond normal consumer credit risk—and then with an interest premium.
• Cosignatory	Effective, provided provisions are made for low-income borrowers.
• Government	Necessary—lessened only by creditworthy cosignatories; cost depends on likely defaults; can assume defaulted loans or pay up-front premium.
• Some combination of the above	As in government, plus cosignatory.
• Borrower, via a risk premium	Only for the naturally creditworthy; interest premiums for generally available loans would be too high.

continued

Table 7.1 Continued

Element	Implications for program design
6. Loan limits	
• Tuition fees only	Leaves problem with uncovered living expenses; also expensive and needs a capital market.
• Estimated living expenses	Good if tuition fees can be kept low (as in Nordic countries).
• Tuition fees plus estimated living expenses	Very costly to the government and large debts for graduates.
7. Subsidization	
• *Aims* of subsidization can be (a) equity, (b) populism (i.e., for all), and (c) manpower planning	Equity can increase participation among the poor or other targeted groups. Populism—low interest rates (high subsidy) for all—achieves little, but politically popular among students. Manpower planning can work if well targeted.
• *Levels* of subsidization are (a) high—low or no interest, (b) moderate—equal to the prevailing rate of inflation, (c) minimal—set at or near the government's borrowing rate, and (d) no subsidization (commercial-credit rates of interest)	Subsidization is a governmental expenditure and so has opportunity costs—even if the only opportunity costs to be considered are other uses of subsidies for student aid. The higher the subsidies that do not achieve a priority policy aim, the less money that is available for other forms and aims. Thus, for example, low interest rates for all borrowers is a tradeoff for, say, larger targeted grants for equity aims or low lifetime-earnings protection via targeted repayment forgiveness.

• *Forms* of subsidization are (a) in-school, (b) grace period, (c) repayment period, (d) forgiveness for low lifetime earnings, and (e) forgiveness for proper practice and venue	In-school interest subsidy may be more politically important—and thus be accorded a higher priority—than low interest during repayment. Targeted repayment forgiveness, if truly effective, may also be a cost-effective form of subsidization for certain policy aims (such as teachers, physicians, or nurses in rural areas).

8. Nature of repayment obligation

• *Form* of the obligation is (a) fixed schedule, (b) income contingent, or (c) hybrid	See text for differences—which are frequently exaggerated. A hybrid version can provide greater simplicity and certainty to the lender of a fixed-schedule obligation, while affording low earners the protection of knowing that repayments will not exceed a certain percentage of earnings.
• *Shape* of the obligation (a) follows earning growth (by definition) in the income contingent form, but (b) can be shaped to rise over time to approximate income growth in fixed-schedule and hybrid obligations	The shape of the repayment schedule is a policy parameter only in fixed-schedule and hybrid repayment obligations. It can be made to approximate earnings growth by tilting the repayment schedule upwards over time to approximate projected average earnings growth.
• *Duration* in the income contingent form *varies*, depending on debt, percentage of income required, and rate of interest; duration in the fixed-schedule form is *set*, with the percent of income (repayment burden) varying	Like shape, the duration of the repayment obligation is a policy parameter only in fixed-schedule and hybrid forms. The longer the duration, the smaller the monthly repayments and the less the burden—but the longer the duration, the greater the total amounts to be repaid. Duration needs to be set according to aggregate indebtedness to make the monthly burdens tolerable for the average borrower.

All of the different policy aims have implications for eligibility. Restricting eligibility to needy students, for example, focuses available public resources on a clear public policy goal, but it is nevertheless costly and perforce limits public-sector savings or reallocation possibilities, and thus curtails the benefits of cost-sharing. Limiting eligibility to public-sector students may be politically popular and financially necessary, but such a policy also limits a potentially cost-effective form of governmental subsidization to the private sector, which in turn might provide a cost-effective way to generate higher educational capacity in countries with enrollment demand surging beyond the available public-sector capacity. Limiting eligibility to academically meritorious students might be politically popular with metropolitan elites, conservative politicians, and university faculty, and it is an obvious way to ration extremely limited governmental resources, but it is almost certainly regressive and cost-ineffective. Similarly, question #5 above, dealing with the ultimate bearer of default risk, is one of the more critical elements of student loan scheme design. If the government does not provide some form of guarantee, the only recourse is a strict requirement of parental (or other) cosignatories, or a restriction of lending to only the most creditworthy students—which, in turn, does little or nothing for the policy aims of advancing participation or cost-sharing.

Moreover (and related to the interconnections among the design elements shown in table 7.1), annual loan limits will be necessary in low- and middle-income countries to ration limited loan funds. In such cases, the political temptation may be to spread the limited funds as widely as possible, which, in turn, may restrict the effectiveness of the loan scheme for all borrowers. Or a policy response to the necessity of rationing may be to limit loans mainly to students from middle- and upper-income families who need only a small amount of borrowing to supplement the monies they receive from their parents. Such a policy solution may maximize the enrollment impact per dollar of governmental funds but do little to increase access among the poorest or most marginalized students. In contrast to these loan-limit policies that are driven by the need to ration limited amounts of total possible lending, the constraints on annual or aggregate borrowing in high-income countries with adequate provisions for risk and generally sufficient amounts of loan capital, such as Canada or the United States, may be more a form of consumer protection: that is, to prevent students from taking on unmanageable levels of debt.

The form and amount of subsidization may, as suggested above, be its single most critical design element. The problem loan subsidies pose to the effective design of loan schemes is that subsidies tend to be hidden, as in highly subsidized interest rates and costly guarantees, and thus fall only on future governments (and on future citizens and future politicians). All of the loan scheme policy aims require some level of subsidization, but, depending on the purpose (or mix of purposes), some forms are more cost-effective than others. For example, governmental guarantees or other forms of governmental risk absorption are probably cost-effective ways to increase the participation of low-income and other potential student borrowers who are on the margin of participation. On the other hand, substantial interest rate subsidies, because of their very great cost, are almost certainly a cost-ineffective use of public money, particularly for programs designed to reach all students; they may even be a cost-ineffective way to reach low-income and other students on the participation margin, particularly if the default rates are also very high. Thus the element of interest subsidization—which, in many countries, is more of a political issue than a financial one and which, along with the likelihood of repayment recovery, contributes greatly to ultimate governmental costs—influences the total volume of lending, the criteria for eligibility, and the possible purposes that can be accommodated in a loan scheme.

Finally, there are a set of crucial policy decisions regarding the form, shape, and duration of the repayment obligation that must be made in order to create a legally enforceable (and saleable or collateralized) loan contract, but that are not particularly essential to the policy aim or the underlying cost of the loan scheme to the government. But the form of the repayment obligation (discussed in chapter 6)—particularly the difference between fixed-schedule and income contingent forms of obligation—is becoming a major focus of debate, especially in the political and policy debates surrounding the implementation of new loan programs. It therefore merits additional attention in the section below.

The Applicability of Income Contingent Loans

An increasingly important question in the construction of national student financial assistance and student loan policies is the applicability of income contingent loans, which seem increasingly to be capturing the fascination of policymakers and politicians. As provided in Australia, New Zealand, and South Africa, as adopted in the constituent countries of the United Kingdom (although abandoned by Scotland in 2008), and as recommended in much of the higher educational policy literature, income contingent loans (sometimes mistakenly referred to as graduate taxes) have certain theoretical as well as practical advantages. However, some of these commonly touted advantages are not in themselves properties of income contingency, per se, but of features that can as easily be built into conventional fixed-schedule loan forms (e.g., repayment collection by employers at the time of wage or salary payments, similar to the withholding of taxes). For analysts contemplating new governmental student loan programs, it is well to keep in mind four qualifications, or caveats, to the all-too-common presumption of the superiority of the income contingent loan form.[3]

First, an income contingent loan is still a loan and, in spite of some presentations to the contrary, it is not any cheaper per se—for most student borrowers —than a conventional loan merely because the repayment obligation is expressed as a percentage of income or earnings. For most student borrowers, the cheapness or expensiveness of a loan—not to be confused with the manageability of its repayments—is measured by its true simple annual interest rate (or, alternatively, by the discounted present value of the repayment stream). On the other hand, manageability is measured by the ease of the individual repayments. Manageability can always be enhanced by increasing subsidization, although only at considerable cost to the taxpayer. Manageability can also be enhanced by reducing the individual repayments (for a conventional loan) or by lowering the percent-of-income to be repaid (for an income contingent loan), in either case extending the repayment period and increasing the total dollars to be repaid, but not affecting the true cost of an unsubsidized or minimally subsidized loan.

Second, an income contingent loan ought not to be viewed as a substitute for a tuition fee, but rather as merely another way of deferring it—like deferring any of the other necessary expense of higher educational participation by borrowing. If a student incurs a monetary obligation for attending an institution of higher education that can be paid in the future, income contingently or otherwise, then for all practical purposes there is an effective tuition fee. In some cases, as in the United States, it is assumed that parents (or perhaps students) pay the tuition up front, but they may take out either a parental or a student loan to do so (and which, in the case of a US Direct Student Loan, may be converted to an income contingent repayment schedule at the initiation of the repayment process, if the student so chooses). In other countries, the deferred amount due, or loan, passes directly from the lender (generally the government) to the university (or into the university's budget appropriation) without ever passing through the student's hands and perhaps never even being perceived quite like the combination of tuition fees and student loans that such a policy really represents. In still other cases—Australia being a good example—students and their parents are given the choice of accepting an income contingent loan, which goes directly to the university and is repaid by the student, or of paying up front, in which case the fees are likely to be paid by the parents (but at a considerable discount). However, a cost-sharing obligation that is entirely in the form of an income contingent loan and is presented (or is allowed to be perceived) as being in lieu of a tuition fee, without a strong incentive to pay up front, almost certainly discourages, and may all but preclude, a parental contribution to the costs of instruction, thus effectively shifting the higher educational cost burden only to the student (Johnstone 2004b).

Third, some of the attractiveness attributed to income contingency—specifically, the presumed convenience to the borrower and the allegedly greater certainty of repayment (and thus of lower defaults) to the lender, or to the government—comes primarily from the government's willingness to employ the same policies and procedures of mandatory, employer-collected income-tax withholding (and often pension or insurance contributions) to the cause of collecting student indebtedness. However, this machinery—including the power to mandate employers to collect such sums at the point of wage and salary payments, as well as the government's power to verify compliance and punish transgressors—could, in theory, also be applied to the collection of conventional fixed-schedule loans. In and of itself, this observation does not deny the theoretical attractiveness of these provisions, nor does it deny certain other theoretical attractions of income contingency. But if the government can compel employers to collect student loans (of any form), it can also compel employers to collect any payment owed by citizens, the effective collection of which is deemed to be of overriding public importance: local taxes, for example, or child support, or the cost of automobile insurance, thus conceivably weakening the primary purpose of tax collection, which is to make possible necessary public expenditures. (Furthermore, an obvious corollary to this observation is that a government that has difficulty collecting taxes and pension contributions from its citizens—which surely describes a problem in most developing and many transitional countries—can hardly be expected to be able to collect payments on an income contingent student loan.)

Finally, an income contingent loan presents some complications not found in conventional fixed-schedule, or mortgage-type, loans. Most of these arise from the need to stipulate precisely, and to then be able to verify, the income that is effectively to be taxed in order to arrive at the proper repayment amount. Multiple sources of income, highly variable income, income that tends not to get reported all, and income that can be easily shifted between a borrower and a nonborrower member of the family all constitute substantial problems for the viability of an income contingent loan scheme. Highly industrialized countries—with extensive reporting and monitoring of virtually all income and with a culture of voluntary income-tax compliance—may be able to overcome these problems, as Australia and New Zealand seem to have done and as the constituent countries of the United Kingdom seem convinced they can do. For other countries, including most of the developing and many of the transitional countries where sources of income or earnings are frequently multiple, highly variable, and often unreported, the problem of establishing the necessary repayment obligation may be considerable, virtually inviting misrepresentation of income and almost certain repayment shortfalls.

In summary, then, income contingent loans, such as those modeled after the Australian Higher Education Contribution Scheme (HECS) would seem to work well when[4]

- a government, by downplaying (or not mentioning at all) the politically treacherous concept of tuition fees, is able to get an element of cost-sharing that it would likely be politically unable to implement were it to advocate openly even for the relatively modest, deferred tuition fees that such plans generally call for;
- a government, by stressing the deferred obligation of the student, is in a financial position to forego the potential of more up-front tuition and to minimize the role of parents (even affluent ones) as an important partner in sharing the costs of instruction;
- a state does not currently need even the students' deferred revenue, but is able to tax or borrow sufficiently to keep the universities open and the students fed and housed, and to accept payment only in the future—in essence becoming the lender—with a limited ability to tap private capital markets; and
- the majority of student borrowers (that is, students who become obligated to future income contingent payments) will have a single

employer that will pay them a periodic and relatively regular salary and that is also sufficiently large, sophisticated, and legally compliant enough so it can be counted upon to take the correct amount out of the borrower's paycheck, year in and year out.

Conversely, income contingent loans would seem to be less applicable when

- nongovernmental revenue is needed immediately, making parental contributions to tuition (even with some discounting and excluding amounts from low-income families) an important source of necessary revenue supplementation;
- the scarcity of governmental revenue precludes the government from being the sole lender, thus placing a premium on student loans that have some (albeit discounted) value in the private capital market;
- many graduates (borrowers) are likely to hold multiple short-term jobs, to be employed in the informal economic sector where records are most unreliable, or to be emigrating; and
- there is no tradition of voluntary, reliable self-reporting of income, and state systems for monitoring and verifying income—for the purpose of income-tax withholding or pension or social security contributions—are nonexistent or unreliable.

Examples of Student Loan Schemes

Drawing on, and providing examples of, the aforementioned principles, the following are some current student loan programs.

Australia: In Australia, students enrolled in Commonwealth-supported places may pay their student contributions up front and receive a 20 percent discount, make a partial up-front payment and take out a Higher Education Contribution Scheme (HECS)–Higher Education Loan Programme (HELP) loan for the rest or take out a HECS-HELP loan for the full amount. The HECS-HELP loan covers the full amount of tuition (as established by the university) up to limits set by the government within three discipline-related bands. The upper limits in 2008 were set at A$5,095 [US$3,665] for Band #1 (humanities, social and behavioral sciences, languages, and visual and performing arts); A$7,260 [US$5,223] for Band #2 (engineering, mathematics, science, and computer science); and A$8,499 [US$6,114] for Band #3 (medicine, law, accounting, and economics).

A student's accumulated HECS-HELP debt is adjusted annually on June 1, in line with changes in the cost of living as measured by the Consumer Price Index to maintain its real value. Therefore, the debt carries a zero real rate of interest. Repayments are income contingent on annual incomes above A$39,825 [US$28,651]. Repayment rates range from 4 percent to a maximum of 8 percent on annual incomes in excess of A$73,960 [US$53,209]. Repayments are collected as income surtaxes by employers or are paid along with the estimated or year-end taxes due. There is no forgiveness based on age or on the passage of years since the borrowing took place. According to the definitions in the previous chapter, HECS is not a true graduate tax, as individual accounts and balances owed are maintained on each borrower. However, enlisting the national tax system gives HECS the appearance of a graduate tax and assures both a low administrative cost for servicing as well as a very low default rate.

Australia also has a student loan program for non-Commonwealth-supported —that is, non-HECS-eligible—students to cover tuition fees. This program, called FEE-HELP, has a lifetime limit per student of A$81,600 [US$58,705] (or A$102,000 [US$73,381] for medicine, dentistry, and veterinary medicine), collected in the same way as HECS-HELP. Similar to HECS-HELP, debts accrued under FEE-HELP are linked to the Consumer Price Index; however, unlike HECS-HELP, FEE-HELP loans carry a 20 percent loan fee.

Canada: The Canada Student Loan Program is jointly administered by the federal and provincial governments. If a student is a resident of Alberta, British Colombia, Manitoba, Nova Scotia, Prince Edward Island, or the Yukon, he or she gets two loans (one from the federal government for up to 60 percent of assessed need, serviced by the National Student Loans Service Centre, and one from the provincial student loan office for up to the remaining 40 percent, serviced by a financial institution). If the student is from a province that has an integrated student loan program, he or she gets only one loan, administered at the provincial level. The National Student Loans Service Centre (NSLSC) is responsible for the disbursement of both federal and provincial funds as well as the repayment of the integrated student loan.

Student loans are means-tested and available to all students in public and private colleges and universities to cover tuition fees and living costs. Students may receive a maximum of C$350 peer week [US$289] for a maximum of 340 weeks. The federal and provincial governments pay interest on the loans while the students are in school. Interest on the federal student loan portion is prime rate plus 2.5 percent and interest on the provincial student loan portion is prime rate plus 1 percent. Students begin repayment after a six-month grace period following graduation. Repayments are made on a fixed schedule and may take up to 15 years. Interest relief is available for graduates with temporary financial difficulties.

Chile: The most recent and comprehensive student loan program in Chile is the Crédito de la Ley 20.027 para Financiamiento de Estudios de Educatión Superior, established in 2005. This is a means-tested loan available to cover the tuition fees of all higher educational students (public and private) in accredited institutions. The scheme is administered by an autonomous body, the Comisión Administradora del Sistema de Créditos para Estudios Superiores, made up of the Minister of Education, the Budget Director of the Treasury, the General Treasurer of the Republic, the Executive Vice President of the Corporación de Fomento de la Producción de Chile (CORFO), and three representatives from education institutions.

Private financial institutions provide funds for the scheme and make payments directly to the higher educational institutions. They also manage debt collection. The loans are guaranteed by the state (risk of nonrepayment) and the higher educational institution (risk of dropouts). The former guarantees up to 90 percent of the capital plus interest, through the Treasury. The latter must cover the risk of dropouts by borrowers, through a financial instrument approved by the Comisión that covers up to 90 percent of the capital plus interest on the loan for a student's first year, up to 70 percent for the second year, and 60 percent for the third year.

While the scheme provides an in-school grace period during which neither the principal nor the interest is paid, it also offers the option of paying the interest in advance to reduce the interest rate. For example, if a student pays 70 percent of the interest that was compounded during his or her degree in advance, the interest rate is reduced by 0.5 percent. Repayment begins 18 months after the student has finished his or her degree, in a series of 240 monthly installments. The payments are divided into three time periods, with those in the first period being slightly lower than those in the second, which are again lower than those in the third, to mirror the student's expected increase in earnings over time. The maximum time period for repayment is 20 years, and it is possible to pay off the debt ahead of time. The interest rate is calculated on the government's long-term borrowing rate.

Chile has two additional student loan programs, both of which are aimed at students studying in one of the 25 traditional universities that are part of the Council of Chilean University Presidents: Crédito CORFO, a means-tested loan aimed at middle class students, and the Fondo Solidario de Crédito Universitario, a means-tested loan that covers tuition fees.

China: China's loan programs have undergone many modifications since their experimental beginnings in six cities in 1999. The Government-Subsidized Student Loan Scheme (GSSLS), as modified in 2004, provides loans of up to 6,000 Yuan [US$1,739] a year to needy students (officially acknowledged to be 20 percent of higher educational enrollment) for tuition fees and living expenses. Interest rates are fixed either at prime or the government borrowing rate and interest is accrued from the origination of the loan. The maximum grace period is two years after graduation and the maximum repayment period is six years after that, which is an extension over the previous four-year repayment period whose monthly payments were far too high. The loans are disbursed by participating banks, and the risk is shared by the government and the banks. Cosignatories are not required for the GSSLS.

There are also nonsubsidized student loans available under the General-Commercial Student Loan Scheme (GCSLS), available for children of the more-affluent families, that require a parental cosignatory (Shen and Li 2003). These loans range from 2,000 to 20,000 Yuan [US$580–$5,797] per year and carry commercial interest rates. The repayment period for the GCSL loans is flexible.

China recently (2009) developed the Student Resident Loan for low-income students whose home is in the same region as the financial institution offering the loan. The loan covers tuition fees, lodging, and other living costs and carries a commercial rate of interest. The government covers the interest during the in-school years.

France: In September 2008, the Ministry of Higher Education and Research launched a new state-guaranteed student loan program that does not require a third-party guarantee and is available to all higher educational students. The Ministry has created a guarantee fund administered by OSEO, a public holding company, to which it makes a yearly contribution. The fund covers part (up to 70%) of the default risk associated with the loans. So far there are two partner banks, CETELEM and the Banque Populaire, who disburse the loans at a market interest rate. The Ministry is aiming to provide 60,000 loans averaging €7,500 [US$8,175] each during 2009. Repayments must be made within 10 years of the first loan allocation, but they may be deferred in part or in total (Ministère de l'Enseignement supérieur et de la Recherche and OSEO 2008).

The Ministry also funds a very small system of interest-free student loans (called prêts d'honneur) that are administered by the Centre des Oeuvres Universitaires. These loans range between €800 and €3,000 [US$870–$3,260] and may be taken out only once. The loans must be repaid within 10 years and reach a very limited number of students (Chevaillier and Paul 2006).

Germany: Germany has an extensive system of means-tested, or need-based, study assistance (known colloquially as BAföG) made up of a 50 percent non-repayable grant and a 50 percent interest-free loan that has to be repaid within twenty years, beginning five years after graduation. The federal government and the Länder (states) provide the funds for BAföG in a 65:35 ratio.

BAföG is differentiated according to several aspects pertaining to living costs and the monthly maximum is €643 [US$721]. Standard BAföG applications are submitted through the universities' Financial Aid Offices, which decide which students are eligible for a BAföG grant/loan (described above) or a BAföG bank loan.

Under the low-interest BAföG bank loan, eligible students receive monthly loan disbursements from the KfW Förderbank (part of the KfW Bankengruppe, a public law institution guaranteed by the federal government) for which no security is required. Starting with the disbursement of the first loan installment, interest is compounded at a variable rate, based on the six-month European Interbank Offered Rate (EURIBOR) plus a 1 percent fee to cover administrative expenses. Once repayment begins (after a six-month grace period), students may negotiate a fixed interest rate with the KfW Förderbank for the remaining term of the loan (limited to no more than 10 years) and must pay it back in equal monthly installments of at least €105 [US$118]. Students' interest-bearing bank loans must be paid before the interest-free BAföG loan and both must be paid within 22 years.

Students may also apply for a federally funded Bildungskredit, or student loan, through the Federal Administration Office (BVA). The non-means-tested Bildungskredit is granted to cover expenses that the BAföG does not cover and it requires no security. The loan is disbursed in monthly installments of €300 [US$337] for a maximum of 24 months. Interest is compounded from the date of disbursement at a variable rate, based on the six-month EURIBOR, and includes a 1 percent fee to cover administrative expenses. Repayment is due in monthly installments of €120 [US$135].

German students (and EU citizens who have lived in Germany for three years) may also apply to a sales partner of the KfW Förderbank for a non-means-tested student loan for living expenses. These loans provide from €100 to €650 [US$112–$730] per month for living expenses during a student's first course of study and can cover such costs for up to 10 (and in some cases even 14) semesters. The loan carries a variable interest rate and is adjusted every six months to the current capital market interest rates. A maximum interest-rate level for 15 years is guaranteed in the contract agreement. Interest payments may be deferred during the grace period of six to 23 months. Borrowers have up to 25 years to repay the loan. The sales partner earns €238 [US$267] for its services, which are prefinanced by the KfW and become part of the loan.

Hungary: The Hungarian Student Loan Center (Diákhitel Központ), a limited-share, state-owned company, awards both state-financed and privately funded loans to students who are registered in accredited public and private higher educational institutions in Hungary or the European Economic Area (EEA). The loans are meant to cover tuition fees and living costs. The Student Loan Center has capitalized the loan program in several different ways. In the 2001–2 and 2002–3 academic years, loans were taken out by the state-owned investment bank and a subsidy was allocated from the central budget. In 2003–4, bonds were issued, which furnished a large percentage of the necessary funds. But there was a mismatch between short-term borrowing (bonds had a maximum maturity of three years) and long-term lending. In 2005, the European Investment Bank began to provide long-term loans at favorable interest rates.

The state provides a guarantee for all of the Student Loan Center's payment obligations undertaken to finance the loan scheme (though there is no guarantee for repayment of the individual loans, the government incurs a substantial contingent liability on behalf of the Student Loan Center). The Loan Center adds a risk premium to cover credit risks (default or losses due to loan write-offs when a borrower retires, becomes disabled, or dies) and operating costs. The risk premium may not exceed 4.5 percent. In the past seven years, the risk premium has varied between 1 and 2 percent.

The maximum amounts are set by decree. In 2006–7, academic-year loans ranged from HUF 100,000 to HUF 300,000 per month [US$778–$2,334] for state-financed students and were HUF 400,000 per month [US$3,113] for self-financed students.

Repayment begins after a three-month grace period and, for two years, is set at 6 to 8 percent of the previous year's minimum wage. After the second year, students must pay either 6 to 8 percent of their average gross monthly income two years before the current year, or 6 to 8 percent of the minimum wage, until the loan is repaid. If the borrower takes a parental leave or a temporary-disability leave, he or she may request a suspension of repayments. The government may cover the interest payments of borrowers with young children who receive a maternity allowance or a childcare allowance. The debt is cancelled if a borrower reaches retirement age, becomes eligible for a permanent-disability pension, or dies.

The Student Loan Center set up an arrangement with higher educational institutions to deal with the "improvement contribution" that was to be implemented for state-funded students in the fall of 2008. Those with student loans were to be able to defer payment of their up-front improvement contributions. The important contribution was rejected in a national referendum in March 2008.

Japan: The Japan Student Services Organization (JASSO)—a newly created, independent administrative institution—administers the recently revised student loan system. The system is made up of two types of student loans: the first-class scholarship loan that is interest free and awarded on the basis of merit and need, and the second-class scholarship that is interest free during in-school years (during repayment, the interest rate is fixed at the rate agreed upon at the initiation of repayment or is assessed every five years) and awarded on the basis of economic need.

When applying for the loan, students can choose between the personal guaranty system and the institutional system, whereby the Japan Educational Exchanges and Services (JEES) cosigns the loan and the student pays JEES monthly default insurance, ranging from ¥1,000 to ¥7,000 [US$8–$54). The loans themselves range from ¥45,000 to ¥51,000 [US$347–$394] per month, based on residency (i.e., living at home or independently), in the first-class scholarship program and from ¥30,000 to ¥100,000 [US$232–$772] per month, also based on residency, in the second-class scholarship program. Loan repayment must begin after a grace period of six months following completion of the student's academic program. Repayment is on a fixed monthly schedule of payments and must be completed within 20 years. Loans are collected automatically from the student's bank or postal account. Both classes of loans add 10 percent annual interest to overdue installments (excluding interest), prorated by the number of days the payment is delayed. First-class loans may be forgiven when students receive outstanding academic results (Shibata 2006).

Kenya: Kenya began its current Higher Education Loan Scheme under a quasi-public Higher Education Loans Board (HELB) in 1995, resurrecting a student loan program that had failed in the 1970s through a combination of extremely high defaults and apparent administrative incompetence (or at least a lack of readiness to administer such a program). At present, loan amounts are means-tested and cover about three-quarters of the yearly higher educational costs that must be borne by a student and his or her family. When the student loan program was introduced in 1995, students received a maximum amount of KES 42,000 [US$1,423]. This amount was increased in the 2005–6 fiscal year to a maximum loan amount for the very poorest students of KES 60,000 [US$2,032] and a minimum of KES 35,000 [US$1,186]. Once HELB determines that a student should be awarded a loan, the board pays KES 8,000 [US$271] towards the student's tuition costs directly to the university. The remaining loan funds are paid to the student (through his or her bank account) for food and lodging costs and other living expenses.

Since September 2008, loans are no longer limited to students in the Module I (government-sponsored) programs and in private universities; funds may also be borrowed by fee-paying students in the Module II (self-paying) track. Interest is set at 4 percent and begins to accrue upon disbursement of the loan. After graduation, students are entitled to a one-year grace period before repayment begins. If the borrower is formally employed, he or she has to authorize his or her employer to deduct the loan repayment and submit it to HELB. Loan repayments may not exceed one-quarter of the borrower's monthly salary.

The key to this new loan program lies in its extraordinary effort to recover payments, aided by new legislation that mandates employers to deduct the repayment amounts due from employees. (The new law also mandates employers to collect outstanding loans from the earlier 1974 Kenyan student loan program.) In addition, HELB works together with the Kenya Revenue Authority (KRA) and the National Health Insurance Fund (NHIF) to recover loans by identifying loan recipients who are working in both the private and public sectors and requiring them to begin repayment.

The Higher Education Loans Board has begun to explore the possibility of floating a KES 7 billion [US$237 million] bond to raise additional capital and reduce its exclusive reliance on government funding.

The Netherlands: In principle, all full-time students in the Netherlands are entitled to a basic grant for a nominal-duration program that is intended to cover both study costs and living expenses. This grant is, in fact, initially a loan that is converted into a nonrepayable grant only if the student meets study-progress requirements (for example, passing 50 percent of his or her exams in the first year). The amount that students receive depends on whether they live at home with their parents (€74.11 per month [US$82] in 2004) or on their own (€228.20 per month [US$254]).

Depending on parental income, a student may also be entitled to a means-tested student loan of up to €253.27 per month [US$281] (an additional €237.30 [US$264] can be borrowed to replace assumed parental contributions) that had an interest rate of 3.35 percent in 2004. This loan is not turned into a grant, and repayment must begin after a grace period of two years. Repayment is spread over 15 years, with minimum monthly installments of €45 [US$50] (Vossensteyn 2004). When graduates have problems repaying their study debts, they can ask for an annual means test. This may reduce (or even cancel) their repayment obligations for one year. All of the debt that remains after the 15-year repayment period is forgiven.

Portugal: A student loan system aimed at all higher educational students was introduced in 2007. It provides loans ranging from €1,000 to €5000 [US$1,408–$7,042] per year, with an overall maximum of €25,000 [US$35,210], at a fixed interest rate equal to the Euro Interest Rate Swap (EURIRS) plus a maximum spread of 1 percent (which includes a mutual guarantee commission of 0.35%). The spread is narrowed by 0.35 percentage points for students whose yearly classification is equal to or above 70 percent of the best possible academic score, and by 0.80 points for students who are equal to or above 80 percent. Interest only is collected during the in-school years and a one-year grace period. Repayment of the principal begins after the grace period ends and lasts up to a maximum of 10 years (twice the duration of the course of study).

The loans are made within the context of the mutual guarantee system that was set up in 2005 to provide support to small enterprises. Under the new student loan system, banks provide the loans to students and acquire shares in a mutual guarantee company (there are three involved at present), in an amount equal to 0.5 percent of the total loan guarantee, in return for the guarantee that the company provides. The banks also provide the mutual guarantee companies with a mutual guarantee commission of 35 basis points per year (already included in the interest rate charged by the bank to the borrower). The government guarantees 10 percent of the loans (providing €150 million to the Mutual Counter-Guarantee Fund).

At present, about 3,000 loans have been made, amounting to €33.7 million [US$47.4 million]. The government is aiming to increase new loans by 25 percent per year.

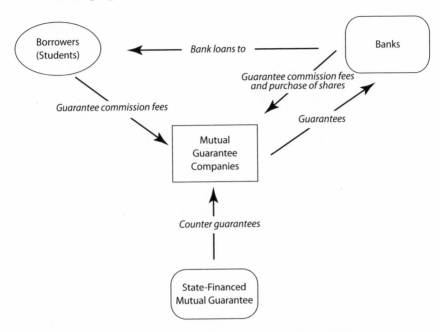

Student loan system in Portugal, with mutual guarantees (Heitor 2008)

South Africa: Student loans are awarded to public university students by the governmentally sponsored National Student Financial Aid Scheme (NSFAS). In 2006, loan amounts ranged between R 2,000 [US$517] and R 32,500 [US$8,398], and were need based. The interest rate, 7 percent in 2007, is relatively high (inflation plus two percentage points), with no in-school interest subsidy. However, fully 40 percent of the amount borrowed can be converted to a grant if the student passes all subjects, with this forgiveness prorated if only some subjects are passed.

Repayment of loans starts when an individual has full-time, permanent employment and his or her annual salary is at least R 26,300 [US$6,795], which is considered the threshold level of income. The repayment rate starts at 3 percent to 8 percent of one's salary, and the repayment period varies according to individual circumstances. There is no maximum repayment period, and interest continues to accrue even during times of unemployment or when one's salary is below R 26,300 [US$6,795].

Special legislation (TEFSA Act 121 of 1993) allows NSFAS to require employers to deduct loan repayments from the monthly salaries of graduates. The national tax and pension contribution systems are not used for collection, but the government has authorized the tax agency to report borrower incomes to NSFAS for income verification purposes (Jackson 2002).

The scheme's primary source of funds (75%) is the National Department of Education. However, international donors such as the European Union played a significant role in capitalizing the scheme in its early years. NSFAS continues to have a strong relationship with the international donor community.

Sweden: Sweden (along with other Scandinavian countries) has relied on student loan programs since the 1960s to cover student living costs and to free parents from the obligation of paying for these costs. (The university is tuition free, as the government already pays all instructional costs.) Swedish student loans are generally available—that is, all who wish to can avail themselves of the opportunity—with no risk rating or cosignatory requirement. The amount of the loan is based the student's own income or assets, and students may borrow up to SEK 1,148 per week [US$124].

Repayment of the loan begins not less than 6 months after the final receipt of study assistance. The maximum repayment period is 25 years or until the borrower reaches the age of 60. Interest is compounded, starting from the first payment. Since 2001, all borrowers must pay at least 5 percent of their income towards loan repayment, and the annual amount of payment increases each year by 2 percent. The government fixes the rate of interest annually at the government rate minus a 30 percent subsidy. The system also permits income contingent repayment.

United Kingdom: Students in England and Northern Ireland may either pay their tuition fees up front or apply to the Student Loans Company (via their local authority) for a student loan for tuition fees. The Student Loans Company pays the student fees directly to the college on the student's behalf. The loans accrue interest (4.8% in 2008), which is linked to a rate of inflation in line with the Retail Prices Index. The loan becomes due for repayment when a student has left a higher educational institution and is earning more than £15,000 [US$23,076] per year. Borrowers must pay 9 percent of their income in excess of £15,000 [US$23,076] each year.

Students may also take out means-tested maintenance loans that carry a zero real interest of 4.8 percent interest rate (reflecting current inflation rates). These loans, like the deferred fees, are repayable once the student has left the university and starts earning more than £15,000 [US$23,076] per year. Repayments (which are linked to earnings) are made through deductions by the employer through the PAYE tax system. Loan balances for both tuition fees and maintenance loans are written off 25 years after repayment commences.

United States: Loans and parental contributions are the bedrock of very extensive reliance on cost-sharing in the United States. Through 2008, the United States provided mainly conventional fixed-schedule loans, available to all students with some financial need (including some students from upper-middle-income families attending very expensive private colleges and universities) at minimally subsidized rates of interest. Through 2009, governmentally sponsored Stafford student loans were supplied either by participating banks or other financial institutions via the Federal Family Education Loan Program (FFELP), or directly by the federal government through the Federal Direct Loan Program (FDLP) if the college or university a student attended was a participant in that program. As of 2009, there is a proposal from the administration to phase out FFELP and provide all governmentally subsidized or guaranteed student loans through the direct loan program.

Whether or not this change in the origination and source of capital occurs (and there is strong political opposition to the proposed phase-out of FFELP), the interest rates and repayment periods are the same under both Stafford programs. The federal government guarantees subsidized student loans and pays all interest during the in-school years, as well as during a grace period for those with financial need (and it effectively does the same with the direct loans). The interest rate on loans made after July 1, 2006, is fixed at 6.8 percent. Students have a six-month grace period—starting the day after they graduate, leave school, or drop below half-time enrollment—during which they do not have to make payments. Students have from 10 to 25 years to repay their loan, depending on the repayment plan chosen. Under the standard repayment plan monthly payments are fixed for up to 10 years. Under the graduated repayment plan, monthly payments start off lower and then slowly increase every two years; most loans must be paid off in 10 years. Under the extended fixed or extended graduated repayment plan, fixed or graduated monthly payments may be stretched out for up to 25 years. For the Income Contingent Loan (ICL) option (available only on direct loans, and used mainly by borrowers under threat of default), the monthly payment is adjusted each year, based on annual income, family size, and the total amount of the loan. After 25 years, any unpaid loan amount is forgiven.

As mentioned in the preceding chapter, a hybrid fixed-schedule–income contingent student loan plan became available in the summer of 2009 under the Income-Based Repayment (IBR) option. The IBR limits loan repayments to 15 percent of the borrower's adjusted gross income in excess of 150 percent of the official poverty line (as adjusted annually and as applicable to the borrower's family size), thus moving borrowers with high debts and low incomes to an income contingent repayment schedule, with any remaining debts forgiven after 25 years. The take-up on the older ICL program—available only through direct loans (which will continue to be available alongside the more generous IBR one)—was very small; it remains to be seem whether the IBR option proves more attractive (as loan analysts believe it will be).

Unsubsidized Stafford loans that do not require demonstrated financial need are also available. They carry the implicit (but not insubstantial) subsidy of a governmental guarantee and the benefit of an interest rate near the government's borrowing rate, but they are otherwise unsubsidized. The borrower is responsible for interest on the loan. Generally, interest accumulates on the unsubsidized loan and is capitalized and added to the principal balance. A student can choose to make monthly interest payments during in-school and grace periods. Repayment terms are the same as for the subsidized Stafford Loans.

Much of the capital and loan origination—at least through 2009, and as long as the options under FFELP persist—is provided by the private banking sector, which in turn sells much of its student loan portfolio to private secondary markets. In participating colleges and universities, the federal government lends to students directly via the Federal Direct Loan Program and, in turn, either sells the notes in the private capital market or taps the federal government's general borrowing capability. Student borrowers in the FDLP can elect to repay their loans according to an income contingent repayment schedule, but as yet, relatively few have chosen this repayment option (which is *not* collected by employers along with income-tax withholding and insurance/pension contributions, and which mainly features a kind of assured refinancing that stretches out the repayment period, with very little ultimate low-earnings protection).

The federal government also makes Perkins loan allocations to eligible institutions so that they may provide low-interest loans to needy students, although the institutions must supply an additional 25 percent to the total loan allocation. Perkins loans are means-tested and provide students with up to $4,000 per year. Students have a nine-month grace period following graduation and then ten years for loan repayment. These loans carry a subsidized 5 percent interest rate paid by the federal government during in-school years and the grace period.

Table 7.2 summarizes several viable student loan schemes according to the design scheme elements (questions) used at the start of this chapter and in table 7.1.

The Role of Student Lending in Effective Higher Educational Finance

The following are some summary points implied by the theory of cost-sharing, the potential role of student loans, and the experiences (for the good or otherwise) of some of the student loan schemes described above.

1. Student loans have the potential both to increase higher educational accessibility and to allow some portion of the costs of instruction and of student living to be shifted to the student, to be paid as he or she enters the workforce. In these ways, student loans, both in theory and in practice, can provide additional revenue to higher education for the purposes of enhancing capacity, quality, and participation.

2. Student loans serve a variety of purposes, including: (a) putting money in the hands of students, thus promoting access; (b) shifting a portion of higher educational costs onto the student and possibly increasing the total amount of revenue available to higher education; (c) supporting (or purposefully declining to support) certain higher educational sectors, including private and even proprietary, or profitmaking, institutions; and (d) influencing postgraduation behavior by the conversion of grants to loans, or visa versa, depending on whether the graduate, with a potential repayment obligation, pursues certain occupations or practices in certain venues.

3. Student loans are an essential ingredient in any comprehensive policy of cost-sharing: that is, shifting a portion of the costs of higher education, including the expenses of student living, from a predominant and increasingly unsustainable reliance on the government (or taxpayer) to being shared with parents and students. For most countries and most institutions of higher education, the absence of some way for students to share in the substantial and rising costs of higher education means that such costs will have to be

covered by taxpayers and parents alone. In such cases, higher educational accessibility is likely to be limited to the most academically talented and the children of the affluent. Hence very many potentially talented students are likely to be left out, to the detriment of society, the economy, and the causes of opportunity and social justice.

4. Student loans as a policy tool to increase participation and widen access should always be accompanied by a variety of forms of subsidization, including a judicious use of grants, especially where there is genuine evidence of student debt aversion, as well as the effective grants represented by minimal interest rate subsidization, repayment forbearance, and eventual forgiveness in cases of lifetime low incomes or other conditions contributing to unmanageable repayment burdens. Financial assistance, including student loan schemes, should also be accompanied by other access policies, such as attention to the quality of middle and secondary schools, sensitivity to access barriers that may be rooted in ethnic or linguistic marginalization, dropout-prevention programs, appropriate postsecondary-sector diversification, attention to private-sector growth and quality, and programs to enhance completion and success for students once they have matriculated.

5. In keeping with the call for a comprehensive approach to increasing participation and widening access, a financially sustainable and politically realistic policy of cost-sharing, including tuition fees, should be implemented, along with targeted financial assistance policies such as student loan schemes and the other access policies mentioned above.

6. If student loans are to be a part of a comprehensive package of cost-sharing and financial assistance, loans for the target population should be provided in adequate amounts to cover tuition fees plus a minimal amount for student maintenance (less grants, expected parental contributions, and realistic expectations of term-time or summer earnings). The goal is to provide sufficient lending to permit higher educational participation without lessening a reasonable expected parental contribution or, where possible, reasonable part-time student employment.

7. The repayment obligation should be spread over just enough time so the monthly payments are manageable. Benchmarks should be established as to what constitutes a manageable loan repayment, but something like a maximum of 10 to 15 percent of earnings might be considered for a start. The fixed schedule of repayments may be graduated to increase over time at the option of the borrower.

Table 7.2   Examples of student loan programs

Element	United States	Kenya
1. Aim(s)	Maximize participation under cost-sharing; influence postgraduate practice and venue	Increase participation within wider cost-sharing policy
2. Eligibility	Generally available but means-tested; no cosignatories or tests of creditworthiness	Needy public and private sector students
3. Source(s) of capital	Banks, secondary markets, and government	Government
4. Originator(s) and mode(s) of disbursement	Banks and other approved lenders and higher educational institutions (via Direct Student Loans and Perkins loans) Loans disburseed to students through their colleges or universities	Higher Education Loans Board (HELB), a semiautonomous government institution established by an act of Parliament Tuition fees disbursed directly to universities by HELB and the balance disbursed to students
5. Ultimate bearers of risk	Government guarantee and lender (via an interest premium)	Government and cosignatories
6. Loans amounts and limits	Vary, according to first year, subsequent years, aggregate undergraduate loans, and total aggregate loans	Maximum award is three-quarters of tuition and maintenance costs

South Africa	China	Australia (HECS-HELP)
Increase participation of needy students	Increase participation of needy students	Cost-sharing
Needy public-sector students	Poor students in regular higher educational institutions	Students enrolled in Commonwealth-supported places in public universities
Primary source of funds (75%) is Department of Education	State-owned banks and commercial banks	Government
Financial aid offices at institutions test eligibility of applicants; determine size of award; make award and send approved loan agreement forms to the National Student Financial Aid Scheme (NSFAS) NSFAS approves loans and pays institutions directly	Banks originate loans and disburse them to students	Government Commonwealth then pays an amount equivalent to the loans directly to the institution
Government	Government and banks	Government
Loans usually cover tuition costs, but in cases of extreme need they may also cover living costs and traveling expenses Awarded based on means-testing, using estimated costs of attendance minus expected family contribution to arrive at award level	Tuition and living expenses	Up to the student contribution level set by the higher educational institution that the student is attending

continued

Table 7.2   Continued

Element	United States	Kenya
7. Amount and form of subsidization	Subsidized loans with minimal subsidization in repayment and zero interest during in-school and grace periods; also unsubsidized loans	Subsidized interest rate; no interest accrued during grace period (in-school years and one year after graduation)
8. Nature, shape, and duration of repayment period	• Loans can be conventional (Stafford and Perkins), hybrid fixed-schedule–income contingent (IBR), or income contingent (option on Stafford direct loans) Interest rates fixed Maximum grace period of six months (Stafford and IBR) or nine months (Perkins) Stafford loans: borrowers can choose a fixed (maximum 10-year) or graduated (maximum 25-year) repayment plan IRB loans: maximum 25-year repayment period (15 years if borrowers work in a recognized public service capacity), with repayments limited to 15 percent of borrower's adjusted gross income in excess of 150 percent of the poverty line Perkins loans: maximum 10-year repayment period	Conventional loan If in formal employment, the borrower has to authorize employer to deduct the loan repayment and remit it to the HELB Loan repayments may not exceed one-quarter of the borrower's monthly salary

South Africa	China	Australia
In some universities, students who pass all courses at the end of the year qualify for a 40 percent rebate on loans, and those who pass half of their courses can receive a 20 percent rebate	Government subsidizes 100 percent of the interest during in-school years	Subsidized interest rate (zero real interest)
Income contingent loan Interest variable at the rate of inflation, plus an additional 2 percent to cover adminis-trative and long-term unemployment/default costs Interest charged from origination of loan until completion of loan repayment Repayment of loan starts when an indi-vidual is in full-time permanent employ-ment and his or her annual salary is at least R 26,300 (US$6,796) Repayment rate starts at 3 percent to 8 percent of salary Special legislation allows NSFAS to require employers to deduct loan repayments from monthly salaries of graduates	Conventional loan Interest rate fixed at prime or government borrowing rate from the origination of the loan Maximum grace period is two years after graduation Maximum repayment period is six years	Income contingent loan Borrower must make compulsory repayment through the tax system when his or her yearly income reaches a minimum threshold (A$38,148 [US$27,444] in the 2006–7 income year) Zero real interest rate, indexed to CPI each year and compounded from the time of loan disbursement

8. If the loan form is a fixed schedule (that is, not income contingent), the scheduled repayments should be automatically deferrable in the event of unemployment, prolonged illness or loss of work, and other such demonstrated criteria. Borrowers needing a repayment deferment should be placed on an extended repayment schedule and have their monthly repayments lowered. Provision should be made to forgive the remaining indebtedness of a borrower after a certain extension beyond the originally scheduled repayment period if he or she is still unable to repay the initial debt at the required rate of interest. (Thus low earners will pay more-or-less income contingently for most of the life of the loan.)

9. Student loans will always be expensive, and a loan scheme should not be launched with the mistaken notion that it will ever become self-funded (that is, with repayments sufficient to finance all new lending). In fact, all student loan schemes that are generally available are costly to the government. These costs include (a) the costs of necessary guarantees to cover the inherently high risk of default; (b) the cost of subsidization to bring the effective interest rate down below either the prevailing rate of consumer debt generally or close to the government's own borrowing rate; (c) the cost of administration, including the costs for means-testing, origination, and collection; and (d) the costs of any debt forgiveness, whether such debts are forgiven to encourage academic success or postgraduation behavior, or to reflect low lifetime earnings (or the failure of a student's higher education to pay off sufficiently to repay his or her indebtedness without undue burden).

10. It is imperative to minimize these costs—consistent with the policy objectives of the student loan program—both because they can be very large and because excessive costs of student lending carry implicit opportunity costs in such forms as the forgoing of a larger number of loans, or a greater number of grants, that might have been possible for the same amount of taxpayer subsidization with a more cost-effective student loan program.

11. Three sources of costs that most student loan schemes can lessen without compromising their purposes are (a) reducing the base interest subsidization to a rate closer to the government's own borrowing costs; (b) minimizing servicing and collection costs with good lender practices (possibly through privatization of this portion of student lending); and (c) minimizing defaults by making sure that the student borrower views the initial loan as a real obligation by requiring some form of a repayment plan to be agreed upon to prior to graduation, by engaging in good collection practices, and possibly by re-

quiring or encouraging repayments to be made through employer deductions at the time of wage and salary payments.

12. To lessen the government's financial exposure, the risk of default should be shared between the government and cosignatories. Some cosignatory requirements may need to be limited to moral persuasion and the loss of one's credit reputation, so as to avoid losing those parents—and thus losing the children from those who are able to borrow—who may have insufficient assets to pledge.

13. The origination of the loans should generally be vested in a public corporation that is accountable to, but insulated from, the government as much as possible. This public corporation should be legally able to set the terms and conditions of the student loans, hire and fire its own staff (including the chief operating officer) without political interference, execute contracts, and raise capital in the private capital market. In too many cases, the boards of student loan agencies and top agency personnel are constrained by politicians who either (or both) do not understand the underlying economics of loans and repayments or are afraid of alienating voters (especially volatile student bodies) by supporting the interest rates, rationing, and collection methods that are essential to real cost-sharing. Therefore, in addition to insulating the student loan agency as much as possible from politics, there need to be ongoing efforts to educate (as well as to listen to) key stakeholders—such as governmental and opposition politicians, top civil servants, students, and the general public—on the difficult decisions and complex tradeoffs involving higher educational quality, accessibility, and the needs of society and the economy. Universities and other higher educational institutions should also be involved in and committed to this process, fulfilling certain responsibilities such as means-testing and requiring mandatory repayment obligation counseling before the borrower can receive his or her degree. Institutions should also bear some of the financial consequences resulting from excessive defaults.

In summary, effective student loan programs are possible and can enhance both institutional financial viability and student accessibility and participation. However, student loans are exceedingly complex and require both proper design and good execution. Unfortunately, too many student loan programs have failed because of both poor design and poor execution. We hope that this chapter can contribute to the policy planning required to begin new student loan programs and to reform existing ones.

NOTES

1. BAföG is the abbreviation for *Bundesausbildungsförderungsgesetz*, or Federal Law for the Promotion of Education.

2. See Johnstone 2006a and 2006b for an elaboration of the theoretical tradeoffs between a dollar volume of general subsidies (e.g., to allow free or very low tuition fees for all students), the same dollar volume of targeted subsidies (i.e., grants, whether means-tested or rationed in some other way), and, finally, the same dollar volume of effective subsidies imbedded within subsidized student loans.

3. Johnstone (2004a, 2004b, 2006b, 2006c) has criticized not the income contingent repayment obligation itself, but the overselling of income contingency and the attribution of strengths to income contingency that can be built into fixed-schedule loans as well.

4. See Chapman 2006a, 2006b; Chapman and Ryan 2002.

REFERENCES

Chapman, Bruce. 2006a. *Government Managing Risk: Income Contingent Loans for Social and Economic Progress.* London: Routledge.

————. 2006b. Income Related Student Loans: Concepts, International Reforms and Administrative Challenges. In *Cost-Sharing and Accessibility in Western Higher Education: A Fairer Deal?* ed. Pedro N. Teixeira, D. Bruce Johnstone, Maria J. Rosa, and Hans Vossensteyn. Douro Series, Higher Education Dynamics, vol. 14. Dordrecht, The Netherlands: Springer.

Chapman, Bruce, and Chris Ryan. 2002. Income Contingent Financing of Student Charges for Higher Education: Assessing the Australian Innovation. Special international issue of *Welsh Journal of Education* 11 (1):64–81.

Chevaillier, Thierry, and Jean-Jacques Paul. 2006. Accessibility and Equity in a State-Funded System of Higher Education: The French Case. In *Cost-Sharing and Accessibility in Higher Education: A Fairer Deal?* ed. Pedro N. Teixeira, D. Bruce Johnstone, Maria J. Rosa, and Hans Vossensteyn. Douro Series, Higher Education Dynamics, vol. 14. Dordrecht, The Netherlands: Springer.

Heitor, Manuel. The Portuguese Loan System. Presentation at Conference on Increasing Accessibility to Higher Education, June 2, 2008, Lisbon, Portugal.

Jackson, Roy. 2002. The National Student Financial Aid Scheme of South Africa (NAFAS): How and Why It Works. Special international issue of *Welsh Journal of Education* 11 (1):82–94.

Johnstone, D. Bruce. 2004a. The Applicability of Income Contingent Loans in Developing and Transitional Countries. *Journal of Educational Planning and Administration* [New Delhi, India] 18 (2):159–174.

————. 2004b. The Economics and Politics of Cost-Sharing in Higher Education: Comparative Perspectives. *Economics of Education Review* 20 (4):403–410.

————. 2006a. Cost-Sharing and the Cost-Effectiveness of Grants and Loan Subsidies to Higher Education. In *Cost-Sharing and Accessibility in Western Higher Education: A Fairer Deal?* ed. Pedro N. Teixeira, D. Bruce Johnstone, Maria J. Rosa, and Hans Vossensteyn. Douro Series, Higher Education Dynamics, vol. 14. Dordrecht, The Netherlands: Springer.

―――. 2006b. *Financing Higher Education: Cost-Sharing in International Perspective.* Boston: Boston College Center for International Higher Education and Sense Publishers.

―――. 2006c. Higher Educational Accessibility and Financial Viability: The Role of Student Loans. In *Higher Education in the World 2006: The Financing of Universities,* ed. J. Tres and F. López-Segrera. Barcelona: Palgrave Macmillan.

Ministère de l'Enseignement supérieur et de la Recherche, and OSEO. 2008. Fiche de Présentation du Prêt Étudiant. www.oseo.fr/notre_mission/garantie_pret_etudiant/.

Shen, Hong, and Wenli Li. 2003. A Review of the Student Loan Scheme in China. In *Policy Research and Dialogue: Student Loan Schemes in Asia,* ed. UNESCO Bangkok. Bangkok and Paris: UNESCO Bangkok and International Institute for Educational Planning.

Shibata, Masayuki. 2008. Student Financial Aid Policy in Japan. In *Report of the International Conference on Worldwide Perspectives of Financial Assistance Policies: Searching Relevance to Future Policy Reform for Japanese Higher Education.* CRDHE Working Paper, vol. 2. Tokyo: University of Tokyo, Center for Research and Development of Higher Education.

Vossensteyn, Hans. 2004. Fiscal Stress: Worldwide Trends in Higher Education Finance. *Journal of Student Financial Aid* 34 (1):39–55.

CHAPTER EIGHT

Cost-Sharing, Financial Assistance, and Student Behavior

The arguments for and against cost-sharing—that is, shifting a portion of the costs of instruction or the expenses of student maintenance from governments, or taxpayers, to parents and/or students—depend in the end on assumptions regarding what impacts tuition fees and other higher educational expenses borne by the student and family have on actual student enrollment behavior. Although the proponents or defenders of tuition fees and other forms of cost-sharing may justify their policy recommendations on the rationales of equity, efficiency, or the sheer need for revenue, as outlined in preceding chapters, such recommendations and any actual policy changes in the direction of greater cost-sharing also depend on the assumption that a shift of some costs to students and/or parents will not substantially lessen or otherwise detrimentally alter the higher educational participation of academically able and interested students from low-income families or other disadvantaged backgrounds. This assumption in turn depends on the proposition that some policy-driven combination of means-tested, or targeted, grants or student loans, generally in combination with a continued subsidy for most of the costs of instruction (that is, with an assumption of relatively modest public-sector tuition fees of no more than, say, 20%–40% of full instructional costs), and sometimes in combination with targeted subsidies for food, lodging, and other necessary expenses, will make up for the lack of financial wherewithal in low-income families and maintain not just the theoretical opportunity, but the actual fact of higher educational participation among all social and economic classes.

In the Nordic countries or other nations (such as Australia or the constituent countries of the United Kingdom) that lack an officially expected parental contribution, the policy of assuring continued access and opportunity relies on the presuppositions that all academically able and interested students can find loans—that is, that student loans are generally available (i.e., not restricted only to creditworthy students or students with creditworthy cosignatories)—and, furthermore, that all students needing to borrow or otherwise defer their higher educational expenses will be willing to take on a reasonable amount of indebtedness in exchange for the advantage of having an opportunity for higher education. In other words, any country that relies on students bearing a portion of the costs either of instruction or of student maintenance—that is, relying on both the ability and the willingness of students to incur some indebtedness in order to access higher educational opportunities—needs to assume that no specific groups of these otherwise academically able and interested students (such as females, or students from low-income families, or students from certain cultures or ethnicities) are so averse to debt as to effectively preclude them from accessing these higher educational opportunities.

The opponents of cost-sharing, however—that is, those who continue to press for no or only nominal tuition fees and for substantial governmental subsidization of a student's food and lodging—may be ideologically committed to the proposition that higher education, like elementary education, should be fully funded by the government, but they generally also contend that *any* level of tuition fees, even with a governmental policy of financial assistance, will preclude higher educational opportunities for some groups of otherwise deserving students. This opposition would be particularly strong—and quite unassailable—in a country that lacked any substantial amount of targeted student financial assistance. However, as virtually all countries profess to at least some level of targeted financial assistance, the opposition to increasing the share of higher educational costs to be borne by parents and/or students is generally more nuanced and may take any or all of the following forms of argument:

- The available financial assistance is inadequate, forcing children of the poor to have to live in unreasonable poverty, or to drop out periodically for want of money, or to have to work excessive hours and thereby delay their academic progress or neglect their studies, or, even worse, to underestimate altogether the private returns to the higher educational experience and thus to make a seemingly economically rational—albeit incorrect—decision not to attend at all (or to drop out).

- The available financial assistance, while possibly adequate at the time that cost-sharing policies were introduced, will likely fail to keep up with the inevitably rising expenses of tuition fees and costs of living, thereby eroding over time the ability of this financial assistance to maintain its promise of access and wide-scale participation—thus constituting a good reason for strenuous opposition to the implementation of cost-sharing in the first place.

- The available financial assistance, while allowing access to certain low-tuition-fee public institutions (perhaps only to lower-status, short-cycle institutions), is insufficient to provide children of the poor with the option of attending the best (oftentimes, especially in the United States, the private) institutions of higher education, thereby giving such students equivalent access, perhaps, but not really equal experiences.

- The high tuition fees and other expenses associated with a higher educational experience—while possibly surmountable through available financial assistance at the time a young person in high school might apply, be accepted, and matriculate—may seem so high to both the student and his or her parent(s) in the middle school years, and the financial assistance opportunities seem so distant (if they are even known at all), that the student never aspires to a higher education, never takes the proper university preparatory courses, and never applies him- or herself academically until it is too late. The opportunity for higher education is thereby lost, or at least severely diminished, not because of seemingly out-of-reach tuition fees and other expenses at the time of high school graduation (costs that might well have been overcome by available financial assistance), but lost many years before by a disconnect between the vivid specter of higher education's substantial tuition fees and the far less vivid (and even confusing) promise of future financial assistance.

- The available financial assistance depends too much on the willingness of the student to assume debt, so while an educational debt for young persons from middle- and upper-middle-class cultures might be entirely reasonable given the probable private returns (both monetary and nonmonetary) from a higher education, there are cultures that are debt averse, and this culturally specific debt aversion deprives students from those cultures of the opportunity for a higher education that depends on student loans or deferred tuition fees.

In short, both the arguments for and the arguments against tuition fees and other elements of cost-sharing—quite aside from politically and ideologically contested assumptions about equity and financial necessity—rely on complex assumptions about student behavior: specifically, how the expenses of higher education, and especially how changes in tuition fees and the costs of student living—as modified by financial assistance, including both grants and loans and the degree of loan subsidization—affect decisions to

- aspire to higher education early enough to take the proper college preparatory curriculum, succeed academically, and go through the necessary steps of applying to a college or university and applying for available financial assistance;
- matriculate and persevere in attending some college or university;
- apply to and matriculate in the *right* college or university (even if it is more expensive or farther from home, and even if it requires more educational debt or part-time employment);
- have the opportunity to live in a college residence or to otherwise live independently—which in many countries has been a part of the total college or university experience—instead of having to live at home with parents solely for financial reasons; and
- have a true choice in attending a higher educational institution full time, which allows a student to complete a degree quickly and devote more time to studies, or attending part-time, which means spending a lengthier period in school, with more time for employment (and thus more earnings) and likely a higher standard of student living.

Methodological Complexities and Difficulties in Researching Student Behavior

A tuition fee is a price, albeit generally a very subsidized one, for what is generally a very highly sought-after product in a supply-constrained market. Both of these qualifications make a tuition fee quite unlike a true price that clears the market: for example, the price of oranges in a competitive market, where basic economic price theory tells us that an increase or a decrease in the price will decrease or increase the quantity of oranges demanded as well as the supply offered until a new equilibrium is reached. Economists study what they term the *price elasticity of demand*, in which price elasticity is a measure of the responsiveness of the quantity demanded (or the total revenue) to a change in price. A price-elastic good is one in which the quantity demanded is sensitive to a variation in price—such as the previously mentioned oranges in the marketplace; a price-inelastic good or service is one in which the quantity demanded will remain essentially the same in the face of increases (or decreases) in price—such as essential medicines or foodstuffs like bread.

Extending this principle to tuition fee policies, then, politicians and policy analysts are interested in the degree to which the imposition of tuition fees where they did not heretofore exist, or an increase in tuition fees where they have previously existed, will cause a drop in the quantity demanded (i.e., enrollments) and thus lose some of the higher-educated population that society or the economy presumably needs. It is both observable and supported by research (e.g., Vossensteyn 2005) that a highly subsidized, greatly demanded, and supply-constrained good like higher education will not see any substantial decline in aggregate enrollments with a relatively modest imposition of, or expansion in, tuition fees. The issue, rather, is the degree to which a rise in tuition fees causes a decline in enrollments and higher educational opportunities among the poor or those otherwise ambivalent about the decision to enroll (in a sense, to purchase an education) in the first place, and thus diminish the policy objective not so much of enrollments in the aggregate, but the principle of access to or equal opportunity for a higher education.

To further complicate the question, however, in any country in which the policy objective of access depends on financial assistance, the relevant tuition fee price is not simply the tuition fee itself, or the change in the size of tuition fees, but the change in *net* tuition fees: that is, after the application of financial assistance. At this point, policy formulation and policy research begin to become more complicated. For example, policy analysts want to know what size grant or loan is needed to offset a tuition increase and whether there is likely to be a difference between the net price effect of financial assistance in the form of grants as opposed to financial assistance in the form of loans or deferred tuition fees. Further, would there be a difference between the likely response to a highly subsidized loan as opposed to a less-subsidized one when both loans would place the same amount of money (or discounts) in the hands of the students, even though the true costs—as measured by the discounted present values of the repayment streams—would be quite different?

There has been a great deal of research into the price elasticity of demand for higher education, although this research has mainly been in the United States and some other OECD countries. On the whole, the research is methodologically limited, at least for the purpose of guiding good policy in the politically volatile policy arenas of cost-sharing and setting or raising tuition fees. One of these limitations is a preoccupation with tuition fees (or net tuition fees), as though these are the only prices—or, better, the only expenses essential to attending college—that might affect enrollment behavior. In fact, at least in public higher educational sectors throughout the world, food, lodging, travel, and the other necessary costs of student living (and the likely annual increases in such expenses) are far greater than the relatively modest tuition fees that prevail in most countries (or the equally modest enlargement of these fees), and are thus far more likely to impact enrollment behavior than changes in public tuition fees. However, as Heller (2001) points out, tuition fees and financial assistance are the principal enrollment-affecting factors under the direct control of governments, and thus they receive the bulk of both analytical and political attention.

A more serious limitation of most of the price elasticity research on tuition is the use of aggregate enrollments as the principal, and sometime the sole, dependant variable. Thus a typical research finding in such studies is that a tuition fee increase of x dollars will likely lead to an aggregate enrollment decline of y percent or a total of z students (e.g., Leslie and Brinkman 1989). The first problem with such a conclusion is that, at least in the United States, it is so contrary to observations: in most years colleges and universities experience rises in tuition fees (sometimes quite dramatic ones), yet enrollments almost never decline. The principal reason, of course, is that the typical amount of the tuition fee increases, at least in the public sector, are actually quite small in comparison to the total price tag of a year's worth of living expenses, and they are particularly modest in comparison with the perceived value of this highly sought-after and still highly subsidized product.

Another reason for the general absence of observed aggregate enrollment decline in response to a rise in public tuition fees in the United States is that there are so many ways of absorbing a public-sector tuition fee increase of, say, several hundred dollars: alterations in cost-of-living expenditures, additional borrowing, extra hours of part-time employment, moving back home with one's parents, or even changing institutions. These are not trivial behavioral responses, and some of them (e.g., having to change institutions, or borrow more, or spend more time in outside employment) may be detrimental to the higher educational process and thus be a legitimate object of policy interest and research (e.g., Simpson 2005). However, most of the research on tuition price elasticity has confined itself to discernable changes in aggregate enrollment and essentially ignored these other, more likely, and still significant behavioral responses to a change in net tuition fees. For example, in the absence of research, Unger (2004) can only speculate on whether, in Austria, the 6 percent growth in the proportion of working students and the expansion in the average number of hours worked per week since 1998 has been due to the introduction of tuition fees in 2001.

A similar methodological limitation in some of the earlier studies that concentrated only on aggregate enrollment and observed little or no response to a relatively small change in the price of this greatly demanded and highly subsidized product (i.e., public higher education), is that any behavioral response would be almost certain to differ very substantially according to the socioeconomic status of the family. Obviously, middle- and upper-middle-income families can absorb what is most frequently a relatively small hike in tuition fees: probably through spending a bit more of their current income or even, if required, with some additional borrowing or dipping into savings. But financially dependent children of low-income families may have a much harder time doing so, and therefore a much more complex enrollment decision to make. Still, their behavioral response is more likely to be borrowing more, adding extra part-time employment, spending less, dropping to part-time-student status, or at worst, dropping out for a semester, rather than dropping out altogether or declining to enroll in the first place. However, whatever the students' behavioral responses to the normal yearly fluctuations in tuition fees might be, any significant responses are almost certain to be confined mainly to those on the socioeconomic margin.

Methodologically, research into tuition fee price elasticity, like so much of social science research, is limited mainly to quasi-experimental statistical techniques. In other words, policymakers would have more robust information on which to make tuition fee and financial assistance policies if they could increase or decrease tuition fees (or financial assistance) in certain randomly selected colleges and universities, or apply these increases only to random samples of students and then test for behavioral differences between the experimental and the control populations, as in the biomedical model of experimental research. Since such experiments are exceedingly difficult, ethically dubious, or altogether impossible in the study of student enrollment responses to tuition fees, researchers must employ other statistical techniques to attempt to control for all the factors that might influence student enrollment behavior in order to isolate, within some parameters of statistical probability, the likely effect of a change in tuition fees (or in financial assistance). At best—even with a sufficient sample size, many other measurable independent variables, and careful controls—such econometric studies still mainly only suggest the percentage of aggregate enrollment variance among groups in the population that may be attributable to a rise or fall in tuition fees.

In response to this difficulty in assessing actual enrollment behavior, some researchers looking into the question of student behavioral response to policy changes in tuition fees and financial assistance have resorted to surveys of existing or prospective college or university students and posed hypothetical questions about their likely responses to such policy changes. This research has some use in guiding policy in the politically sensitive arenas of tuition fees and financial assistance, and it is frequently all the information there is coming directly from students. However, aside from the obvious problems that must be overcome in any survey research (such as sample bias, sample size, statistical power, nonresponse bias, and the like), there are at least two sources of response bias that are a function of the specific issue of policy changes in tuition fees or financial assistance. The first is the likelihood that at least some students will interpret a supposedly hypothetical question about their response to a hike in tuition fees as a probe from policymakers, and such students may well conclude that a response of "no effect" is akin to an invitation for policymakers to precede with a fee increase that is presumably desired by the respondents. A more politically savvy response, therefore, might be for students to say that they would of course have to drop out altogether—an answer which, they might assume, would at least reinforce a hoped-for political opposition to the proposed increase.

A second inherent response bias in the issue of student behavior can arise when students who have dropped out are queried about why they have done so. In fact, dropping out may be a function of many factors, including academic difficulties, academic boredom or disinterest, or personal problems (what adults might term "youthful irresponsibility") arising from their sudden release from parental supervision. All of these reasons, however, attribute the cause for this behavior to the student, along with some implication of failure or blame. A more socially and personally acceptable rationale for dropping out, however, is for a student to attribute the reason for this action to others—such as to the policymakers who increased tuition fees or who did not provide sufficient financial assistance. This in no way suggests that financial difficulties are not a legitimate reason—albeit generally one among others—either for dropping out or perhaps for deciding not to enroll in the first place. However, as there are many politicians and students leaders, especially in those countries where cost-sharing is still so politically and ideologically contested, who will wish to discredit tuition fees on the basis of their alleged barrier to widely accepted political values such as access and participation, it is well to be cautious about making critical policy decisions on the basis of such research without adding some perspective (and perhaps a pinch of skepticism).

Conceptual Complexities in Assessing Student Enrollment Behavior

Complexities in the assessment of student behavioral responses to policies regarding cost-sharing, tuition fees, and financial assistance can be conceptual as well as methodological. For example, the very policy premise that cost-sharing ought not to preclude otherwise academically able and interested students from accessing higher educational opportunities is attractive, and perhaps even obvious on its face, but in practice it is conceptually complex. In virtually all countries, children from low-income backgrounds—whose parents may be unlikely to have finished high school, much less to have had the advantage of a higher education—are far less likely statistically to aspire to a higher education, or to have had the learning advantages of a home with educated parents, or to have been educated at a neighborhood school with the best teachers and educationally aspiring peers. Therefore, to the extent that finishing high school and going on to a college or university requires not only hard academic work, but may also require assuming an educational debt and perhaps needing to take a part-time, generally low-paying job, it is entirely natural (and virtually inevitable) that young people from such backgrounds will (again, at least statistically) be not only less academically prepared, but will also seem less academically ambitious, or more academically ambivalent, than their age peers from more educationally advantaged backgrounds. It also stands to reason that this greater ambivalence might be at least partially overcome by requiring less debt or less part-time employment on their part: that is, either by asking such students to pay lower tuition fees or by giving them financial assistance that consists only of grants rather than loans. The policy issue, then, is the degree to which students from very low-income (or otherwise disadvantaged) backgrounds should be held to less-stringent cost-sharing requirements— such as expecting less educational debt or not as much part-time or summer employment—than other students with equivalent financial needs who may have had the advantages of better academic preparation and a more robust higher educational aspiration in preparation for the sacrifices entailed in securing a college or university degree.

Another conceptual question, especially in countries where there is a great diversity of higher educational opportunities—differing in selectivity and prestige and therefore in status and doors to be opened—is the extent of the desired higher educational opportunities. Should they merely provide access to some institution of higher education, which may be the one that is least selective and has the lowest cost, or should financial assistance bring the best higher educational opportunities within range of all students, even if this requires a great deal of taxpayer-borne financial assistance and even if it effectively obviates one purpose of cost-sharing, which is to supplement scarce public revenue? This is at least in part a question involving suppositions about student behavior, in that it requires knowledge of (or at least assumptions about) the degree of public subsidization required to overcome the presumed lesser academic preparation and aspirations that are associated with students from low-income or otherwise disadvantaged backgrounds.

Finally, to the degree that debt aversion does exist and is associated with certain socioeconomic classes, ethnicities, or cultural backgrounds, and to the extent that this aversion goes beyond a mere dislike of debt and results in actual behavior not to matriculate if matriculation requires some assumption of

Chile: A Case Study of Policy and Enrollment Behavior

Chile's experience with higher educational participation offers an illustrative case of the dynamics of changes in university pricing. Higher education was free until 1980, but it was very limited and elitist and was offered by only eight traditional universities (comprised of two state universities and six state-financed private universities). In 1980, higher educational reforms were introduced that reorganized the public higher educational sector into 25 traditional universities eligible for state funding (the traditional 8, 3 new Catholic universities, and 14 new state institutions), deregulated the private higher educational sector, and introduced significant tuition fees in all public institutions, along with a means-tested student loan program to cover tuition fees in the 25 traditional universities (Brunner 1993; Matear 2006).

Enrollments in universities with public funding grew rapidly in the subsequent ten years (13%), despite the high tuition fees. The overall participation rate of the relevant age group in higher education grew from 9 to 16 percent (Brunner 1993, 1997; Vargas 2003) and there was little change in the socioeconomic composition of the students (Brunner and Briones 1992).

The return to a democratic government in 1990 led to the consolidation of Chile's market model for higher education and the introduction of some corrections (Brunner 1997). Between 1992 and 1996, tertiary enrollments grew by almost 50 percent for the richest income quintile and by 34 percent for the 4th quintile; however, they barely moved at all for the lowest income quintile (Holm-Nielsen, Zúñiga, and Hansen 2002). Poor students continued to have difficulty qualifying for the more academically demanding public universities, and these students did not have sufficient money to enroll in private universities.

Additional student financial assistance policies were added and old ones reformed in an effort to remove the financial barriers for low-income students. Between 1997 and 2003, public support for student financial assistance rose by 87 percent (Holm-Nielsen 2005). In 2002, students were no longer required to provide cosignatories for their loans and in 2006, financial support was extended to students in the new private universities (Matear 2006). The new policies have contributed to dramatic increases in overall access in the last twenty years (from 16% of 18- to 24-year-olds in 1990 to 37.5% in 2004), and a not insignificant portion of this growth has been in the lowest income quintile (from 4.4% of the relevant-aged, low-income population in 1990 to 14.5% in 2003). Overall, in Chile there has been a move toward greater equity in access to education among the various socioeconomic groups, alongside its marketization/privatization of the higher educational sector and success in meeting this goal that exceeds that of its neighbors—including those like Brazil that retain free higher education. Chile's example would argue that when introduced with adequate means-tested student financial aid (whether via grants or loans), tuition fees do not necessarily have a negative effect on enrollment or on the socioeconomic composition of the students.

debt, policymakers need to decide just how far the government should go in dealing with this debt aversion. Should the government replace, just for these students, what would otherwise have been an expectation of some level of student indebtedness with an outright grant, at considerably greater cost to the taxpayer? In short, is it appropriate public policy to treat an allegedly debt-averse student more favorably than a student who accepts the appropriateness of an investment in his or her higher education? Some scholars of student behavioral response to tuition fees and financial assistance (e.g., Vossensteyn 2005) doubt whether some students' declared aversion to debt is a significant determinant of actual enrollment behavior. Others, most notably Callender (2003; Callender and Jackson 2008) in the United Kingdom, allege that debt aversion is real. They contend that it is a fairly widespread cultural phenomenon within many of the UK minority cultures—even if its actual impact on enrollment behavior is complex and not altogether clear—and that equitable public policy needs to recognize it as such in order to provide genuinely equivalent higher educational opportunities. An opposing view maintains that a willingness to assume appropriate levels of debt—quite aside from the extent of debt aversion or its actual impact of enrollment behavior—is simply a feature of modernity, not unlike the acceptance of certain social mores, or current tastes in dress or music, or the use of credit cards, or indeed the aspiration to higher education itself. This skeptical perspective suggests that the taxpayer should not be expected to subsidize such a particular and arguably self-servingly cultural norm as debt aversion, even if it can be linked to the enrollment behavior of some students. In short, like most of the research on student behavioral responses to tuition fees and varieties of grant and loans, research on debt aversion does not yet appear sufficiently definitive even for scholarly consensus, much less to make a major impact on higher educational policies dealing with student financial assistance.

Research on Student Enrollment Behavior

For all of these conceptual and methodological complexities, and for all of their less-than-definitive and sometimes even contradictory findings, there is a large body of research on student enrollment behavior in response to tuition fee and financial assistance policies. For example, research studies in Australia (Andrews 1999; Chapman and Ryan 2003), Austria (Pechar 2004; Unger 2004), Canada (Junor and Usher 2002; Educational Policy Institute 2008; Johnson

2008), China (Li and Min 2000; Li 2007), the Netherlands (Jongbloed 2005), New Zealand (LaRocque 2003), the United Kingdom (Vossensteyn 2005; Brown and Ramsden 2008), and the United States (Leslie and Brinkman 1989; Heller 1997) confirm that at the macro level, the demand for higher education is relatively inelastic in the face of price increases—or, as in the case of Ireland in 1995, even in the face of tuition fees being scrapped altogether. However, in some countries, including Canada and the United States, or at certain tuition fee levels, there may be a discernable impact on enrollment behavior for children and families of low socioeconomic status and from some ethnic or minority racial groups.

Additionally, the meta-analysis of early research by Leslie and Brinkman (1989)—as well as more recent research from such scholars as McPherson, Schapiro, and Winston (1993); Heller (1999); Vossensteyn (2005); and Vossensteyn and Jong (2006)—conclude that increasing or decreasing grants or tuition-fee discounts—that is, what might be viewed, at least in the United States, as lowering or raising net tuition fees—have similar effects on aggregate enrollments as do the commensurate changes in the tuition fees themselves. However, they have found—again mainly for low-income students—that the deterrent impact of tuition fees on enrollment behavior is about twice as strong as the attractive power of grants.

In general, research confirms that the response of low-income students and students from ethnic minorities to grants and scholarships, similar to their response to changes in tuition fees alone, is significantly stronger than that of middle- and upper-income students. This research also suggests that different types of financial aid may have varying impacts on enrollment behavior and that grants may have a stronger influence on college enrollment than loans, work-study, or tax credits (Heller 2001; Vossensteyn 2005; Long 2008). In the United States, some research has found grants to be especially effective for enhancing African American and lower-income student matriculation. Some research has also found grants to be more effective than loans in promoting persistence among low-income students and infers from this finding that grants should have a similar advantage in terms of enrollment decisions (Usher 2006). However, most net price theory research does not take loans into account and therefore does not provide information on the degree to which loans could have had the same impact as grants (Educational Policy Institute 2008).

Research on student enrollment behavior has examined the impact of tuition fees and student financial assistance on enrollments and enrollment behavior. It has also attempted to evaluate the claim that certain groups of students—mainly ethnic and cultural minorities—are debt averse to such an extent that they will not borrow to access higher education and will either find other, less educationally sound ways to raise the required funds or will not enroll at all. Several conclusions can be drawn from such research:

1. At the aggregate level, the demand for education is relatively inelastic in the face of price changes.
2. In some countries, this demand inelasticity does not vary according to student characteristics (socioeconomic class, ethnic group, or race), while in others—including the United States—price changes appear to have a greater effect on students from lower socioeconomic classes and on minority students.
3. In some countries, even in nations where student enrollment is not impacted by price change, student behavior may vary as a result of price changes. Such behavioral alterations may include switching from full- to part-time programs, taking time off to earn money, working longer hours in off-campus employment or making adjustments to reduce living costs (moving home, getting a roommate, doing without cellular phones or computers, etc.).
4. Grants appear to have a stronger positive impact on student enrollment than do loans, although the research is not conclusive.
5. While there is no doubt that debt aversion exists among some cultures, and while students alleging debt aversion prefer not to take up loans, there is no conclusive evidence that this aversion translates into actual behavior and precludes students from enrolling in higher education. There is evidence, however, that debt-averse students may avoid debt through other cost-reduction strategies, such as attending less-expensive programs.
6. Behavioral economics offers a theoretical approach that can move beyond general price theory and human capital theory to explain student responses to changes in tuition fees and student financial assistance policies.
7. It is clear that more longitudinal research is needed on the impact of cost-sharing and student financial assistance policies on higher educational accessibility, enrollment behavior and student behavior.

In summary, research has attempted to discern the effects of cost-sharing, and especially the effects of the imposition of, or increases in, tuition fees on student enrollment behavior. Such research is important and should continue. However, behaviors as complex as the decision to enroll in some college or university, as well as deciding where to enroll, whether to attend full- or part-time, and the like, are difficult to discern using empirical research at its best— and such choices are all the more complicated and limited when confounded by political and ideological agendas. And with due respect to the many competent researchers, of both quantitative and qualitative bent, who have labored on the methodologically complex issue of enrollment response to changes in tuition fees and student assistance, their results are not likely to have much impact on or even be of interest to policymakers. even though critical decisions concerning tuition fees, grants, loans, and other subsidies lie in the latter's hands.

Cost-Sharing and Student Behavior

Ultimately, student enrollment behavior in connection with policies that attempt to shift more of the higher educational costs to parent and students—in conjunction with financial assistance in the form of targeted grants and generally available student loans—rests on the degree to which such increasing costs will still allow and encourage students (particularly lower-income students) to

- aspire to and prepare for higher education while in middle and secondary school, knowing that higher education is financially possible and will almost certainly, although by no means inevitably, pay off;
- matriculate and complete a degree in *an appropriate* college or university;
- with additional indebtedness, and with even more parental sacrifice, matriculate and complete a degree in the *best possible* college or university;
- attend a higher educational institution without having to engage in excessive outside employment;
- live in a college or university residence or otherwise live independently as a young adult (if this is the prevailing college-going culture) without excessive *deprivation*; and

- attend a college or university and live as most other students do
  without incurring excessive *debt* (that is, keeping debt at levels that
  most graduates will be able to repay).

Clearly, all these behavioral aims are both subjective and aspirational. Appropriate levels of parental contribution, or term-time employment, or reasonable student debt loads—like appropriate standards of student living and per-student university expenditures—will depend on many factors, including a country's wealth (per-capita GDP), its current level of massification (gross tertiary-level enrollment rate), the degree of price and status differentiation among alternative higher educational institutions, and the cultural acceptance of credit and debt. These appropriate levels and standards will also depend on the extent to which the priority of social equity—as opposed, rather, to competition or individualism or meritocracy—is embedded in a country's sociopolitical system. What is excessive deprivation to a young student in a wealthy OECD country might not be so to a young student in sub-Saharan Africa. A degree of equality between institutions or among students that may be prized in Scandinavia might be considered excessive and stifling in England or the United States. The "best possible" college or university has a very different meaning in the United States, where institutions of higher education strive to differentiate themselves by status and often by price, than it would in most of continental Europe, where there is little institutional differentiation in price and, until the end of the first decade of the twenty-first century, supposedly little differentiation in status. And the challenge of maintaining high levels of both academic preparation and higher educational aspirations in secondary schools is much greater in the United States—with its pockets of urban poverty and failing schools, exacerbated by the peculiarly American constitutional principle of local school control—than in a country where the nature and the financing of basic education through high school is a national responsibility and where low income may be common but is not likely to be as associated with dysfunctional families, crime-ridden neighborhoods, failing schools, and racial discrimination.

For all of the complexities in examining student behavior in the face of different tuition fee and financial assistance policies, however, and for all of the country-specific variations in parental, student, and governmental assumptions and expectations regarding higher educational accessibility, several broadly applicable policy conclusions about student behavior may be appropriate:

1. Policies to widen access and participation cannot depend solely on
    policies dealing with either finance or admission standards at the
    point of college or university entry. The goal of equitable access to
    higher educational opportunities must begin in the middle and
    secondary schools, where academic preparation, study habits, and
    higher educational aspirations are formed, and must include (if such
    be the case) learning that financial assistance will be available and
    that higher education is not an aspiration merely for the wealthy.

2. The possible financial barriers to higher educational participation
    include both the expenses of student living and the costs (if any)
    associated with tuition and other fees paid to the college or univer-
    sity (or deferred and paid later to the state). In almost all countries,
    including the United States, and notwithstanding the political
    theater associated with policies surrounding tuition fees, the ex-
    penses of student maintenance are usually far greater, and thus
    more significant to the issue of financial accessibility, than are
    tuition fees.

3. A governmental policy of widening higher educational participation
    to include more students, especially from lower-income families,
    requires financial assistance in the form of targeted (i.e., means-
    tested) grants and generally available loans (i.e., available without
    regard to the creditworthiness of either the family or the student).
    In addition, the imposition of tuition fees where they did not
    heretofore exist, or of very sharp rises in tuition fees where they
    have existed, requires a commensurate increase in financial assis-
    tance, either in the form of additional targeted grants or additionally
    available student loans (or other payment-deferral arrangements).

4. By and large, higher education is quite price inelastic: that is, the
    imposition of, or increases in, tuition fees are unlikely to lead to
    changes in enrollment behavior, either to preclude potential students
    from enrolling or to cause enrolled students to abandon their higher
    education. This general price inelasticity (at least of public higher
    education) exists because a postsecondary education is greatly valued
    by students and their families alike and is, furthermore, highly sub-
    sidized in almost all countries. Therefore, most students will accom-
    modate an imposition of, or an increase in, tuition fees (or other
    elements in the total expenses associated with going to college) with

additional funds from parents or other family members, or extra borrowing, or more part-time employment, or reductions in their living expenses.

5. Low-income families, however, may be unable (or, in certain circumstances, unwilling) to come up with additional funds, demonstrating tuition price elasticity. Therefore, it is imperative for there to be either commensurate increases in grants or in available funds to borrow.

6. Students from low-income families, at least in most countries and most cultures, will not only be more sensitive to tuition fee and other cost/expense hikes, but will also be more likely (again, at least statistically) to exhibit less academic preparation, a reduced awareness of the full returns from higher education, and more ambivalence regarding the sacrifices required, including the assumption of debt. Therefore, the matriculation and higher educational persistence of low-income students is more likely to be responsive to grants than to loans, and countries that are financially able to do so should consider *front-loading* grants: that is, providing a greater proportion of total financial assistance in the form of grants as opposed to loans in the early years, when dropping out is more likely (and when successful debt recovery is unlikely anyway).

7. Certain cultures may be more debt averse, or more averse to indebtedness for, say, daughters. A reasonable accommodation to such a disinclination to borrow is to limit student indebtedness to amounts (and interest rates and repayment periods) that can be amortized with the prevailing salaries of college and university graduates and to provide either income contingency or the hybrid types of repayment deferment or forbearance that were discussed in chapter 6, in order to assure borrowers that reasonable levels of student indebtedness will not become unmanageable or require default.

8. Policies of cost-sharing and financial assistance need to recognize that assumptions about parental financial responsibility, as well as assumptions about the minimal costs/expenses of student living based on the typical 18- to 24-year-old bachelor's degree student with no dependents, are inadequate for most students at graduate or advanced professional levels of education, or for students returning to finish undergraduate work after years in the workforce or military service. Thus minimally subsidized student loans may have to carry much of

the greater costs of student maintenance, as well as what are often higher tuition fees, at such levels of university education.

9. In the end, however, tuition fee policies—including regular increases in fees to maintain more-or-less constant shares of instructional costs by means of sufficient targeted grants and generally available loans—are not incompatible with wide participation and access, even for potential students from low-income families. The argument frequently presented by opponents of any augmentation to cost-sharing is that tuition fees will automatically exclude deserving students from low-income families or ethnic minorities, but this notion is supported neither by research nor by observation.

REFERENCES

Andrews, Les. 1999. *Does HECS Deter? Factors Affecting University Participation by Low SES Groups*. Canberra: Higher Education Division, Department of Education, Training and Youth Affairs.
Brown, Nigel, and Brian Ramsden. 2008. *Variable Tuition Fees in England: Assessing the Impact on Students and Higher Education Institutions*. London: Universities UK.
Brunner, José Joaquín. 1993. Chile's Higher Education: Between Market and State. *Higher Education Policy* 25:35–43.
———. 1997. From State to Market Coordination: The Chilean Case. *Higher Education Policy* 10 (3/4):225–247.
Brunner, José Joaquín, and Guillermo Briones. 1992. *Higher Education in Chile: Effects of the 1980 Reform*. PHREE Working Paper. Washington, DC: World Bank.
Callendar, Claire. 2003. *Attitudes to Debt: School Leavers and Further Education Students' Attitudes to Debt and Their Impact on Participation in Higher Education*. London: Universities UK and Higher Education Funding Council for England.
Callender, Claire, and Jonathan Jackson. 2008. Does the Fear of Debt Constrain Choice of University and Subject of Study? *Studies in Higher Education* 33 (4):405–429.
Chapman, Bruce, and Chris Ryan. 2003. Higher Education Financing and Student Access: A Review of the Literature. Working paper, Research School of Social Sciences, Australian National University, Canberra, ACT.
Educational Policy Institute. 2008. *Access, Persistence, and Barriers in Postsecondary Education: A Literature Review and Outline of Future Research*. Toronto: Higher Education Quality Council of Ontario.
Heller, Donald E. 1997. Student Price Response in Higher Education: An Update to Leslie and Brinkman. *Journal of Higher Education in Africa* 38 (6):624–659.
———. 1999. The Effects of Tuition and State Financial Aid on Public College Enrollment. *Review of Higher Education* 23 (1):65–89.
———. 2001. *Debts and Decisions: Student Loans and Their Relationship to Graduate School and Career Choice*. Education New Agenda Series. Indianapolis: Lumina Foundation for Education.

Holm-Nielsen, Lauritz B. 2005. Supply/Demand Side Financing: Dichotomy or Continuum? Paper read at the KEDI—World Bank International Forum: Financing Reforms for Tertiary Education in the Knowledge Economy, 8 April 2005, Seoul, Republic of Korea.

Holm-Nielsen, Lauritz B., Patricia García Zúñiga, and Thomas Nikolaj Hansen. 2002. *Chile—Human Resources for the Knowledge Economy.* LCSHD Paper Series. Washington, DC: World Bank, Latin America and the Caribbean Regional Office.

Johnson, David. 2008. Inter-Provincial Variation in University Tuition and the Decision to Continue to Attend University: Evidence from Youth in Transition Survey in Canada. Measuring the Effectiveness of Student Aid Research Paper. http://www.mesa-project.org/research.html.

Jongbloed, Ben. 2005. Strengthening Consumer Choice in Higher Education. In *Cost-Sharing and Accessibility in Higher Education: A Fairer Deal?* ed. Pedro N. Teixeira, D. Bruce Johnstone, Maria J. Rosa, and Hans Vossensteyn. Douro Series, Higher Education Dynamics, vol. 14. Dordrecht, The Netherlands: Springer.

Junor, Sean, and Alexander Usher. 2002. *The Price of Knowledge: Access and Student Finance in Canada.* Canada Millennium Scholarship Foundation Research Series. Montreal: Canada Millennium Scholarship Foundation.

LaRocque, Norman. 2003. *Who Should Pay? Tuition Fees and Tertiary Education Financing in New Zealand.* Wellington: Education Forum.

Leslie, Larry L., and Paul T. Brinkman. 1989. *The Economic Value of Higher Education.* New York: Macmillan.

Li, Wenli. 2007. Family Background, Financial Constraints and Higher Education Attendance in China. *Economics of Education Review* 26:725–735.

Li, Wenli, and Weifang Min. 2000. Tuition, Private Demand and Higher Education Expansion in China. Working paper, School of Education, Peking University.

Long, Bridget Terry. 2008. The Effectiveness of Financial Aid in Improving College Enrollment: Lessons for Policy. Working paper, Harvard Graduate School of Education, Cambridge, MA. http://gseacademic.harvard.edu/~longbr/college_information.htm.

Matear, Ann. 2006. Barriers to Equitable Access: Higher Education Policy and Practice in Chile since 1990. *Higher Education Policy* 19:31–49.

McPherson, Michael S., Morton Owen Schapiro, and Gordon C. Winston. 1993. *Paying the Piper: Productivity, Incentives, and Financing in U.S. Higher Education.* Ann Arbor: University of Michigan Press.

Pechar, Hans. 2004. Tuition Fees and Student Participation: Lessons from Austria. Paper read at the International Conference on Accessibility of Higher Education: Challenges for Transition Countries, 29–30 June 2004, Moscow.

Simpson, Bobby Jo. 2005. The Effects of the Increase in SUNY Undergraduate Tuition in the 2003–2004 Academic Year on Undergraduates at the University at Buffalo. Ph.D. diss., Department of Educational Leadership, State University of New York at Buffalo.

Unger, Martin. 2004. The Introduction of Tuition Fees in Austria: Some Empirical Effects. Paper read at Public Higher Education Under Pressure: 2nd International Workshop on Reform of Higher Education in Six Countries, 8–9 July 2004, Vienna, Austria.

Usher, Alex. 2006. *Grants for Students: What They Do, Why They Work.* Canadian Higher Education Report Series. Toronto: Educational Policy Institute.

Vargas, Andrea Repetto. 2003. *Access Barriers for Poor and Indigenous People in Chilean Higher Education.* LCSHD Paper Series. Washington, DC: World Bank, Latin America and the Caribbean Regional Office.

Vossensteyn, Hans. 2005. Perceptions of Student Price-Responsiveness. University of Twente, Enschede, The Netherlands. http://www.utwente.nl/cheps/publications/.

Vossensteyn, Hans, and Uulkje de Jong. 2006. Student Financing in the Netherlands: A Behavioural Economic Perspective. In *Cost-Sharing and Accessibility in Higher Education: A Fairer Deal?* ed. Pedro N. Teixeira, D. Bruce Johnstone, Maria J. Rosa, and Hans Vossensteyn. Douro Series, Higher Education Dynamics, vol. 14. Dordrecht, The Netherlands: Springer.

CHAPTER NINE

Cost-Sharing in Practice Worldwide

The shift of higher educational costs from governments and taxpayers to parents and students, as we have asserted and as will become more vivid in this chapter and in the appendix, has increased throughout the world in the last decades of the twentieth and the first decade of the twenty-first centuries. However, the widely divergent rationales for cost-sharing outlined in chapter 3 differ very much in salience, depending on the particular country and on its stage of economic development, wealth, and level of industrialization; its higher educational history and level of higher educational participation; its dominant political ideology; and the size and significance of its nonstate, or private, higher educational sector (if any).

The predictors or antecedents for an acceptance or a resistance to cost-sharing are complex and inconsistent. For example, the acceptance of cost-sharing would seem to be furthered by a history of good-quality private, tuition-fee-supported higher education. Such a history, at least in theory, should make families accustomed to paying tuition fees—if not by the families themselves, then by their neighbors: Japan and the United States are clear examples (although the expensive public-sector tuition fees in Japan are relatively recent). At the same time, the prevalence of a substantial and frequently high-quality, fee-dependent private sector in much of Latin America has not lead to an acceptance of tuition fees in the public sector, even though the benefits of free higher education are known to be disproportionately enjoyed by the children of the wealthy and otherwise advantaged.

A country's acceptance of cost-sharing would also seem to be advanced by the vigor of its free-market capitalism (i.e., its level of acceptance of the competition, individualism, inequalities, and economic instabilities that inevitably accompany capitalism). Free-market capitalism, at least in theory, should promote either (or both) private higher education and the privatization of public higher education. Vigorous free-market capitalism may also strengthen political opposition to continuous increases in public budgets and taxes—as opposed to command economies or welfare-state capitalism, in which very high levels of taxation and governmental employment are more apt to be taken for granted. The United States is a good example of such a vigorously capitalistic political economy that has an expensive but generally robust sector of private higher education and is also generally (if often reluctantly) supportive of tuition fees and the other elements of cost-sharing in its public sectors. And the United Kingdom, while featuring (to Americans) relatively low—and, since 2006, only deferred rather than up-front—tuition fees, is probably the most vigorously free-market country in Europe and has supported this position by its adoption, albeit with great reluctance and with some backsliding, of the first other-than-nominal tuition fees in Europe. The Nordic countries, with their welfare-state, or soft, version of capitalism, continue to resist any tuition fees, although Sweden plans to introduce tuition fees for non-European students in 2010. At the same time, however, tuition fees also continue to meet great resistance in most of the rest of capitalistic Western Europe. Furthermore —and also contrary to the assumed association of vigorous capitalism with a greater acceptance of cost-sharing—Scotland in 1998, followed by England and Wales in 2006, gave in to this same political resistance by shifting from up-front to deferred tuition fees. Ireland in 1996—in the very midst of its economic renaissance—appeared to have abandoned tuition fees, although it retained a very high level of other fees, ranging from €600 to €800 [US$588–$784], and by 2009, with the apparent end of the Irish economic miracle, the country is considering a resumption of tuition fees. And even in the aggressively capitalistic United States, regular increases in tuition fees meet with great political resistance—albeit generally with eventual acceptance in most states.

Finally, the acceptance of cost-sharing might seem to be furthered by substantial rates of higher educational participation. At the same time, high participation rates (for example, in the range of 30%–50% of the relevant age cohort) seem to have an uneven, if not at times a counterintuitive, impact on the acceptance of or resistance to cost-sharing in public higher education. The classic equity rationale for cost-sharing is predicated on the assumption that higher educational participation is disproportionately enjoyed by the children of the wealthy and otherwise advantaged, while the tax revenues that support it often come disproportionately from the middle and lower socioeconomic classes. A low rate of participation, mainly by the children of the wealthy, strengthens cost-sharing's equity rationale, while a very high level of participation, especially when this participation is relatively evenly spread across socioeconomic strata, undermines the equity argument. The substantial across-the-board participation in the Nordic countries is a confirming example of nations seemingly unmoved by any equity rationale in support of tuition fees. Similarly, but with an opposite effect, the ready acceptance of tuition fees by the ruling Communist party in China as early as 1997, when higher educational participation was clearly inequitably distributed (albeit less by wealth, per se, than by family education and position) reaffirms the equity rational in favor of tuition fees, convincingly trumping any Marxist or Maoist ideology of free higher education regardless of the distribution of its benefits.

On the other hand, when participation is very low—as in Francophone Africa, with rates well below 5 percent of the eligible population cohort and clearly inequitably distributed—the costs of higher education may simply seem not worth the political battle of attempting to shift higher educational costs from the government to parents and/or students—in spite of the supposed salience of the equity rationale—especially when the opponents are students (always a politically dangerous force in sub-Saharan Africa) and the elite (whether by wealth or political connections). When student numbers begin to rise and the financial austerity of the universities becomes truly crippling (despite frequent prodding by the World Bank), such very low-income plus low-participation-rate countries might begin to implement (or to reinstate) tuition fees, theoretically supported by the equity rationale, but these nations may balance their attempt at increased cost-sharing by inaugurating student loan schemes that—as in Ghana in 1988, Ethiopia in 2003, and Tanzania in 2005—may have little chance of being collected, but that may buy some very temporary peace with the World Bank, the students, and the politicians alike. China's example, seemingly to the contrary, where an initially low level of participation and a legacy of Communism nevertheless brought about a fairly steep tuition fee, may be a reflection more of the political power of the Party's leadership, which was better able to withstand the populist attraction of entitlements than the more openly, albeit fragile, democratic governments of other low-income, low-participation-rate countries.

In short, the introduction of cost-sharing may be shrouded by the generally complex and contested ideologies that frequently—especially on the part of political actors—obscure the motives for shifting costs that used to be governmental to parents and/or students. But the spread of cost-sharing, especially the adoption of tuition fees, is unmistakable and seemingly inexorable, at least in the non-Nordic world (and even Sweden plans to begin charging tuition fees for non-EU international students in 2010). Thus in most countries, the combination of rising higher educational cost pressures, ascendant liberal (or market-oriented) ideologies, and the success of cost-sharing policies in boosting higher educational revenues with little or no loss in accessibility together have furthered the worldwide shift of higher educational costs from being mainly or even exclusively the responsibility of governments (or taxpayers) to being shared as well with parents and students.

The United States is probably the poster country on behalf of cost-sharing, melding high-quality instruction and research and a substantial degree of higher educational participation with a cost-effective balance of university and other-than-university sectors, and with the significant financial support of parents, students, and philanthropy. The United States can be accorded this place because of its combination of

- extensive sector diversification, with some 40 percent of first-time postsecondary students entering at the level of the two-year community college;
- an extensive and robust tuition-fee-dependent private sector, constituting nearly 70 percent of the institutions and 22 percent of all US higher educational enrollment, and including both open-access and highly selective colleges and universities;
- tuition fees in all public colleges and universities, generally encompassing from 20 to 45 percent of undergraduate instructional costs;
- a broad range of financial assistance from federal (i.e., central governmental), state, institutional, and other private sources, and including

grants (mainly means-tested), loans (federally guaranteed and comprised of both means-tested subsidized and unsubsidized loans), and education tax credits, totaling some $143.4 billion in 2007–8 (College Board 2008);[1] and

- extensive philanthropic support for higher education—both in endowments, exceeding $149 billion in 2007 (National Association of College and University Business Officers 2008), and in annual support to both the private and the public sectors, adding some $29.75 billion to college and university coffers in 2007 (Council for Aid to Education 2008).

Although comparative aggregate statistics for public versus private financial support of higher education are unreliable because of the complications and inconsistent treatment of instructional versus other-than-instructional pur-poses, a similarly inconsistent treatment of externally funded research and medical/clinical operations, and the complexities of allocating and accurately reporting full compensation costs (including pensions and insurance), we believe it is safe to conclude that the United States gets more higher education—including both instruction/learning and research/scholarship—per direct public (tax) dollar than any other highly industrialized country because of this extraordinary level of nongovernmental revenues from parents, students. and philanthropists (or donors). Japan might be in relatively close second place because of its extensive private sector and its relatively high tuition fees in both the private and the public sectors. But Japan has far less revenue support from either endowments or current philanthropy. Australia, Canada, and New Zealand also have comparatively expensive tuition fees in their public sectors, but they generally have insignificant private sectors and also relatively negligible philanthropic support.

Europe may remain the most resistant region of the world to this trend of augmented cost-sharing, and especially to the trend of expanded tuition fees. However, by the end of 2008, most European nations other than the Nordic countries, even including six of the German Länder, had some form of tuition fees, however nominal, supporting their costs of instruction (CESifo Group 2007). Resistance to tuition fees in Europe has been strengthened by the region's affluence, its democratic institutions (and the great populist appeal of free higher education), and by the fact that students and/or parents, at least in most countries, are already paying for the expensive European costs of student maintenance. At the same time, the massification of higher education, which is a phenomenon in all countries, but which has been furthered in some European nations by a tradition of university admission as an entitlement for all graduates of academic secondary schools, has accelerated the trajectory of rising costs and revenue needs and has therefore supported the financial case for some kind of governmental revenue supplementation. In addition, the emergence of a more unified and more aggressively competitive Europe (especially on the European continent) has reinforced its need to compete more effectively with the leading public and private universities of the Canada, the United Kingdom, and the United States. The historic resistance to tuition fees is thus (slowly) giving way in most of other-than-Nordic continental Europe to a combination of higher education's voracious revenue needs and heightened recognition that free higher education alone does not assure equal access to quality higher education, nor do tuition fees, when allied with targeted financial assistance, necessarily diminish access.

This adoption of tuition fees extends to Russia and the other republics emerging from the former Soviet Union, as well as to the formerly Communist countries of Eastern and Central Europe that have been politically unable to abandon free higher education for the most academically well-qualified students. At the same time, they have nonetheless clearly moved in the direction of greater cost-sharing via such indirect but more politically acceptable mechanisms as freezing cost-of-living grants, increasing fees for food and lodging, and enlarging the numbers and the proportions of students admitted in the privately sponsored, or fee-paying, tracks (in addition to the political and legal acceptance of greater numbers of private, tuition-fee-supported institutions).

The Anglophone OECD countries of Australia, Canada, New Zealand, the United States, and the constituent countries of the United Kingdom (with some backsliding in the United Kingdom, especially in Scotland) have been leaders in the growth of tuition fees in public higher education, although only the United States also features a significant, high-priced, and generally high-quality tuition-fee-dependent private sector. The Anglophone countries, for all that they champion vigorous capitalism, free-market strategies, and New Public Management (see chapter 2 for a discussion of the latter), also feature a widely accepted political commitment to accessibility, with extensive financial assistance as well as a self-conscious, albeit politically contested, acceptance of a need to go well beyond financial assistance and embrace affirmative action, or preference policies, in order to raise the higher educational participation of those marginalized by socioeconomic class or ethnicity or by immigrant status.

Cost-sharing has also come to the former Socialist and Communist countries of Asia: from the highest tuition fees in the world (relative to per-capita income) in the case of Mongolia, to the implementation of near-universal tuition fees and substantial fees for food and lodging in China, to the more reluctant and indirect emergence of cost-sharing in India—this latter with both a rapid rise in private, tuition-fee-supported higher education and the start of tuition fees in some of India's public universities (which, however, have always had a myriad of other fees).

In free-market Asia, Japan features both a reliance on tuition-fee-dependent private higher education plus expanded tuition fees in the public sector, with financial assistance available only through loans. Korea and the Philippines also rely heavily on demand-absorbing private sectors to relieve their governments of many of the costs of their extensive higher educational provisions. The future of cost-sharing in India, the other newly emerging Asian giant, is complicated by its democratic, federal system of governance that seems to entrench the status quo, including a very large public sector, heavy governmental regulation, and continuing efforts to eradicate class- and caste-based inequalities with various entitlements and preferences.

In Latin American, the traditions of vacillating populism and *dirigism* (economic control and planning by the state) conflict with a surging higher educational demand and its consequent need for additional revenue. In 2009, Latin America featured public tuition fees that were mainly low but that varied widely, ranging from no tuition fees in Argentina, Brazil, Peru, and Uruguay (and, of course, Cuba); to nominal or moderate fees in Colombia and Mexico; to high tuition fees in Chile. Many South American countries rely extensively on fee-dependent, primarily demand-absorbing private sectors. This uneven but vibrant private sector may be a useful reminder of the fact that very many families will pay tuition fees when they must or when they want the higher quality that some private institutions are believed to provide—and thus a reminder that public sector colleges and universities in many Latin American countries are theoretically walking away from this revenue.

Finally, even the African continent is moving in the direction of greater cost-sharing, although with enormous political ambivalence. On the one side there are arguments pushing for tuition fees and other elements of cost-sharing: an almost desperate need for nongovernmental revenue, combined with very socially and politically compelling alternative needs for what few tax revenues there are, and further augmented by the disproportionate higher educational participation of the children of the (albeit relatively small) middle- and upper-middle classes. On the other side there is resistance to cost-sharing, especially in the form of tuition fees in the public sector: the combination of fragile democracies with immense poverty plus the legacy of African socialism makes any political advocacy of tuition fees politically dangerous. The continent's European colonial legacy compounds this political ambivalence: African countries (and politicians) can look at their vastly richer former colonial masters and observe many of these nations (especially France) continuing to resist tuition fees. Aside from South Africa and Kenya, the absence of workable, generally available student loan programs (at least as of the close of 2009) and the political and technical difficulties of targeting, or means-testing, financial assistance further contribute to the difficulties of implementing tuition fee policies in sub-Saharan Africa. At the same time, these constraints are beginning to fall to the universities' escalating desperation for revenue, the mounting pressures for additional higher educational capacity, and, in a growing number of countries, a continuing (albeit mixed) embrace of the *Washington Consensus* of liberal, market-oriented political economies.

Cost-sharing, then, is a worldwide trend that requires coordinating politically sensitive and technically complex tuition fee and financial assistance policies in order to augment university revenues while preserving (and preferably increasing) equity and accessibility. A policy of cost-sharing also requires some form of governmental stance towards the provision of private higher education, which has unexpectedly burst upon the scene in the decades before and after the turn of the twenty-first century. This especially applies in the former Communist world, where private forms of higher education were, of course, previously prohibited, but where a substantial level of higher educational expectations, a constrained supply of state-sponsored higher education, the difficulties of taxation (and, thus, limited public revenues), and the sluggish pace of curricular and other reforms in the established universities have combined to open significant market space for private, tuition-fee-dependent higher education.

We will conclude this chapter with some descriptive tables of the 2009 status of cost-sharing in selected countries in several regions, organized according to their levels of industrialization, their predominant political-economic systems, and their per-capita income. We shall look specifically at cost-sharing in four categories of nations: advanced industrialized countries, transitional countries, middle-income countries, and low-income countries. The countries selected for inclusion—both in the chapter tables that immediately follow as well as in the fuller descriptions provided in the appendix—are drawn from the country studies of the International Comparative Higher Education Finance and Accessibility Project of the University at Buffalo's Center for Comparative and Global Studies in Education, which has been the scholarly home of the authors and the many advanced graduate students who assisted in the compilation of the data underlying much of this book.[2] We have sought to include nations that are politically, economically, and educationally significant: that is, those likely to be models for other, frequently smaller countries with similar political and ideological leanings and similar levels of economic development and industrialization. However, inclusion or omission is partly by chance, at times dependent on the language facilities of our student research assistants or on other essentially opportunistic factors. Thus the countries that are included, while representative of their groups, are neither statistically random nor scientifically stratified samples.

The tabular country descriptions of the form and extent of cost-sharing can be specified by considering the following factors for each country:

1. *Tuition fees*: Specifically, whether a policy of tuition fees is officially expected of parents (or extended families) or, instead, is expected primarily of students (and thus is deferred in the form of loans, whether or not they are acknowledged to be such), as well as the extent of these tuition fees (i.e., the approximate proportion of institutional costs such fees are expected to cover).

2. *Means-tested expected parental (or extended family) contributions*: Specifically, whether these expected contributions—presumably means-tested, or targeted to low-income families—are to cover tuition fees (as described above), or the costs of student maintenance, or both.

3. *Governmental student financial assistance*: Specifically, whether this governmental financial assistance (as opposed to any philanthropically or institutionally provided aid or any tuition fee discounts) is in the form of means-tested grants, or generally available (and thus inevitably subsidized) student loans, or subsidies for food or lodging or other expenses of student living.

4. *The extent, official encouragement, and financial support of private higher education*: The extent of private higher education, as indicated (where data exist) by the approximate percentage of postsecondary enrollments in various private sectors, as well as the principal mode or modes of support (e.g., direct subsidies to private institutions, competitive access to publicly supported research; access to subsidized capital in the form of low-interest loans; private students' eligibility for governmentally subsidized financial assistance in the forms of grants, loans, and the like).

Advanced Industrialized Countries

The advanced industrialized countries in this summary include Australia, Canada, Japan, Korea, New Zealand, the United States, and Western Europe. Other industrialized countries within the Organisation for Economic Co-operation and Development (OECD) may be included in subsequent sections under in the classifications of transitional countries, such as Russia and the formerly Communist countries of Eastern and Central Europe, or middle-income countries, such as Argentina, Brazil, and Chile.

Higher Educational Variations in Advanced Industrialized Countries

Common features of advanced industrialized countries are high levels of industrialization, high per-capita levels of GDP, well-developed and efficient systems of taxation, and extensive public sectors, as well as a long-standing embrace of capitalism and liberal democracy. These countries also have well-established universities formed on the classical Humboldtian university model, with traditions of scholarship rooted mainly (although not exclusively) within the universities (France and Germany are exceptions, with extensive state-supported research institutes more-or-less independent of the established universities).

The advanced industrialized countries also exhibit important differences in their systems of higher education. These include differences in system structures (that is, the form and extent of nonuniversity institutions), institutional governance, the relationship of universities and other institutions of higher education to the state, and finance, including the extent and forms of cost-sharing:

- *Sector diversification*: The different and uneven forms of nonuniversity institutions include the two-year community colleges, the public and private comprehensive colleges and universities (granting baccalaureate and master's degrees), and the liberal arts colleges found in the United States; the German and Austrian Fachhochschulen; the French Instituts Universitaires de Technologie (IUT); and the Dutch Hogeschoolen (HBO). There is minimal nonuniversity development in Spain or Italy. The United Kingdom (before devolution) appeared to be backsliding on sector diversification when, in 1990, it abolished the binary line that had created a very sharp distinction between the universities and the polytechnics. However, the nation's move toward competitive research funding via a research assessment exercise has preserved considerable financial and status differentiation even within the nominally unified university sectors. The now-devolved constituent countries of the United Kingdom also feature short-cycle sectors for further education.
- *Internal governance*: The internal governance systems of the universities in advanced industrialized countries are all built on a model of substantial faculty influence (called *shared governance* in the United States), but with differing apportionments of authority between faculty, the state (or ministry), and institutional management. Management, for example, can be a French or German university rector, an American university president, or a British university vice-chancellor, with the power of chief executive officers in both the US and the UK systems strengthened by having ultimate authority vested in an external board of governors or trustees, as opposed to being determined by faculty election, as is the case for a continental European university rector. Since the idea of cost-sharing and a more ready acceptance of tuition fees tend to be associated with strong management, external (i.e., governing board) authority, and liberal (i.e., market-oriented) policies, the greater acceptance of cost-sharing in the Anglo-American model of university management is predictable.
- *Relationship to the state*: The relationship of universities to the state varies in advanced industrialized countries. At one extreme, the state has full ownership (as with any other state agency), with the faculty and staff as civil servants, and with extensive governmental controls

over both aggregate and line-item spending, all of which have been characteristic of universities on the European continent. At the other extreme, ownership is by a board of trustees, which has the status of a private (albeit generally a private nonprofit) corporation, as is found in the great private universities of the United States. In between, and spread along continua of ownership, control, and financial dependence on the state, various models of public corporations can be found, where the ownership is clearly vested in the state but where universities (as public corporations) have the authority, for example, to employ faculty and staff, own real property and other assets (such as endowments), make contracts, and establish tuition and other fees (Johnstone 2002).

In this regard, the movement toward public corporatization is another trend with clear implications for the more ready acceptance of, and even institutional advocacy for, cost-sharing. Japan began to move in the direction of public corporatization of their national universities in 2004, which included a clear mandate to the university presidents to supplement a declared decline in state revenue with nongovernmental revenue, implying higher and more differentiated tuition fees (Johnstone 2008). In 2008, France began the process of passing much greater autonomy to their universities under the Universities' Freedoms and Responsibilities Law. The French national students' union (UNEF) immediately (and predictably) protested on the grounds that this new autonomy could lead French universities to begin to select their students (formerly entitled to admission by an academic high school degree), raise fees (formerly not permitted), differentiate salaries and other benefits of the faculty and staff (who were formerly civil servants), and take other steps, including the creation of foundations to raise philanthropic donations, that would lead to a differentiation among the 80+ French universities that are theoretically equal (Marshall 2009).

- *Private higher education*: Finally, the number of private universities and colleges varies greatly in advanced industrialized countries. This range extends from the United States, with a vast array of high-quality, highly selective, and highly autonomous private nonprofit colleges and universities, all of which are private corporations; to the minimal number and significance of private universities in Europe; to the extensive number of private colleges and universities in Japan that are substantially autonomous (although less so than US private colleges and universities), but only a few of which are highly selective or prestigious or are otherwise thought to be models for Japan's top national (public) universities.

Cost-Sharing in Advanced Industrialized Countries

A comparison of cost-sharing in the universities of advanced industrialized countries is shown in table 9.1. Specific country details are provided in the appendix, as these details change so rapidly as to make their inclusion in a chapter problematic.

Table 9.1 displays the great variation in cost-sharing policies within selected advanced industrialized countries. Tuition fee policies are shown in the initial two columns. The first indicates whether there are regular tuition fees in the public colleges and universities and, if so, whether they are up front and generally expected of parents (assuming their financial capability to pay these fees), or deferred and expected of students (via the repayment of loans). Tuition fees are up front and thus expected primarily from parents or families in Austria, Canada, six of the German Länder, Japan, Korea, the Netherlands, Portugal, and the United States. Tuition fees are deferred and thus expected mainly from students via loans (in all cases featuring income contingent repayment obligations) in Australia, England, and New Zealand. The second column under tuition fee policies indicates the extent of these fees, ranging from no fees of any sort in the Nordic countries of Norway and Sweden and in Scotland, which abandoned its deferred tuition fee in 2008; to no tuition fees as such but substantial other fees expected of all students in Ireland and France; to levels of tuition fees ranging in academic year 2007–8 from moderate ($1,500–$3,000) in the Netherlands and Portugal to high (more than $3,000) in Australia, Canada, England, Japan, Korea, and the United States.

The means-tested expected parental contributions column reinforces the fact that in all cases where countries expect parental, or family, contributions for the up-front payment of tuition fees, they also expect parental contributions for the costs of student living (assuming a means-tested ability to pay, and further assuming that the student is a financially dependent child). It also indicates that parental contributions for student living expenses—although not for tuition fees—are expected in Australia, England, France, those German Länder that are still without tuition fees, Ireland, New Zealand, and Scotland—

Table 9.1 Sharing of higher educational costs in advanced industrialized countries

Country	Tuition fee policies		Means-tested expected parental contributions	
	Up front or deferred	Extent of fee[1]	To tuition fees	To student living costs
Australia	Deferred[4]	High	Discount for up-front payment of deferred fees	Yes
Austria	Up front	Nominal	Yes	Yes
Canada	Up front by province	High	Yes	Yes
England	Deferred	High	No	Yes
France	No	Minimal; substantial other fees	No	Yes
Germany	Up front in six Länder and no tuition fees in others	Nominal	Yes (for certain Länder)	Yes
Ireland	No	Minimal; substantial other fees	No	Yes
Japan	Up front	High	Yes	Yes
Korea, Rep.	Up front	High	Yes	Yes
Netherlands	Up front	Moderate[10]	Yes	Yes

	Governmental financial assistance		Officially encouraged and supported private sector	
Means-tested grants	Generally available loans	Food, lodging, and other subsidies	Mode of support[2]	Size of private sector[3]
For living costs	For tuition fees	Transportation allowances and rent assistance for needy students	Direct (to recognized private institutions) and indirect	Minimal (<1%)
For tuition fees and living costs	For tuition fees	Travel and transportation allowances	Indirect[5]	Minimal
For tuition fees and living costs	For tuition fees and living costs	No	Direct and indirect	Minimal
For living costs	For tuition fees and living costs[6]	No	Indirect	Minimal[7]
For living costs	Fees and living costs	Student housing subsidy	Direct to certain Grandes Écoles and indirect	Medium[8] (13%)
Federal and Länder BAföG	Repayable portion of BAföG	No	Direct[9] and indirect	Minimal (3% and 7%)
For living costs	No	No	Indirect to eligible institutions	Minimal (7%)
No	For tuition fees and living costs	No	Direct and indirect	Extensive (77%)
No	For tuition fees	No	Direct and indirect	Extensive (78%)
Basic grant for study and living costs[11] and supplementary means-tested grant for living costs	For tuition fees and living costs	Student rent subsidy	Direct to three private universities and indirect to others	Minimal

continued

Table 9.1   Continued

Country	Tuition fee policies		Means-tested expected parental contributions	
	Up front or deferred	Extent of fee[1]	To tuition fees	To student living costs
New Zealand	Deferred	Moderate to high	No	Yes
Norway	No	NA	No	No
Portugal	Up front	Moderate	Yes	Yes
Scotland	No	NA	No	Yes
Sweden	No	NA	No	No[15]
United States	Up front	High	Yes	Yes

1. Nominal <$1,000; moderate up to $3,000; high >$3,000. Calculated using World Bank global purchasing power parities (World Bank 2009).

2. Indirect (via student financial assistance) versus direct (operational or capital funding).

3. PROPHE's *92 Country Data Summary: 2000–2007* used for enrollment in private higher educational institutions as a percentage of total higher educational enrollments to divide them into minimal (<10%), medium (10%–25%), and extensive (>25%) for Germany, Ireland, Japan, New Zealand, Portugal, and the United States (PROPHE 2008). OECD/UNESCO's world education indicators on enrollments in private tertiary institutions as a percentage of total tertiary enrollments used for Australia, France, and Ireland (OECD and UNESCO 2005). Nasjonalt organ for kvalitet i utdanningen data used for Norway (NOKUT 2008).

4. Commonwealth-supported students may defer tuition fees using the HECS-HELP income contingent loan scheme, or they (and/or their parents) may pay their tuition fees up front with a 20 percent discount. Fee-paying students may defer their tuition fees using the FEE-HELP income contingent loan scheme or pay their tuition fees up front.

5. Federal direct support to private higher educational institutions forbidden, but municipalities and Bundesländer provide some direct support.

6. Two-thirds of which is not income assessed.

7. There is only one private university in the higher educational sector. All other private institutions are in the further education sector, where they do not receive any direct public support unless they are affiliated with a recognized higher educational provider.

Governmental financial assistance			Officially encouraged and supported private sector	
Means-tested grants	Generally available loans	Food, lodging, and other subsidies	Mode of support[2]	Size of private sector[3]
For living costs	For tuition fees and living costs	Lodging benefits for needy students	Direct and indirect	Minimal (9%)[12]
For living costs	For living costs[13]	No	Indirect	Minimal (<10%)
For living costs	For tuition fees and living costs	Subsidies for food and lodging	Direct and indirect	Extensive (26%)
For living costs	For living costs[14]	No	Direct and/or indirect, depending on the institution	Minimal
For living costs	For living costs	No	Direct and indirect	Minimal
For tuition fees and living costs	For tuition fees and living costs	No	Direct and indirect	Medium (23%)[16]

8. Made up of 5 private universities, 14 private colleges, and some private and mixed public/private Grandes Écoles. Private institutions are divided into those that are grant-assisted (these are subsidized by regional or local authorities, have their teaching staffs paid by the state, and also get indirect support through student financial assistance) and those that are independent private higher educational institutions (these receive no direct public support, but they do get indirect support in the form of student financial assistance).

9. Some private-sector higher educational institutions receive support for operational expenses from their Länder and capital investment funds from their Länder and the federal government.

10. But in cases where students are not eligible for state support, they (or their parents) have to pay a tuition fee set by the institution.

11. Non-means-tested basic grant, which is initially a loan that is then converted to a grant if the student meets the study progress requirements.

12. No private universities.

13. Upon graduation, up to 40 percent converted to a grant.

14. Partially means-tested.

15. Grants for living costs are means-tested on the student's means. Parental means are irrelevant.

16. Very diverse, ranging from elite colleges to open-admission institutions.

leaving only the Nordic countries (only Norway and Sweden are shown in table 9.1) with no expectation of parental contributions either for tuition fees or for the expenses of student living.

The third set of columns, related to governmental financial assistance, shows some form of means-tested grants, from either the national or the provincial (or state or Länder) levels of government, for either tuition fees or living costs or both, in all of the countries covered in table 9.1—with the exception of Korea and Japan, which rely entirely on generally available student loans. All of the countries shown in table 9.1 except Ireland feature generally available loans, although the loans provided in France and Austria are small, both in average amounts and in the percentage of take up, and therefore play a relatively minor role in providing access to higher education. A new state-guaranteed student loan program was launched by the French government in September 2008, however, and it aims to make 60,000 loans in 2009.

The fourth set of columns illustrates the extent of private higher education in the advanced industrialized countries represented in table 9.1. Japan and Korea have private sectors that are both extensive and significant. The private sector of higher education in the United States, while smaller in relative size than in Japan and Korea, might in some ways be considered extensive because of the significance of its undergraduate selectivity and the scholarly prestige of the faculty in leading private colleges and universities. The advanced industrialized countries—with exception of Japan, Korea, and the United States, and including virtually all of Europe—are most notable for the small size and general insignificance of their private higher educational sectors (OECD and UNESCO 2005; Nasjonalt organ for kvalitet i utdanningen 2008; PROPHE 2008).

Altogether, the advanced industrialized countries included in this tabular presentation represent considerable diversity in their acceptance of tuition fees as a significant source of supplemental revenue, as well as whether tuition fees, if they are to be accepted, should be expected from parents (up front) or students (deferred). These countries also exhibit large variations in terms of the extent and significance of private higher education. At the same time, advanced industrialized countries seem to be converging—not only in the structuring of their national higher educational systems (i.e., in degree format and with greater competition and market orientation) but, with exception of the Nordic countries, in turning to parents and/or students for some of the revenue needed to keep up with the trajectory of rapidly increasing higher educational costs and revenue needs.

Transitional Countries

Transitional is a label given to former Communist countries following the breakup of the Soviet Union in the late 1980s and early 1990s, which lead to an independent Russian Federation and 14 other effectively independent and sovereign states: the Baltic states of Estonia, Latvia, and Lithuania; the Euro-Russian states of Belarus, Moldova, and the Ukraine; the Caucasian states of Armenia, Azerbaijan, and Georgia; and the central Asian states of Kazakhstan, Kyrgyzstan, Tajikistan, Turkmenistan, and Uzbekistan. The Eastern and Central European countries that were held in the grip of the former Soviet Union prior to its formal dissolution in 1991 are also generally labeled transitional, including Bulgaria, Czechoslovakia (now the Czech Republic and Slovakia), East Germany (quickly reabsorbed into the Federal Republic of Germany), Hungary, Poland, and Romania. Similarly labeled transitional, or at least post-Socialist, are the states emerging from the breakup of the former Yugoslavia, consisting of Bosnia and Herzegovina, Croatia, Macedonia, Montenegro, Serbia, and Slovenia. Finally, albeit with very different higher educational histories since the abandonment of their formerly rigid Marxist economic systems, are the Asian transitional countries of China, Mongolia, and Vietnam.

These post-Communist countries have been transitioning *from* governmental ownership of virtually all means of production, effective prohibition of all but the smallest forms of private enterprise; governmental provision of many free services and transfers, such as education up to and including higher education (with free or heavily subsidized food and lodging for university students), health care, pensions, and the like; and governmental establishment and regulation of prices and wages—and transitioning *to* the privatization of state-owned enterprises, encouragement of private enterprise and the ownership of real property, permission for foreign direct investment, and determination of most prices and wages by the market.

In the post-Soviet and Eastern and Central European states, as well as Mongolia, transitional also implies the demise of governmental control by the established state Communist parties and a switch to democratic governments through elections (albeit frequently based on personalities rather than on established party ideologies and platforms, and, in some transitional countries, with effective control maintained by former Communist Party apparatchiks). The Communist parties of China and Vietnam, however, have not relinquished control over the apparatus of their governments, although some observers believe there to be a form of democratization within the parties themselves. At the same time, while all of the transitional countries have abandoned such orthodox communist tenets as state ownership of the principal means of production, central planning, and control of virtually all prices and wages, and have also accepted a prominent role for markets (and thus a form of capitalism), continuing governmental ownership and control of such sectors as utilities, transportation, and petroleum, along with heavy governmental regulation and minimal roles played by private nonprofit entities and other forms of nongovernmental organizations, suggest market socialism more than free-market capitalism in some transitional countries.

Higher Education under Communism and in Transition

The higher educational systems of the countries we now label transitional were modeled on higher education in the Soviet Union: that is, featuring strong governmental/ministerial and party control, commensurately weak faculty or university/managerial (i.e., rector or president) authority, and minimal regard for the academic interests or needs of individual students. Furthermore, the governmental ownership and control of universities in the former Soviet model was fragmented among a higher educational ministry (sometimes associated with basic education or science) and other ministries (such as health, transportation, petroleum, mining, tourism, and the like), and was further dissociated from most basic research, which was undertaken within the separate state-controlled academies and institutes to serve state needs. University curricula were strong in math, science, and engineering and generally weak in the humanities and social sciences (especially in economics), where teaching and research were distorted by party ideology and the officially proclaimed needs of the state. Admission to programs, especially in universities controlled by the production ministries, was limited to the numbers projected in the economic plans of the ministries and carried a virtual assurance of employment (and commensurately restricted opportunities in other endeavors). Since faculty and staff were civil servants, and appointments were vetted and protected by a parallel Communist Party management within each university, there was virtually no ability (or felt need) on the part of rectors, presidents, or deans to reallocate resources, institute new programs, seek nongovernmental revenues, or otherwise engage in institutional entrepreneurship. Especially significant to our themes of cost-sharing, tuition fees, and financial assistance, higher education was free of tuition fees, and both lodging and food were also heavily subsidized.

When the transitional countries broke free of the grip of party ideology and embraced private enterprise and markets, the effect on universities was profound—but financially it was mainly negative. Gross domestic products in Russia and the other post-Soviet countries (less so in the Central and Eastern European transitional countries) plummeted in the 1990s. Governmental revenues, suddenly deprived of the technically and politically easy value-added, or turnover, taxes on state-owned enterprises, declined even more. Universities, formerly dependent on now-scarce governmental revenues and subsidized energy, entered a period of profound austerity.

With the loss of the ideological authority of the Communist Party and of central governmental revenue, higher educational authority—especially in the post-Soviet and European transitional countries—gravitated to university presidents and rectors (and, in the Russian Federation, also to the subject provinces: krays, oblasts, autonomous republics, and other units). Rectors and deans aggressively sought nongovernmental revenues from fees on lodging and canteens, leases, and fees from special nondegree courses and other forms of faculty and institutional entrepreneurship, as well as from the dual track tuition fee system, which allowed a parallel track of fee-paying students while preserving free higher education for regularly admitted, or governmentally sponsored, students. Cost-sharing, then, in a sense was both forced upon the universities (by the loss of governmental revenue and the ensuing austerity) and simultaneously allowed to happen (by the loss of governmental and official Communist Party authority and the consequent rise of executive, or managerial, authority).

The Special Case of China. As an example of one of the many differences between the Asian and the Soviet and Central and Eastern European transitional countries, China in particular never experienced the latter nations' extreme economic dislocation or the virtual hemorrhage of revenue from critical state sectors such as higher education. China parlayed its state form of market socialism and its enormous supply of low-cost, well-disciplined labor into a formidable export manufacturing machine, with its economy growing at an average annual rate of 9 percent in the decades before and after the turn of the century. Vietnam, while beginning from a stage of economic development far behind its European counterparts, has also experienced robust economic growth since the start of its liberalization. Chinese higher education has seen enormous growth since the transition to its form of market socialism, increasing its overall tertiary education enrollments to some 23.4 million in 2006 and its participation rate from 6.4 percent in 1999 to 21.6 percent in 2006 (Xiaoyung and Abbott 2008).

The Chinese higher educational system (like China's overall experience with Communism)—both before and after the 1949 Revolution and after the liberalization beginning in the 1980s—is also quite distinct from the higher educational institutions and systems of Russia, or the other transitional states emerging from the former Soviet Union, or from Central and Eastern Europe (and even from the other Asian transitional countries). Chinese higher education under Mao Zedong (that is, prior to the post-Mao economic reforms) had many features in common with higher education in the old Soviet Union, including the fragmentation of universities, with many under the control of production ministries; a Communist Party administration parallel and actually superior to a university's president and deans; a rigid and ideologically controlled curriculum relatively strong in mathematics, science and engineering and weak in the humanities and social sciences; and free higher education, including free food and lodging. At the same time, there have always been significant differences between higher education in China and in the states emerging from the former Soviet Union or Eastern or Central Europe.

For example, with the exception of Peking, Fudan, and a few of the other universities that, in the early twentieth century, had been modeled after the classical Western university, there were relatively few Western-type universities in China before its 1949 Communist Revolution—as opposed to the very many Western universities in Eastern and Central Europe—fewer even than in Russia before its 1917 Revolution. Furthermore, the Chinese system of higher education that emerged in the 1950s and early 1960s, modeled on the Soviet experience, was all but destroyed by the Cultural Revolution of the mid- and late 1960s. Consequently, when China fully opened it doors and began its great economic experimentation and liberalization in the late 1970s and early 1980s, and when Chinese students and scholars began to pour into the universities of Great Britain, the United States, and other Western countries, the Chinese universities were almost starting from scratch—and able to model themselves quite explicitly on the US university format.

Another difference is that China's embrace of market socialism was deliberate, cautious, pragmatic, and top down—in distinct contrast to the sudden and chaotic embrace of markets and the effective collapse of central planning and economic authority in Russia and the other states emerging from the former Soviet Union. This same pragmatism and measured policy reform permeated the universities as well as the guiding precepts about higher educational reform handed down by the Chinese government. For decisions having to do with finances, for example—unlike universities in Europe, Latin America, or even the United States, and quite unlike the universities in Russia or Eastern and Central Europe or the other transitional countries—there was little effective resistance from either faculty or students to the adoption of tuition fees or to massive structural alterations in curriculum or university governance.

Thus, when the Chinese government, following a new Communist Party manifesto, declared that higher education was partly a private good and that both tuition fees as well as fees for food and lodging should be assessed on nearly all Chinese university students, the government changed from a dual track tuition system, which had been similar to that of the other transitional countries, to a policy of tuition fees expected from nearly all Chinese students, beginning in 1997. Although the maximum percentage of instructional costs to be covered by tuition fees has been set by the Ministry at 25 percent of per-student instructional costs—and accepting the variability and even unreliability of comparative university financial statistics noted earlier in this chapter—Shen (2008) reported that the percentage of university operating revenue from tuition fees increased from just over 6 percent in 1993 to 23 percent in 1999 and more than 31 percent in 2005, suggesting, at a minimum, the growing importance of tuition fees in the financing of higher education in China.

China began making student loans on a small scale as early as 1987, but it launched a more serious six-city experimental student loan program in 1999, which it then expanded to two nationwide loan schemes: the Government Subsidized Student Loans Scheme and the General-Commercial Student Loan Scheme. However, the growth of loans and other forms of student assistance has lagged considerably behind the extraordinary explosion of student numbers in China. Thus tuition fees, which are expected from parents, represent a substantial cost for very many families, especially in rural areas and among the new urban workers. However, imposing a heavy (and new) burden of tuition fees and other expenses for higher education in the first decade or so after 1997 may have been possible for three reasons: (1) the historic Chinese cultural reverence for education and for scholars; (2) the nation's one child policy, which limited the higher educational expenses for most families; and

(3) the academic selectivity of both universities and academic secondary schools, which together weeded out most of the rural and urban poor and left a university-eligible population limited mainly to the emerging Chinese middle class.

The Special Case of the Central and Eastern European Transitional Countries. Central and Eastern European transitional countries, on the other hand, are nations that turned away from Communism and Soviet domination in the late 1980s but had had Western-type classical universities from the nineteenth century through the post–World War II Soviet domination, when they were transformed into institutions more nearly resembling the leading universities of the Soviet Union. In the nearly two decades since the liberalization of these Central and Eastern European transitional countries, there have been marked changes, many of them incorporating elements of cost-sharing.

The period immediately after liberalization saw significant austerity due to disruptions in their general economies and especially in the ability of their governments to collect taxes. Marek Kwiek, a Polish economist and analyst of higher educational finance in Poland and other Central and Eastern European transitional countries, describes Poland's cost-side attempts to close the gap between expanding revenue needs and limited available public revenues as including the "freezing of salaries (in a highly inflationary economy of the 1990s), the limitation or elimination of expenditures except for basic ones (thus very limited expenditures on books, equipment, and generally on all non-salary items), and cutting of maintenance and repair work . . . lowering [the faculty-student ratio] by increasing class sizes (especially for part-time students)." He then goes on to describe the revenue-side solutions.

> Revenue-side solutions to the chronic underfunding of Polish public higher education included various forms of cost-sharing (from among Johnstone's catalog): a special tuition-paying track in nominally free (by constitution) public institutions—fee-paying nonregular weekend mode of studies; the imposition of "user charges" to the expenses of what were once heavily subsidized residence and dining halls; the reduction of student grants and scholarships. Of special interest is another form of cost sharing [the deliberate limitation of capacity in the free public universities and the expansion of a demand-absorbing private sector]. (2009, p. 19)

Cost-Sharing in China, Russia, and the European Transitional Countries

A comparison of cost-sharing in the universities of China, Russia, and several of the Central and Eastern European transitional countries is shown in table 9.2. As with the advanced industrialized countries, more detailed information for selected countries is provided in the appendix. Some summary points follow.

Table 9.2 shows that all of the selected transitional countries, with the exception of China and Vietnam, have the form of up-front tuition fee that we have previously termed dual track. With free higher education in most transitional countries guaranteed by constitutions and higher educational framework laws, and with politicians unable or unwilling to confront the popular aversion to tuition fees directly, governments turned to the dual track tuition fee technique that reserved free higher education only for regularly admitted, governmentally sponsored students and paved the way for the admission of privately sponsored students who paid tuition fees. The dual track tuition policy, then, preserved the pretense of free public higher education, at least for governmentally sponsored students who attained this status by a test of academic merit. But it also allowed public colleges and universities to charge tuition fees to other students—usually part-time, evening, or weekend students. And if the dual track tuition revenue did indeed *supplement* rather than merely *replace* governmental (tax) revenue, the consequence was added quality, or added capacity, or both. In Russia, by the early 2000s dual track tuition revenue was contributing as much as 50 percent of all university revenues (Bain 2001), and Kwiek (2009) reports almost as much impact in Poland.

In accord with its designation as a special case among the transitional countries, China also initially implemented a dual track system, but in 1997 it accepted both the logic and the financial advantage of across-the-board tuition fees. We speculated above on some of the reasons why Chinese families, in spite of that nation's still very low average per-capita income, seemed able to afford these new (as of 1997) tuition fees. Another speculation, which goes more to the political ability of the Chinese government to raise tuition fees when the post-Soviet and European transitional countries seem (as of 2009) to be unable to do so, is the pragmatic and technocratic grip of the Chinese Communist Party and the still-tight control of student demonstrations—in contrast to the unruly politics and more politicized universities of the newly democratic post-Soviet and European transitional countries.

Table 9.2 Sharing of higher educational costs in transitional countries

Country	Tuition fee policies		Means-tested expected parental contributions	
	Up front or deferred	Extent of fee[1]	To tuition fees	To student living costs
China	Up front	Moderate	Yes	Yes
Czech Republic	Dual track	Nominal for fee-paying students	For fee-paying students	Yes
Hungary	Dual track	Moderate to high for fee-paying students	For self-financed students	For self-financed students
Poland	Dual track	High for fee-paying students	For fee-paying students	Yes
Romania	Dual track	Nominal to moderate for fee-paying students	For self-financed students	For self-financed students
Russia	Dual track	Moderate to high for fee-paying students	For self-financed students	Yes
Vietnam	Up front	Nominal	Yes	Yes

1. Nominal <$1,000; moderate up to $3,000; high >$3,000. Calculated using World Bank global purchasing power parities (World Bank 2009).
   2. Indirect (via student financial assistance) versus direct (operational or capital funding).

Governmental financial assistance			Officially encouraged and supported private sector	
Means-tested grants	Generally available loans	Food, lodging, and other subsidies	Mode of support[2]	Size of private sector[3]
For tuition fees	For tuition fees and living costs	Subsidized food	Indirect	Minimal (9%)
For living costs	No	Subsidies for food and lodging and heath insurance; public transportation discounts	Direct and indirect	Minimal (9%)
For tuition fees and living costs	For tuition fees and living costs	Free lodging for state-financed students	Direct and indirect	Medium (14%)
For living costs	For tuition fees (for fee-paying and private students) and living costs	Subsidized food and lodging for state-financed students	Direct and indirect	Extensive (30%)
For living costs	Under consideration as of 2008–9	Subsidized food and lodging for state-financed students	Direct	Medium (23%)
For living costs (for state-financed students)	For tuition fees and living costs via experimental loan schemes	Subsidized lodging	Direct	Medium (15%)
Merit-based tuition waivers and subsides for living costs; social scholarships for living costs	For tuition fees and living costs	Subsidized lodging	Some direct	Medium (10%)

3. PROPHE's *92 Country Data Summary: 2000–2007* used for enrollment in private higher educational institutions as a percentage of total higher educational enrollments to divide them into minimal (<10%), medium (10%–25%), and extensive (>25%) for China, the Czech Republic, Hungary, Poland, Romania, Russia, and Vietnam (PROPHE 2008).

Dual track tuition fees can be opposed on several grounds. Many on the Far Left dislike any form of tuition fees. A number of economists and policy analysts who are inclined to support the principle of cost-sharing and tuition fees also disapprove of the dual track form on equity grounds, claiming that such tuition fees favor the most academically prepared and thus tend to reward disproportionately the sons and daughters of the well educated and the privileged. Others believe that free higher education for the most academically prepared and ambitious is simply an extravagance, as it almost certainly does not alter enrollment behavior, and, therefore, that it can be assigned an opportunity cost—foregoing forms of means-tested, or targeted, grants that will make a difference in behavior and further the policy aim of more equal higher educational opportunity.

Kwiek (2009) and Matějů and colleagues (2008) persuasively argue that the barrier to access is more likely to be insufficient capacity than the imposition of, or even an increase in, tuition fees. Kwiek demonstrates that enrollments rose dramatically in Poland and other Central and Eastern European transitional countries, due to the opening of private institutions and the additional capacity in existing public universities made possible by supplementary revenue from fee-paying students. The expansion of higher education that was made possible in both the public and private sectors through tuition fee revenue—across the board tuition fees in the private sector and dual track fees in the public sector—did not diminish access, at least not in Poland (Kwiek 2009) or the Czech Republic (Matějů et al. 2008). In fact, Kwiek notes that in Poland, the numbers and proportions of students from families where neither parent had attended a university rose after additional revenue began to flow into both the private and public sectors.

Interestingly, none of the transitional countries portrayed in table 9.2 have turned to the deferred form of tuition fee that has been gaining so much attention in highly industrialized and middle-income countries such as Australia, Chile, England, New Zealand, and South Africa. The reason for this may have to do with the transitional countries' greater need for current revenue, as opposed merely to assets of some uncertain value on the government's books in the form of deferred tuition fee repayment obligations. Parents in the transitional countries who are financially able to do so also seem to be willing to pay the dual track tuition fee, perhaps because it is generally less than the alternative private-sector tuition fees, and perhaps also because free higher education is no longer considered a right, as it was under the former Communist ideologies, but is something that is earned in a highly competitive quest (and the price of failure is the need to buy university admission).

Financial assistance in most transitional countries continues to be either in the form of cost-of-living stipends or of access to subsidized food and lodging. However, stipends in most transitional nations have been cut or frozen; thus their purchasing power is diminished in these countries' inflationary economies. Yet financial assistance is very necessary, most particularly for those in fee-paying tracks and private-sector institutions, but also for those governmentally sponsored students for whom there is insufficient space in subsidized university lodging. Therefore, in addition to China, which as of 2009 had two well-developed and large-scale student loan programs, Hungary, Poland, and Vietnam have launched student loan schemes. Russia continues to struggle with several student loan schemes that seem (as of 2009) to have not yet been successful, except for students who can offer creditworthy cosignatories. Romania (as of 2009) is deliberating on a proposal within the Ministry (on which we worked as consultants to the World Bank in 2008). In short, as of 2009, student loan schemes are still—except for China and Hungary—in the early stages of development in transitional countries.

Table 9.2 also shows the contribution to access and enrollments made by the emerging private sectors in key transitional countries. Private higher education is extensive in Poland, and smaller but significant in Hungary, Romania, Russia, and Vietnam (PROPHE 2008). Absent the long histories (and sometimes the significant endowments) that characterize the prestigious private universities of Canada, Japan, Korea, the United States, and some of the Latin American countries, private higher education in most of the transitional countries is likely to be more entrepreneurial, efficient, and professionally oriented, and also typically lower in prestige than that in the public universities. It is difficult to predict the future role of the private sectors in transitional countries, especially in light of seriously declining youth demographics (at least in Russia and the Central and Eastern European transitional countries), increasing attention to accreditation and the conditions required for nonprofit status, and likely continued improvements in the quality and responsiveness of the public-sector colleges and universities. In light of these threats from the public sector, it is possible that many of the smaller, more specialized, and totally tuition-fee-dependent private institutions that have emerged in this period of transition will not be able to stay in business. At the same time, even if some (or even many) fold in the next decade or two or three, these nimble and entrepreneurial private institutions will have done a service for their countries and for the public-sector universities that will have learned much from their examples.

In summary, at the time of their liberalization, universities and systems in the transitional countries needed a great deal of additional revenue to meet the pent-up higher educational demand that had not been accommodated by these nations' highly meritocratic, Communist-era universities, as well as to carry out the structural and curricular changes needed to overcome the academic distortions that were part of the Marxist-Soviet legacy. At the same time, the public sectors (including colleges and universities) in most of the transitional countries experienced great economic austerity, due to the economic dislocations and loss in tax capacity that accompanied the transition from command to market economies. In the transitional countries emerging from the former Soviet Union and in Central and Eastern Europe, constitutions, framework laws, the legacy of entitlements (such as free higher education), and volatile politics all worked to limit the implementation of across-the-board tuition fees (China and Vietnam being distinct exceptions). Although dual track tuition fee revenue, for all of the flaws in the underlying policy, may for the moment be as financially lucrative as China's smaller across-the-board tuition fees for all undergraduates, extending tuition fees to all students—perhaps differentiating the fees by institutions, programs, and levels and supplementing this extension with an expansion of financial assistance and the introduction of student loans schemes—appears in 2009 to be on the policy agendas of most of the transitional countries (or at least of their academic economists and ministerial policy specialists).

Middle-Income Countries

The World Bank (2009) classifies countries by income group according to per-capita gross national income (GNI). By this method, in 2009 54 countries were categorized as lower-middle income, with per-capita GNIs between $936 and $3,705. Another 41 countries were classified as upper-middle income, with per-capita GNIs between $3,706 and $11,455. In table 9.3 we present summaries of cost-sharing in six upper-middle-income countries (Brazil, Chile, Malaysia, Mexico, South Africa, and Turkey) and six lower-middle-income countries (Colombia, Egypt, India, Indonesia, Morocco, and the Philippines). Of the countries we treated as transitional in table 9.2, the Czech Republic and Hungary are high income by the World Bank's income classification, Romania, Russia, and Poland are upper-middle income, and Vietnam is low income. China is included with the lower-middle-income countries, strictly on the basis of its huge population and consequently still-modest per-capita GNI.

As with our summaries for advanced industrialized countries and transitional nations in the preceding sections, we are again interested in overall patterns, leaving cost-sharing details to the appendix. Also as in our preceding sections, we extend the same cautions about applying inferences from our small, essentially opportunistic sample to all of the countries in this broad middle-income category. In fact, there is enormous variability in the 95 countries that the World Bank classifies as middle income—as well as in the dozen countries we have portrayed in table 9.3.

Higher Educational Variations in Middle-Income Countries

Classification as (either lower- or upper-) middle income also says nothing about a nation's stage of economic development or rate of GDP growth, or about such relevant measures of its economy as the degree of income inequality, the extent of urban or rural deprivation, or the general condition of education or the status of educational participation. These middle-income countries exhibit substantial within-country income inequalities as well as considerable differences between nations, such as in the average per-capita GNIs in Chile and Indonesia. As a consequence, there will be extraordinary differences in the standards of living for the Brazilian or Chilean middle and upper-middle classes, for example, and the rural populations in, say, China, India, Indonesia, and the Philippines.

There are also differences within the middle-income countries in the maturity and sophistication of key governmental agencies and activities—such as taxation, regulation, budgeting, and accounting—as well as in the analytical and statistical capabilities within these agencies. However, even if their economies are struggling and their politics are occasionally paralyzing, most if not all middle-income countries are fully capable, for example, of devising and executing sophisticated means-testing systems or securitizing student loan paper.

At the same time, the extent of poverty is extreme, particularly in the rural areas of the lower-middle-income countries, but also in many of the upper-middle-income nations, such as the rural areas and urban slums of Brazil, Malaysia, South Africa, or Turkey. In reference to our themes of higher educational capacity, accessibility, and affordability, then, the challenge of accessibility in many of the middle-income countries begins with poor elementary and secondary schools, minimally trained teachers, parents with little formal education, and oftentimes the added complications of indigenous languages and ethnic and regional tensions—before even proceeding to the possible additional access barriers of insufficient capacity and affordability. Therefore, while we will continue to maintain the feasibility, as well as the general desirability, of modest cost-sharing—particularly in light of the demographic- and participation-driven college and university enrollment expansion in most of these countries—we must begin with an acknowledgment that large proportions of the families in middle-income countries will have little or nothing to spare either for tuition fees or for their children's living expenses away from home. This may be of little immediate consequence to nations in which most of the children of the very poor drop out before completing secondary school, as in some of the lower-middle-income countries. In fact, the more disproportionately the middle- and upper-middle classes are represented in a country's colleges and universities, the stronger the equity case will be for tuition fees and the less this tuition fee revenue will need to be reduced to pay for means-tested financial assistance for low-income families. But expanding enrollments are inevitable in most of the middle-income countries. Higher education must therefore increase its efficiency as well as its revenue to provide additional capacity and more of the necessary financial assistance.

Cost-Sharing in Middle-Income Countries

Table 9.3 displays variations in cost-sharing in 12 middle-income countries, with half each selected from the lower-middle-income and higher-middle-income brackets, as outlined above. Most of the middle-income countries in this table have up-front tuition fees, although many are nominal. Chile, probably the most market-oriented and liberalized country in Latin America, has relatively high tuition fees, but this is a regional exception; the rest of Latin America in 2008–9 featured either modest (and still heavily contested) tuition fees, as in Mexico, or the absence of public-sector tuition fees altogether, as in Brazil. A still-vivid demonstration of the politics and passions that surround the issue of tuition fees in Latin America is the example of the National Autonomous University of Mexico (UNAM), which was closed down for most of 1999 and badly damaged by the violent opposition to a proposal to increase tuition fees from less than a US dime (where they had been frozen for nearly 50 years) to approximately $70 per semester.[3]

In addition to Brazil, the other country in table 9.3 that, at least as of 2009, was still without tuition fees was Morocco, in spite of tuition fees being on the government's agenda (and blessed by the King) since 2000. As the Moroccan dilemma is a textbook example of the confluence of factors exacerbating higher educational austerity in middle-income countries, we quote from our report to the World Bank on the Moroccan student financial assistance system.

> [The diverging trajectories of higher educational revenue needs and available governmental revenue are] especially acute in Morocco due to the combination of: (1) a very rapidly increasing number of secondary-school graduates (due less to increasing population than to increasing rates of educational participation); (2) the legal obligation (as well as the political pressure) to accommodate all high school graduates in the public university system; (3) the lack of attractive alternatives to the public universities (such as public colleges or other nonuniversities, or private universities) to absorb more of the lycée graduates at other-than-governmental expense; (4) the need for increased financial assistance (due to the freezing of the cost-of-living stipend for nearly twenty years and to the increasing numbers—especially at the margin of the increasing participation—of students from low-income and rural families); (5) the need for increased capital and operating revenues both for increased university capacity and increased quality; and (6) the absence—as yet—of any significant cost-sharing in the form of either tuition fees or more nearly market rate fees for governmentally provided food and lodging with which to supplement the increasingly inadequate available governmental revenue. (Johnstone, Ait Si Mhamed, and Marcucci 2006)

The unwillingness of the Moroccan government to implement tuition fees in spite of its unmet higher educational revenue needs is, of course, political; but the politics of tuition fees in Morocco goes beyond the mere attractiveness of a popular entitlement. Morocco is part of Francophone North Africa, and the fact that France, with far greater wealth, still rejects tuition fees cannot be entirely ignored. Yet Morocco has indirectly implemented cost-sharing in the forms of a dramatic decline in the purchasing power of its means-tested cost-of-living stipends (frozen since 1977) and a freeze in the capacity of subsidized food and lodging through the *cités universitaires*, which are no longer able to feed and house all of the legitimately needy students (Ait Si Mhamed 2006).

Dual track tuition fees, found in many of the transitional countries and also in low-income East Africa, are much less prevalent in the (nontransitional)

Table 9.3 Sharing of higher educational costs in middle-income countries

Country	Tuition fee policies		Means-tested expected parental contributions	
	Up front or deferred	Extent of fee[1]	To tuition fees	To student living costs
Brazil	No	NA	No	Yes
Chile	Up front	High	Yes	Yes
Colombia	Up front	Nominal to moderate	Yes	Yes
Egypt	Dual track	Moderate for fee-paying students	For fee-paying programs	Yes
India	Up front	Nominal	Yes	Yes
Indonesia	Up front	Nominal	Yes	Yes
Malaysia	Up front	Nominal	Yes	Yes
Mexico	Up front	Nominal to moderate	Yes	Yes
Morocco	No	NA	NA	Yes
Philippines	Up front	Moderate	Yes	Yes
South Africa	Up front	High	Yes	Yes
Turkey	Up front	Nominal	Yes	Yes

1. Nominal <$1,000; moderate up to $3,000; high >$3,000. Calculated using World Bank global purchasing power parities (World Bank 2009).
2. Indirect (via student financial assistance) versus direct (operational or capital funding).
3. PROPHE's _92 Country Data Summary: 2000–2007_ used for enrollment in private higher educational institutions as a percentage of total higher educational enrollments to divide them into minimal (<10%), medium (10%–25%), and extensive (>25%) for Brazil, Chile, Egypt, India, Indonesia, Malaysia, Mexico, the Philippines, and South Africa (PROPHE 2008). OECD/UNESCO's

Governmental financial assistance			Officially encouraged and supported private sector	
Means-tested grants	Generally available loans	Food, lodging, and other subsidies	Mode of support[2]	Size of private sector[3]
Only for private-sector students	Only for private-sector students	No	Direct and indirect	Extensive (73%)
For tuition fees and living costs	For tuition fees and living costs	No	Direct[4] and indirect	Extensive (73%)
For living costs	For tuition fees	No	Indirect	Extensive (51%)
No	No	Subsidized food and lodging	No	Medium (19%)
For tuition fees (very few)	For tuition fees and living costs	No	Direct to some	Extensive (31%)
For living costs	No	No	Direct	Extensive (71%)
No	For tuition fees and living costs	No	Indirect	Extensive (39%)
For living costs	For tuition fees and living costs	No	Indirect	Extensive (33%)
For living costs	Under consideration as of 2008–9	Subsidized food and lodging for scholarship holders	Indirect	Minimal (5%)
For tuition fees and living costs	For tuition fees and living costs	Subsidized lodging	Direct	Extensive (75%)
For living costs for students from the provinces	For tuition fees and, rarely, for living costs[6]	For students with financial assistance	No	Minimal (5%)
No	For tuition fees and living costs	No	Direct	Minimal (3%)

world education indicators on enrollments in private tertiary institutions as a percentage of total tertiary enrollments used for Turkey (OECD and UNESCO 2005). Data for Colombia and Morocco came from ICHEFA Project research.

    4. To some via subsidies and to others via competitive research grants.

    5. Mix of elite and non-elite institutions.

    6. Forty percent becomes a grant upon successful completion.

middle-income countries. Egypt does allow universities to admit some students on a fee-paying basis, but a distinctive feature in the Egyptian dual track policy is the high tuition fee charged for programs taught in English or French, as opposed to Arabic. Unlike the merit-based dual track systems that tend to privilege the better prepared with free higher education, this Egyptian policy charges higher tuition fees to those who tend to be more privileged: that is, who have had an English or French secondary education and who are in programs such as management (taught in English) that will lead to more lucrative jobs.

Cost-sharing via encouraging (and sometimes indirectly subsidizing) a private sector is another common feature of middle-income countries, as indicated in the last column in table 9.3. Private higher education is especially notable in East Asia and Latin America (PROPHE 2008). The Philippines depends more on private higher education than any other country, and private higher education is also extensive in India, Indonesia, and Malaysia (as it is in the highly industrialized East Asian countries of Japan and Korea, as presented in table 9.1 and discussed above). Brazil, Chile, Colombia, and Mexico (and most other Latin American countries) also have large and well-established systems of private (mainly not-for-profit) colleges and universities, many established by the Roman Catholic Church, but others by academic entrepreneurs. A few are clearly prestigious; many principally serve a demand-absorbing function.

Lastly, middle-income countries have a mixed record with regard to financial assistance. Of the countries summarized in table 9.3, Chile, the Philippines and South Africa have comprehensive programs including both means-tested grants and loans. Turkey has a well-established student loan scheme. Colombia has an extensive student loan program as well as a sophisticated system of means-testing. Singular among the other Latin American countries included in table 9.3, Brazil in 2008 had grants and loans only for private-sector students. Mexico has a national program of means-tested grants for students in public colleges and universities, as well as a number of small loan schemes, many established for private universities or consortia and some only for certain states, but it is still without a national, comprehensive, generally available student loan scheme. Morocco as of 2009 had only a cost-of-living stipend that had been badly eroded by twenty years of inflation, plus subsidized food and lodging plagued with insufficient capacity.

In summary—and again with caution about drawing patterns with regard to countries that display such a wide variation in wealth, economic growth rates, demographics, participation rates, and political-economic systems—the middle-income countries have the mixed blessing of a sophisticated and well-educated elite, many of whom attended top universities in the highly industrialized countries, who have very substantial higher educational aspirations for their children, their universities, and their countries. For most middle-income countries, these aspirations are fueled by simultaneously rapid increases in the size of their college-age cohorts and in the participation rate of these rapidly increasing cohorts. Their aspirations are exceedingly expensive, at the very time that other costly and both politically and socially compelling needs are coming before their beleaguered governments and hard-pressed taxpayers.

The dilemma of higher educational finance in middle-income countries calls for a combination of cost-side and revenue-side solutions:

1. Modest tuition fees (possibly differentiated by instructional cost, market demand, and level)
2. Modest grants or discounts that are that are cost-effectively targeted, or means-tested, and that keep pace with increases in tuition fees
3. Means-tested, generally available student loans at minimally subsidized interest rates that can be recovered cost-effectively in amounts sufficient to provide reasonable access to students whose families are unable to assist them financially
4. Efforts to cut instructional costs without damaging educational quality, such as the cost-effective use of instructional technology, distance learning, and more reliance generally on out-of-class learning
5. Efforts to reduce expensive student maintenance by decentralizing facilities (perhaps in conjunction with distance learning technologies) and facilitating living at home, at least for the first two or three years of postsecondary education

These prescriptions, as well as those we offered for the advanced industrialized and transitional countries, are not so very difficult; the true dilemma lies more in the politics of convincing not only politicians, but also faculty, staff, and students.

Low-Income Countries

By the same World Bank scheme used to classify middle-income economies for the section above, the Bank in 2008 categorized 49 nations with a GNI of less than $935 per capita as having low-income economies.[4] We summarize the following low-income countries in table 9.4: Burkina Faso, Ethiopia, Ghana, Kenya, Mozambique, Namibia, Nigeria, Pakistan, Tanzania, Uganda, and Uzbekistan. The countries classified as low income by the World Bank are overwhelmingly in sub-Saharan Africa, with only a few in Asia and Oceania, and only one, Haiti, in the Western Hemisphere. Uzbekistan can also be classified as transitional, but we did not include it with the countries discussed in table 9.2, as it has more in common with the low-income countries than with most other transitional countries.

Characteristics of Low-Income Countries

Low-income countries are characterized by

- high levels of extreme poverty;[5]
- high levels (the highest in the world) of inequality in both wealth and income;
- poor health and nutrition, poor schools, and low educational attainment, frequently confounded with ethnic and linguistic marginalization;
- low levels of industrialization, adverse terms of trade, high unemployment (including among university graduates), import dependence, and (generally) low and sometimes negative rates of growth;
- low levels of public infrastructure, including roads, telecommunications, sanitation, public health facilities, and educational facilities, including those for higher education;
- greatly constrained public treasuries, due to so little taxable income and wealth as well as to the prevalence of taxation avoidance and dependence on donor nations and organizations; and
- political instability, considerable corruption, and low levels of nonprofit and volunteer activities or other elements of civil societies.

The World Bank's *2006 World Development Report* underlined the extreme poverty of these nations, indicating for low-income countries an annual per-capita Gross National Income of $510 by exchange rates and $2,260 by purchasing power parities (World Bank 2006). Chen and Ravallion (2008) of the World Bank, using 2005 estimates of purchasing power parities in the developing world, estimated that 1.4 billion people in 2005, or one-quarter of the world's population, lived below the World Bank's poverty line of $1.25 a day, and that some 2.6 billion people consume less than $2 a day. The poverty rate in East Asia, formerly the highest in the world, fell from 80 percent to 20 percent from the early 80s to 2005, while it remained level at about 50 percent in sub-Saharan Africa, although population growth in Africa increased the number living under this poverty index to some 380 million. Added to this are the constraints on these nations' treasuries. The combination of limited public revenues and the extraordinarily high levels of unmet needs—including basic education, public health (made especially compelling in sub-Saharan Africa due to the HIV and AIDS pandemics), welfare, and all public infrastructure—magnifies the opportunity costs of any additional revenues for higher education, no matter how compelling the need.

Higher education in many low-income countries, in turn, is characterized by

- a rapidly increasing demand for places, due to high birth rates and to expanding proportions of college-level-age young people who are completing academic secondary schools with aspirations for higher education;
- limited higher educational capacity, especially in universities, but also relative underdevelopment of short-cycle nonuniversity institutions;
- expectedly high levels of austerity, with overcrowded lecture theaters, heavy teaching loads, and inadequate resources for books and journals, equipment, computers, and telecommunications;
- large proportions of these nations' already inadequate governmental budgets for higher education absorbed by student maintenance expenditures and never even available for the support of instruction;
- curricula considered by many to be elitist and academic expectations seen as unreasonable (although the academic preparedness of entering students from many of the secondary schools is also low, compounded by difficulties with the languages used in the universities, which may be English, French, or Portuguese); and
- great resistance to cost-sharing due to the poverty of most of the students, compounded by the legacies of socialist experiments and the political volatility of students, especially over tuition fees and other matters concerning their personal finances.

In short, the low-income countries are especially caught in the trap that we have identified: the diverging trajectories of surging higher educational costs and revenue needs and extremely limited available public revenues. At the same time, the kind of governmental revenue supplementation that cost-sharing promises, at least in theory, is constrained by the volatile politics of cost-sharing and tuition fees; the technical problems of means-testing, or targeting; limited financial assistance available to students for whom such assistance is most likely to make a difference in accessibility; and low recovery rates on student loan schemes.

Cost-Sharing in Low-Income Countries

In table 9.4 we summarize the key elements of cost-sharing in 12 low-income countries.

The first column in this table shows the prevalence of tuition fees in the selected low-income countries. However, for the two countries (Burkina Faso and Mozambique) in which the tuition fee is up front—that is, expected at the time of matriculation, supplied mainly by parents, and available for institutional budgets—the fee is very nominal and, at least anecdotally, is frequently not paid anyway. Ethiopia, Namibia, and Tanzania have versions of deferred tuition fees, where the fee is to be repaid after graduation in the form of income contingent repayments. In chapter 6 we discussed the questionable suitability of income contingent repayment schemes in very low-income countries, where the amount of one's income is so often unknown to the government and where university graduates are likely to emigrate (or at least be out of the county for substantial periods). If they remain in the country and are not employed by the government, they may have multiple employers, or be self-employed, or be able to split earnings between members of a single household, or otherwise underreport their earnings. In short, and as we discussed in greater length in chapter 6, there are many reasons to be concerned about the financial viability of income contingent repayment recovery in low-income countries. And while the relatively few examples of such schemes, other than in upper-middle-income South Africa, were, in 2009, still too new to have reliable evidence on their likely cost recoveries, the generally abysmal record of conventional fixed-schedule student loan schemes in sub-Saharan Africa—again with the exception of South Africa and possibly of Kenya—does not provide a great deal of confidence. Furthermore, even if the repayments were to be recovered in some substantial measure in the future, there is no indication that colleges and universities will benefit from them, because the loans—that is, the deferred tuition fees—are still only bookkeeping entries, with no new capital other than limited new infusions from the government's operating budget.

Other low-income countries summarized in table 9.4—Ghana, Kenya, Pakistan, Uganda, and Uzbekistan—employ some form of dual track tuition fee. Particularly if the fee-paying track is substantial (as in Uganda's Makerere University, where the African notion of dual track, or parallel, tuition fees began), it can be a substantial revenue source to supplement limited governmental funds (Ssebuwufu 2003). We have commented in earlier chapters about the questionable equity implications of the dual track concept: that is, the practice of providing free higher education to the most academically prepared and academically ambitious, regardless of financial need, while charging tuition fees to those who may have scored only a little lower on the entrance examination. At the same time, a dual track tuition fee policy may be the most technically and politically feasible way to implement a policy of tuition fees. If the fee-paying track gets large enough, relative to the governmentally sponsored free track—as in Uganda's Makerere University, where the fee-paying track consists of about 80 percent of the entering students—the tuition-fee-free track begins to resemble the merit scholarships that politicians and faculty seem to love (for quite different reasons), and this may be a small price to pay for surmounting political and popular resistance to the very notion of tuition fees. And when such a *fee-tilted* dual track policy is accompanied by a financially viable student loan scheme—which admittedly is a challenge for any low-income country— the dual track tuition fee policy can generate additional revenue, expand capacity, and possibly even maintain or even enhance accessibility.

Nigeria (as of 2009) had no tuition fees in its national universities, but this country does have up-front tuition fees in its state universities—which seems mainly to be a function of the more volatile politics of tuition fees at the national level, where the students are, ironically but not unusually, likely to be better able to afford a modest tuition fee. The rejection of cost-sharing altogether in a low-income country such as Nigeria, which does have a middle and even an upper class that can afford tuition fees, seems to be a waste of higher educational revenue that low-income countries can ill afford.

Means-tested grants and loans are a technical problem for most low-income countries in which many incomes, other than for civil servants and perhaps employees of large companies, come from self-employment, or are earned in family venues, or are seasonal, and are thus often relatively easy to hide (in short, for all of the reasons why income contingent loans present problems in low-income countries). Yet means-testing, or targeting, is an essential policy tool for the disbursement of many kinds of services and transfer payments,

Table 9.4 Sharing of higher educational costs in low-income countries

| Country | Tuition fee policies | | Means-tested expected parental contributions | |
	Up front or deferred	Extent of fee[1]	To tuition fees	To student living costs
Burkina Faso	Up front	Nominal	Yes	Yes
Ethiopia	Deferred	Moderate	No	No
Ghana	Dual track	Moderate for fee-paying students	For fee-paying students	Yes
Kenya	Dual track	Nominal for Module I students and moderate for Module II students	Yes	Yes
Mozambique	Up front	Nominal	Yes	Yes
Namibia	Deferred	Moderate	Yes	Yes
Nigeria	No (at federal level) and up front (at state level)	Ranges from nominal to high for state universities	Yes (at state level)	Yes (at both levels)
Pakistan	Dual track	Nominal to moderate	Yes	Yes

Governmental financial assistance			Officially encouraged and supported private sector	
Means-tested grants	Generally available loans	Food, lodging, and other subsidies	Mode of support[2]	Size of private sector[3]
For tuition fees and living costs	For tuition fees and living costs	Food and health subsidies	Some direct	Medium
No	For tuition fees and living costs	No	No	Medium (24%)
No	For living costs	Subsidized, but limited, lodging	Direct (competitive funds) and indirect	Minimal (3%)
For tuition fees	For tuition fees and living costs for Module I students and students in the private sector	Subsidized food and lodging for Module I students	Indirect	Medium (24%)
Some for tuition fees and living costs	No	Subsidized food and lodging, mainly for scholarship holders	Direct and indirect	Extensive (26%)
No	For tuition fees	Subsidized lodging	No	Minimal
Yes (at state level)	Unclear	Subsidized lodging in federal universities	No	Minimal (8%)
For tuition fees and living costs	No	Subsidized food and lodging for government-sponsored students	Direct and Indirect	Medium (23%)

continued

Table 9.4   Continued

| Country | Tuition fee policies | | Means-tested expected parental contributions | |
	Up front or deferred	Extent of fee[1]	To tuition fees	To student living costs
Tanzania	Deferred	Nominal for public-sponsored students and moderate for fee-paying students	Yes (only up to 60% can be deferred)	No
Uganda	Dual track	Free for state-sponsored students and moderate for private-entry-scheme students	For fee-paying students	For fee-paying students
Uzbekistan	Dual track	Moderate for fee-paying students	For fee-paying students	Yes

1. Nominal <$1,000; moderate up to $3,000; high >$3,000. Calculated using World Bank global purchasing power parities (World Bank 2009).
2. Indirect (via student financial assistance) versus direct (operational or capital funding).
3. PROPHE's *92 Country Data Summary: 2000–2007* used for enrollment in private higher educational institutions as a percentage of total higher educational enrollments to divide them into minimal (<10%), medium (10%–25%), and extensive (>25%) for Pakistan (PROPHE 2008). Ng'ethe, Subotzky, and Afeti (2008) used for Ghana (enrollments in universities and polytechnics; the proportion of private enrollments increases to 11% if only university enrollments are

and thus deserves the time and expense that developing it will take. The following summary of five principles useful in the creation of means-testing schemes in low-income countries comes from Tekleselassie and Johnstone (2004) and Johnstone (2006).

1. Means-testing in developing countries must combine (a) voluntary reporting of income and assets with (b) some stipulated set of verifiable categorical indicators, or attributes, both to measure additional capacity to pay and

Governmental financial assistance			Officially encouraged and supported private sector	
Means-tested grants	Generally available loans	Food, lodging, and other subsidies	Mode of support[2]	Size of private sector[3]
No	For tuition fees and living costs	Subsidized lodging	Indirect	Medium (11%)
No	No	Free food and lodging for state-sponsored students	No	Extensive (35%)
Monthly scholarship for living costs	For fee-paying students	Subsidized food and lodging	No	Minimal

considered, as there are no private polytechnic institutions), Kenya (universities, polytechnics, and postsecondary colleges; if polytechnics are excluded, the proportion of private enrollments increases to 27%, as there are no private polytechnics), Mozambique (universities and polytechnics), Nigeria (excluding postsecondary colleges), Tanzania (enrollments in universities and polytechnics, excluding open-university enrollments; the proportion of private enrollments increases to 17% if only university enrollments are considered, as there are no private polytechnics), and Uganda (universities and postsecondary colleges). Data for Burkina Faso, Ethiopia, Namibia, and Uzbekistan came from ICHEFA Project research.

also to corroborate voluntary reports and other measures of income and asset values, enforced by (c) a system of random-sample verification and (d) appropriate sanctions.

2. All means-testing schemes—even the ones used in advanced industrialized countries such as the United States—involve compromises and imperfections. The means-testing schemes that are even conceivable in Africa, particularly at this initial stage, will be imperfect and will involve compromises on

both of the essential goals of equity and efficiency. At the same time, experience from developed nations suggest that a thoughtful, comprehensive, and transparent policy, even in the absence of all of the supporting data, traditions, and systems that have existed for decades in many of the OECD countries, can minimize those avoidable imperfections in means-testing schemes that emerge simply from a failure to have thought through the kinds of complications we have discussed and to have devised some—any—clear and workable resolution.

3. Means-testing, or needs-analysis, schemes need not be perfect, but they must be clear and predictable. In the end, a truly effective and efficient system of targeting must rely substantially on voluntary participation and compliance. This, in turn, requires people to believe that such a system, however much it may disadvantage them, is both essentially fair and unacceptably costly to evade or misrepresent. This calls for systems that are (a) predictable and clear, and (b) actually convey confidence and motivation. The inevitably complex and imperfect multiple indicators and verification procedures of means-testing have the potential not only to anger the politically powerful, but also to discourage low-income and ethnic or linguistic-minority parents and students from coming forward and participating in the application procedures (i.e., *incomplete take up*). Providing technical support for needy families as they fill out an application for financial assistance is equally important. This will add costs, but it will help assure both the vertical and the horizontal equity of higher educational subsidy targeting.

4. The development and especially the implementation of cost-sharing and targeting schemes require adequate participation by local constituencies, including religious authorities, local governments, community organizations, and cultural groups. For example, an assessment of the appropriate family unit needs to be sensitive to cultural and religious mores, including the acceptance, for example, of the practice of polygamy. A workable and enforceable scheme for determining expected family contributions, then, must thus go beyond the central government to grassroots constituencies—both to solidify political acceptance of policies that are almost inherently unpopular and also to appropriate local mechanisms of verification and enforcement.

5. A workable and cost-effective scheme of cost-sharing, accompanied by means-tested student financial assistance, requires the participation not just of the higher educational ministry, but also of a host of existing governmental ministries and agencies—such as those involved in secondary education, tax

collection, the census, immigration, the postal service, welfare and other social services, and other agencies at both the central and provincial levels. All of these bodies—and their top governmental officials and civil servants—have their own, often overwhelming, problems. Therefore, the formation and successful execution of a scheme of cost-sharing and revenue diversification requires a strong and committed government.

Seven of the low-income countries portrayed in table 9.4 carry some kind of generally available loan scheme. Student loans, however, present a major technical problem for low-income countries. Student loan schemes were first introduced in sub-Saharan Africa in Nigeria in 1973 and Kenya in 1974. Both of these loan schemes had the apparent primary objective of putting money in students' hands to cover living expenses (there were as yet no tuition fees), under the assumption that these loans would in theory be (or could be made to seem to be) less expensive to their hard-pressed treasuries than outright grants. At the same time, cost-sharing—that is, the attempt to recover anything near to the original cost of the loan—was apparently not a serious objective and repayments were few. Nigeria essentially abandoned its initial plan, but it has been attempting since 2007 to restart it as an Education Trust Fund. The original Kenyan student loan plan, having recovered little in the way of repayments, was totally revised in 1995 and put under the control of the Higher Education Loans Board, with an explicit cost-sharing objective. Other loan programs (Prêts FONER) were introduced in Burkina Faso, but the recovery has been exceedingly low (Some 2008). Ghana introduced a loan program with technical assistance from the World Bank, but it depended on guarantees from the national pension fund, thus putting both the viability of the loan scheme and the pensions of cosignatories in jeopardy. This scheme has since been changed and placed under a new Students Loan Trust Fund. Ethiopia (in 2003) and Namibia (in 1996) adopted income contingent loan schemes, presumably modeled after the Australian Higher Education Loan Scheme; these have not, as of 2009, been credibly evaluated, but their fiscal viability remains questionable for the reasons presented in chapter 6.

The problems with student loan schemes in low-income countries are those presented in chapter 6 for all countries—only more so.[6] Student loans in all countries carry an above-average lending risk because of the recipients' lack of credit experience and long delays between receipt of the loan and the initiation of repayments (assuming the student was truly aware of taking out a loan in the first place—which they frequently are not, especially with deferred tuition fees). Various factors may be compounding these issues (which are especially problematic in low-income countries): a high rate of unemployment and the extreme mobility of recent graduates, the difficulties of tracking individuals (who generally do not want to be tracked), the absence of comprehensive credit reporting, and uneven legal systems that either do not permit the attachment of wages or that tend not to prosecute student-debt arrearage at all. The level of agency experience and professionalism in the technically complex tasks of skip-tracing and collecting have been uneven in low-income countries. Furthermore, the design of student loan schemes in many of the low-income countries (as in countries at any stage of economic development) may be such that cost recovery would be minimal even with a low rate of default, due to interest rates that have frequently been set at levels that are far below the prevailing cost of money—as in the 4 percent interest rate charged on student loans in Kenya when the government's borrowing rate in 2008 was 8 percent and the rates on consumer debt would have been far higher.

Most of these problems are present, and some are exacerbated, when the repayment obligation is set as a percentage of future income (or income contingently) and when the income contingent repayment obligation is coupled with an employer deduction from the borrower's pay, as in the loan programs in Ethiopia and Namibia. These problems, discussed in chapter 6, arise especially in low-income countries because of, for example, the frequency of seasonal, dual, and self-employment; the resistance of very small businesses and partnerships in accommodating the collection of repayment obligations; the likelihood of family-owned businesses and wage-splitting; and the prevalence of emigration and frequent periods out-of-country (Johnstone 2004, 2006).

Finally, to complete this less-than-sanguine portrayal of the ability of student loan schemes to help solve the austerity of higher educational finance in low-income countries, even if their design is appropriate (i.e., with interest rates close to the government's own borrowing rate) and even if defaults remain manageable (i.e., in the neighborhood of consumer debt levels), to our knowledge no generally available student loan scheme in a low-income country has managed to tap the world credit markets—thus requiring all loan disbursements to be made from a combination of repayments and exceedingly scarce new governmental appropriations.

Except for South Africa, which is an upper-middle-income country, Kenya may have the only student loan scheme in sub-Saharan Africa that in 2009 appeared to be somewhat successfully achieving the difficult dual objectives that were discussed in chapter 6, namely (1) enhancing accessibility by putting much-needed money into the students' hands; and (2) contributing a real source of revenue (in addition to supplemental governmental and parental/family revenue) to expand university quality and capacity and, in the end, to enhance higher educational access and equity. There remain for Kenya the two challenges of lessening the scheme's excessive, built-in interest subsidization and of turning student loan repayment obligations into genuine assets so they can be sold. There also remains, for all the sub-Saharan African countries contemplating student loan schemes, the underlying fact that student loan schemes at their best will be only marginally helpful in solving the true underlying dilemma of low-income-country higher educational finance, which is the rapidly diverging trajectories between higher educational costs and needed revenues and limited available governmental revenue. Nevertheless, the imperative of finding nongovernmental revenue and the fact that student loans can work (as shown in chapters 6 and 7) suggest that low-income countries need to continue adopting and perfecting student loan schemes.

Finally, table 9.4 demonstrates the size and significance of private sectors in the 12 low-income countries shown here. It is difficult to detect patterns in this array. Ethiopia, Kenya, Mozambique, and Uganda (all in East Africa), as well as Pakistan, all have private colleges and universities absorbing between one-quarter and one-third of their postsecondary student populations (Ng'ethe, Subotzky, and Afeti 2008; PROPHE 2008). None is significant in the sense of prestige or in an ability to attract significant numbers of students from other countries (unlike some private universities in Latin America and other middle-income countries). But the viability of private colleges and universities, even (in some countries) without significant public revenues, serves to illustrate the feasibility of tuition fees even as they absorb some of the higher educational enrollment demand.

NOTES

1. These are preliminary figures for academic year 2007–8 in constant 2007 dollars. Included in the total are some $28.909 billion in governmental (federal and state) grants, another $29.066 billion in institutional grants and discounts, and another $10.440 billion in private and employer grants; some $65.543 billion in governmentally sponsored

and guaranteed loans, including $28.440 billion in subsidized and $26.513 billion in unsubsidized student loans, as well as $10.590 in parent loans; and an estimated $7.040 billion in education benefits (College Board 2008, table 1, p. 5).

2. As of 2009, the full country studies as well as many of the papers cited throughout this book can be found on the Web site of the ICHEFA Project at www.gse.buffalo.edu/org/IntHigherEdFinance/.

3. This opposition did have a deeper political agenda, as many of the Mexican state universities had had more than nominal tuition fees for years. But UNAM was highly symbolic of the opposition to cost sharing, and this opposition was also partly against the government generally, rather than just to this one governmental action.

4. The World Bank provides financial and technical assistance to developing countries. It is composed of two development institutions: the International Bank for Reconstruction and Development (IBRD), which focuses on middle-income and creditworthy poor countries, and the International Development Association (IDA), which focuses on the poorest and least creditworthy countries (essentially, those classified as low income and the object of this section).

5. Statistics that purport to measure the poverty of families in low-income countries can be misleading, because of the difficulty of reflecting the true purchasing power of local currencies when they tend to have an exceedingly low exchange value. Thus per-capita income figures, especially in low-income countries, are better expressed in purchasing power parities that compare, for example, what the Ghanaian cedi will purchase in Ghana with what the US dollar will purchase in the United States. Per-capita incomes expressed in purchasing power parities (PPPs) will virtually always be larger (that is, show less destitution) than per-capita incomes using regular exchange rates.

6. Much of the following on the problems of collecting student loans in low-income countries is taken from a workbook that we developed for a small, six-nation, invitational conference held in Arusha, Tanzania, in February 2008, entitled *Making Student Loans Work in East Africa*. The conference was organized by the University of Buffalo's International Comparative Higher Education Finance and Accessibility Project.

REFERENCES

Ait Si Mhamed, Ali. 2006. Cost-Sharing in Moroccan Higher Education: Perceptions and Attitudes of Students and Parents. Ph.D. diss., Department of Educational Leadership and Policy, State University of New York at Buffalo.
Bain, Olga. 2001. The Costs of Higher Education to Students and Parents in Russia: Tuition Policy Issues. *Peabody Journal of Education* 76 (3&4):57–80.
CESifo Group. 2007. Tuition Fees in Europe 2007/2008. *CESifo DICE Report [Database for Institutional Comparisons in Europe]* 4/2007. www.cesifo-group.de/portal/page/portal/ifoHome/b-publ/b2journal.
Chen, Shaohua, and Martin Ravallion. 2008. *The Developing World Is Poorer Than We Thought, but No Less Successful in the Fight Against Poverty.* Policy Research Working Paper. Washington, DC: World Bank.
College Board. 2008. *Trends in Student Aid 2008.* New York: College Board.

Council for Aid to Education. 2008. Contributions to Colleges and Universities Up by 6.3 Percent to $29.75 billion. www.cae.org/content/pdf/VSE 2007 Survey Press Release.pdf.

Johnstone, D. Bruce. 2002. Privatization. In *Higher Education in the United States: An Encyclopedia*, ed. James J. F. Forest and Kevin Kinser. Santa Barbara: ABC-CLIO.

———. 2004. The Applicability of Income Contingent Loans in Developing and Transitional Countries. *Journal of Educational Planning and Administration* [New Delhi, India] 18 (2):159–174.

———. 2006. *Financing Higher Education: Cost-Sharing in International Perspective*. Boston: Boston College Center for International Higher Education and Sense Publishers.

———. 2008. Higher Educational Cost-Sharing and Financial Assistance in Japan: Policy Options in an International Context. In *Report of the International Conference on Worldwide Perspectives of Financial Assistance Policies: Searching Relevance to Future Policy Reform for Japanese Higher Education*. CRDHE Working Paper, vol. 2. Tokyo: University of Tokyo, Center for Research and Development of Higher Education.

Johnstone, D. Bruce, Ali Ait Si Mhamed, and Pamela Marcucci. 2006. *Reforming the Moroccan University Student Financial Aid System: A Technical Report to the World Bank*. Washington, DC: World Bank.

Kwiek, Marek. 2009. Two Decades of Privatization in Polish Higher Education: Cost-Sharing, Equity and Access. In *Financing Access and Equity in Higher Education*, ed. Jane Knight. Rotterdam: Sense Publishers.

Marshall, Jane. 2009. France: Universities Move to Autonomy. *University World News* 58 (11 January). www.universityworldnews.com.

Matějů, Petr, Simona Weidnerova, Thomas Konecny, and Hans Vossensteyn. 2008. *Student Financing, Opportunity Growth, and Equity in Access to Higher Education*. Prague: Institute for Social and Economic Analysis.

Nasjonalt organ for kvalitet i utdanningen [NOKUT]. 2008. *Higher Education in Norway*. www.nokut.no/sw456.asp/ [accessed 27 May 2008].

National Association of College and University Business Officers. 2008. *2007 NACUBO Endowment Study*. Washington, DC: NACUBO.

Ng'ethe, Njuguna, George Subotzky, and George Afeti. 2008. *Differentiation and Articulation in Tertiary Education Systems: A Study of 12 Countries*. World Bank Working Papers 145. Washington, DC: World Bank.

OECD and UNESCO. 2005. *World Education Indicators*. www.uis.unesco.org/ev.php?ID=6192_201&ID2=DO_TOPIC/ [accessed 10 March 2009].

PROPHE [Program for Research on Private Higher Education]. 2008. *PROPHE 92 Country Data Summary: 2000–2007*. www.albany.edu/dept/eaps/prophe/data/international.html [accessed 15 January 2009].

Shen, Hong. 2008. Access to Higher Education through Student Loans: The Choice of Needy Students in China. Paper presented at the Asia-Pacific Sub-Regional Preparatory Conference for the 2009 World Conference on Higher Education, 25–26 September, Macao SAR, People's Republic of China. www.unescobkk.org/fileadmin/user_upload/apeid/workshops/macao08/papers/2-d-1.pdf.

Some, Touorouzou. 2008. Student Loans in Ghana and Burkina Faso: How to Square the Circle. In *Education and Social Development: Global Issues and Analyses*, ed. Ali A. Abdi and Shibao Guo. Rotterdam: Sense Publishers.

Ssebuwufu, John P. M. 2003. University Financing and Management Reforms: The Experience of Makerere University. In *Financing of Higher Education in Eastern and Southern Africa: Diversifying Revenue and Expanding Accessibility*, ed. Burton L. M. Mwamila, Issa Omari, and Eva Mbuya. Dar es Salaam: University of Dar es Salaam.

Tekleselassie, Abebayehu, and D. Bruce Johnstone. 2004. Means-Testing: The Dilemma of Targeting Subsidies in African Higher Education. *Journal of Higher Education in Africa* 2 (2):135–158.

World Bank. 2006. *2006 World Development Report*. Washington, DC: World Bank.

———. 2009. Country Classification, Data & Statistics. http://web.worldbank.org [accessed 14 January 2009].

Xiaoyung, Ma, and Malcolm Abbott. 2008. China's Tertiary Education Expansion. *International Higher Education* 53 (Fall):17–20.

CHAPTER TEN

Cost-Sharing and the Future of International Higher Educational Finance

This book has been concerned with the financing of higher education world-wide and with some of its discernable trends, particularly the increase in cost-sharing—that is, the shift of higher educational costs from governments and taxpayers to parents and students—at least from the perspective of the end of the first decade of the twenty-first century. We will finish our discussions with some conjectures about the financial future of higher education, some of the forces that may shape this future, and the place of cost-sharing and other policy options within this future, however dimly perceived. Let us first turn toward some of these forces that have been shaping, and will almost certainly continue to shape, the future of higher education and how we will pay for it. In the limited space of a concluding chapter, we will briefly mention five forces that seem particularly salient: surging enrollments and enrollment demand, increasing higher educational costs and revenue needs, the growing liberalism of the world economy, increasing globalization, and declining governmental revenues.

Forces Shaping Higher Education

Surging Enrollments and Enrollment Demand

The spread of cost-sharing is occurring in the context of worldwide trends affecting the demand for, and the costs of, higher education, as well as following more country-specific trends in politics, ideologies, and public-sector management. This worldwide trend of surging demand for higher education is partly a function of the increasingly knowledge-based economies of most countries —or at least of the widespread aspirations to move in the direction of such economies. Higher education is viewed as one of the major engines—perhaps even *the* major engine—for the economic development of any country, which is a major rationale for public investments in higher education. The growth of knowledge-based economies are also the source of the current (as of 2009) preoccupation, at least in the wealthier countries, for universities to attain some kind of world-class stature, as recognized by international rankings such as those Shanghai Jiao Tong University's *Academic Ranking of World Universities* or the Times Higher Education Supplement's *World University Rankings*.

Individual students and their parents are also demanding access to higher education in growing numbers. In some countries (and anticipating our eventual segue into the worldwide increase in cost-sharing), this demand reflects a greater willingness to pay for at least some (and, in the case of private higher education, for all or nearly all) of the costs of instruction. In countries that continue to resist cost-sharing, the demand is more simply manifested in burgeoning applications for higher education, especially in the university sectors. And in countries where university admission is an entitlement for all academic secondary-school graduates, such as in much of continental Europe, escalating demand is manifested by the increasing numbers of students showing up to register and trying, often in vain, to find a seat in the lecture theaters. Although most of this surging demand is private—that is, originating from the personal decisions of students (encouraged by their families) to finish secondary school and at least aspire to higher education, rather than from a governmental edict or public master plan—the rise in demand may go well beyond the needs of the above-mentioned knowledge economies for specific numbers of trained workers. Many countries are experiencing greater numbers of unemployed and underemployed college and university graduates. At the same time, a rising demand for higher educational places in excess of labor market needs is at least in part a consequence of intensified competition for a limited number of good jobs, as well as a consequence of the use of higher educational attainment partly as a screening device for the allocation of the available good jobs (in addition to an increasing demand stemming from greater social status and the sheer enjoyment of learning, quite apart from any labor market benefits).

In this context, the numbers of students in some form of higher, or postsecondary, education worldwide have risen in the past century from an estimated 500,000 in the early 1900s to well over 100 million in the early years of the twenty-first century (Schofer and Meyer 2005), and a 2006 estimate projected that the number might reach 120 million by 2010 (Daniel, Kanwar, and Ulvalic-Trumbic 2006). While such figures, for multiple reasons, are heartening, the cost implications are daunting.

Increasing Costs and Revenue Needs

Along with, and greatly magnified by, this surging worldwide demand for higher education is the rapid escalation of higher educational costs—or at least of higher education's revenue needs. The tendency of unit, or per-student, costs in higher education to rise at rates in excess of the prevailing rates of inflation is at the heart of this escalation (as described in chapter 1)—unless this natural rate of increase is dampened by the failure of higher educational wage rates to keep pace with wages in the larger economy, or unless colleges and universities are forced to bear considerable disinvestments in faculty and staff (i.e., declining faculty-student ratios), in the maintenance of their physical plant, and in a failure to replenish investments in technology, equipment, and library resources. In this way, higher education is like the other labor-intensive sectors of any economy. But rising unit cost pressures are especially great in sectors that are technology-intensive (and thus even more costly). For higher education, this expanding use of technology, unlike the infusions of technology into most sectors of the economy, adds to, rather than diminishes, its already rapidly rising unit costs. The rate of acceleration in unit, or per-student, costs is further magnified by the surging enrollments mentioned above, creating what we have previously termed the underlying divergence between higher educational cost trajectories (or the trajectories of revenue needs) and those of the revenues themselves. In most countries, higher educational costs will be considerably in excess of the prevailing rates of inflation and—especially significant to the theme of this book—in excess of the likely trajectories of any augmented public revenues.

Increasing Liberalization of the World's Economies

The unlikelihood of public revenues keeping up with higher education's expanding revenue needs is partly a function of the sheer size of the (mainly public) higher educational enterprise in most countries, compounded by the rates of growth of these revenue needs and exacerbated by more country-specific trends in politics, ideologies, and public-sector management. For example, the collapse of communism both as a political and as an economic system has been accompanied in many countries (including some former Communist countries) by an increasing *liberalization*: that is, an orientation to free markets, smaller governments and public sectors, and less taxation.[1] On the one hand, liberalism—by its predilection for smaller governments and lower taxes—contributes to the austerity of public sectors in general, and of public colleges and universities in particular. On the other hand, these same predilections are also leading many governments and public institutions of higher education to surmount, or at least to better cope with, financial austerity. The movement in the direction of liberalism does this in part by turning toward

- *corporatization*—meaning the conversion of public universities from state agencies to public corporations able to hire faculty and staff (rather than having them be employed as civil servants), comingle and carry over funds, execute contracts, issue debt, and—significantly, albeit generally within some limits—set tuition fees;
- *privatization*—meaning contracting out to private providers many of the public universities' essentially nonacademic functions (such as the provision of student lodging and food services) and operations (such as printing, maintenance, and telecommunications);
- *new public management* (NPM)—meaning the adoption of budgetary and managerial practices associated with private enterprise, such as flexible budgeting, cost centers, the carry-forward of funds from one fiscal year to the next, a high degree of attention to marketing, and the like; and
- *the encouragement of private colleges and universities*—first by a legal permission to operate, then by accreditation, and finally by entitlement to public funds, either directly (e.g., awarding a grant per full-time equivalent student or per graduate) or indirectly (e.g.,

making students eligible for financial assistance or allowing the faculty or the institution to be eligible for research grants).

Increasing Globalization

Liberalization, in turn, has contributed to, and been accelerated by, increasing *globalization*. Globalization is an internationalization—that is, a fundamental decline in the significance of countries and national borders—of information and knowledge (made possible by telecommunications that can send billions of digitized bits of information per second by optical fiber or microwave for fractions of pennies per mile); capital (the flows of claims on wealth between savers and either borrowers or investors); and production (which is increasingly technical, capital-rich, and mobile, with a predisposition to locating where politics are stable, labor is low cost, contracts are enforceable, and tax and regulatory climates are benign). While globalization is credited with adding to the wealth of many countries, it also may help foster the depression of tax revenue, as both production and capital are drawn to lower-wage and lower-tax jurisdictions. Globalization thus complements the predilection of (European style) liberalism for smaller governments and lower taxes and, indirectly, has a role in public-sector austerity and the case for revenue diversification and cost-sharing. More directly related to the topic of higher education, globalization, in association with increasingly knowledge-based economies, also contributes to the greater value placed on higher education, and especially on leading universities, in the wealthy nations (and particularly on the leading universities in the English-speaking world).

Increasingly Limited Governmental Revenues

The limited ability (or likelihood) of governmental, or tax-originating, revenues maintaining government's share of the rapidly rising trajectory of higher education's revenue needs can be diminished even further by the ascendancies of both liberalism and globalization, even if the overall wealth of a country's economy is expanding (although this latter event seems less likely, in light of the virtually worldwide economic downturn at the time we were writing). But the growing inability of tax revenues to keep pace with higher education's increasing needs is also a function of the sheer difficulty of raising taxes both cost effectively and progressively in most economies, regardless of the prevailing political ideology. Finally (and also quite apart from political and ideological trends), the difficulty of diverting ever larger amounts of tax revenues to higher education is also a function of increasing competition from other politically and socially compelling public needs—which, in developing countries, can be especially wrenching.

The Rise of Cost-Sharing

The above-mentioned trends—surging enrollments, mounting costs (and therefore greater revenue needs), the rise of liberalism and globalization, and increasingly limited governmental revenues—all lead to the diverging trajectories of higher education's costs and revenue needs and the available governmental revenues. Costs press upward sharply, especially where naturally rising unit costs are accelerated by surging higher educational demand, while revenues are limited by sluggish economies, the difficulty of collecting taxes, and competition from other compelling social needs. This situation has prompted all nations to search for other-than-governmental revenues for higher education—with the most obvious, albeit politically contested, source being some combination of parents and/or students. This is what we described in chapter 3 as the need-for-revenue rationale for cost-sharing—with the latter term reflecting both the simple fact that the underlying costs of higher education are shared by governments (or taxpayers), parents, students, and philanthropists, as well as a description of a worldwide policy trend where these costs are being increasingly shifted from governments to parents and students.

Beyond the sheer need for supplemental revenue, most economists and higher educational policy analysts point to an equity rationale for cost-sharing: observing that higher education is virtually everywhere partaken of disproportionately by the sons and daughters of the wealthy and privileged (who would certainly pay at least a share of the costs if they had to), while tax revenues come from all citizens (and in very many instances come disproportionately from the middle and lower socioeconomic classes). Finally, there is an efficiency rationale: a belief that charging some tuition fees would make students take their studies more seriously and make colleges and universities more efficient and responsive in their provision of higher education.

Signs of this policy trend toward greater cost-sharing are everywhere. In the United States, the *costs* of college, public as well as private, have been increasing at annual rates far in excess of the rates of inflation, and the *prices* of college (that is, tuition fees)—especially in public colleges and universities where states have not kept pace with their shares of these growing per-student costs—

have been escalating even faster, with little or no relief in sight and with student debt loads already at worrisome levels. Cost-sharing, as we saw in chapter 9, is encroaching into Europe, once the last bastion of free higher education, with tuition fees by 2009 even entering into some of the German Länder. Of the formerly Communist countries, China, Mongolia, and Vietnam have long since abandoned their previous ideology that higher education (and food and lodging) all were to be free, while Russia and most of the former Soviet Republics, as well as most of formerly Communist/Socialist Central and Eastern Europe, have managed to preserve free higher education only for a handful of the academic elite, who tend (ironically but not surprisingly) to be the sons and daughters of the privileged, while most others must pay. And in sub-Saharan Africa, it is not just free instruction that is slipping away, but free or highly subsidized food and lodging, as well as the long-since-abandoned pocket money that once went to a handful of privileged students in these otherwise struggling economies.

In the meantime, while governments everywhere struggle with the surging costs of higher education and attempt to shift some of these costs onto students and parents, tuition fees remain a veritable third rail of politics in many countries, with students, politicians, and once-privileged parents protesting the loss of the so-called free higher education that was thought to be a birthright. And with some education beyond high school thought nearly everywhere to be a key to a healthy democracy and a vibrant civil society, as well as a boon to a competitive economy and a major factor in socioeconomic mobility, the already expensive and rising costs of postsecondary education are becoming both a social and a political problem. Thus governments are attempting to gain precious revenue without compromising participation and equitable access by combining cost-sharing (most often in the form of tuition fees) with means-tested grants and student loans. However, as we saw in chapter 4, the challenges of equitable and cost-effective family-income targeting, or means-testing, are extremely difficult, especially in countries with little reliable information on incomes or where incomes tend to be multiple, uncertain, frequently noncash, and easy to hide. And the challenge of a student loan program that not only meets the financial needs of students and parents but is actually recoverable— with minimal losses and a minimum of interest subsidization—is truly formidable, as demonstrated by the dozens of failed student loan programs.

In short, the story of higher educational finance and the worldwide shift of costs from exclusive or near-exclusive reliance on government, or the taxpayer, to parents and/or students is a story replete with financial stakes, matters of equity and social justice, issues of management and competence, and fiercely contested politics and ideologies. It is the viewpoint of the authors that cost-sharing for almost all countries is not only an imperative for the financial health of their colleges and universities, but it can also bring about enhanced efficiency, equity, and responsiveness. At the same time, the authors know well the sheer technical difficulties of advancing such policies, in addition to the extraordinary and almost inevitable political resistance and turbulence that generally (and understandably) accompanies even the discussion, not to mention the actual implementation, of tuition fees and other cost-sharing policies.

A Caveat—with Hope for the Future

Cost-sharing is no miracle cure. The 49 countries identified in chapter 9 as low income are already facing crushing poverty and demands on their scarce public revenue that cannot be accommodated, not to mention the specter of continuously surging enrollment demand for a higher education that many of them can neither afford nor effectively utilize. The 2.6 billion persons estimated by the World Bank to be living on less than $2 a day (Chen and Ravallion 2008) have little or nothing to share. And the track record to date of student loan programs in sub-Saharan Africa and some low-income countries in Asia, in spite of our own work to help some of them succeed, does not yet provide much hope for several of the solutions we have been suggesting. Perhaps this is just another lamentation over the plight of the impoverished, overpopulated, frequently resource-poor, and ill-governed regions of the globe. But it is perplexing and troubling to look at higher education's potential to contribute so much to solving the world's problems and then to observe the seemingly worsening higher educational austerity in so many countries and the limited ability of our conventional policy tools, including cost-sharing, to close the gap between voracious revenue needs and available revenues.

And even in the highly industrialized world, including the United States, limits on, and the intense competition for, governmental revenue and the capacity constraints of colleges and universities are being matched by ceilings on parental ability or willingness to contribute and by limits on student indebtedness. Decreasing university budgets, rising student-faculty ratios, and declining faculty morale are being met with growing student anger, political resistance to the perpetual increases in tuition fees, larger and more worrisome student debt loads, and governments unable to reconcile their desire to have world-class universities with their inability to fund them—together with their suspicions that the enterprise should not have to cost so much anyway!

Nevertheless, we need to remember and take heart from the fact that the main force behind the most daunting of these problems, which is an ever-greater higher educational austerity in the poorest countries with the fastest-growing youth populations, can still be a very good thing. These surging enrollments, even if the labor market cannot immediately absorb them, promise a likelihood of strengthened democratic institutions, more civil tolerance, greater individual opportunities, and the future underpinnings of economic growth and better lives. We will not back away from the theme of this book, which is that a more *appropriate* (oftentimes, but not always, a *greater*) sharing of the high and rising costs of higher education with families and students can bring additional revenue, quality, capacity—and equity—to our colleges, universities, and other postsecondary institutions. But we also need to reiterate that our advocacy of cost-sharing is always an advocacy for its ability to supplement and augment governmental revenue, never to replace it. Governments must continue to recognize the worth of higher education, to the individual and to society alike, the value of expanding participation in this enterprise, and the facts that higher education is expensive and that its revenue needs will continue to grow. And financial assistance, in the form of targeted grants and loans, must always be a feature of any policy of higher educational cost-sharing.

Finally, we need to keep other solutions to the dilemma of higher educational austerity on the policy table. There are additional cost-side savings that can be achieved, particularly in some of the higher educational institutions that are almost certainly not needed for, and may not be fully capable of, the kinds of knowledge-creating capacities that are essential to the very costly production functions of a classical research university. In this same light, there are almost certainly savings (or *dampened cost trajectories*) to be made in more enlightened forms of sector diversification, which expands shorter-cycle, less-costly, and more labor-market-relevant forms of postsecondary education without losing track of the goal of equitable access.

We hope that this book can make a contribution to these policy discussions, possible solutions, and necessary decisions.

NOTE

1. We prefer the term *liberalism*—which, at least in its European meaning, has clear connotations of an orientation toward freer markets, less regulation, and generally smaller government—to the more ideologically packed and even more politically hostile term *neoliberalism*, which is favored by many critical academics. In either case, this sense of the term is quite distinct from—and to some extent almost opposite to—its prevailing American usage, which connotes big governments, extensive regulation, large public sectors, and high taxes.

REFERENCES

Chen, Shaohua, and Martin Ravallion. 2008. *The Developing World Is Poorer Than We Thought, but No Less Successful in the Fight Against Poverty.* Policy Research Working Paper. Washington, DC: World Bank.
Daniel, John, Asha Kanwar, and Stamenka Ulvalic-Trumbic. 2006. A Tectonic Shift in Global Higher Education. *Change* (July/August): 16–23.
Schofer, Evan, and John W. Meyer. 2005. The Worldwide Expansion of Higher Education in the Twentieth Century. *American Sociological Review* 70:898–920.

Appendix
Selected Country Examples of Cost-Sharing

These country examples are synthesized (and, at times, updated) versions of the country profiles drafted within the context of the International Comparative Higher Education Finance and Accessibility Project at the State University of New York at Buffalo. The profiles, together with their bibliographical references, can be accessed at www.gse.buffalo.edu/org/IntHigher EdFinance/. It should also be noted that the student loan programs in Australia, Canada, Chile, China, Germany, Hungary, Japan, Kenya, the Netherlands, South Africa, Sweden, the United Kingdom, and the United States are not included here, as they were described in chapter 7.

Advanced Industrialized Countries

Austria

The Austrian higher educational sector is comprised of universities, fine arts universities (formerly fine arts colleges), Fachhochschulen, and other postsecondary institutions, all of which are funded mainly by the federal government. There are a total of 21 public universities that enrolled 209,410 students in 2006. The 2002 Universities Act (Universitätsgesetz) granted universities complete autonomy from the state in handling their internal affairs and drafting their statutes, although the state continues to finance them. The federal government has recently (2006) moved from lump-sum funding to performance based-funding using performance agreements, which are negotiated every three years.

Before 2000, university students had free access to the universities, as tuition fees at state-run higher educational institutions were abolished in 1972 by the Higher Education Tuition Fees Law (Hochschultaxengesetz). However, in 2000 the government announced that starting the following academic year, students of both universities and Fachhochschulen would be required to pay a "study contribution" of ATS 10,000 [€727 or US$836*].

Not surprisingly, the inauguration of tuition fees—the first in recent years in a German-speaking country—was controversial. University leaders were generally caught off guard. Although the initial fees were modest, student leaders object to the very principle of tuition. Furthermore, as the expected revenue stream from the new tuition fees was

---

* All currency conversions in the appendix use the World Bank's 2005 International Comparison Program's global purchasing power parity (PPP) estimates, except when amounts are given in US dollars by the reporting government agency.

equal to the revenue cutback in the 2001 state budget for the universities, the tuition fees were seen as benefiting not the universities, but either other governmental programs or the Austrian taxpayer.

Several social policy measures were introduced in the 2001–2 academic year to compensate for the introduction of tuition fees. These included adding extra financial aid allocations, extending the range of students who were entitled to receive study grants, and introducing subsidized loans. In 2004–5, more than 47,000 students received financial aid and, of these, approximately 44,250 received study grants.

The direct aid outlined in the 1992 Student Support Act (Studienförderungsgesetz) is means-tested and linked to academic performance;* this assistance includes study grants, transportation allowances, a travel allowance, aid for studies abroad, and so forth. In 2005 the maximum study grants ranged from €424 per month (US$487) for single students to €666 (US$765) for students with children, and they are paid over the entire calendar year.

As part of the 2001–2 changes, study allowances were introduced for needy students, to help them cover their tuition fees. Study allowances are applied for at the same time as study grants. The specific amount is based on the degree of need demonstrated by the individual student and is calculated using similar parameters to those used for study grants.

Indirect aid, which is not means-tested, includes family allowances, insurance coverage (either under the parents' health insurance or through self-insurance), statutory accident insurance, and tax breaks granted to parents whose children study in the tertiary sector.

Those students who are not eligible for study grants may apply for subsidized bank loans to cover their tuition fees for a maximum of 14 semesters, with the government paying approximately 2 percent of the interest.

Australia

Australia's higher educational financial system, and the government's role in it, has changed dramatically since the early 1970s. Prior to 1974, students were expected to pay partial fees. These were removed in 1974, and for more than 10 years Australian higher education was free of tuition fees, except for some contributions demanded from students to fund student facilities. Tuition fees began to appear again in 1985. First, the government established a Higher Education Administration Charge (A$250 per student), followed by the introduction of tuition fees for certain Australian postgraduate students in 1986.

Since 1989, most Australian students contribute to the cost of their higher education through the Higher Education Contribution Scheme (HECS), introduced in the Higher Education Funding Act of 1988, whereby Commonwealth-funded students take out loans for all or part of their student contribution. The scheme is administered by the Department of Education, Science, and Training (DEST), the Australian Tax Office, and higher educational institutions. In its first years of operation, all undergraduates paid HECS at

* A satisfactory academic performance means that examinations have been passed according to curricula requirements (i.e., passing a set percentage of the total number of mandatory credit hours for courses and exams per semester), and that the legal duration of studies has not been significantly exceeded.

the rate of about 23 percent of the average costs of study. In 1997, the uniform-tuition-fee aspect was removed from the scheme. HECS was increased and differentiated into three cost bands, based on a combination of the relative cost of course delivery and the relative profitability (i.e., the rate of return) of certain programs. The package of reforms introduced in 2003 includes a partial fee deregulation that starting in January 2005 and has allowed institutions to set student contribution levels within a range from A$0 to a maximum set by the Australian government. In 2009, student contribution levels range from A$0–A$5,201 [US$3,715] for Band 1 courses (social studies, humanities, etc.), from A$0–A$7,412 for Band 2 courses (accounting, economics, etc.), and from A$0–A$8,677 (US$6,197) for Band 3 courses (law and medicine).

Since 1989, universities have also been able to offer fee-paying slots to Australian undergraduates. These places can only be offered on the condition that universities have met their enrollment targets for Commonwealth-funded students and that the total number of domestic fee-paying students will be limited to 35 percent of the total number of places. In 2004, there were close to 14,000 Australian undergraduates in full-fee-paying openings.

Not surprisingly, the introduction of tuition fees paralleled a significant decrease in government support for higher education. Between 1989 and 2002, this support for education fell from 77.2 to 53.8 percent of costs. In 2005–6, the Australian government contributed about 41 percent of the total revenue received, and it budgeted A$11 billion (US$7.85 million) in new support for higher education from 2004 to 2014.

Economic pressure, coupled with a huge expansion in demand for higher education, has led Australian higher educational institutions to seek alternative sources of revenue. They actively compete for fee-paying students and have been recruiting international students for the added tuition fee revenues. In 2003, the revenue received from fees and charges contributed about 22 percent of the sector's total income. Overseas students comprised 24 percent of the total number of students attending Australian universities in 2004. Universities are also seeking extra funding through research earnings, summer programs, and overseas campuses.

In Australia, there are a variety of public and university financial grants, scholarships, bursaries, and loan support schemes (see chapter 7 on Australia's HECS-HELP student loan scheme) available to tertiary students in both the higher educational and the vocational education and training sectors to cover living expenses. A Youth Allowance is available for eligible full-time students aged 16 to 25; full-time students over the age of 25 if they were getting a Youth Allowance before they turned 25 and they are still pursuing the same course of study; and young people up to the age of 21 who are combining a part-time job and part-time study. Financial assistance under the Austudy program is available to eligible full-time students aged 25 and older who are enrolled in an approved course of study. Both Youth Allowance and Austudy payments are subject to income and assets tests, as well as to a parental means test if the student does not qualify as being financially independent. There is also Abstudy, which provides financial assistance for Aboriginal and Torres Strait Islander Australians who undertake full- and part-time study. The Abstudy living allowance is a fortnightly means-tested payment.

In 2004, the government introduced the Commonwealth Learning Scholarships Programme to assist students from low socioeconomic backgrounds with the costs of higher education. Two types of merit-based scholarships are available to full-time undergraduate students: the Commonwealth Education Costs Scholarship (CECS), allocated by the institutions, is for educational costs of up to A$2,000 [US$1,428] per year; and the Commonwealth Accommodation Scholarships (CAS), paid directly to the student, is for accommodation costs of up to A$4,000 [US$2,857] per year. In 2004, 2,500 new CECSs and 3,000 CASs were provided. By 2008, over 8,600 new CECSs and CASs will be awarded each year. Starting in 2005, the government now allows individual higher educational institutions to award Exemption Scholarships (at their own expense) that make selected students exempt from paying tuition fees.

Additional benefits are also available to students receiving these kinds of financial assistance, including fare allowances for transportation between home and the educational institutions, a Health Care Card to help with medical costs, a pharmaceutical allowance to help cover the cost of certain prescriptions, a remote area allowance for students living in remote parts of Australia, and an interest-free Advance Payment of up to A$500 [US$357]. Students aged 16 to 24 may also be eligible for Rent Assistance if they live away from home while studying.

Canada

Provincial and territorial governments provide most of the direct funding for postsecondary public education in Canada. The balance of public postsecondary education income is obtained from tuition fees, research grants, contracts with business and industry, government research contracts, donations, and investment income. Since the early 1990s, university tuition fees have accounted for a growing proportion of university revenues. Average undergraduate university tuition fees rose by 76 percent through the 1990s, or by 6 percent a year in inflation-adjusted dollars. In the late 1990s, increases in average general undergraduate tuition fee rates slowed, while tuition fee hikes in professional, graduate, or second-entry programs surged. Average undergraduate tuition fees in Canada rose from C$1,600 in 1990 to C$3,550 in 2001 (in 2000 Canadian dollars) to US$3,700 in 2008 (in 2005 PPP).

The average student can cover his or her costs using summer earnings and debt financing. During the summer, nine out of ten students are employed, earning (on average) a total of C$4,000 [US$3,333], of which approximately C$1,200 [US$1,000] is saved. In the total pool of student income, students rely most upon employment (37%), followed by government loans (13%), family support (16%, including parental contributions, other family or spousal contributions, and family loans), private loans (7%), government nonrepayable aid (5%), and other grants (5%).

Since 1995, the total governmental (i.e., federal and provincial) expenditure on postsecondary education has remained unchanged in real dollars; however, it has shifted from funding educational institutions to funding individual students. The country has three interlocking sets of financial assistance programs—the Canada Student Loans system, provincial student assistance systems (loans and grants), and the Canada Millennium Scholarship Foundation's millennium bursaries—all of which can be applied for through a student's provincial or territorial government. Applications are assessed on the basis of eligibility and need. Generally, the neediest applicants receive provincial grants and Canada Millennium Scholarship bursaries, and those with less need receive loans. Seventy percent of all assistance is through loans. (See chapter 7 for more on Canadian student loans.)

Four different organizations have administered grants in Canada: the federal government (Canada Study Grants), various provinces (provincial grants), postsecondary institutions, and the Canada Millennium Scholarship Foundation. In most provinces and territories (with the exception of the Northwest Territories, Nunavut, and Quebec, who all operate their own student assistance plans), students who complete an integrated student loan application at the provincial level are considered for the full range of federal and provincial grants, bursaries, and scholarships.

The Canada Millennium Scholarship Foundation was phased out in the fall of 2009, and the government introduced a new consolidated Canada Student Grant Program that increased the financial resources available. Under this new program, low-income students receive an up-front grant of C$250 (US$208) per month and middle-income students receive C$100 [US$83] per month. The government is also investing C$123 million [US$147 million] to streamline and modernize the Canada Student Loans Program.

Canadian colleges and universities spend almost C$100 million [US$83 million] per year on undergraduate merit-based student financial assistance and another C$100 million [US$83 million] on need-based awards. Nationally, over 50 percent of institutional merit awards and 80 percent of all need-based awards are distributed by universities in the province of Ontario.

In addition to governmental grants and loans, there are other sources of student financial aid, including the Work-Study Program, funded by the government in certain provinces, whereby eligible students work on campus and receive an hourly wage and non-need-based tax assistance: tax deferrals on educational savings, tax exemptions on scholarship and bursary income up to C$3,000 [US$2,500], and tax credits for tuition fees and for enrollment at recognized education institutions.

Japan

The Japanese higher educational sector is characterized by its dual structure, composed of a limited public sector controlled by national and local governments and a very large tuition-fee-supported private sector. The Japanese higher educational system has recently undergone dramatic changes. Reforms, passed in 2004, granted public corporation status to the 87 national universities. While they are still a part of the public sector, they are independently managed and their staffs are no longer civil servants. The national universities are also able to set their own tuition fee levels, although the amount may not exceed 110 percent of the standard tuition fee set by the Ministry of Education and the Ministry of Finance. In 2005, the standard fee was raised to ¥535,800 [US$4,134] and most national university corporations raised their tuition fees accordingly, despite a promise to the contrary made by the Japan Association of National Universities (an organization established in 1950, made up of national university presidents).

Private institutions are, in principle, self-financed by tuition fees, application and entrance fees, donations, and income from auxiliary services. However, subsidies for current expenditures are granted by the national government through the Promotion and Mutual Aid Corporation for Private Schools of Japan, primarily to maintain and improve educational and research conditions and to ease the financial burden of the students. The Corporation also offers long-term, low-interest loans for funds needed to improve facilities and equipment in private higher educational institutions. In addition, the national government provides direct grants to private institutions of higher education for the purchase of educational and research equipment to promote the distinctive education and research offered in these private institutions. Nonetheless, state subsidies for private universities have been decreasing since 1980.

Japan has not developed a system of student grants, and most assistance is delivered via student loans (see chapter 7).

The Netherlands

The Netherlands has a binary system of higher education: wetenschappelijk onderwijs (WO) offered by universities, and hoger beroepsonderwijs (HBO) offered by Universities of Professional Education (UPEs). In addition, the Open University (a state establishment) offers open distance learning courses at both the HBO and the university levels. Central (in US parlance, federal) government grants are awarded as a lump sum to each university. In addition to these direct public funds, universities generate income from tuition fees, which are centrally fixed at a uniform rate (7% of total income), research councils (5% of total income), and contract activities (19% of total income).

In the Netherlands, there are approximately 60 private higher educational institutions that offer some 500 programs (mainly in professional education) and enroll approximately 35,000 students. These are divided into government-funded and non-government-funded private higher educational sectors. Three religious-based private universities are funded directly by the government, while seven universities fall into the non-government-funded private sector, including five theological institutions, the University for Business Administration at Nijenrode, and the Humanistic University at Utrecht.

The Ministry of Education, Culture, and Science sets tuition fees in the Netherlands. Student liability for these fees depends on whether or not a student is eligible for support. Students with support pay a centrally determined tuition fee rate; students without support pay tuition fees set by the institution. Part-time students are not eligible for student support; nor are those full-time students who are not (or who are no longer) entitled to such support, either because their personal incomes exceed the income cutoff point for student support or because they have used up all their entitlements.

In principle, all full-time students in the Netherlands are entitled to a basic grant for the duration of their programs. This grant is, in fact, initially a loan that is converted into a nonrepayable grant only if the student stays in school and completes his or her higher education within ten years. The amount that students receive depends on whether they live at home with their parents (€94 per month [US$104]) or independently (€260 per month [US$289]). Depending on parental income, a student may also be entitled to a means-tested supplementary grant of up to €212 per month [US$236] if living at home or €232 per month [US$258] if living independently.

Students may also take up subsidized loans and tuition fee loans (which are below the market interest rate of 3.35%) of up to €285 per month [US$316] for the former and €1,565 per year [US$1,739] for the latter. These loans are not turned into grants, and repayment must begin after a grace period of two years. Payments are spread over 15 years, with a minimum monthly installment of €45 [US$50]. When graduates have problems repaying this study debt, they can ask for an annual means test, which may reduce their repayment obligations (even to zero) for one year. All debt that remains

Table A.1   Monthly student support allocations,
in Euros, in the Netherlands in 2009

	Living at home	Living away
Basic grant	94 [US$104]	260 [US$289]
Supplementary grant	212 [US$236]	232 [US$258]
Loan	285 [US$317]	285 [US$317]
Tuition loan	131 [US$146]	131 [US$146]

Source: Center for Higher Education Policy Studies [CHEPS], University of Twente, Enschede, The Netherlands. www.utwente.nl/ cheps/.

after the 15-year repayment period is forgiven. (See chapter 7 for more on student loans in the Netherlands.)

Parents and students make up the difference between the standard budget allowed by the government and that which is commonly accepted to be a student's actual (substantially higher) budget. Students may earn up to €13,000 [US$14,444] per year without affecting their grant eligibility.

Sweden

Social equality in higher education is an important objective in the many policies and reforms in Sweden over the past 50 years. These are aimed not just at eliminating financial barriers to education, but also at actively drawing students from underprivileged social backgrounds into the higher educational system. The financial reforms of the mid-1960s included the creation of a new support system, made up of grants and loans. that enshrined the principle of students' financial independence from their parents.

More recently, in 2001, the Swedish Parliament passed an open higher education bill to broaden access and introduce new paths to higher education. As part of its efforts to widen access, the government has stated that its goal is seeing that 50 percent of each age cohort enters higher education by the age of 25. In 2003–4, the participation rate was approximately 47.3 percent.

In Sweden, all higher education is undertaken at universities and university colleges, with no distinction made between a university and a nonuniversity education. Ninety percent of undergraduate studies, postgraduate studies, and research are carried out at the 13 state universities and 23 university colleges. Alongside the public universities and colleges, there are a small number of privately run higher educational institutions that receive government grant funds. These include the Stockholm School of Economics, Chalmers University of Technology and University College of Jonkoping. In addition, there are some 10 smaller private institutions which have the right to award certain higher education degrees.

From the late 1970s to the late 1980s, the Swedish higher educational system had a nearly constant capacity of between 40,000 and 45,000 entrants per year. Thereafter, there has been a steady expansion in the total number of places for undergraduate studies. By 2004, student enrollment had grown to 302,600.

Table A.2   Amount of student assistance
(in Swedish kroner) payable to full-time
students in 2009

	Amount per week
General grant	671 [US$72]
Loan	1,284 [US$139]
Total	1,955 [US$212]
Higher grant	1,566 [US$169]
Supplementary loan	423 [US$46]

Source: Centrala studiestödsnämnden [CSN], Sundvall,
Sweden. Information on Swedish Study Assistance.
www.csn.se [accessed 19 August 2009].

Higher education in Sweden is free of charge for all students, except for a small fee paid to the student union for social services. Approximately 86 percent of the funding for undergraduate programs comes from state grants.

A fundamental principle in Swedish higher education is that all students who need help to finance their studies should receive such assistance from the central government. This aid takes the form of student grants and loans. About 30 percent of the total amount is in the form of a nonrepayable grant that, like the loan portion, is inflation indexed. Table A.2 shows the student assistance available to full-time students in the 2004–5 academic year.

A student must fulfill certain requirements to receive this assistance. For example, grants and loans may be reduced if the student's own income becomes too substantial. However, the economic situation of the student's parents or spouse is not taken into account. A student is entitled to a higher grant if he or she is 25 or older and attending a municipally run course of adult education studies. A supplementary loan is available to students who are studying full time and have received a below-minimum level of income during the twelve months that preceded the initiation of their studies. They may obtain this loan for a maximum of 120 weeks. (See chapter 7 for more on student loans in Sweden.)

United Kingdom

Higher education in the United Kingdom has devolved (since 1999 for Scotland and 2004 for Wales), and each constituent country sets its own policy and decides on its own funding methodology via its individual funding council (the Higher Education Funding Council for England, the Scottish Funding Council, the Higher Education Funding Council for Wales, and the Department for Employment and Learning in Northern Ireland). There has been a rapid expansion in the UK higher educational sector during the last three decades. By 2005–6 there were more than 1.7 million students studying in higher educational institutions, the participation rate was about 44 percent, and total government spending on higher education in 2005–6 was £6.5 billion [US$10 billion].

Between 1989 and 1997, during the rapid expansion period of the higher educational sector, public per-student funding fell by around 36 percent (this trend was not reversed until 2000–1), putting a considerable strain on universities and colleges. In an effort to address this pressure, the National Committee of Inquiry into Higher Education (the Dearing Committee) made a number of recommendations in its report, *Higher Education in the Learning Society—The Report of the National Committee of Inquiry into Higher Education*, including a proposal that full-time students in higher education should pay some of the costs of their tuition fees. In response to the Dearing Report, in 1997 the government announced that it would require means-tested contributions to tuition fees by full-time UK and EU undergraduates, introduce a new system of income contingent loans, and abolish maintenance grants. The revenue generated from student fees and maintenance was destined to be spent on supporting improved access and higher standards in both further and higher education.

Consequently, in the 1998–99 academic year a tuition fee of £1,000 [US$1,538] for full-time UK and EU undergraduate students was introduced, and it has been increased yearly to keep pace with inflation. How much of this tuition fee a student paid depended on assessed family-residual income, and students from the lowest-income families did not pay any tuition fees.

A new level of regional autonomy was granted to Scotland in 1999, and the newly formed Scottish Parliament began work immediately to roll back tuition fees in Scotland. By 2001, Scotland abolished up-front tuition fees and replaced them with an income contingent loan (referred to as a graduate contribution) that would be paid after graduation (see Scotland below).

On January 22, 2003, Charles Clarke, the Secretary of State for Education and Skills, announced the publication of a White Paper, "The Future of Higher Education," that set out the government's plans for radical reform and investment in universities and higher educational colleges. In terms of higher educational finance and the United Kingdom's cost-sharing strategy, this White Paper sought to increase the resources available to higher educational institutions without jeopardizing the government's access goals.

After extensive public consultation, the Higher Education Act was passed in 2004. Among other things, it gave those English universities that had signed an Access Agreement with the new Office for Fair Access the power to charge a student contribution of between £0 and £3,000 [$US4,615] per year for each program of study, as of September 2006. Maximum fees (until 2010 at the earliest) may not rise by more than the rate of inflation. The Act abolished the up-front payment of tuition fees and replaced it with a new income contingent loan scheme that allows every student to defer payment of their fees until after they have graduated and have started to earn a minimum of £15,000 [US$23,076]. Payment is through the tax system and is linked to a student's ability to pay. Each Access Agreement identifies the steps that the university will undertake to improve higher educational access, including the provision of financial help so that students from all backgrounds can apply. (See chapter 7 for more on student loans in the United Kingdom.)

The Higher Education Act also gave the National Assembly for Wales the authority to decide on the tuition fee and student support policies to be applied in Wales. In order to review policy options, the Welsh Executive commissioned an independent report (the Rees report) on the devolution of the student support system and the tuition fee regime in Wales. The Rees report proposed the introduction of deferred flexible fees (along the lines of the English system), accompanied by a National Bursary Scheme that would award means-tested, targeted bursaries to low-income students. (See below for more on Wales.)

Table A.3   Tuition fees in the United Kingdom in 2008–9

England	Flexible fees up to £3,145 [US$5,240]
Wales	Flexible fees up to £3,145 [US$5,240]
Scotland	Free higher education
Northern Ireland	Flexible fees up to £3,145 [US$5,240]

Sources:
Student Finance England. www.direct.gov.uk/en/EducationAnd
Learning/.
Student Finance Wales. www.studentfinancewales.co.uk.
Student Awards Agency for Scotland. www.saas.gov.uk.
Student Finance Northern Ireland. www.studentfinanceni.co.uk.

In Northern Ireland, Higher Education (Northern Ireland) Order 2005, passed in April 2005, introduced variable deferred tuition fees, to be instituted in 2006, along the same lines as those introduced in England.

Student Financial Assistance in England and Northern Ireland

Higher educational reforms in the United Kingdom also changed the student financial assistance system. Students in England and Northern Ireland may pay their tuition fees up front or apply to the Student Loans Company (via their local authority) for a student loan for tuition fees. The Student Loans Company pays the student fees directly to the college, on the student's behalf. The loans accrue interest (2.4% in 2006), which is linked to the rate of inflation in line with the Retail Prices Index. The loan becomes due for repayment when a student has left higher education and is earning more than £15,000 [US$23,076] per year. Borrowers must pay 9 percent of their income each year that they earn over £15,000.

Financial assistance is also available for living costs, in the form of a means-tested nonrepayable Maintenance Grant for up to a maximum of £2,700 [US$4,153] (a maximum of £3,200 [US$4,923] in Northern Ireland). Students with annual family incomes exceeding £37,500 [US$57,692] may not receive maintenance grants, but they are eligible to receive student loans for maintenance. (See chapter 7 for more information on student loans in the United Kingdom.)

Those English and Northern Irish institutions that charge more than £2,700 [US$4,153] per year in fees must provide additional bursaries of at least £300 [US$461] to students who are eligible for the full maintenance grant of £2,700 [US$4,153].

Student Financial Assistance in Scotland

After a new level of regional autonomy was granted to Scotland in 1999, the Scottish Parliament's Cubie Report (published in December 1999) proposed a Graduate Endowment Scheme, and up-front tuition fees for new Scottish students studying in Scotland were abolished, starting in 2001–2. In place of tuition fees, students were required to pledge to "contribute" £2,289 [US$3,521] (in 2006–7) after graduation to an entity called the Graduate Endowment Fund of Scotland. Students could pay their Graduate Endowment contribution in a lump sum up front, or pay part of it up front and apply for a student loan for the rest, or apply for a student loan from the Student Loans Company for the full amount. Payments toward this contribution obligation began as soon as the graduate's annual income reached £15,000 [US$23,076], and they were made on an income contingent basis, conforming to the provisions of the UK income contingent student loan plan (with a 2.4% rate of interest). However, this program was scrapped as of February 2008.

Support is also available for living costs. Students may apply for a means-tested Young Students' Bursary of £2,455 [US$3,776] for living costs, as well as for a partly means-tested student loan for living costs (maximum of £4,300 [US$6,615] if living away from home and £3,405 [US$5,238] if living at their parents' home). Mature students may apply for partly income-assessed student loans for living costs (up to a maximum of £4,300 [US$6,615] for a 30-week course) and for income-assessed nonrepayable supplementary grants.

Student Financial Assistance in Wales

Following in the footsteps of Scotland, the Higher Education Act 2004 gave the National Assembly for Wales the authority to decide what level of tuition fees and student support will apply in Wales. An annual deferred flexible tuition fee was introduced as of the 2007–8 academic year. Starting in 2007, all Welsh students (irrespective of income) studying at a Welsh institution are entitled to a tuition fee grant of up to £1,800 [US$2,769], to be paid directly to the institution. A Welsh student who studies elsewhere in the United Kingdom will be charged tuition fees according to the fee regime in the country of study and will be eligible for a loan from Student Finance Wales to cover these fees. This loan is to be repaid in the same way as the student's study loan.

Welsh students from families whose annual income is less than £37,425 [US$57,577] are entitled to means-tested Assembly Learning Grants to meet general living expenses. Students from families with an annual household income of £17,500 [US$26,923] or less are entitled to the full £2,700 [US$4,153] grant, while those from families with an income between £17,500 [US$26,923] and £37,425 [US$57,577] are eligible for partial grants. Student loans are also available to cover living costs (see chapter 7).

Additional financial contingency funds are available through a student's college or university. These funds allow the institution to award discretionary assistance to students who are experiencing financial difficulties or who would otherwise not be able to afford a higher education.

United States

Higher education in the United States is the responsibility of the states, rather than the federal government, and state universities, since their inception, have charged tuition fees to students and their families. The underlying per-student costs are high in most public US colleges and universities, and the share borne by parents and students—particularly prior to netting out the effects of grants and other forms of price discounting—is also higher than in other countries. For public four-year institutions, the average 2006–7 undergraduate tuition fees ranged from $4,000 to $9,000 (considerably more for out-of-state students), and dormitory and board costs amounted to about $7,000 for a student living on campus. Tuition fees at private four-year institutions ranged from $18,000 to as high as $35,000.

These expenses are considered a family, or parental, financial responsibility, at least for the traditional-age, dependent student through the baccalaureate degree—but only to the limit of what an Expected Family Contribution (EFC) calculates as the parents' ability to pay. This EFC is established by the US Congress, and it is the basis for awarding federal need-based (i.e., means-tested) Pell Grants, as well as for calculating a student's eligibility for federally guaranteed and partially subsidized student loans. The EFC—arrived at either by the Federal Methodology or through similar (but somewhat more financially demanding) private needs-analysis systems, such as the College Board's College Scholarship Service (CSS)—is then subtracted from a student's estimated total higher educational expenses, to yield an institution- and family-specific financial need. This remaining financial need must then be filled by some combination of

- additional family resources, such as relatives, or family borrowing;
- institutional financial assistance, which is especially prevalent in the better-endowed US private colleges and universities;
- state scholarships and grants, such as New York State's Tuition Assistance Program;
- student earnings from summer or term-time employment (which a majority of US students use to fill the financial gap); and/or
- federal grants and student loans.

The US financial assistance system may be more accurately described as a nonsystem, albeit somewhat implicitly coordinated. This system, or nonsystem, consists of independent sources of grants, loans, and work-study assistance from the federal government, the 50 state governments, most colleges and universities (through their endowments and associated foundations), hundreds of corporate and local philanthropic funds that have financial aid as one of their programs areas, and a wide range of guaranteed and partially subsidized student loans. The role of the federal government in the system is twofold. First, it uses grants and loan subsidies to make up for funds that low- and middle-income families can neither afford nor are able or willing to borrow, in order to bring at least moderate-tuition-fee, state-sponsored public education within reach of any student who is also willing to contribute through loans and term-time and summer earnings. Second, it also makes minimally subsidized or unsubsidized student loans widely available, and at sufficient amounts, to bring more-expensive private higher education within reach for the student whose parents have contributed up to a reasonable limit of funds (often with considerable indebtedness or depletion of assets) and who is also personally willing to assume substantial student indebtedness.

Financial aid to students from the federal government is mainly in one of four forms:

1. Grants, including, most importantly, Pell Grants
2. Federally guaranteed loans (subsidized Stafford Loans, unsubsidized Stafford Loans, Federal District Loans, PLUS Loans, consolidation loans)
3. Federal Perkins Loans
4. Federal work-study funds

In 2003–4, federal financial assistance—either as Pell Grants or student loans or both —reached 48 percent of all US undergraduates. Among students enrolled full-time for the full academic year, 28 percent of all US undergraduates received a federal grant and 34 percent (or their parents) received a federal loan. At the federal level, loan aid (described in chapter 6), estimated in 2006–7 at nearly $60 billion, makes up almost 70 percent of all federal student assistance. (For more on student loans in the United States, see chapter 7.)

Through grants to participating postsecondary schools, the federal work-study program provides need-based, part-time employment for undergraduate students requiring financial assistance. Schools must provide one dollar for every three provided by the government, and the program encourages schools to place students in community-service positions.

Every state offers need-based grants to its resident undergraduates. Certain states have signed reciprocity agreements that allow these grants to be taken across state borders or even offered to students from other states.

A major trend in US student financial assistance has been the substantial and sudden growth in various forms of non-need-based assistance from federal, state, and institutional sources. Some of this is in the form of merit-based grants. However, most non-need-based assistance is in the form of tax benefits, either from the deductibility of tuition fee payments (HOPE Scholarships and Lifetime Learning Credits) or from the tax deductibility of earnings from tuition fee savings plans. While estimates of the effective cost of these benefits are difficult and controversial, the College Board estimated the "lost tax" cost of HOPE scholarships and Lifetime Learning tax credits at $5.8 billion in 2006–7.

Transitional Countries

China

Higher educational institutions in China are financed primarily by state appropriations associated with funds from other channels. In 2005, the country's total overall educational expenditure was 841,884 billion Yuan [US$244,024 billion] of which 516,108 billion Yuan [US$149,597 billion] came from a state appropriation. Of this amount, the expenditure on public (state) education equaled 2.82 percent of the gross domestic product (it was 3.01% in 2006), much lower than the world average level. In 2005, China's total higher educational expenditure was 255,023 billion Yuan [US$73,920 billion], including 109,084 billion Yuan [US$31,619 billion] from the state appropriation.

Although public funding is still the most important fiscal source for public higher educational institutions, it is gradually declining, and a diversified higher educational financing system is being established. The proportion of public funds within total expenditures decreased from 91.81 percent in 1993 to 67.24 percent in 1999, then to 42.77 percent in 2005. At the same time, the percentage of tuition and other fees within total expenditures on higher education rose from 6.18 percent in 1993, to 23.35 percent in 1999, and to 31.05 percent in 2005. Institutional revenues in China come from the following sources: state appropriations, earmarked education levies, tuition fees plus other fees, entrepreneurial earnings, donations, educational foundations, contracted research, educational loans, and capital markets.

The concept of cost-sharing was introduced to China in the late 1980s. To cope with financial austerity and to meet the huge demand for higher education, the central government implemented a dual track enrollment policy during the late 1980s and early 1990s. The majority of students did not need to pay tuition and dormitory fees. Others, who scored below the cutoff line in the national college entrance examinations, had to pay for their higher education. Since 1997, all regular higher educational institutions charge students tuition and other fees.

At present, while tuition fees may only represent up to a maximum of 25 percent of the annual per-student cost (as set by the Ministry of Education), the average total amount of fees charged nationwide is higher. Institutional tuition fee standards are approved by either the central government or provincial ones, depending on each institution's affiliation. Tuition fees vary according to institution, program, and location. Tuition fees for students in the six national normal universities (Peking Normal, East China Normal, Centre China Normal, East–North Normal, Shanxi Normal, and West–South Normal), which are affiliated with the Ministry of Education, have been waived since the fall semester of 2007.

With the implementation of, and increase in, tuition and other fees in higher educational institutions, a student financial aid system was initiated in recent years. Financial aid to students includes: (1) grants—the State Grant program was established in 2002 to award funds to excellent needy undergraduate students in regular higher educational institutions; (2) scholarships—merit-based scholarships are one of the main types of aid available to college students since 1986; (3) work-study—in 1994, "regulations on building work-study funds in regular higher education institutions" were issued to require all institutions to construct work-study fund programs aimed at helping poor students; (4) tuition fee waivers—only a very limited number of needy students may get this kind of aid; and (5) student loans—the first loan program began in 1986. In the late 1990s, two loan programs—the General-Commercial Student Loans Scheme (GCSL) and the Government Subsidized Student Loans Scheme (GSSL)—were proposed and implemented throughout the country. (See chapter 7 for more on student loans in China.)

The Czech Republic

The Czech Republic is one of the transition, or post-Communist, countries where higher educational reform was implemented; it accompanied the nation's transition from an authoritarian to a democratic political system and from a command-type to a market-driven economy. Tertiary education in the Czech Republic includes advanced vocational and university education and is available to all applicants who have passed both their secondary-school-leaving exam and the entrance examination for their institution of choice.

There are three types of higher educational institutions in the Czech Republic: public, state, and private. Tertiary educational institutions are divided into university (28 institutions, 24 of which were public, and 2 state run, in 2005) and nonuniversity types (36 private institutions). Public higher education is offered by universities and colleges. Higher education is free—except for students who have exceeded the standard length of study, are going for a second degree, or are studying in a program offered in a foreign language. Besides public colleges, there are two state colleges: the Police Academy of the Czech Republic and the University of Defense.

Private colleges must receive accreditation from the Ministry of Education, Youth, and Sports. The first private colleges were set up around the year 2000. The most popular subjects offered by these colleges are business, finance, and law. The quality of the programs is guaranteed by the Ministry of Education, Youth, and Sports.

In addition to university- and nonuniversity-type tertiary educational institutions, there are 174 tertiary professional schools (114 regional, 1 state, 47 private, and 12 religious), which provide students with advanced technical knowledge and generally take three to three and one-half years to complete.

In 2006, 50 percent of the tertiary-aged cohort was in tertiary education, with 292,520 students enrolled in public universities and 31,755 in private institutions (less than 10% of all students).

After 1994, when new mechanisms for financing tertiary education were implemented, the number of students at public universities grew steadily—from 132,000 initially to 274,000 in 2004. The number of students enrolled in bachelor's degree programs in the Czech Republic grew very slowly until 2002, when the Higher Education Act was amended to set a binding time schedule for the implementation of the 29-nation Bologna Declaration (pertaining to European higher education).

Public expenditure on education was 4.4 percent of GDP in 2004, and 10 percent of the Czech Republic's total governmental expenditure. Twenty percent of the nation's educational expenditures are distributed to tertiary education. Public spending per student is 30.6 percent of GDP per capita. Private expenditures on tertiary education represented 15 percent of total expenditures on educational institutions in 2004.

The total state subsidy for a particular institution is based primarily on its teaching and research performance, although the most significant change in recent years has been the declining importance of formula funding. In 1997, almost 70 percent of the budget for higher educational institutions was funded through teaching formulas; by 2005, this had dropped to 53 percent.

Public institutions account for more than 90 percent of students, and the vast majority of their revenues come from public sources. Other income sources include property revenues, services to students, extra teaching activities, research and development activities, and study-related fees. Students and their families cover the cost of their school fees, accommodation, and food.

The 2005 amendment of the Higher Education Act introduced a social stipend for university students, which is provided by their institutions using resources from the state. It also transformed the Grant for Students' Accommodation from an in-kind contribution via subsidized dormitories into a student scholarship that is distributed by the various institutions according to their own rules. Students can use the scholarships to pay student hostel fees or to rent private accommodation.

The Czech Republic represents a typical example of a system where the state's responsibility for financing higher education through institutional funding is supplemented by the families' responsibility for their students' living expenses. Elements of the student welfare system in the Czech Republic include a scholarship, exemption from or a reduction in tuition fees, and individual tax benefits. Families with students in higher educational institutions can also get other benefits, such as child allowances and tax relief. Furthermore, there are several forms of student support, such as subsidized accommodations and meals, health insurance, public transportation discounts, pension insurance, and health insurance in the case of illness.

Private institutions educate less than 10 percent of the students in the Czech Republic and are legally obliged to be financially self-supporting. Usually some 90 percent of their income comes from student fees. In some cases, part of the tuition fees may be financed by means of subsidies. Students also pay all costs for school materials, accommodation, and food.

The 2000 amendment to the Higher Education Act was aimed at solving the most acute structural and fiscal problems of tertiary education. It allowed universities to invest capital into private joint ventures and spinoff companies. Because of continued strong opposition to tuition fees, the amendment legalized a type of dual track system, which some universities were in fact already operating. Students in the lifelong learning programs, for which universities were already allowed to charge tuition fees, are now allowed to take courses in accredited programs and accumulate regular credits; under certain conditions these credits can be converted into a regular diploma.

Hungary

Higher educational enrollments in Hungary quadrupled between 1989 and 2005, with most of the enrollment growth taking place in the public sector. The rise in student numbers was not accompanied by a proportionate increase in budget subsidies. On the contrary, funding for higher education, which currently consumes approximately 1 percent of GDP, has declined. Therefore, higher educational institutions have been forced to spend their internal reserves and make use of nongovernmental revenues.

In 1996, a system of normative financing was introduced—the first step towards the distribution of support awarded for achievement, with this distribution accomplished in a more transparent manner. Standards were established for state support on a per-student basis, differentiated by the 15 major branches of training (public and nonpublic institutions receive the same support per student, but the latter do not receive additional funds for maintenance, etc.).

Hungary's new system of financing assumes that institutions of higher education will become more self-sufficient. To further this aim, in 1995 tuition fees were introduced in public institutions, at a monthly rate of HUF 2,000 [US$15] for full-time students. In 1996, differentiated fees were introduced, and in 1998, education became free for first degree, state-funded, full-time students. Since 1996, public higher educational institutions have been allowed to accept self-financed students who are responsible for covering their own tuition fees (annual tuition fees range from HUF 180,000 to HUF 800,000 [US$1,401–$6,226]), food and lodging, book purchases, and other expenses. The higher educational institutions can set their own tuition fees, and they differentiate these fees across fields of study. According to Act CXXXIX of 2005 on Higher Education, by the Ministry of Education, state-funded students must equal 35 percent of the total number of students admitted three years prior to the year concerned (the due year).

State-funded students do not have to pay a tuition fee and most receive free accommodation in the university dorms (however, space constraints mean that some of them do not).

In the spring of 2008, the government tried to introduce moderate (US$550) yearly student "improvement contributions" (to be paid by all students starting in the fall of 2008) as part of its deficit-cutting reform package. However, a nationwide referendum in March 2008 rejected the package and Parliament, as required by the referendum, voted to ban tuition fees. No Parliamentary votes to alter the laws affected by the referendum may be made for three years.

With regard to scholarships for undergraduate students, in mid-2007 the Ministry of Education decided to allot 35 to 40 percent of its scholarship funds to needy students, and about 60 percent of its scholarship funds to merit-based students. The standard yearly scholarship is about HUF 116,500 [US$907].

Students may receive monetary or in-kind benefits relative to their financial standing, income situation, and academic performance, including dormitory placement or an accommodation grant, a maintenance grant and other bursaries (including a study grant and a Scholarship of the Republic of Hungary), social grants, and textbook grants. Student may also qualify for work study. (For information on student loans in Hungary, see chapter 7.)

Poland

The fall of Communism brought about many changes in Poland's higher educational system, including greater academic freedom, curricular reform, the development of more market-oriented curricula, and the emergence of a private sector. Between 1990 and 2007, enrollment in Poland's higher educational institutions grew fivefold, to close to 2 million students. This growth has been accompanied by new academic programs, new faculty pay schemes, a new system of accreditation, an expansion in facilities, a dramatic increase in the enrollment rate (from less than 10% to close to 40%) and the emergence (with government encouragement) of a significant private higher educational sector. In 2007, 640,000 of the country's 2 million students were in private sector institutions.

In 1999, a revised higher educational framework law was presented that consolidated what was previously contained in three separate higher education acts. The law made one ministry responsible for supervising all nonmilitary higher educational institutions, and it included provisions to allow for the payment of tuition fees for evening and weekend studies, part-time studies, and postgraduate studies at public higher institutions.

Polish higher education, both state and nonstate (private), includes universities, technical universities, maritime schools, academic economics, high pedagogical schools, academies of agriculture, academies of medicine, academies of theology, military academies, music schools, schools of art, theater schools, and academies of physical education.

The radical changes in all Polish institutions brought about by the end of the country's command economy has greatly affected the governance and management of universities and other institutions of higher education. As in all of the countries of the former Soviet Union and the Socialist/Communist countries of Eastern and Central Europe, these changes involved decentralization and the devolution of authority from the central government to the institution and its management. The rise of a market economy and commercialism brought about a new level of responsiveness both to students and their families, as well as to emerging business enterprises as consumers and users of higher education. In addition, the economic, political, and cultural reintegration of Poland with the rest of Europe—right at the time that all of European higher education was undergoing reforms in the direction of greater institutional autonomy, conformity of degrees, and more reliance on nongovernmental revenues—has accelerated the changes in Polish higher education.

Although the underlying legal guarantee of free education continues to constrain Polish universities from diversifying revenues through the imposition of tuition fees and other fees, there are exceptions and loopholes. As mentioned above, the 1999 Act on Higher Education authorized charging tuition fees (not to exceed 10 percent of an average monthly salary) to pay for the verification of knowledge, the certification of qualifications, and some "extra services." In addition, beginning in November 2000, the revised framework law allowed state-owned higher educational institutions to request tuition fees for selected study programs, such as evening and extramural studies.

State funding is distributed to the Polish universities according to an algorithm that is closely related to enrollments. In addition, most of the public universities receive approximately 25 percent of their total operating budgets from other external sources, including tuition fees from part-time and continuing education programs. External income is divided between the central administration and the relevant faculties at most universities on a 30:70 basis.

The nonpublic higher educational system is not financed from the state budget, with the exception of KUL (the Catholic University of Lublin) and PAT (the Pontifical Academy of Theology) in Cracow. Due to past laws, these two institutions are subsidized from the state budget in the same way as public higher educational institutions (except for investments). Private institutions may, however, receive small public competitive research grants, and they may also garner indirect government support from their full-time day students who are eligible to receive scholarship aid from the state budget.

Higher educational spending's share of Poland's state budget was 3.21 percent in 1990, 2.36 percent in 1994, and 3.86 percent in 2001.

Financial support services for students in higher educational institutions subsidized by the state budget are financed within these institutions' fiscal support funds for students. The scope and forms of these services are laid down by

- the Government Regulation of 22 January 1991 on financial support for full-time day students at higher educational institutions operating under on the Act of 12 September 1990; and
- the Regulation of the Minister of National Education of 23 September 1998 on financial support for full-time day students at vocational training colleges.

Full-time day students of public higher educational institutions are entitled to social financial support, special aid for disabled persons, scholarships awarded for academic results, accommodation subsidies, and meal subsidies. Full-time day students at public universities and colleges who achieve the best academic results and are highly academically active are entitled to apply for a Minister's Scholarship for academic achievements.

Loans made to students in accordance with the Student Credit and Loan Act of July 1998 are a supplementary form of financial support. All students in public and private institutions can apply for loans, and from the academic year 1998–99 to the year 2001–2, around 174,700 students benefited from this available credit.

Russia

Higher education in Russia is under the jurisdiction of the Ministry of General Education and Science, which is responsible for the accreditation of higher educational institutions and for the development and maintenance of state educational standards. As of 2007, there were over 6 million students in approximately 658 state-owned institutions and 450 private, accredited, university-level institutions.

According to the regulations that guide Russian higher education, there are three basic kinds of higher educational institutions. Universities offer a wide spectrum of programs at all levels of education: undergraduate, graduate, and continuing. Universities are leading research centers in fundamental fields that combine learning, teaching, and research. Academies are higher educational institutions that provide postsecondary education at all levels and conduct research mainly in one branch of science, technology, or culture (Academy of Mining, Academy of Architecture, Academy of Arts, etc.). Institutes are independent higher educational institutions, or parts (structural divisions) of universities, or academies that offer professional education programs.

The Constitution and the Russian Federation Law on Education guarantee open and free access to Higher Education on a competitive basis. Significant recent reforms, which took effect in 2009, have replaced the old individual high school exams and university entrance tests with a Unified State Examination (a standardized test similar to the SAT used in the United States) and have substituted a bachelor's and master's degree system for Russia's previous three-level undergraduate study cycle.

In 2003, state expenditures on education in Russia were 3.8 percent of its GNP; spending on tertiary education was approximately 70 billion rubles in 2006 (0.25% of GDP—much lower than the OECD average of 1.7%). State universities receive between 70 and 80 percent of their budgets from the federal budget, with the remainder coming from research, grants and overhead, tuition fees, and other educational services (such as renting out facilities and additional services provided to the population).

Russia's tuition fee policy may be described as dual track, which corresponds to its dual track admissions policy. In 1992, the Russian Federation Law on Education legalized tuition fee charges under conditions that were extended in the 1996 Law on Education; in addition, the 1992 law introduced the concept of higher educational cost-sharing. The 1992 Law on Education guarantees the right of free access to public higher education on a competitive basis, and it sets the quota of students who are to be awarded free tuition and given modest scholarships from the federal budget. The law also provides legal grounds for the admission of fee-paying students, who have passed the entrance exam but whose scores are not good enough to qualify for state support. Instruction on a fee-paying basis is geared to the market value of a program and the prestige of the institution, rather than on actually incurred costs. Law, economics, business management, and foreign languages are the most expensive fields, since they provide training for high-demand careers. In contrast, science and engineering are the least expensive. By 2005, over 55 percent of all students enrolled in public higher educational institutions paid tuition fees (compared to only 13% in 1995–96). In April 2004, the State Duma cancelled the requirement that universities have a minimum of 25 percent of their students be those whose tuition fees are paid for by the State.

Many public institutions have come to depend on tuition fee revenues as their second major income source, after state allocations. The size of this additional revenue generation varies by institution and by year, ranging from 20 to 60 percent. The dual track tuition fee policy has allowed a substantial increase in enrollments in higher educational institutions, with the system tripling its enrollments between 1992 (when the policy was introduced) and 2005.

Vietnam

The Vietnamese higher educational system is diversified and multilevel, with approximately 275 public and 47 nonpublic universities and colleges. Among the public institutions, large multidisciplinary universities dominate. Fourteen of these, designated as key universities, enroll almost one-third of all higher educational students.

Enrollments are growing very rapidly. Total student enrollment rose from 162,000 in 1992–93, to approximately 1 million in 2001–2 ,and to 1.6 million in 2008 (a higher educational gross enrollment rate of 10%). This expansion is a result of the dramatic growth in the number of students in areas such as economics, business administration, law, English, and computer science.

While the Ministry of Education and Training (MOET) is directly responsible for the management of the larger and more important universities and colleges and controls academic matters for all higher educational institutions, a recent education reform (Decree 85) has allowed local educational authorities more power over other aspects higher education and universities more autonomy over financing, research, and human resources.

Governmental funds are directly distributed to public institutions according to formulas. At the National Meeting of the Rectors of Colleges and Universities in 1987, MOET announced its intention to expand higher educational enrollments by allowing the admission of fee-paying students in excess of the centrally planned quota for which scholarship support funding is available.

Among regular students, the number paying tuition fees grew very quickly compared with the number sponsored by the state. The latter did not change significantly between the 1987–99 and 1998–99 academic years, while the number of tuition-fee-paying students grew to become four times larger than the number of scholarship students. Among irregular (part-time or in-service) training groups, most students pay tuition fees; the rest may get tuition fee assistance from their organizations. Most of the country's students are paying some form of tuition fee.

Access to higher education in Vietnam is influenced by factors such as income level, social status of the student's parents, region, race, religion, ethnicity, and gender. Since the open-door policy was implemented, access for students from low-income families has increased, and about 30 percent of four-year-program students come from peasant families. At the same time, 75 percent of the population lives in rural areas. Moreover, ethnic minorities have even less access to higher education. These people usually live in remote areas and belong to low-income groups; moreover, according to their culture, rural girls are additionally disadvantaged in their access to higher education, as compared with boys. There is no evidence showing any worsening of this situation in recent years, but there is a feeling that the opportunity for ethnic minorities to access higher education is decreasing.

Tuition fees vary from institution to institution and from program to program. In 2008, the government set a tuition fee ceiling at a maximum of 6 percent of average family income, up from a previous ceiling of VND 180,000 [US$38] per month, with tuition fee maximums differentiated according to seven disciplinary categories.

Ten years ago the government publicly subsidized the cost of student living. Presently, a crowded dormitory room at the minimum cost is the only subsidy some higher educational institutions can provide for a limited number of students, especially the ones with scholarships. Staying in inexpensive private housing is the only choice for other students. However, housing, food, and other related items are also becoming expensive, and the amount spent on them can surpass the amount of tuition fees that students pay in public universities. Tuition fees, living costs, and other school-related expenses represent a significant burden even for middle-income families.

All government scholarships include tuition fee waivers, while only some of them provide subsidies for housing, food, and learning materials. Merit scholarships—based purely on academic grades, with no allowance made for a family's income level—are intended to reward high achievement. Depending on their academic accomplishments during the previous school year, students may receive all, half, or one-fourth of their living expenses for the next year. A "full" scholarship covers only one-third of the real cost of student living in municipal higher educational institutions, and half of the maintenance costs in rural ones. Social scholarships are reserved for disadvantaged students, including war invalids, orphans, certain ethnic minorities, and student from mountainous regions.

A governmental student loan scheme, whereby students could borrow money to cover tuition fees and living expenses, was announced in 2006 and has been recently revised. Under the previous program, students could only borrow VND 300,000 [US$64] per month from the Vietnam Bank for Social Policy. That amount has now been increased to VND 800,000 [US$170] and the interest reduced from 0.65 percent to 0.5 percent. Students will have a one-year grace period after they complete their studies.

Middle-Income Countries

Chile

As of 2005, the postsecondary system in Chile consisted of 64 universities (25 traditional universities and 39 new private universities without direct public subsidy); 48 professional institutes, all of them private; and 117 private technical training centers. In 2005, 72 percent of the students enrolled in postsecondary institutions were enrolled in either public or private universities.

Tuition fees for higher education were introduced as part of the country's 1981 educational reforms. There is no set policy for tuition fees or any other fees, and each institution has the freedom to set up both without government restrictions. As of 2007, tuition fees in public institutions ranged from 1.7 million Chilean pesos [US$5,101] to 2.7 million pesos [US$8,101].

The government has shown a considerable commitment to improving the access of low-income students to tertiary education. In 2005, 170,000 students (out of a total of 600,000 in the higher educational system) received public financial aid, with a total (between grants and loans) of 83 billion Chilean pesos [US$249 million] set aside in the 2005 budget. (See chapter 7 for more on student loans in Chile.)

A variety of state-funded, need- and merit-based grants are available to pay tuition fees and living expenses. The most important of these are outlined in table A.4.

India

The cost of higher education in India is supported by the central and state government sectors and by the nongovernmental sector (including students and/or parents and the

Table A.4 Grant opportunities for Chilean higher educational students

Grant	Targeted group	Use	Amount
Beca Bicentenario	Needy students	To cover part or all of the tuition fees in one of the 25 traditional universities	According to need
Beca Juan Gómez Millas	Needy, academically meritorious students who have graduated from a municipal educational establishment	Tuition fees in traditional public or autonomous private higher educational institutions	Up to 1 million pesos [US$3,000]
Beca de Alimentación para Educación Superíor	Needy students	Food	1,300–1,400 pesos [US$3.89–$4.19] per day for 10 months
Beca Pedagogía	Students who will study education in accredited higher educational institutions	Tuition fees	Up to 1 million pesos [US$3,000] (needy students may also receive a complementary grant for books and materials)
Beca de Excelencia Académica	Top five percent of graduates from subsidized establishments	To be used toward tuition fees	Up to 1 million pesos [US$3,000]
Beca de Mantención para Educación Superíor	Needy students who have received either the Beca Bicentenario, the Beca Juan Gómez Millas, or the Beca de Excelencia Académica	Living expenses	Monthly allowances of 25,000 pesos [US$75] for food and 14,500 pesos [US$44] for living expenses

Beca Nuevo Milenio	Needy students who are pursuing technical degrees	Tuition fees in eligible institutions	Up to 300,000 pesos [US$900]
Beca Hijos de Profesionales de la Educación	Needy children of teachers	Tuition fees in traditional public or autonomous private higher educational institutions	Up to 500,000 pesos [US$1,500]
Beca Presidente de la República	Needy students	Living expenses	Monthly stipend of 46,640 pesos [US$140]
Beca Zonas Extremas	Students from isolated areas	Living and transportation expenses	Monthly stipend of 70,338 pesos [US$211] plus transportation costs
Beca Estudiantes de Ascendencia Indígena	Needy indigenous students (priority given to those who study agricultural sciences)	Living expenses	506,142 pesos [US$1,519] (in 2006)
Beca para Puntajes Nacionales	Needy and academically excellent students (who receive the highest scores on the PSU examinations, i.e., the University Selection Test) who have graduated from a municipal educational establishment	Tuition fees	1 million pesos [US$3,000]

Source: Gobierno de Chile, Ministero de Educación, powerpoint presentation [not dated].

rest of the community). The 16 central universities receive maintenance and development grants from the central government through the University Grants Commission (UGC), while other universities and colleges receive maintenance funds from state governments and some development grants from the UGC.

Private colleges are either privately managed but publicly funded (aided colleges) or both privately managed and funded (unaided colleges). Aided private colleges are required to admit 50 percent of their students based on their performance on entrance exams (free seats). These students are not required to pay any extra fees or tuition fees. The other 50 percent of their students are admitted based on their willingness to pay these tuition fees (payment seats). Unaided private colleges establish their own fee levels (below a government-set ceiling) that are generally extremely high in comparison to the aided private colleges and government colleges.

To finance higher educational expansion, the government has consistently increased its share in the total expenditures on higher education, from 49.1 percent in 1950–51 to more than 90 percent in 1999. Students pay a small fee that constitutes 10 to 15 percent of the institution's budget. However, data suggest that fee contributions may vary considerably between central and state institutions, with student fees contributing a significant amount of income in some state universities, while in others violent student resistance to the introduction of tuition fees has delayed their implementation.

The higher educational financing system is beginning to change, and a policy of fostering financial independence in universities and degree colleges (reducing government allocations to the universities and increasing user fees) has been in place since 1997. Despite policy pronouncements over the last six years, however, it is only fairly recently that action has been taken. While the UGC has the legal right to set tuition and other fees, it has not done so in practice, leaving it up to the individual state governments and institutions to take the initiative. There is a gradual trend towards cost recovery (with special care being taken to frame policies to assist low-income and disadvantaged students). Professional and private educational institutions have come to accept this change more readily, because these students are often from economically stronger families and are more certain of gainful employment upon completion of their education.

A report was presented by the Prime Minister's Task Force on Education in April 2000 that recommended, among other measures, full cost recovery in higher education—asserting that students and parents can bear the costs of higher education and that the central and state governments should only fund those disciplines that have no market orientation. In May 2000, the Human Resources Development Ministry decided that higher educational institutions' fee levels should rise 7 percent in that academic session, with a 1 percent increase each subsequent year.

To offset the fee hike, in April 2001, the Indian government announced a new educational loan program, the merit-based Educational Loan Scheme, that covers fee and nonfee expenditures related to study. The maximum amount awarded by participating banks is Rs 750,000 [US$51,020] for studies in India and Rs 1,500,000 [US$102,041] for studies abroad. The program does not require collateral for the first Rs 400,000 [US$27,211] loaned, and it charges an interest rate tied to the lending rate set by the Reserve Bank of India (12% for amounts up to Rs 400,000 [US$27,211]). Larger loan amounts carry higher interest rates. The interest rate is not compounded during the repayment holiday/moratorium (course period plus one year, or six months after getting a job, whichever is earlier). Some banks will not make loans to students whose families earn less than Rs 3,072 [US$209] per month, which disqualifies most Indians, since there is no provision for governmental underwriting.

South Africa

The government and its appointed agencies, such as the National Student Financial Aid Scheme (NSFAS) and the Tertiary Education Fund for South Africa (TEFSA), dominate higher educational finance in South Africa. The private sector also plays a significant, though limited, role in financing higher education.

Government financing of higher education is guided by the principles of shared costs, equity and redress (compensation for the damage done to Blacks, Coloreds, and Asians during the Apartheid era), and development. The principle of shared costs (i.e., cost-sharing) states that other than in a few specialized colleges, the government and students and/or their parents must share the costs of higher education, because of the envisaged higher private returns. However, in colleges and other higher educational institutions that produce "pure public goods," the government is responsible for all financing.

The past ten years have seen decreasing state funding for public higher education in real terms. It declined as a percentage of GDP from 0.82 percent in 1996 to 0.67 percent in 2006. Higher educational institutions have dealt with these decreases by raising their tuition fees.

A new funding framework (NFF), composed of block grants and earmarked grants, was introduced and promulgated in 2003. Earmarked funding is mostly geared toward the student loan program, while the four types of block grants are related to goals and performance through teaching and research.

State departments and provincial legislatures provide financial assistance to students in the form of bursaries. In some cases these bursaries may need to be repaid, but in most cases the requirement is that the recipients work for the department or province that granted the bursary for a certain period of time after graduation. (See chapter 7 for information on the national-level student loans scheme, the NSFAS.)

Individual institutions also offer work-study programs to needy students. For example, at the University of Western Cape, in the first semester students receive 40 percent of the money they earned, while 60 percent is allocated to their fees. In the second semester, students receive 20 percent and 80 percent is allocated to their fees, until the fee account is settled in full. Thereafter students receive full payment.

Most banks in South Africa offer student loans at competitive interest rates, although these rates vary, depending on the bank. Some banks offer loans to students in any year of study, while others offer loans from the second year on. Students are generally expected to make interest-only payments for the duration of their studies (unless they are part time—then they have to start repaying the capital immediately) and to start capital repayments upon graduation.

Low-Income Countries

Kenya

Like most African countries, higher education in Kenya was historically free, with the government covering both tuition fees and living expenses, and it enjoyed relatively generous funding compared to other levels of education. This trend began to shift in the 1990s and has continued ever since. In 2006–7, for example, while public expenditures on basic education increased by 9.8 percent, those for higher education decreased by 9.4 percent.

Cost-sharing in Kenyan higher education was first introduced in 1991, as a response to the ever-declining state budget, which did not keep pace with the high student intake when the first cohort of 8–4–4 students (eight years of primary schooling, followed by four years of secondary education, and then a four-year bachelor's degree program) entered the university. Under the country's new cost-sharing policy, students and/or their parents are required to cover both tuition fees and the cost of maintenance. A student loan program was also established to enable needy students to access higher educational institutions.

However, the resources generated by these cost-sharing measures were insufficient, given the severely limited number of students. Therefore, in 1998, a dual track tuition fee policy was introduced via the self-sponsored, or Module II, programs that admitted students who qualified for admission, but not for government-subsidized places, on a fee-paying basis.

In Kenya, the assumed average cost of each degree program is KES 120,000 [US$4,068] per year, of which the government covers KES 70,000 [US$2,373] for a Module I (government-sponsored) student, leaving the remaining KES 50,000 [US$1,695] for the student to raise from the Kenyan Higher Education Loan board (HELB) or private sources. The Module II students (admitted on a self-paying basis) gain entry to universities according to criteria that vary from institution to institution. While they are eligible for a means-tested Higher Education Loan, such loans cover only a portion of their more expensive tuition fees, and they have to raise the money for the remaining portion by themselves.

In addition to loans (described in chapter 7), needy students also receive bursaries. The Ministry of Education disburses about KES 82 million [US$2.7 million] each fiscal year to HELB. HELB identifies needy students through means-testing and awards bursaries according to each student's level of need. Funds are paid directly to the universities and go towards tuition fee costs. The maximum amount that a student can receive in the form of bursaries is KES 8,000 [US$271]. It is important to note, however, that students in private universities do not receive bursaries from HELB; they apply instead to the Ministry of Education for funds.

Students in both private and public universities can also apply for grants or bursaries from the Constituency Development Fund (CDF). The CDF was created through an Act of Parliament in 2003 to finance community-based projects, with the overall goal of alleviating poverty. Needy students from various constituencies can apply for the bursaries, which account for 10 percent of the total CDF.

Pakistan

Higher education in Pakistan is characterized by tremendous demand and a private sector that has been growing rapidly to keep up with this demand in the face of the public sector's inability to do so by itself. The government has recognized the importance of private higher education and has made it relatively easy for the private sector to establish new colleges and universities, easing the ban on private higher education in the late

1970s and passing supportive legislation in some provinces. Private institutions can be established under either a federal or a provincial charter and are regulated by the Higher Education Commission. Their main source of income is student tuition fees, and while they are free to set their own fee levels, they must grant fee exemptions or scholarships to at least 10 percent of their students.

While public provincial universities are administered by the provincial governments, all universities (federal and provincial) are funded by the central government through the Higher Education Commission, or HEC (which replaced the University Grants Commission in 2002). HEC also oversees the academic programs of all public and private institutions and prescribes all operational guidelines. As of 2004–5 there were 107 public and private degree granting institutions in Pakistan, (including 49 general universities in the public sector and 36 universities in the private sector), as well as a vast number of other specialized public and private degree-granting institutes (including 1,882 intermediate and degree colleges—of which 1,025 are public—and 1,324 technical/professional institutes—of which the majority are private).

Starting in 2006–7, HEC university grants are allocated on the basis of enrollments and grading/performance. In the previous two years they included two additional components: across-the-board increases due to cost adjustments, and adjustments to remove historic inequalities. While HEC spending on higher education grew by 300 percent between 2001–2 and 2005–6 after years of underfunding, much of this increase was absorbed by expanded student enrollments, and less than 0.5 percent of the country's GDP was spent on education. In 2004–5, 14 percent of the total educational budget was expended on higher education.

Public higher educational institutions also receive small grants from provincial governments (accounting for about 8% of their revenue in 2005–6) and generate third-party revenues from examinations, tuition fees, and other fees. The lion's share of revenue (63%), however, is provided by the government.

Higher education in Pakistan can be divided into university higher education and nonuniversity education; the latter is provided by polytechnics, technical and commercial institutes, and colleges. Only 2.38 percent of young people aged 18–23 were enrolled in a university in Pakistan in 2004–5. As of 2006–7, there are an estimated 400,000 students in private and public universities, 250,000 students in degree-awarding and affiliated colleges, and 900,000 in all other forms of postsecondary education.

Students may receive need-based financial assistance from their institutions (by law, all universities must use at least 10% of their fee income to support needy students)—in the form of tuition fee waivers or housing grants—or from national grant schemes that cover tuition fees and living expenses for public and private students.

Selected Bibliography

This is a selected bibliography that includes the more general books, compilations, and reports on higher education finance and cost-sharing by major authors in the field. We have steered away from including country-specific selections and chapters or articles that are part of compilations or special journal issues. These may be found in the references section at the end of each chapter when cited in the text. For a more extensive annotated bibliography on cost-sharing, please visit our Web site at www.gse.buffalo.edu/org/IntHigherEdFinance/project_publications.html/.

Barr, Nicholas. 2005. Financing Higher Education. *Finance and Development* 42 (2). www .imf.org/external/pubs/ft/fandd/2005/06/index.htm.

Callender, Claire, and Jonathan Jackson. 2008. Does the Fear of Debt Constrain Choice of University and Subject of Study? *Studies in Higher Education* 33 (4):405–429.

Chapman, Bruce. 2006. *Government Managing Risk: Income Contingent Loans for Social and Economic Progress.* London: Routledge.

Colclough, Christopher, and James Manor. 1991. *States or Markets? An Assessment of Neo-Liberal Approaches to Education Policy.* Oxford: Clarendon Press.

College Board. 2008a. *Trends in College Pricing.* Washington, DC: College Board.

———. 2008b. *Trends in Student Aid 2008.* New York: College Board.

Court, David. 1999. *Financing Higher Education in Africa: Makerere; The Quiet Revolution.* Washington, DC: World Bank.

Cunningham, Alisa F., and Deborah A. Santiago. 2008. *Student Aversion to Borrowing: Who Borrows and Who Doesn't.* Washington, DC: Institute for Higher Education Policy.

Dynarski, Susan M. 2003. Does Aid Matter? Measuring the Effect of Student Aid on College Attendance and Completion. *American Economic Review* 93 (1):279–288.

Ehrenberg, Ronald G. 2003. *Tuition Rising: Why College Costs So Much.* Cambridge, MA: Harvard University Press.

Finnie, Ross, Alex Usher, and Hans Vossensteyn. 2004. *Meeting the Need: A New Architecture for Canada's Student Financial Aid System.* Toronto: Educational Policy Institute.

Fossey, Richard, and Mark Bateman, eds. 1988. *Condemning Students to Debt: College Loans and Public Policy.* New York: Teachers College Press.

Heller, Donald E. 1999. The Effects of Tuition and State Financial Aid on Public College Enrollment. *Review of Higher Education* 23 (1):65–89.

Johnstone, D. Bruce. 1972. *New Patterns for College Lending: Income Contingent Loans.* New York: Teachers College Press.

———. 1986. *Sharing the Costs of Higher Education: Student Financial Assistance in the United Kingdom, the Federal Republic of Germany, France, Sweden, and the United States.* New York: College Entrance Examination Board.

———. 2004a. The Applicability of Income Contingent Loans in Developing and Transitional Countries. *Journal of Educational Planning and Administration* [New Delhi, India] 18 (2):159–174.

———. 2004b. The Economics and Politics of Cost-Sharing in Higher Education: Comparative Perspectives. *Economics of Education Review* 20 (4):403–410.

———. 2005. Fear and Loathing of Tuition Fees: An American Perspective on Higher Education Finance in the UK. *Perspectives* 9 (1):12–16.

———. 2006. *Financing Higher Education: Cost-Sharing in International Perspective.* Boston: Boston College Center for International Higher Education and Sense Publishers.

Johnstone, D. Bruce, and Pamela N. Marcucci. 2007. *Financially Sustainable Student Loan Programs: The Management of Risk in the Quest for Private Capital.* Washington DC: Institute for Higher Educational Policy, Global Center on the Private Financing of Higher Education.

Johnstone, D. Bruce, and Damtew Teferra, eds. 2004. Cost-Sharing and Other Forms of Revenue Supplementation in African Higher Education. Special issue of *Journal of Higher Education in Africa* 2 (2).

Jongbloed, Ben. 2004. Tuition Fees in Europe and Australia: Theory, Trends and Policies. In *Higher Education: Handbook of Theory and Research*, ed. John C. Smart. Dordrecht, The Netherlands: Kluwer Academic Publishers.

Kirshstein, Rita, Andrea Berger, Elana Benatar, and David Rhodes. 2004. *Workforce Contingent Financial Aid: How States Link Financial Aid to Employment.* Indianapolis: Lumina Foundation for Education.

Knight, Jane, ed. 2009. *Financing Access and Equity in Higher Education.* Rotterdam: Sense Publishers.

Leslie, Larry L., and Paul T. Brinkman. 1987. Student Price Response in Higher Education: The Student Demand Studies. *Journal of Higher Education* 58 (2):181–204.

Levy, Daniel C. 2002. *Unanticipated Development: Perspectives on Private Higher Education's Emerging Roles.* PROPHE [Program for Research on Private Higher Education] Working Paper Series. Albany: State University of New York at Albany.

Li, Wenli. 2007. Family Background, Financial Constraints and Higher Education Attendance in China. *Economics of Education Review* 26:725–735.

Long, Bridget Terry, and Erin Riley. 2007. Financial Aid: A Broken Bridge to College Access? *Harvard Educational Review* 77(1):39–63.

Loonin, Deanne. 2008. *Income-Based Payment: Making It Work for Student Loan Borrowers.* Boston: Student Loan Borrower Assistance Project, National Consumer Law Center.

Marcucci, Pamela, and D. Bruce Johnstone. 2007. Tuition Fee Policies in a Comparative Perspective: Theoretical and Political Rationales. *Journal of Higher Education Policy and Management* 29 (1):25–40.

Marcucci, Pamela, D. Bruce Johnstone, and Mary Ngolovoi. 2008. Higher Educational Cost-Sharing, Dual Track Tuition Fees, and Higher Educational Access: The East African Experience. *Peabody Journal of Education* 83 (1):101–116.

McMahon, W. 1988. Potential Resource Recovery in Higher Education in the Developing Countries and the Parents' Expected Contribution. *Economics of Education Review* 7 (1):135–152.

Palacios Lleras, Miguel. 2004. *Investing in Human Capital: A Capital Markets Approach to Student Funding.* Cambridge: Cambridge University Press.

Palfreyman, David. 2004. *The Economics of Higher Education: Affordability and Access; Costing, Pricing and Accountability.* Oxford: Oxford Centre for Higher Education Policy Studies.

Schwarzenberger, Astrid, ed. 2008. *Public/Private Funding of Higher Education: A Social Balance.* Hanover: Higher Education Information Systems (HIS).

Shen, Hong. 2008. Access to Higher Education through Student Loans: The Choice of Needy Students in China. Paper presented at the Asia-Pacific Sub-Regional Preparatory Conference for the 2009 World Conference on Higher Education, 25–26 September, Macao SAR, People's Republic of China. www.unescobkk.org/fileadmin/user_upload/apeid/workshops/macao08/papers/2-d-1.pdf.

Shen, Hua, and Adrian Ziderman. 2007. *Student Loans Repayment and Recovery: International Comparisons.* Bonn: Institute for the Study of Labor.

St. John, Edward P. 2003. *Refinancing the College Dream: Access, Equal Opportunity, and Justice for Taxpayers.* Baltimore: Johns Hopkins University Press.

Swail, Watson Scott, and Donald E. Heller. 2004. *Changes in Tuition Policy: Natural Policy Experiments in Five Countries.* Millennium Research Series. Montreal: Canada Millennium Scholarship Foundation.

Teixeira, Pedro, D. Bruce Johnstone, Maria J. Rosa, and Hans Vossensteyn, eds. 2006. *Cost-Sharing and Accessibility in Higher Education: A Fairer Deal?* Douro Series, Higher Education Dynamics, vol. 14. Dordrecht, The Netherlands: Springer.

Usher, Alex. 2005a. *Much Ado About a Very Small Idea.* Toronto: Educational Policy Institute.

———. 2005b. *Understanding International Debt Management/Repayment Programs and Their Effect on the Repayment of Student Financial Assistance.* Toronto: Educational Policy Institute.

Vossensteyn, Hans. 2004. Fiscal Stress: Worldwide Trends in Higher Education Finance. *Journal of Student Financial Aid* 34 (1):39–55.

———. 2005. Perceptions of Student Price-Responsiveness. University of Twente, Enschede, The Netherlands. http://www.utwente.nl/cheps/publications/.

Woodhall, Maureen, ed. 2002. Paying for Learning: The Debate on Student Fees, Grants and Loans in International Perspective [editorial]. Special international issue of *Welsh Journal of Education* 11 (1):1–9.

Ziderman, Adrian. 2002. Alternative Objectives of National Student Loan Schemes. Special international issue of *Welsh Journal of Education* 11 (1):37–47.

Index